THE HANDBOOK
OF FOLKLORE

THE HANDBOOK
OF FOLKLORE

CHARLOTTE SOPHIA BURNE

SENATE

ERRATA.

Page 11, line 9 from bottom. *For* part in mysteries *read* innermost mysteries.

Page 11, line 8 from bottom. *For* through an initiation-rite *read* part in an initiation-rite.

Handbook of Folklore

First published in 1914 by Sidgwick & Jackson Ltd,
London

Copyright © Charlotte Sophia Burne 1914

This edition first published in 1995 by Senate,
an imprint of Random House UK Ltd,
Random House, 20 Vauxhall Bridge Road,
London SW1V 2SA

Reprinted 1996

ISBN 1 85958 157 9

Printed and bound in Guernsey by
The Guernsey Press Co Ltd

PREFACE.

THIS book is not written for the use of members of Anthropological Expeditions, whose work demands far more thorough acquaintance with the subject than could possibly be conveyed in a single volume. It is addressed to officers of the public services, to missionaries, travellers, settlers, and others whose lot is cast among uncivilized or half-civilized populations abroad; to residents in country places at home; to medical men, philanthropic workers, and all educated persons whose lives and duties bring them into touch with the uneducated. Such persons have it in their power to contribute very greatly to the advance of an important study, the value of which is as yet hardly fully appreciated; and it is believed that they will be willing to do so, if only the way is pointed out to them. To do this is the aim of the *Handbook of Folklore*.

The genesis of the book is somewhat complicated. The scheme of classification devised by Sir Laurence Gomme for the original edition of 1890 has been retained, with only such modifications of detail as experience and extended knowledge have shown to be desirable. That its retention should have been found possible, in spite of the great development of the study during the last quarter of a century, is no small testimony to the prescience of its author. Beyond this, a few passages here and there, and the list of Types of Indo-European Folk-tales, represent all that has been preserved from the first edition. The earlier chapters are founded on a manuscript which Mr. E. Sidney Hartland began some years ago with a view to a new edition, but which for various reasons was never completed. This he generously placed at the disposal of the Folklore Society, and the whole work has had the benefit of his wide range of reading, and of his suggestions and advice. The debt it owes to his unwearied kindness can hardly be over-estimated.

The account of Chinese Ancestor-worship in chapter vi, (p. 87), is by Mr. A. R. Wright, F.S.A. ; that of the religious system of the North American tribes in chapter vii, (p. 115), by Miss Freire-Marreco ; that of the English Village Community in chapter xi, (p. 188), by Mr. F. M. Stenton, M.A. Oxon., Professor of History at University College, Reading. Chapter xv, (Games), is by Miss Moutray Read ; and chapter xii, (Rites of Individual Life), is based on a draft by Mr. Stanley Casson, formerly Secretary of the Oxford Anthropological Society. Dr. W. H. R. Rivers has kindly supplied the material for the accounts of the Classificatory System of Relationship and the Genealogical Method of Enquiry, (pp. 166-170)—subjects peculiarly his own. For the rest I am myself responsible.

Dr. A. C. Haddon, Dr. R. R. Marett, Dr. W. H. R. Rivers, Dr. C. G. Seligmann, and Mr. W. Crooke have kindly read various portions of the work in MS., and have contributed valuable hints and criticisms. The whole Council of the Folklore Society have had the opportunity of reading it in proof. MS. notes received from these sources are in many cases indicated by initials. But the final responsibility of selection or rejection has rested on my own shoulders, and for whatever flaws or weaknesses may be found in the work, the blame must lie at my door, for I have throughout retained the woman's privilege of the last word.

Omissions there doubtless are, but I would ask readers to take the Questionary into consideration before making sure of this in any particular instance. Only the main points of each topic are touched on in the text : the Questionary is designed to supplement it, and to suggest further details in each case.

Repetitions are unavoidable, however carefully one's matter may be arranged. Life is not lived in water-tight compartments, and the folklore which is its outcome and expression cannot be fitted into insulated pigeon-holes. One thing in folklore always involves another. The most ordinary story of an apparition involves questions of the nature of the phantom itself, of the kind of place where it appeared, the person to whom it was visible, and the " witching hour " at which it was seen.

When a gardener, in accordance with the traditional lore of his craft, swears at his lettuce or radish-seed and thrashes his young walnut-trees, or sows his peas in the wane of the moon and his potatoes on Good Friday, and utterly declines to root up the parsley-bed, he is putting in practice time-honoured beliefs, not only about trees and plants, but about life and death and the influence of sacred days and of the heavenly bodies. When the mourners at the funeral feast tell the bees of their bereavement, they are acting on ancient imaginings as to the nature of a future life and on their own actual beliefs as to the sagacity of the lower animals, as well as carrying out a traditional part of the funeral rites. A whole philosophy of Nature was bound up in the constitution of ancient Ireland when the Stone of Tara proclaimed the destined successor to the throne of Leinster. The more we look into the matter, the more the truth is borne in upon us that Folklore is an essential unity ; or, in other words, that Social Anthropology—" new Presbyter is but old Priest writ large "—is not an arbitrary selection of unrelated topics, but a homogeneous science which will some day come to its own.

C. S. B.

TABLE OF CONTENTS.

PAGE

INTRODUCTION

I. WHAT FOLKLORE IS 1

II. HOW TO COLLECT AND RECORD FOLKLORE 6

PART I. BELIEF AND PRACTICE

CHAPTER

I. THE EARTH AND THE SKY . . . 23

II. THE VEGETABLE WORLD 31

III. THE ANIMAL WORLD 40

IV. HUMAN BEINGS 47

V. THINGS MADE BY MAN 64

VI. THE SOUL AND ANOTHER LIFE . . 75

VII. SUPERHUMAN BEINGS 90

Worship, p. 99. Cult as a Moral Sanction, (Australia, Andamans), p. 109. Rudimentary Worship of Nature-Powers, (Bushmen), p. 111. The Cult of Mystic Power, (North America), p. 115. Systematic Polytheism without Idolatry, (Uganda), p. 117. Heterogeneous Polytheism with Idolatry, (India), p. 121.

VIII. OMENS AND DIVINATION 124

IX. THE MAGIC ART 134

X. DISEASE AND LEECHCRAFT . . . 152

PART II. CUSTOMS

CHAPTER   PAGE
XI. Social and Political Institutions . 161

The Tribe in Australia, p. 174. Mother-right in a
North American Tribe, p. 175. The Tribe in Europe,
p. 176. Aristocracy, (Polynesia), p. 178. Barbarian
Monarchy, (Bushongo), p. 179. Secret Societies, p. 183.
The Village Community in Europe, p. 188.

XII. Rites of Individual Life .   .   . 193

XIII. Occupations and Industries   .   . 220

XIV. Calendar Fasts and Festivals .   . 236

XV. Games, Sports, and Pastimes   .   . 248

PART III. STORIES, SONGS, AND SAYINGS

XVI. Stories ; (*a*) Told as True, (*b*) Told
for Amusement 261

XVII. Songs and Ballads 271

XVIII. Proverbs and Riddles 280

XIX. Proverbial Rhymes and Local Sayings 287

APPENDICES

A. Terminology 295

B. Questionary 301

C. Types of Indo-European Folktales .   . 344

D. Authorities Cited 356

INTRODUCTION.

I. WHAT FOLKLORE IS.

THE word *Folk-Lore*—literally, "*the learning of the people*"—was coined in 1846 by the late Mr. W. J. Thoms to replace the earlier expression "popular antiquities." It has established itself as the generic term under which the traditional Beliefs, Customs, Stories, Songs, and Sayings current among backward peoples, or retained by the uncultured classes of more advanced peoples, are comprehended and included. It comprises early and barbaric beliefs about the world of Nature, animate and inanimate ; about human nature and things made by man ; about a spirit world and man's relations with it ; about witch-craft, spells, charms, amulets, luck, omens, disease, and death. It further includes customs and rites as to marriage and inheritance, childhood and adult life, and as to festivals, war-fare, hunting, fishing, cattle-keeping, etc. ; also myths, legends, folk-tales, ballads, songs, proverbs, riddles, and nursery rhymes. In short, it covers everything which makes part of the mental equipment of the folk as distinguished from their technical skill. It is not the form of the plough which excites the attention of the folklorist, but the rites practised by the ploughman when putting it into the soil : not the make of the net or the harpoon, but the taboos observed by the fisher-man at sea : not the architecture of the bridge or the dwelling, but the sacrifice which accompanies its erection and the social life of those who use it. Folklore, in fact, is the ex-pression of the psychology of early man, whether in the fields of philosophy, religion, science, and medicine, in social organization and ceremonial, or in the more strictly intellectual regions of history, poetry, and other literature.

Within all human societies, whether savage or civilized, we may naturally expect to find old beliefs, old customs, old memories, which are relics of an unrecorded past. Such sayings and doings, wherever found, wherever told or practised, have this common " note," that they are sanctioned and perpetuated, not by experimental knowledge or scientifically-ascertained facts, not by positive law or authentic history, nor by the written record which is the necessary condition of any of these, but simply by habit and tradition. And the scientific study of folklore consists in bringing modern scientific methods of accurate observation and inductive reasoning to bear upon these varied forms of Tradition, just as they have been brought to bear upon other phenomena.

The study of this traditional lore began with the observation that among the less cultured inhabitants of all the countries of modern Europe there exists a vast body of curious beliefs, customs, and stories, orally handed down from generation to generation, and essentially the property of the unlearned and backward portion of the community.

It was then noted that similar, and even identical beliefs, customs, and stories, are current among savage and barbaric nations. Numerous illustrations of this fact will be found in the ensuing pages. This similarity may reasonably be accounted for by the hypothesis that such ideas and practices among civilized peoples must be derived, by inheritance or otherwise, from a savage or barbaric state of society. They have accordingly received the technical name of " survivals ; " and the establishment of the existence of " survival in culture " as an observable phenomenon may be taken as the first-fruits of the scientific study of folklore.

But the matter does not end there. Further study and examination of these traditional Beliefs, Customs, and Stories, in all their variations and in connection with their different settings and surroundings, ought to show us how far their characteristics are common to humanity and how far they are due to the influences of race and environment ; and should thus advance the study of Ethnology. A careful record of the geographical distribution of folklore in the United Kingdom should, for example, form a valuable contribution to our knowledge of the Ethnology of our own islands. We may look to learn what events or circumstances affect and modify racial folklore, what is the effect of contact, whether by way of commerce or of conquest, between peoples of varying degrees of civilization, and what amount of credit may be attached to tradition—using the word in the common but restricted sense of unwritten history. Eventually we may hope to adjust the balance between circumstance and character, and to arrive at the causes which retain some races in a state of arrested progress while others develop a highly-organized civilization. Thus a most important chapter will be added to the History of mankind. Further, the study of rudimentary economic and political forms should enable us to trace the lines of development of the several systems of civilized nations from their source, and to fathom the reasons of their strength or weakness ; and should thus contribute to the progress of Sociology. And finally, in the domain of Psychology we may look to ascertain far more clearly than at present the early workings of the mind of man ; to learn how unsophisticated man regards the facts of life and nature, and how he reasons about them ; to discover what have been the processes by which religion, morals, philosophy, science, art, and literature have been developed from crude and barbaric beginnings ; nay, even perhaps what have been the very germs and origins out of which they have sprung.

The conception of man's past history which has resulted from, and now directs, the study of folklore, has already made its impress on modern philosophical thought, and it would be difficult to over-estimate the additions to the sum of human knowledge which may be made in course of years by a continuance of the study on these lines. Meanwhile one very practical result should follow from it, namely, the improved treatment by governing nations of the subject-races under their sway. In the words of Sir Richard Temple (*FL.J.*, iv. 209), "we cannot understand the latter rightly unless we deeply study them, and it must be remembered that close acquaintance and a right understanding beget sympathy, and sympathy begets good government; and who is there to say that a scientific study which promotes this, and indeed to some extent renders it possible, is not a practical one?"

The subjects comprehended under the name of Folklore may be arranged in three principal groups with sub-headings as follows:

I. *Belief and Practice* relating to:

   (1) The Earth and the Sky.
   (2) The Vegetable World.
   (3) The Animal World.
   (4) Human Beings.
   (5) Things made by Man.
   (6) The Soul and Another Life.
   (7) Superhuman Beings, (Gods, Godlings, and Others).
   (8) Omens and Divination.
   (9) The Magic Art.
   (10) Disease and Leechcraft.

II. *Customs*.

   (1) Social and Political Institutions.
   (2) Rites of Individual Life.
   (3) Occupations and Industries.
   (4) Calendar Fasts and Festivals.
   (5) Games, Sports, and Pastimes.

III. *Stories, Songs and Sayings*.

   (1) Stories: (*a*) told as true; (*b*) told for amusement.
   (2) Songs and Ballads.
   (3) Proverbs and Riddles.
   (4) Proverbial Rhymes and Local Sayings.

It will be observed that this classification is of a purely objective character. No attempt is made to docket any of the observances or sayings in accordance with what might be presumed to be their primary meaning or origin. The present Handbook is intended as an introduction for the student and a guide for the collector, and in such a work it is necessary to avoid committing the novice to theories which the advance of knowledge may afterwards oblige him to unlearn. The attempt, therefore, has been made throughout the following pages to steer clear of theory as far as may be. Not that it is possible to study any subject without becoming acquainted with some, at least, of the theories formed by previous students. But such theories as have been touched upon are either obvious inferences from facts, or points noted as requiring further investigation ; and as such, and not as proven foundations on which to erect further structures, the worker is invited to consider them.

For above all things a collector of folklore should work independently of theory. The thought of a people finds its outward expression in manners and customs, in song and story. If these be carefully and literally recorded by an unprejudiced observer in the field, the thought which originally prompted them may often be more satisfactorily ascertained by the student at home, who has access to evidence from many lands. and so has a far wider area for induction at his command. And if at first the meaning of the evidence be misinterpreted, the record of observed facts nevertheless remains intact until the coming of some thinker of deeper insight. For instance, the relations of Religion and Magic are still under discussion. Everybody will agree that some practices are magical ; as to others, theorists may differ. But if they are simply set down as customs practised on certain occasions, without any attempt to refer them to their psychological source, the facts are put on record for future use, unobscured by the observer's personal prepossessions or opinions, and the settlement of the question is advanced far more than if each item were labelled as " magical " or " religious," and perchance labelled wrong ! The first point is to ascertain and record the actual concrete facts ; the interpretation of them must follow later.

II. How to Collect and Record Folklore.

Let it once more be emphatically said that this book is not intended for the members of scientific expeditions, but for travellers or residents among backward folk at home and abroad. The field of research is vast, and " Expeditions " cannot hope to cover it before it is " developed " out of existence. Anyone, then, who can and will observe and record a single fact accurately is doing a service to science.

Whatever country be the scene of operations, the first requisite in collecting folklore is to enter into friendly relations with the folk. Anything in the way of condescension, patronage, or implied superiority will be a fatal barrier to success, and any display of wealth in dress or equipage should be avoided. A kindly, simple, genial manner, much patience in listening, and quick perception of, and compliance with, the local rules of etiquette and courtesy are needful ; and the inquirer must be as careful to do nothing that could be resented as an impertinence or a liberty as he would be in the company of friends—or strangers—of his own class and nation. He must adopt a sympathetic attitude, and show an interest in the people themselves and their concerns generally, not merely in the information he wants to get from them. He should avoid any appearance of undue curiosity, should encourage them to talk, and should listen rather than ask questions. Incredulity and amusement must be concealed at all costs. The enquirer may not be able to rise to the height of a certain Somersetshire parson, and to perjure his soul with " Ah, very likely ! " when assured that the Devil's footmark in a certain rock emits blue lights in thunderstorms. But if he cannot refrain from sarcastic remarks when told that two friends after a convivial evening saw two horses in the stable where only one should be, or suppress smiles when he hears that the necessary qualification for the office of town-crier of the Bushongo is that a man should have been born a twin, he has mistaken his vocation and must not hope to succeed as a practical folklorist.

Sympathy, a true " feeling *with*," and not merely "*for*," the people, is the main secret of success. The greatest possible respect should be shown to all their beliefs and opinions, even the most trivial ; and the visitor should endeavour to attain to a certain passive and receptive frame of mind which will enable him to accept whatever marvels may be told him as if they were true.

One must from the outset recognize the fact that the customs of the lower culture, at home and abroad, eccentric though they may seem to us, are sensible and reasonable from the point of view of the folk who practise them. The difficulty is to grasp that point of view, to discover the under-lying idea, as Miss Kingsley puts it. She relates a case in point from her own experience. When descending a West African river in a canoe manned by natives, a man on the bank suddenly fired at the party. She jumped ashore and demanded " why he had behaved so exceedingly badly ? " It turned out that, as she drolly puts it, " the poor man was merely suffering under domestic affliction. One of his wives had run away with a gentleman from a neighbouring village, and so he had been driven to fire at and attempt to kill a member of any canoe-crew from yet another village that might pass his way ; because, according to the custom of the country, the men of this village would thereby have to join him in attacking the village of the man who had stolen his wife." This apparently unprovoked attack, therefore, was merely a compliance with the native forms of law (*FL. Fjort*, p. iii.).

Miss Kingsley draws the moral that the traveller labours under great disadvantages in forming a true opinion regarding native customs compared to the resident to whom they are familiar. Residents in a locality have undoubtedly a great advantage over visitors ; not only from their familiarity with the speech, the ways, and the modes of thought of the people, and from their friendly acquaintance with individuals, but because there is—or there should be—no doubt of their good will and good intentions, however mysterious may be the curiosity they show. Among savage peoples, an introduction from a white man already known and respected is often of the first importance to inspire the natives with confidence in the stranger's integrity and good faith. Again, the visitor must be indebted to the resident for a sketch of the *carte du pays*, and of the local etiquette as to salutations, interviews, visits, presents, and the like. " It is such small matters as the mode of salutation, forms of address, and politeness, as rules of precedence, hospitality, and decency, as recognition of superstitions however apparently unreasonable—which largely govern social relations, which no stranger can afford to ignore, and which, at the same time, cannot be ascertained and observed correctly without due study," says Sir Richard Temple, addressing the Anthropological Section of the British Association at Birmingham, 1913. " Nothing," he adds, " estranges the administrator from his people more than mistakes on these points." Still less, then, can a casual visitor afford to disregard them.

On the other hand, it may happen that, given the requisite tact, sympathy, and understanding, a stranger may be able to penetrate to the confidence of the people more quickly than a resident who is too far removed from them by social rank or official position. To take one instance out of many, Mr. Cecil Sharp in Somersetshire collected a number of traditional songs from the dependents of a family who were utterly ignorant of their retainers' musical skill. The family in question welcomed the knowledge, and added the airs to their own repertory, but it sometimes happens in such cases that the resident treats the revelations made to the newcomer with surprise and incredulity. " I've known so-and-so for thirty years, and *I* never heard of anything of the sort." He does not realize his limitations, nor perceive that they are the penalty he pays for greatness—or perhaps for incuriousness and want of observation. At home, the local pressman, the parish doctor, the veterinary surgeon, the land-steward, the intelligent master-workman, are better situated for collecting folklore than the squire and the parson ; and abroad, the trader and the settler may learn things that are hidden from the missionary and the Civil Servant. Yet much valuable information about social institutions and ceremonies may be gained and recorded by those who cannot easily obtain personal confidences, and they should not neglect the opportunities they have because others are not open to them.

There is great difference in the comparative ease of investigating the several groups of subjects included in folklore. The collector will be wise to begin his own studies with the Beliefs treated of in the first part of the present volume, so as to familiarize himself with the attitude of the folk and their methods of thinking and reasoning, and to learn something of the principles of animatism, animism, the unity of nature, " virtue," sanctity, contagion, sympathy, and the like, which make up the natural philosophy of the lower culture. But in the actual work of collection he had better begin with Custom, with the social and political institutions and the rites connected therewith, (represented in England by the relics of the old village system and the local manorial customs). If the enquirer is judicious and takes care not to awaken fears of annexation or increased taxation, the natives are not likely to resent enquiry into their social customs ; nor will European folk be affronted by interest shown in their public festivals, their ancient monuments, and the legends connected therewith. In fact, their local pride is often flattered by it ; and the local sports and ceremonies, as well as the children's games, may be investigated without difficulty. Some hints on personal observation of local rites are given in chapter vii. The visitor should enquire for and take advantage of all opportunities of witnessing such things, so as to be able to speak from personal knowledge. In this way a considerable body of notes on custom and legend may be got together, and acquaintances formed which may pave the way for more.

But Beliefs are a more difficult matter. They crop up incidentally and unexpectedly,—in a law-court, beside a sick-bed, on a journey or a sporting expedition ; and they must be gathered just as occasion occurs. A lady living in Needwood Forest sent her garden-boy to the house with a branch of blackthorn in flower. It never arrived there. She did not know it till afterwards, but it is held unlucky in that neigh-bourhood to take blackthorn into the house. Another lady, in the Punjâb, was asked by her gardener to shoot a parrot that was destroying his best vegetables. By the time she had got her sun-hat on, the *chuprassi* had forestalled her. Called to order afterwards by his master, he explained in deep distress that he had had no alternative. He knew that the Memsahib was "in hope," and had she taken life it would have en-dangered the life of the unborn. In New Guinea one afternoon towards dusk Dr. Seligmann had occasion to send the native boy who was his companion back to a village about a mile distant. The boy consented but asked that he might be allowed to carry a knife as a protection,—from what was not clear, but it was from no bodily foe. In such ways as these does belief betray itself, and there can be no more genuine or unimpeachable kind of evidence.

One may also note the taboos and other prohibitions observed, and enquire into the reasons for them. Every taboo must have, or must formerly have had, a belief at the back of it.

The importance of these little items of belief is not always fully recognized. We sometimes find them mentioned only as corroborative evidence of some important hypothesis arrived at on other grounds, whereas they are really the very foundation-stone of the whole structure of folklore. The main difficulty of instituting any direct quest for them is that the believer is often reserved in proportion to the reality of his belief, and not merely friendly but confidential relations are generally needed before he can be drawn out on the

subject. To betray previous and sympathetic knowledge on
kindred subjects is the best key to the lock.

The magico-religious rites which are built upon these beliefs
are for the most part shrouded in secrecy, and even payment
will not always secure admission to them. Sometimes they
are the property of an esoteric circle not limited by nationality,
and then a professor belonging to another race may be welcomed. Dr. Hildburgh, hearing that a certain Sinhalese was
a professional wizard, took the man into his service, made
known his own interest in and acquaintance with sundry
forms of magic art, and in consequence obtained much information from him and other " devil-dancers " concerning
their secret rites. The negro " conjurer " King Alexander
went so far as to deny all knowledge of magic till Miss Owen
told him that she knew the ingredients of " a trick that
could strike like lightning." Instantly he recognized a
fellow-professor,—one, too, who could injure him if disobliged
—and agreed to give her the sort of information she desired
(*FL. Congr.* 1891, p. 242).

Still more sacred and jealously guarded are the rites and
beliefs of clans and tribes, of local secret societies, and other
social groups. Mr. Sproat lived for two years in Vancouver
Island before he succeeded in discovering " a whole characteristic system of religious doctrines " which the people
had carefully hidden from the white man up till then. It
was twelve years before Mr. Batchelor discovered the serpent-
cult of the Ainu. Sir E. B. Tylor gives a list of similar instances
(*Prim. Cult.* i. 422). Only the initiated are admitted to the
part in mysteries. The late Dr. A. W. Howitt took
through an initiation-rite in Australia, after which he was
informed of the existence of a divinity whose very name had
been concealed from him before, though he had already
collected a mass of information about native customs (*J.A.I.*
1885, p. 301 *sqq.* ; cf. *Kurnai and Kamilaroi*, 1881, p. 192).

" The unspoiled savage," says Dr. Haddon, " is firmly
impressed with the sanctity of the more important ceremonies
and of all that pertains to them, and he also possesses remark-

able reticence and self-control." And of the Hindoo, Mr. Crooke says that " he lives in a world of reticence and mystery. . . . Even his own name and that of his wife and child he does not care to disclose, and he usually has a second name in reserve which no one but his *Guru* or spiritual adviser . . . knows. When you reach a higher grade than that of the mere rustic, the tendency to this kind of reticence is still more clearly marked." (*FL*. xiii. 307.)

How to enter on the subject of folklore at all is a difficulty to many. An excellent way of utilizing a necessarily short stay in a town is to haunt the stalls and little shops in the by-streets in search of amulets sold there, when enquiry and comparison will naturally lead to further communications. (Some physiological knowledge is useful in collecting amulets.) The conversational gambits recommended by one expert are to spill salt and feign annoyance, or to pick up a pin and express satisfaction. A former President of the Folklore Society once successfully authenticated the existence of a " belief " by admiring an old oak cradle in a cottage kitchen, making as if to touch it, then recoiling,—" Oh, but I suppose you would not like me to touch it ? " " Eh dear no ! " said the owner, falling into the trap, " I've had eleven already, and I've only been married fourteen years ! "—the true inwardness of which is that rocking an empty cradle brings a baby to fill it. But ingenious and earnest collectors will make all roads lead to Rome. " You can begin talking about the weather and make the conversation lead up to anything you like," says Mr. S. O. Addy (*FL*. xiii. 298). The mutual misery of waiting helplessly for a train on the platform of a country railway station served Sir John Rhŷs as an opportunity for extracting fairy-tales from a Welsh marketwoman. Admiration of an old church may enable one to draw out the sexton on bells and burial-customs, and interest in the children's games leads to acquaintance with their parents. " Hours spent in playing cats' cradle are not wasted," says Dr. W. H. R. Rivers, whose genealogical method described in chapter xi. is probably the best of all means of getting on friendly terms with most of the lower races, though there are a few who regard questions about relationships as highly improper. And in any country a stranger can put up at the village inn, or its equivalent, and join in friendly gossip with the loungers there. A light for a pipe, requested or offered, makes an excellent opening, and leads easily to conversation on the convenience of lucifer matches, other methods of getting a light, fires kept continually burning, objections to giving light or fire at certain times, stories of the origin of fire. A whole group of interested listeners would probably be attracted before this stage was reached.

Common sense is necessary in the choice of subjects of enquiry, for not every person knows every kind of folklore. Some customs are observed by men, others by women ; others again are peculiar to special trades. A life of incessant toil kills games and sports, and irregular occupation encourages them. Household customs are best observed by old-established families in solitary homesteads, but it needs a fairly large community to keep up public rites and festivals. Young women are the best authorities on love-songs, charms, omens, and simple methods of divination ; old women on nursery songs and tales, and all the lore connected with birth, death, and sickness. (A medical training is often very useful in obtaining their confidence.) Every man is more likely to be an authority on matters connected with his own craft than on anything else. One must talk to the hunter about birds and beasts, to the woodcutter about trees, to the gardener about plants, to the shepherd and the cowherd about sheep and cattle, to the housewife about baking and washing. The fundamental rule is to cultivate the habit of observation and work always from the concrete to the abstract.

When an informant is once started it is best to listen as much and to talk as little as possible. When our friend has run himself down is the time to go back over the narration, asking for details on points which have not been made clear, and endeavouring as far as may be to ascertain the " What ? How ? When ? and Where ? " of each item. The " why ? "

of any given observance is likely to be " because my grand-father did so " ; the " what for ? " is what is wanted above all, and it is not easy to discover this, unless the details of the rite itself reveal it on closer observation. The enquirer must not cross-examine the witnesses too closely, for this may either offend them by implying doubt of their word, or make them suspicious of his motives. He must avoid leading questions above all things ; they may be assented to in order to save trouble, or under the impression that assent is what is expected, or simply from want of comprehension ; and they have this further disadvantage, that they enable the person to whom they were addressed to say on a future occasion, " I have heard of " such a thing ; *i.e.* from a previous interrogator. Questions in the *negative* form are especially apt to be misunderstood. (N.B.—The Questionary at the end of this volume is meant for the collector's private use, not for a set of examination papers for his informants.) It is necessary to be careful not to tire the witnesses, who are probably unused to continuous mental exertion, and easily get confused. To test the credi-bility of a witness one may recur to the subject a few days later—" What was it you were telling me the other day about so-and-so ? " and see whether his statement varies. Or, better, one may cautiously draw out another man on the same subject.

Father Augustin de Clercq, speaking from many years' experience as a missionary in the Belgian Congo, tells us that intelligent free men of good standing, who are held in respect by their neighbours, make the best informants. Pupils at the mission schools have generally been removed from their surroundings too young to be fully informed about them ; natives in the service of white men have often forgotten a good deal, perhaps unconsciously to themselves. Information from professional interpreters and from natives locally resident but belonging to other tribes should be re-ceived with caution ; they are apt to be imperfectly in-formed and to make mistakes. Mission pupils, he further warns us, should not be desired to write down information in their own words, as they will unconsciously give it a Christian colouring ; but they may be set to write out proverbs, songs, and even stories, until they are sufficiently aware of what you want to be able to reproduce accurately what they hear from uneducated neighbours. Trained natives working independently of each other in the different missions of a district might thus collect much matter of the highest value (*Anthropos*, vol. viii. pp. 13, 14, 19).

As to the general trustworthiness of information ; first, it may be taken as pretty nearly for granted that all uneducated people will instinctively tell lies if they are frightened. That is to say, they will feign ignorance and deny what they really know. The Hindoo peasant, afraid of being dispossessed of his heritage if he discloses the particulars of his title, or the old Englishwoman, afraid of putting herself within reach of the law if she avows acquaintance with a reputed witch, will take refuge in denials and negatives, equally with the savage who lives in dread of vengeance, human or divine, if he discloses tribal secrets. Secondly, many people, especially such as belong to obsequious subject-races, like to " give pleasant answers," and will complaisantly agree to any suggestion made to them. But few are ingenious enough to invent information, as it is sometimes suggested that they do, and as it seems the imaginative Celtic nations really do (see " Fiona Macleod " in *Nineteenth Century*, Nov. 1900) ; though their inventions appear to be directed to putting the too-inquisitive Sassanach off the scent rather than to " pleasing and surprising " him. In fact, the suggestion of invention comes chiefly from persons to whom the whole subject is new and startling.

On the other hand, ignorance may be real, not pretended. Where everything is preserved by tradition alone, the frequent statement that " our fathers knew more than we " may entirely correspond to facts, especially when some great crisis of war or migration has recently affected the social life. Among some peoples there is a recognized ownership of folk-tales and songs, or of certain customs, and it is necessary to go to headquarters for them. And again, it must be recognized that individual natives differ in talents and characteristics as well as white men. There are clever people and stupid people among them as among ourselves ; people who interest themselves in the history and meaning of things, and people who give no heed to them. A man who is honestly ignorant will often direct the enquirer to a more likely informant. This is to some extent a test of good faith. Sooner or later, both at home and abroad, the proverbial " intelligent native " will turn up, who will comprehend the enquirer's purpose and may be employed to collect from others.

The collector must be on his guard against assuming that a practice does not exist, a story is not known, or a belief not held, because it has not come under his notice, but, on the other hand, definite evidence of negation should always be noted. " It is as important to record what does not occur in any district as to note what does occur. Savages rarely misinform in this respect. [One cannot always say as much for white men.] I have often been told, ' Me no savvy that, that fashion belong another fellow,' and the place where it occurs may be mentioned." (A. C. H.). Where the tribal or caste organization is strong, local differences are especially apparent.

Observation should extend to the environment of custom or belief. If there are many taboos on women, note whether any special magical powers are attributed to them, and whether the people are markedly warlike ; if any persons are forbidden to touch the bare earth, or there is any horror of spilling blood upon it, note whether the community is specially agricultural. Where rain-making ceremonies are practised, are elemental deities acknowledged ? Where there is a hierarchy of gods, is the political organization elaborate ? If kings and chiefs are surrounded with taboos, is the chieftainship hereditary ? Where totemism prevails, are secret societies found also ? and so on. A careful and intelligent observer will note all such things, and will also endeavour to find out anything he can of the history of a rite or custom—when it is *supposed* to have been introduced, by whom, and whence,—and what, if any, modification in it has been made of late years.

Unless the witnesses fully comprehend the purpose of the enquiry it is unwise to produce one's notebook before them. It may render them suspicious and dry up the stream of information. So Mr. Crooke found in Northern India, though, on the other hand, his native orderly liked to have folk-tales taken down from his dictation, like legal depositions, night after night. Mr. Addy recommends asking leave to write : " That is very interesting ; do you mind my making a note of it ? " Another very successful English collector, before taking notes, always premised that what was told him " would not be made game of, or put in the papers." And when permission has been obtained, the collector must be prepared to take down—or to appear to take down—a great deal of irrelevant matter which his informant thinks interesting, in addition to what he really wants.

Each record should be made as nearly as possible in the witness's own words. Even in England this is necessary, to avoid mistakes and false impressions due to differences of dialect among other causes, *e.g.* the words to *overlook* and to *bewitch* connote very different ideas, and in some counties to " walk " means to move in procession, while in others it means to return as a ghost. Native words which do not exactly correspond to the English equivalents should be left untranslated ; such as, for instance, the Fiote word *nkulu*, soul or mind, which especially conveys the combined ideas of intelligence and voice (*FL.* xvi. 374, 379 *n.*). The name, age, sex, residence and status of the informant should be appended to every note, and it should be stated whether he or she is bilingual. The *names* need not necessarily be published ; it is often desirable to use initials or pseudonyms only.

When an uncivilized country is the scene of action, the observer will do well to provide himself with a copy of *Anthropological Notes and Queries*, (Royal Anthropological Institute,

50 Great Russell Street, London. 5s.). In any part of the world he will find that a camera, and a phonograph for recording songs, are invaluable additions to his kit. Besides its primary purpose, the latter is extremely useful to attract and amuse the people, who will often come for miles to hear their own songs on it.

It is a good plan to carry both a red ink and a black ink pen [or blue and black indelible pencils]. Notes of things personally witnessed, and the first or principal accounts obtained from informants, can be entered in black ink, and subsequent information added in red. When working up notes afterwards, this enables one to form an estimate of the comparative value of conflicting statements. (C. G. S.)

A notebook with detachable leaves is indispensable. Every item of evidence should have a leaf to itself, and the leaves can then easily be detached and sorted at leisure. The scheme of classification used in this volume has been tested by experience, and will, it may be hoped, be found a useful model. Especially it will show the collector and his readers how much ground he has covered and what still remains untouched. For it is not to be supposed that most collectors will be able to examine the whole range of the folklore of any locality, and no one should be deterred from doing a little because he cannot do much. The Editor of *Folk-Lore*, (the Folklore Society's Journal), is always ready to consider, and if possible insert, short communications from those who are unable to offer complete articles or volumes.

In preparing notes for publication, the following five points are of first-rate importance :

1. State whether you communicated with the natives in their own language, or by means of some form of " pidgin English," or through an interpreter.

2. Be scrupulously exact in terminology. Do not call a clan, a tribe ; a fetish, an idol ; a spell, a charm ; and so on. Inaccurate and slovenly expression detracts enormously from the value of work which it has perhaps cost the worker immense trouble to achieve. Many hints on Terminology will

be found throughout this volume, and a short list of accepted terms is given in Appendix A, p. 295.

3. Relate actual incidents in preference to making general statements, and do not be afraid to use the first person singular when giving your own evidence.

4. Distinguish carefully between things which have come under your own observation and those which you have heard of from other people, or read in books. Give exact references to all printed authorities.

5. Keep your evidence entirely distinct from all extraneous matter whatever, and give your own views or comments separately as an Introduction or Conclusion.

PART I.
BELIEF AND PRACTICE.

ἡ πίστις χωρὶς τῶν ἔργων νεκρά ἐστι.

"La théorie sans la pratique devient la métaphysique."
v. GENNEP, *Rites de Passage*.

CHAPTER I.

THE EARTH AND THE SKY.

THE records of prehistoric archæology teach us that man's early progress over the world must have been very slow. At first unarmed and unclad, and subsequently but very inadequately armed and clad, he probably wandered along the banks of the rivers, surrounded by hills and mountains, by dense jungles, by fierce and often gigantic animals. He was exposed to heat and cold, to wind and weather, to storm and tempest. Forces outside himself and beyond his control caused him pain or pleasure, obliged him to move hither or thither for safety, shelter, or subsistence. Little wonder then, that he should attribute a mysterious life and power not only to the heavenly bodies, the winds, the streams, or the waves, but even to silent motionless unchanging objects, such as mountains, crags, boulders, and pebbles ; nay, further, that he should think of them as beings endowed with will and consciousness ; or that finally he should suppose them to be the abodes or manifestations of beings more powerful than himself. That such beliefs were actually held is amply proved by the myths current among primitive and barbarous races. Traces of similar ideas may also be found in the folklore of civilized Europe even down to the present day, as will be seen.

(i) Every here and there in England one may still meet with agricultural labourers who believe that *stones grow*. Suffolk farmers have been heard to state that the earth produces them spontaneously, and a piece of " pudding-stone," or conglomerate, has been pointed out as a *mother-stone*, the parent of small pebbles (*County FL.* vol. i. 2). Particular stones are credited with supernormal powers. The Manx fishermen think that a *white* stone in the ballast brings ill luck to the fishing. Fossil belemnites, wherever found, are used to cure disease or to protect from lightning. Dr. Seligmann speaks of " charm-stones" used by the Koita tribe of Port Moresby, British New Guinea, " immanent in which (and in other natural objects) is a ' virtue' communicable under certain circumstances to other objects with which they are brought into mediate or immediate contact. Either their rarity, their peculiar shape (*e.g.* naturally perforated stones), or some likeness of contour to the things they are to influence, causes them to be known for good charms. A stone shaped like a seed yam, for instance, planted in a garden will cause the yams to produce a good crop. Certain charm-stones," he writes, " —as far as I know these are always of quartz— are so highly charged with magical power that it is not considered safe for them to be touched with the hand, even by a man who is about to bring their power into play. One charm of this sort which I saw was kept in a small bamboo cylinder, out of which it was lifted by means of a bone fork, the pointed end of which was thrust through a loosely netted covering which surrounded the stones." In the darkest corner of a Naga hut Mr. T. C. Hodson was once shown a war-stone for giving victory in battle. It was a rough mass of conglomerate, kept folded in many wrappings, for if a woman were to see it, all its virtue would be lost (Hodson, 117, 189, and oral information). A *Mên-an-tol* or holed standing-stone is, or was, held in Cornwall to have the power of curing disease. Ricketty children are passed nine times through the hole, with the sun ; from east to west and from right to left. A man stands on the one side, a woman on the other, a boy is passed from the woman to the man, a girl from the man to the woman (Courtney, 160). Scrofulous children are passed naked three times through the

Mên-an-tol near Penzance, and then drawn on the grass three times against the sun (Hunt, 415). The *Lia Fail*, or coronation stone of the ancient Kings of Leinster, *roared* when the destined monarch stood on it, recognizing him (it would seem), much as the magnet turns to the Pole or the divining-rod to water. The Holy Stone of Mecca is the centre of religious pilgrimage to all Islam.

(ii) In the New Hebrides " large stones, as they naturally lie, have," says Dr. Codrington, " a high place among the sacred objects." Various tales are told of their origin. Some have individual names ; others none. " Some are *vui* (spirits) who have turned into stones ; some in the sea are men of old times turned into stones ; some were never anything but stones, but have a *vui* connected with them ; some stones above the waterfall are called ' dwellers in the land,' the native people of the stream, and these have all their names. They have much spiritual power, for they are in a way the bodily presentment of the spirits to whom the stream belongs. When men go eel-fishing they secure success by offering a bit of the first they catch upon the appropriate stone." (Codrington, 183).

Mr. (now Sir Everard) im Thurn, speaking of the Indians of Guiana, says that they believe that inanimate objects, such as plants, stones, and rivers, are compounded of body and spirit. " And not only many rocks but also many waterfalls, streams, and indeed material bodies of every sort are supposed to consist each of a body and spirit, as does a man ; and that not all inanimate objects have this dual nature avowedly attributed to them is probably due only to the chance that while all such objects may at any time . . . show signs of a spirit within them, this spirit has not yet been noticed in some cases." (Im Thurn, 355).

We can hardly expect to find the idea of personality in rocks and stones in so crude a form in Europe. But the belief that great standing-stones are transformed human beings is common. The circle known as the Hurlers in Cornwall is believed to be a party of Sabbath-breakers turned to stone. The King and the Whispering Knights among the Rollright Stones in Warwickshire would have conquered England could they have reached Long Compton. Listeners may hear them whispering together, and on certain nights they go down to the spring to drink. (*FL.* vi. 5-51 ; xiii. 292.)

(iii) We may next turn to the beliefs in superhuman inhabitants of crags and mountain tops. Mr. Alldridge, District Commissioner in Sierra Leone, mentions " a mountain known as the Mamba ; an isolated peak which, standing out in bold relief against the surrounding country, naturally produces a very awe-inspiring effect that makes it an object of terror to the people, who believe it to be the dwelling-place of the devil." Nothing would induce the people to cut a track through the dense brush at the foot of the mountain to enable Mr. Alldridge to ascend it. " They would not even accept the present that I hoped would procure me a little bit of the rock ; and they seemed uncommonly glad when I turned to depart without having aroused the anger of the local evil spirit." (Alldridge, 202.) On the other side of the African continent, the Rev. J. Roscoe tells us that the natives of Uganda supposed that certain hills were possessed by the ghosts of wild animals. The people approached them with fear and were careful to appease the lion or leopard spirit when obliged to cross them. Neither the king nor any messenger from him might venture on any of these hills, so they were used as sanctuaries by persons who had incurred his displeasure (Roscoe, 319). The gods of the Todas live amongst the peaks of the Nilgiris. In Europe the hilltops are usually the habitation of giants. Polyphemus lived on Mount Etna, Cader Idris in Wales is the Giant's Chair, the wonderful basaltic rocks on the north coast of Ireland are the Giant's Causeway. In other cases the Devil owns such places ; we have the Devil's Chimney at Cheltenham, the Devil's Dyke on the Downs above Brighton.

In these groups of examples, culled from hundreds that might be adduced from all parts of the world, we get the three stages or varieties of belief glanced at in the opening paragraphs of this chapter. The first group of beliefs cited above exhibits the mental attitude distinguished by Dr. R. R. Marett (*Threshold of Religion*) as *Animatism* ; namely, the attribution of life and personality—but not of a separate or apparitional soul—to what, for us, are inanimate objects, such as mountains, stones or rocks, or the ascription to such objects of mysterious awe-compelling power (termed by M. van Gennep, " dynamism "). In the two latter groups we are confronted with the doctrine of *Animism* or the belief in spiritual beings pervading nature, so luminously expounded by Professor Sir E. B. Tylor in *Primitive Culture*. In group ii. we have spirit conceived of as immanent in matter,—the rock or stream is the *embodiment or manifestation* of a spirit. In group iii. the rock, crag, mountain, or other inanimate object, is the *habitation* of spirits more or less separable from their dwelling-place and visible, if at all, in other shapes. These two forms of animistic belief must not be confounded. The native terms for the several kinds of spiritual beings locally recognized should be used whenever possible ; and when translation is necessary the word " spirit " is best restricted to the spirit embodied in matter, and the separable being, capable of appearing apart from his or her habitation, may be distinguished as the local daemon, or *genius loci*, or even as a godling (cf. chap. vii.). Not that the collector should classify his notes under the several headings of Animatism, Animism, etc., but that he should endeavour to grasp and express the native thought with as much precision as possible.

The following examples of beliefs about springs, rivers, and the heavenly bodies, exhibit the same ideas, and show, moreover, how the conception of a living and powerful personality, transcending human personality and power, may overshadow the more analytic notion of a being compounded of body and spirit. A man was drowned in the (Derbyshire) Derwent in January 1904. " He didna know *Darrant*," commented an old neighbour, with a triumphant tone in her voice, " He said it were nought but a brook. But Darrant got him ! They never saw his head, he threw his arms up,

but Darrant wouldna let him go. Aye, it's a sad pity,—
seven children ! But he shouldna ha' made so light of Darrant. He knows now ! Nought but a brook ! He knows
now ! "—" She talked of the river as if it were a living personage or deity," wrote the narrator, " I could almost imagine
the next step would be to take it offerings." (*FL.* xv. 99.)
The reverence paid to the Ganges throughout Northern India
and the rites performed on its banks, are too well known to
need more than a mention here. " On *l-'ánṣára* (Midsummer)
Day," says Dr. Westermarck (*FL.* xvi. 31), " the people of
the Andjra," a district of Morocco, " bathe in the sea or
rivers ; for on that day all water is endowed with *baraka*,"
(" magic energy " or " benign virtue "), " which removes sickness or misfortune. They also bathe their animals." We
have in the British Isles numerous healing wells, to which
sick persons resort for cure, and hang rags from their clothing
on the surrounding bushes ; " wishing-wells " into which the
votaries drop pins and pebbles, desiring boons ; and " holy
wells " consecrated to some saint, generally a local saint.
Wales is full of stories of spectral ladies, " white," " black,"
" grey," and " green," who appear beside wells, give mysterious
hints of hidden treasure and vanish. The Lady of the Van
Pool in South Wales is a being of a more material type. She
was the ancestress of a long line of distinguished physicians
whose descendants are by no means yet extinct. She came
out of the lake, and returned thither when her human husband
broke the marriage compact. She is still said to appear at
Lammastide gliding over the surface of the pool, and not
many years ago people used to go to the pool at that season
in the hope of catching sight of her (Rhŷs, *Celtic FL.* i. p. 2).

The conception of the treacherous mermaid, the " fair
pretty maid with a comb and a glass in her hand," is widely
spread. The Lorelei of the Rhine will occur to every reader.
English water-demons were more repulsive. " Jenny Green-
teeth " lurked under the weeds of stagnant pools in Shropshire
and Lancashire, and dragged in unwary children. Inland
" mermaids " threatened floods if offended by projects of

drainage. The Tees, the Skrine, the Ribble, and many other rivers have each a spirit, who in popular belief demands human victims. Sometimes the water-demon appears in animal form, as the kelpie, water-horse, or water-bull, of Celtic regions.

The man in the moon, or a woman in the moon is known everywhere in Europe and the hare in the moon is as familiar in the Far East. People in England bow to the new moon, or turn their money, or show it to her the first time of seeing her. It is very unlucky to see the new moon through glass, and children are told that it is wicked to point the finger at the moon or try to count the stars. A girl in Berkshire was said to have been struck dead after doing so (*FL.* xiii. 419). On the continent of Europe, the Magyars forbid sweeping towards the sun ; a girl who throws the sweepings in the direction of the sun will never be married ; a married woman may not appear in face of the sun with uncovered head. The ancient Greeks held that at eclipses the heavenly bodies were threatened by demons, and they shook brass and iron to drive the demons away. Even to-day in Greece the proper way to stop an eclipse of the moon is to cry out, " I see you ! " Similar beliefs and practices survive in Judea and elsewhere.

Among the Ojibways of North America, Peter Jones, himself an Ojibway, tells us that the sun, moon, and stars are adored as gods. " At the rising of the sun the old chiefs and warriors chant their hymns of praise to welcome his return : and at his going thank him for the blessing of light and heat during the day. When a visible eclipse of the sun takes place, the poor Indians are thrown into the greatest alarm. They call it the sun's dying, and suppose that he actually dies. In order to assist in bringing him to life again, they stick coals of fire on the points of their arrows and shoot them upwards into the air, that by these means the expiring sun may be re-animated and re-kindled. . . . I well remember when I was a little boy being told by our aged people that I must never point my finger at the moon, for if I did she would consider it an insult and instantly bite it off." (Jones, 84.) The Sun-dance is the great annual religious solemnity of the Blackfeet Indians. Vows made to the sun in times of trouble or danger are then paid, often at the cost of severe torture to the vow-makers ; offerings are made, prayers uttered, and consecrated food shared by the participants. " The great Sun-god is our father," said Mad Wolf, the greatest orator of the Blackfeet, in dismissing the tribe when the Sun-dance was over ; " he is kind, for he makes the trees to bud and the grass to become green in the springtime. He gave the people good hearts that they also might be kind and help each other." (M'Clintock, 322.)

It will not escape the notice of an observant reader that the European beliefs on these subjects are of similar quality, indeed are sometimes identical, with those of uncivilized peoples, always excepting the actual deification of the heavenly bodies or other material objects—an idea which naturally is no longer to be met with here.

The Questions given in the Appendix cover many points which it is not possible to develop in the text (see p. 302).

CHAPTER II.

THE VEGETABLE WORLD.

MAN must from the earliest times have been indebted to trees and plants for food, shelter, fuel, and clothing. In the search for edible plants and fruits he could not fail to become acquainted also with the poisonous, narcotic, or medicinal qualities of other plants. Between need, fear, and the sense of mystery, the growth of myth and ritual would be practically inevitable. And accordingly we find that in the lower stages of civilization trees and plants are almost more the objects of awe and reverence than are the sun and moon, storm and tempest, mountains and waters. Sensation, consciousness, and personality are ascribed to them ; innate magical or supernatural properties and powers are attributed to certain species. We meet with sacred trees, tree-gods, tree-worship ; stories of human beings transformed into trees ; myths of the descent of mankind, or of families or individuals, from trees.

" The Malays believe that the coco-nut has eyes, and therefore will never fall on anyone's head." (R. V. H. Burne, Singapore, 6th Oct., 1913.) Drovers' sticks in England are often made of holly, because it has the useful property of bringing back runaway cattle if thrown after them (*FL.* xxii. 18, 236). The sacred pole of the Omaha is made partly of ash, partly of cottonwood, both of which they account sacred and mystic trees. The cedar is also a sacred tree among them, and the Teton Dakota believe that the smell of cedar-wood or of the smoke from it drives away ghosts. The Japanese believe that a mulberry-grove will never be struck by lightning, and therefore repeat the word *Kuwabara* (mulberry plantation) during a thunderstorm, to deceive the Thunder-god and so ward off the stroke (Hildburgh, 142).

In most countries we find that certain trees and plants are credited with power to repel lightning, and are used accordingly. Houseleek is encouraged on roofs in France and Germany for this purpose ; sprigs of yew are hung from balconies in Spain with like intent, and are kept in houses in the Hebrides to protect from fire. Pieces of hawthorn gathered on Ascension Day are used in England as a protection against lightning (*FL*. vii. 381).

Many of the beliefs connected with trees and plants are exactly analogous to the case of the New Guinea " charmstones " described in the last chapter.

Their mysterious *virtue*, like that of those stones, is often thought to be communicable to other bodies by contact. In Westphalia, on the 1st of May, and in Dalecarlia, on or about Ascension Day, the young heifers are ceremonially struck with a branch of the mountain-ash or rowan-tree, and in the former locality a formula is recited to the effect that as sap comes into the birch and beech, and as the leaf comes upon the oak, so may milk fill the young cow's udder. The rod or sapling of mountain-ash is then set up over the cowhouse or on the haystack, to remain there through the summer. A similar ceremony is prescribed in the Vedas, for use at the new moon (Kuhn, 161). The mountain-ash (rowan-tree, wicken-tree, or whitty-tree) is used as a protection against witchcraft throughout the British Isles, and in Scotland and Shropshire it is used, as the hazel is in Somerset, for driving horses or cattle. Animals struck with either of these will prosper, but if struck with a willow-rod they will be seized with internal pains ; and children beaten with broom or willow will cease to grow. For the broom never attains to the height of a tree, and the willow is " the very first tree to perish at the heart," to quote the West Midland ballad which relates the mythical reason for its early decay ; and their qualities will be communicated to the creatures struck by them. The birch and the ash, no doubt, owe their repute as instruments of punishment to their tall and slender growth. " Hey, gaffer," said a Cheshire blacksmith to a schoolmaster newly imported—with his tawse—from Scotland, " thou'st bin a-ammerin' our Tum wi' a strap wi' a 'ole in it, 'stead of a stick, an' A wunna 'ave it. Whoy, *what dost think ash-plants was growed fur ?* " (*FL.* xxii. 18.)

Trees and plants themselves are sometimes threatened and beaten into good behaviour. In Guernsey it is held advisable to swear while planting small herbs, " to render them thoroughly efficacious." (*Guernsey FL.* 425.) In England it is said that a young walnut-tree must be thrashed to make it bear. The following ceremony was formerly used at Jugra, near Selangor, to make the durian-trees more productive. On a chosen day the villagers would assemble at the durian-grove and would single out the most barren trees from the rest. One of the local *Pawangs* (wizards) would then strike the trunk of the tree sharply several times with a hatchet, saying, " Will you now bear fruit or not ? If you do not, I shall fell you." The tree would reply, through the mouth of a man who had been stationed for the purpose in a mango-stin-tree hard by, " Yes, I will now bear fruit, I beg you not to fell me." (*M.M.* 198 ; cf. *FL.* xxiv. 247 ff.)

The following is from a private letter dated Rawal Pindi, 13th November, 1911. " I heard the following story up at Chamba (Punjâb). The natives refused to fell a certain tree, because they said there was a *Devi* in it and that when it was cut it began to bleed, and cried out. They could not get anyone to touch it, so at last P., one of the assistants, who told me the story, ordered the Lohār (blacksmith) to make him an axe. The man asked him, did he want it to fell this tree ? and when he said yes, refused to make it, saying that he did not want the Sahib's blood to be on his head. The result was that the tree was not felled at all." (S. F. Burne, R.F.A.) In Balochistan " a *jāl* tree (*Salvadora*

Indica) was inhabited by a jinn which persecuted the family in a house near. My proposal to cut down the tree caused such horror that I gave it up, and a new house had to be built for the family, the old one being abandoned." (M. L. Dames.)

Such animistic beliefs are often attached to species as well as to individual trees. "When an oake is falling," says Aubrey (*Remaines*, 247), "before it falles it gives a kind of shriekes or groanes that may be heard a mile off, as if it were the genius of the oake lamenting. E. Wyld, Esq., hath heard it severall times." In Wales they say the elder bleeds if it is cut (Trevelyan, 103). Burning elder-wood is frequently forbidden in England. In Needwood Forest they say that to burn it would raise the Devil (*FL.* vii. 380). In Lincoln-shire they believe that the *Old Lady* or *Old Girl* is offended by cutting elder-wood without asking her leave, which may be done thus : " Owd Gal, give me some of thy wood an Oi will give thee some of moine, when I graws inter a tree." (*County FL.* v. 20.) The Danish peasants believe that a being called Hyldemoer, or " Elder-mother," dwells in the elder-tree and avenges all injuries done to it. Before they cut it they ask her permission, thus : " Hyldemoer, Hylde-moer, permit me to cut thy branches." (Thorpe, ii. 168.)

When the Bengali wood-cutters go to the jungle to cut wood they take with them a fakir (religious devotee), who performs ceremonies and makes offerings to the jungle-deities. The Maghs, a jungle tribe of Bengal, are most unwilling to fell trees. Nothing but positive orders and the presence of Europeans would induce them to do so. On felling any large tree, one of the party was always ready prepared with a green sprig which he ran and placed in the centre of the stump, when the tree fell, as a propitiation to (or rather as a new home for) the spirit which had been dislodged so roughly, pleading at the same time the orders of the strangers for the work (Crooke, ii. 87). The *tabak* trees of the Malay Peninsula, which produce the rare and valuable gum called *gharu* or eaglewood, are under the care of certain *hantu* or wood-spirits, and it would be hopeless for the uninitiated to attempt

to find *gharu*. Even the *Pawang* has to be very careful,
to burn incense, to recite charms and invocations and offer
sacrifices, to make sure that the eaglewood do not vanish
before it can be secured. " When the tree has been felled,"
says Mr. Skeat, " you must be exceedingly careful to see
that nobody passes between the end of the fallen trunk and
the stump ; whoever does so will surely be killed by the
' eaglewood spirit,' who is supposed to be extremely powerful
and dangerous. I myself received a warning to this effect
from some Labu Malays when I saw one of these trees felled."
(*M.M.* 211.)

The Votiaks of Eastern Russia have sacred woods, where not
a single tree may be cut down, or the god of the place will
avenge the injury. In the midst of such a wood there is
often a hut, or simply an altar, on which animals are offered
in sacrifice (*Rev. des Trad. Pop.*, xi. 248, quoting *Russ. Ethn.
Rev.*).

A specially interesting example of a sacred and inviolable
tree comes from Shropshire. Near Oswestry there grew an
oak tree known as the Mile Oak, which was already " olde "
in 1635, and was popularly associated with the legend of the
eponymous local saint, Oswald King of Northumbria, killed
in battle A.D. 642. When it was cut down by the agent of
the lord of the manor in 1824, a ballad-lament was " made "
and circulated in which this noteworthy verse occurs :

> " *To break a branch was deemed a sin,*
> A bad-luck job for neighbours,
> For *fire, sickness, or the like*
> Would mar their honest labours."
>
> *Shr. FL.*, 241.

Turning from negative to positive forms of veneration, the
following account of a sacred tree on the Rio Negro of South
America (Darwin, p. 71) is worth quoting. " Shortly after
passing the first spring we came in sight of a famous tree
which the Indians reverence as the altar of Wallechu. It
is situated on a high part of the plain, and hence is a land-
mark visible at a great distance. As soon as a tribe of Indians

come in sight of it, they offer their adorations by loud shouts. The tree itself is low, much-branched and thorny : just above the root it has a diameter of about three feet. It stands by itself without any neighbour, and was indeed the first tree we saw ; afterwards we met with a few others of the same kind, but they were far from common. Being winter the tree had no leaves, but in their place numberless threads, by which the various offerings, such as cigars, bread, meat, pieces of cloth, etc., had been suspended. Poor Indians, not having anything better, only pull a thread out of their ponchos, and fasten it to the tree. Richer Indians are accustomed to pour spirits and maté into a certain hole, and likewise to smoke upwards, thinking thus to afford all possible gratification to Wallechu. To complete the scene, the tree was surrounded by the bleached bones of horses which had been slaughtered as sacrifices. All Indians of every age and sex make their offerings ; they then think that their horses will not tire, and that they themselves shall be prosperous. . . . The Gauchos [half-castes] think that the Indians consider the tree as the god itself, but it seems far more probable that they regard it as the altar "—a conclusion which we may perhaps take leave to doubt.

The greatest of the household gods of the Kachàris of Eastern Bengal is Bàthau, whose " living symbol," the *siju* or *hiju* tree (*Euphorbia Splendens*), may be seen growing within a fence of split bamboo in many of the Kachàri homesteads. All offerings made within the house on the altar of Song Ràjà (another household god) are afterwards brought outside and laid at the foot of Bàthau. " The writer has often seen heads of goats, pigs, and fowls, etc., as well as plantains, *tàmul*-nuts, *pàn*-leaves, *gaizà* (a mixture of rice and pulse) humbly laid down for Bàthau's acceptance, and to enlist his influence to preserve the household from disease, famine, and misfortune of all kinds." (Endle, 36.)

Another set of beliefs connects trees and plants with the life and death of man and beast.

In years when nuts are plentiful, babies will abound also.

Primroses and willow catkins may not be gathered; or, if plucked at all, it should be in large quantities, for the number of the poultry hatched in the early spring will be limited by the number of spring flowers brought into the house. Snowdrops may not be brought in at all, as they will make the cows' milk watery and affect the colour of the butter. These are common English country beliefs. A favourite incident of folk-tales is the *life-index*, the tree or plant with which the fate of an individual is bound up. If it withers he sickens, if it is cut down he comes to a violent end. This is a matter of actual belief and practice in West Africa, and in some of the Indo-Oceanic Islands (see *G.B.* iii. 391). Among the English-speaking population on the eastern shore of the Chesapeake, when one of the family leaves home, a bit of " live-for-ever " is stuck in the ground. If the absent one prospers it will take root and grow, if not it will wither and die (Hartland, *L.P.* ii. 37). In Europe we sometimes find it supposed that if any injury should afterwards befall the split ash-tree through which a child has been passed for the cure of infantile hernia, the child will suffer accordingly ; and the practice of planting a tree to commemorate the birth of a child may be a relic of the same belief.

The fate of the kingdom of the Rajas of Gonda was said to be bound up with a *Chilbil* tree there which, like many sacred trees of India, had sprouted from the " tooth-twig " of a saint. The kingdom was to last till the day a monkey sat on the tree. This happened on the morning the Mutiny broke out, which ended in the ruin of the dynasty (Crooke, ii. 92).

In many villages in the district between the upper Cross River and its tributary the Aweyong, there is a large tree surrounded by a circle of rudely-carved stones. Of the stones the natives can give little account, except that they feed them every year at the feast of new yams, and believe that their forefathers offered human sacrifices to them. But the tree, they say, is the " life " of the village. It may not be cut, for when a man dies his spirit goes into it, even if he

have died away from home; and when a woman wants a
child, a sacrifice is offered to it. Each village has its own
tree, and no village can sacrifice to another's tree. This,
although they acknowledge numerous personal gods, and a
" big god" over all who lives in the sky (Partridge, p. 273).

Some peoples attribute the origin of mankind to trees.
A Scandinavian myth recorded in the *Elder Edda* relates that
three of the gods found an ash and an elm lying on the sea-
shore and transformed them into the first human beings.
At Saa in the Solomon Islands, it is said that men sprang
spontaneously from a particular sort of sugar-cane called
tohu-nunu (Codrington, 21). The Andaman Islanders say the
same thing about the bamboo (*oral inf.*). The Amazulu believed
that the first man " broke off " from a bed of reeds (Callaway,
88, 97). The English nursery fable that the new baby was
found in the parsley-bed or under the gooseberry-bush,
compared with these myths, illustrates at once the likeness
and the difference between savage and civilized folklore.
Conversely, transplanting parsley is often believed to cause
a death in the family (*Shr. FL.* 249).

Totem-clans are often named from trees and plants, and
the members of the clan usually believe themselves to be
descended from the plant in question, and pay respect to
the species accordingly (see *Totemism* in chapter iii.). Classical mythology is full of legends of the transformation of
human beings into trees, such as the well-known story of
Philemon and Baucis. Much more might be said on this
subject, and on tree-marriage, tree-burial, the divining-rod,
the magician's wand, the Maypole, the mistletoe-bough, the
use of plants in divination and in medicine. The principles
of animatism, animism, sanctity, contagion, and sympathy
run through them all, as they run through the whole gamut
of folklore. But the foregoing examples are enough, it may
he hoped, to illustrate not only the folklore of trees and plants,
but the idea of the essential unity of the various manifestations
of life and of the sympathy existing between them, which
pervades so much of the philosophy of the Lower Culture.

The collector should be careful to note and describe the appearance of any unfamiliar species of tree or plant, and to give its botanical name if possible. If unversed in botany, he should note the height of the species, and describe the growth, whether straight, curved, or angular ; the bark, rough or smooth ; the leaves, evergreen or deciduous, long, rounded, serrated, pinnate, or pinnatified ; the fruit, nuts, or seed-vessels ; thorns or prickles ; colour of flowers or fruit, or leaves at the change of seasons ; and, if possible, he should procure photographs or specimens of leaves and blossoms or seed-pods, which can be submitted to some expert botanist for identification.

See Questionary, p. 306.

CHAPTER III.

THE ANIMAL WORLD.

(*Beasts, Birds, Reptiles, Fishes, Insects.*)

THE same ideas of the interdependence, the interchange-ability, the essential unity, of all forms and manifestations of life, which appear in the folklore of plants, underlie much of the folklore of animals. There is, for example, the well known European belief in the *werwolf*, the man who is a human being by day and a wolf by night. This is still the theme of popular legends in Wales (Trevelyan, 296). Varied by environment, it appears in India and in the Malay Penin-sula as belief in the *wer-tiger*. " For the time being, the man *is* the tiger," says Mr. Skeat (*P.R.* ii. 191). In South Africa he is the hyena, in Balochistan the black bear, and so on.

The idea of the possibility of such transformation is practi-cally universal. The *Metamorphoses* of Ovid are simply a collection of classical examples of it. Sometimes the power of " shape-shifting," as it has been called, occurs as a special faculty possessed by sorcerers ; sometimes, as in the tale of Circe's lovers, the change is the effect of a curse laid by a sorcerer or sorceress on a victim. In this form it is a familiar incident of European folk-tales, such as *Beauty and the Beast* and the *Frog-Prince*, little romances which turn on the re-covery by the hero of his proper shape. A Bushman folk-tale describes the sensations of the transformed heroine, a wife and mother. " Bring the child quickly ! " she says to her younger sister, " while I am still conscious, for I feel as if I should forget you, *I feel as if my thinking-strings would fall down.*" (Bleek and Lloyd, 89.)

In the folk-tales of many of the lower races the majority of the characters are usually animals, who speak and act like human beings to such an extent that it is plain that the narrators, who tell the stories in all seriousness, have no distinct idea of the boundary line between man and beast. The beast is a beast in one sentence, and a man in the next, without even the necessity for any ceremony of transformation. And in Mota (Banks Islands), certain persons are believed actually to *be* animals or plants at the same time that they are human beings, in consequence of the mysterious influence exercised by some living creature that has rested on their mother's body, or some fruit that has fallen on her loin-cloth, during her pregnancy. The child when born shows its origin by its character, and it must never eat the animal or plant in question ; that would be a kind of cannibalism. (*J.R.A.I.* xxxix. 173.) Closely akin to this is the much more common belief in animal ancestors. This appears in European folk-tales. A Gaelic version of *Cinderella* represents her as the daughter of a sheep (Cox, p. 534). But in Viti Levu, one of the Fiji Islands, the natives can state definitely which of their own great-grandfathers in the eighth or ninth degree was an eel or some other such creature (*J.R.A.I.* xxxix. 158).

This brings us to the peculiar social institution known as *Totemism,* which is so closely bound up with the subject of animal-beliefs that it must be considered here. The word *totem* comes to us from the Red Men of North America, where the totemic system was first observed by a Mr. John Long in 1791. The essential feature of the system is the association of a *whole clan,* or other definite social group, with a *whole species,* or class, of other beings—generally animals, often plants, sometimes inanimate things—which forms the " totem," " augud," " kobong," " nyarong," " siboko," or whatever it may be called, of the human group. The group is (*a*) known, with few exceptions, by the name of the *totem,* and in normal cases its members do not marry anyone of the same name, *i.e.* they are exogamous (see chapter xi.). Exogamy cannot, however, be reckoned as an essential part or distinctive feature of the totemic system. It does not occur in the totemic regions of Polynesia, and it flourishes apart from totemism in other countries. (*b*) The members of the group believe themselves to be related to the totem, or of "one flesh" with it. As a Mabuiag man said to Dr. Haddon : "*augud* all same relation, he belong same family." (*Torres Straits*, v. 184.) Again, an Arunta of the Kangaroo totem-group, looking at his own photograph, said : "That one is just the same as me ; so is a kangaroo." (S. & G., *Centr. Tribes*, p. 202.) Frequently, though not invariably, they believe themselves to be descended from the totem. (*c*) There is believed to be a magico-religious bond between the human group and the *totem*. The members of the group look for protection from their *totem*, and at the same time show respect to it. The manner in which respect is shown varies, but the most usual way is by the prohibition to injure the *totem* ; to kill it, if a living creature ; to eat it, if edible— unless, in some cases, ceremonially. Sometimes totem-groups contain similar lesser groups within themselves, in which case individuals of course acknowledge two or more totems. In other cases, one clan, or corresponding social group, owns more than one totem (see Appendix A, *Terminology*, p. 297).

The totemic system is found not only in North America, but in Australia and many of the Oceanic Islands, among several of the Dravidian tribes of India, and of the Bantus of Africa. Whether it has ever been universal—that is to say, whether all races have passed through a totemic stage of development—is a question still undecided. Single items of similar beliefs are to be found in every quarter of the globe, but whether they are fragmentary survivals of a vanished totemism, or the raw material out of which some peoples have elaborated a totemic structure of society, cannot as yet be determined. Meantime, the collector should carefully note every detail which may have a bearing on the subject ; such as, for example, prohibitions to injure certain birds and their nests—the robin, wren, and swallow in England, the stork on the continent of Europe, etc.

In some of the Australian tribes, together with the regular totemic system, the men reverence a certain kind of bird as their " elder brother," and refuse to injure any of the species, while the women do the same with another kind as their " elder sister " (Howitt, *Native Tribes*, 148). Another practice sometimes found concurrently with totemism is that of acquiring animal protectors by individuals. Among the Omaha and allied tribes, a youth on arriving at manhood was sent forth into the wilds alone to fast and pray to *Wakonda* till he received in answer a vision suited to his special needs. When this came in the form of an animal, as it frequently did, he went forth again within a short time to find and kill one of that species, part of whose remains he preserved thenceforth as his most sacred treasure ; and thereafter accounted the species his " guide, philosopher, and friend " for life (Fletcher, *Omaha Tribe*, p. 128 *sqq.*). Wherever these concomitants of totemism—the " sex-patron " and the " guardian genius " as they have been happily termed by Dr. J. G. Frazer (*Totemism and Exogamy*, iii. 449 *sqq.*)—are met with, their relation to the local totemic system should be carefully examined and recorded.

The combined wisdom and power of animals implied in all these beliefs must not escape our notice. It reappears in a variety of forms. In the Banks Islands (non-totemic) a man can procure a *tamaniu*, an (actual) individual *animal-familiar*, from any man who has, or possesses a stone which has, *mana* (power), for this purpose. The *tamaniu* is kept in confinement and employed to injure the owner's enemy for him. If it dies, the owner dies too (*J.R.A.I.* xxxix. 176). Somewhat analogous to these are the animal-familiars of witches—the toads and black cats of Europe, the badgers of India, the wolves and hyenas of South Africa.

Again, we meet with animal-gods, and with gods incarnated in the form of animals, as in Hindostan, Samoa, and ancient Egypt. It is difficult to distinguish between the two classes. The thought of the lower culture is not clear on such points, or if clear is not easy to us to grasp. A remarkable case is that of the Ainu bear-sacrifice, as it is usually termed, though it might perhaps be better described as a ritual feast. Bear-hunting is a regular and most important part of Ainu life, and the flesh of the bear is freely eaten. A bear-cub is sometimes taken alive and brought up in a hut with the family until nearly full-grown, when it is ceremonially put to death by suffocation after being shot at with blunt arrows. The flesh is exposed for three days at the sacred east window of the hut, and then feasted on with much drunkenness. Before execution the victim's pardon is asked for what they are about to do; it is desired not to be angry, and is assured that many *inao* and plenty of wine will be sent along with it. It is addressed as follows: " O thou divine one, thou wast sent into the world for us to hunt. O thou precious little divinity, we worship thee; pray hear our prayer. We have nourished thee and brought thee up with a deal of pains and trouble, all because we love thee so. Now, as thou hast grown big we are about to send thee to thy father and mother. When thou comest to them, please speak well of us and tell them how kind we have been; please come to us again and we will sacrifice thee." (Batchelor, 487. Cf. Harrison, pp. 87 *sqq.*) The Ainu believe that animals possess souls and will enjoy a future life, but in spite of the epithets applied above to the bear, it does not appear from the evidence that the beast ranks as a god. The Ainu recognize a multiplicity of personal, functional gods, local and general, of varying rank, who are diligently worshipped by prayer and offerings of *inao*, or whittled willow-wands. Their favour is implored at every stage of a bear-hunting expedition and they are thanked if it is successful. They are formally notified of an intended bear-sacrifice, and the skulls of animals killed in hunting are placed with the household *inao* offered to them.

In other cases we find certain species of animals associated with certain gods, as in ancient Greece—the owl with Pallas,

the bear with Artemis, the mouse with Apollo, the pig with
Demeter, etc. Tacitus tells of the sacred white horses kept
by the ancient Germans in a sacred grove, and harnessed
periodically to a sacred chariot, which they drew about the
country attended by priests, who found omens in the animals'
starts and neighs, and " thought themselves the servants,
but the horses the confidants, of the gods." In England
even to this day horses (and also dogs) are credited with
the power of seeing ghosts ; a wish formed on seeing a white
horse will be fulfilled (*Shr. FL.* 208) ; the rider of a piebald
horse knows how to cure whooping-cough, and the idea is
not unfrequently expressed that the animals " have more
knowledge than any Christian ! "

Perhaps hardly enough importance has hitherto been
attached by students to this idea of the superhuman power
and knowledge of animals. Yet it is widely spread. The
Red Men of the Upper Amazon, it is true, are said to dislike
and despise animals, and to regard them from much the
same point of view as a Brahman would a Pariah. But
many of the North American tribes think of animals as
bound together in tribes and communities like human beings,
and acting like human beings, but wielding superhuman power.
In fact, scientific anthropologists personally acquainted with
them have not hesitated to speak of the animals as their
gods. The Skidi Pawnee believed that " only less powerful
than the gods in the heavens were the gods of the earth,
ruled over by lodges of *Nahurak* or animals. . . . In these
lodges the animals were wont to gather together in council
to make or mar the fortunes of men. To these lodges individuals favoured by the gods of the earth were conducted
from time to time and were instructed in the mysteries of
earth-craft. They especially are the patron-gods of the
medicine-men and often of the warrior." (Dorsey, xix.) In
the traditional stories of many of the American tribes, animals
are agents in the formation of the world and its adaptation
to human needs, and are in some sort the Culture-Heroes
of their peoples. The Helpful Animals (*e.g.* Puss in Boots),

so common in the folk-tales of the Old World, belong to the same stage of thought.

The natives of Calabar, who practise a kind of pictographic writing, think that the art was taught to their forefathers by the baboons (*J.R.A.I.* xxxix. 211). Often it is held that animals have a language of their own, that men may learn it, that the animals also understand human speech, that on a certain night in the year they speak the language of men. In Schleswig and Holstein it is believed that any one who goes to the cowshed on Christmas night may hear the oxen talking together and foretelling the deaths of those who are fated to depart before Christmas comes again; and sometimes the listener hears his own name among the list (Thorpe, iii. 7).

What has been said of beasts applies equally to birds, with the addition that, owing of course to their powers of flight and song, they figure more especially as messengers between earth and sky—fire-bringers, soul-bringers, baby-bringers. Neither must insects, reptiles, or fishes be omitted from the collector's investigations, though they cannot be specially dealt with here—the folklore of the serpent alone would furnish matter for a volume.

Any peculiarity of form, colour, or habits—red fur or plumage, cleft lip, hooked beak, migration, or hibernation, etc.—should be noted, as it may often throw light on the association of particular beliefs with particular species. Such peculiarities also often form the subject of stories accounting for their origin.

See Questionary, p. 307.

CHAPTER IV.

HUMAN BEINGS.

FROM the ideas of uncultured man about his surroundings we turn to his ideas about himself, both as an individual and in relation to his fellow-man. Man's own personality and natural powers, their supposed extent, the precautions taken to preserve them from injury, the manner in which they are affected by food, clothing, contact or communication with other persons, must all be considered. This involves touching upon a great variety of practices, some very savage, others very trivial.

Without unduly generalizing, some ideas found as living principles of action in the lower culture may be briefly mentioned. Special magic properties are attributed to particular persons, or thought to reside in particular parts of the body. Blood is looked upon as the essence of vital energy, and saliva as hardly less potent. Union between different persons may be effected, or at least a mutual bond established, by mingling blood, or by sharing food together. The nature and qualities of anything eaten are supposed to pass into, or to be imparted to, the eater. Magic virtue, either to hurt or to heal, may be communicated by touch, by breathing, by saliva, or even by a glance of the eye. The personal name is treated as an integral part of the personality, which generally also includes shadows, reflections, portraits, and effigies; and power may be gained over another by the possession of anything that has belonged to him, or has in any way formed part of his personality. " I could save you or ruin you if I could get hold of so much as one eye-winker or the peeling of one freckle," said the Voodoo conjurer, " King Alexander," to Miss Owen (*Trans. FL. Congr.* 1891, p. 235). Hence the care universally taken of stray hairs or nail-parings. For things that have once formed parts of a whole are held to continue in sympathy though separated. Early in the nineteenth century, a boy in New Hampshire, U.S.A., was badly scalded, and a piece of skin, fully an inch across, sloughed off from the wound. His mother declared that it would never decay during his lifetime, and preserved it carefully among her treasures to the day of her death in 1843, after which his sisters continued to do so ; and though after he had once left home to begin life for himself his family never heard of him again, they satisfied themselves that he was still living, as the bit of skin remained undecayed (*Journ. Amer. FL.* ii. 69). This sympathetic principle forms the basis of most of the common magical practice of every-day life. A mother wishing to wean her baby will be recommended in Shropshire to throw some of her milk into a running stream or into the fire. As it is carried away or consumed, so the rest of the milk will gradually disappear. The principle is even extended from the severed parts of a whole to separate things which have once been in contact with each other : the best illustration of which, as Mr. Hartland observes, is the common form of wart-cure, in which the wart is rubbed with something—a piece of meat, a bean-pod—which is afterwards thrown away, and, as it decays, so will the wart. Thus sympathy may be set up by contagion.

All these principles recur continually in practice. Some instances of their working may be given here.

Professor Haddon exchanged names with a chief in the Torres Straits who belonged to the Crocodile clan, and found himself regarded as a brother crocodile-man on another island. Every member of the Arunta tribe of Central Australia has his or her secret name, which may be either a new one, or that of some celebrated legendary man or woman.

This secret name is never uttered except on the most solemn
occasions, and that of any particular individual is only known
to the fully initiated men of his own local totem group. " To
utter such a name in the hearing of women or of men of
another group would be a most serious breach of tribal custom,
as serious as the most flagrant case of sacrilege amongst
white men. When mentioned at all it is only in a whisper,
and then after taking the most elaborate precautions lest it
should be heard by anyone outside the members of his own
group. The native thinks that a stranger knowing his secret
name would have special power to work him ill by means
of magic." (S. & G., *op. cit.* 139.) Sir Everard im Thurn (220)
says that although the Indians of British Guiana have an
intricate system of names, it is of very little use, in that the
owners have a very strong objection to telling or using them,
apparently on the ground that the name is part of the man,
and that he who knows it has part of the owner of that name
in his power. Among the Ainu we are told " the wife should
not pronounce her husband's name, for the bare fact of
mentioning it is equal to killing him, for it surely takes away
his life." (Batchelor, 252.) A local goddess in India was
accustomed to climb a tree and ask the names of individuals.
They died in consequence. A lid placed over her put a stop
to the mortality (*FL.* v. 280).

The subject of names and effigies is fully discussed by Dr.
Tylor, *Early History of Mankind,* 108-152 ; cf. also Frazer,
G.B. i. 403 *sqq.*, and Clodd, *Tom Tit Tot, passim.* The
importance in the lower culture of the extended idea of
personality which the practices connected with names imply
can hardly be over-estimated.

To turn to the subject of food :—it is a common belief in
the British Isles that pigs can see the wind, and the Shropshire
folk say that anyone who drinks bacon-broth will acquire
the same power (*Shr. FL.* 210). In the Torres Straits, parts
of the bodies—usually the eyes, ears, or cheeks—of enemies
killed in battle are given to boys and young men to eat ; or
blood or sweat may be given to a lad to drink, " to learn

him," " to make him strong and like stone, no afraid ; "
" heart belong boy, no fright." (*Torres Straits*, v. 301, 302.)

" In Mota, one of the Banks Islands, society is divided into
two exogamous groups, the members of which are supposed
to have very different dispositions. Fathers and sons do
not belong to the same group, and they are forbidden to
eat together, lest the sons should acquire the disposition of
their fathers' group.

" In the same island there are secret societies for the practice
of magic arts. The members on joining the society drink
together from the same coco-nut. This forms a mutual bond
which pledges them never to exert their magic powers against
one another." (W. H. R. R.)

The solemn sharing of food together by the bride and
bridegroom constitutes a typical form of marriage ceremony,
the significance of which as a bond of union is very marked
when, as among Servians, Santals, Niam-niams, and others,
the marriage feast is the first and last time in their lives that
a man and a woman eat together (Crawley, 379, 380).

Among the Arabs of Moab, says P. Jaussen (*Coûtumes des
Arabes de Moab*), " the act of eating together is considered
something solemn and sacred " (p. 86). " To make use of
an Arab expression, ' while the salt of the Sheikh of the
Ka'ābneh was in our belly' (*notre ventre*), we had a right
to his protection, and he was obliged to protect us. . . .
This protection, projected in a sense outside the tent over
the person who has taken the food, who has entered into
living communion (*communication de vie*) with the family
and the tribe, and who carries away in his belly the bread
and salt, contributes no little to give security to the desert.
. . . The guest has a right to the protection of him who
receives him into his tent ; but he is required in his turn to
observe certain rules, especially to be loyal and to avoid everything like felony. An Arab who profits by hospitality to commit by treachery a robbery or any other evil deed falls into
supreme contempt and exposes himself to the utmost reprisals."
(pp. 87-89.)

The commingling of blood creates a more permanent bond than the above. Mrs. French Sheldon, F.R.G.S., made the bond of " blood-brotherhood " with no less than thirty-five tribal chiefs during her expedition in East Africa, and with others in the course of her previous travels in the African continent. " It makes the participants, as it were, one person," she writes to us (Oct. 1909), " and commands recognition from every member of the tribe. The ceremony among the Masai and neighbouring tribes consists of the sacrifice of a perfectly white goat whilst the arms (if not the legs) of the two parties are scarified just below the elbow, and as the blood flows the arms are put together, so that there is a (supposititious) fusion of blood, the while complete silence is maintained, whilst the witch-doctor or fetisher incantates, and sometimes sprinkles over and about the wounds some magic powder. The wound—really nothing more than a good pin-prick—is bound up with a leaf of banana or some other glossy leaf. Then each party rolls up in his fingers a little pilule of meal provided by the chief and saturates it in the blood of the goat, which has been stuck in the throat, and although not quite dead, does not survive the ceremony, but provides an exclusive and highly prized viand for the chief and the fetisher. These little pilules are exchanged, and as soon as they have been swallowed, the brotherhood is a *fait accompli*. Then all the witnesses begin to sing and dance—if cavorting round in a disorderly fashion can be called dancing. The initiated is given certain emblems to evidence the existence of his recognised entrance into the tribal fraternity, and sometimes there are also certain signs imparted to be used in order to be recognized and to recognize. The details of the ceremony differ in different regions, but the covenant ensured the same safety as far as I was concerned, and was never violated." Dr. Trumbull, in *The Blood Covenant*, gives details of a variety of similar rites.

Something of a sacred and mystic property is generally ascribed to blood. The Esthonians, like the Jews, will not use blood for food. They think it contains the soul of the animal, which would enter into anyone who tasted it (*G.B.* i. 353). The " devil-dancers " of Southern India become " possessed " by a demon, and utter oracles and prophecies after drinking the blood of a sacrificed goat (*ibid.* 134). The Maori notion is that blood is full of germs ready to turn into malicious spirits (*J.A.I.* xix. 101). The Egyptian fellahîn believe that if the blood of a murdered man, or one accidentally killed, falls on the ground at the place of his death, it gives birth to an *afrît* or local demon (C. G. S.).

Here we may draw attention to the use of blood in some (not all) of the *Intichiuma* rites of the Arunta tribe of Central Australia. It must be explained that, like all Australian blackfellows, the Arunta are totemic, but they are unacquainted with the natural process of the reproduction of species, and believe that every child is the reincarnation of some deceased ancestor. His totem, therefore, is fixed, not by his immediate parentage on either side, but by the totem of the ancestor whose spirit is thought to have entered into his mother desiring to be reborn. The *Intichiuma* are rites performed by men of each totem-group for the purpose of increasing the numbers or quantity of the totem, and the consequent food-supply of the tribe as a whole. Either at the close of the rites or afterwards, the totem-group eat their totem ritually and sparingly. If they did not do so, they say, their power of performing *Intichiuma* would fail. The ceremonies vary considerably, but are always conducted with the utmost solemnity, secrecy, and silence, save for the sound of the songs. In the Emu-group a level space is cleared on the ground and the men allow blood from their arms to drip upon it till they have made the surface " slab and good." They then draw on it representations of certain parts of the Emu—the internal fat, the eggs in different stages ; the *Churinga* or ancestral soul-caskets are set up, and the men sit round the drawings singing magic songs. In the Hakea group (the Hakea is a shrub of which the flowers are used to make a sweet drink) the men assemble under an old and venerated Hakea-tree, round a sacred stone, the soul-casket of a

Hakea ancestress, and a young man is chosen to open a vein in his arm and let it bleed upon the stone, while the others seated round him sing their songs. The rendezvous of the Kangaroo group is the " death-stede " of a famous legendary Kangaroo, whose tail, turned to stone, is still to be seen there. The rocky cliff side overhanging it is painted with kangaroo emblems, and some young men standing on it are bled in the arm, so that the blood runs down upon the painting. The others meanwhile are grouped below, singing. After this they paint their bodies with kangaroo emblems and then hunt a kangaroo, which is killed and solemnly eaten, and some of the fat is smeared on the bodies of the men. On the second day the hunt and the feast are repeated. The men say that the cliff is full of the " spirit-parts " of animal kangaroos, which are impelled by the blood-letting to leave it and be reborn as young kangaroos (S. & G. ch. vi.).

Returning to Europe, we find that in the early nineteenth century old Welsh people believed that the blood is the seat of the soul, and that if any hæmorrhage were not quickly checked, the soul would pass away with the flowing blood (Trevelyan, 306). In the same line of thought is the well-known idea that drawing blood from a witch deprives her of her power.

Power resides also in saliva. " King Alexander " spat " violently and copiously " upon the " luck-ball " he made for Mr. C. G. Leland, to impart to it " his own strong spirit," but when his pupil, Miss Owen, proposed to imitate his example he scornfully replied that she and Mr. Leland had nothing to spit out ! (*Trans. F.L. Congr.* 1891, 233.)

To turn to other parts of the body. Many peoples account the head sacred. Throughout Polynesia and Further India it is thought an indignity to have another person (literally) placed over one's head. The Burmese and Cambodians build their houses with only one story on this account, and Maori chiefs have been known to object to enter a ship's cabin for the same reason (*G.B.* i. 363 *sqq.*). The Baganda think that the soul of a dead man clings to the lower jaw, and preserve the jaw-bone accordingly (Roscoe, pp. 112, 113). The Bihari and others in Eastern Hindustan believe that the "water of life" exists in the little finger (*FL*. xi. 433). Village doctoresses in England say that the forefinger is poisonous, and forbid wounds or sores to be touched by it.

Much power is universally attributed to the eye. When the eyes are painted on a Sinhalese image, what was a lump of stone or clay becomes a "god," and a mirror may be held up to catch the first glance of the "god." (C. G. S.) The belief that some men can cause pregnancy in a woman by breathing or by a glance of the eye has been noted in modern London (*FL*. ix. 83). A godparent's glance at the baptismal water makes the infant grow up like him or her (noted 1837, *Shr. FL*. 286).

"Some persons' eies are very offensive," says Aubrey (*Remaines*, 80) ; "there is *aliquid divinum* in it, more than anyone thinks." Of Tupai, the high priest of Samoa, we read : "His very look was poison ; coco-nut died and bread-fruit withered at his glance" (Turner, p. 23). A certain Yorkshireman afflicted with this power attempted to mitigate its ill effects. "Look, sir," said his neighbour to the author of Carr's *Craven Glossary* (i. 137), "at that pear-tree, it wor some years back, sir, a maast flourishing tree. Ivvry morning, as soon as he first oppans the door, that he may not cast his e'e on onny yan passin' by, he fixes his een o' that pear-tree, and ye plainly see how it's deed away." (The *first* act of any series is usually the important one, and the effect of any kind of "virtue" is enhanced when the agent or the object is still fasting.) Another Yorkshireman habitually walked with his eyes bent on the ground, lest his blighting gaze should fall on a little child or other living thing (*County FL*. ii. 163). A Sinhalese chief was much disturbed because Mrs. Seligmann drank some milk in public. He explained that some envious eye in the crowd was certain to rest upon the draught (C. G. S.). The glance of envy or admiration is supposed in Oriental countries to have the effect of the Evil Eye ; hence it is injudicious to express admiration of a child, horse, or anything else valued by the owner. (Compare " forespeaking " in Scotland.)

Perhaps there is no more widespread or better-known belief than this of the Evil Eye, *mal' occhio, jettatura*. The subject has been dealt with in detail by Mr. F. T. Elworthy, *The Evil Eye*. It must be noted that it is not a matter of " art-magic " or " witch-craft," but a (supposed) natural power inherent in certain persons, whether voluntarily or involuntarily exerted. Collectors in the British Isles, especially, must be careful not to confuse " overlooking " " blinking," or " giving a blink wi' the ill e'e," however intentionally and maliciously done, with " ill-wishing," " cursing," " bewitching," or " putting a spell on " a person or thing (or whatever the local phrase may be), which are feats of witchcraft.

Powers of divination and prophecy also may be innate and not acquired, as, *e.g.* the gift of second-sight among the Scottish Highlanders.

Personal innate power or " virtue " (using the word in the sense in which it occurs in the Authorized Version of the Bible, and in which it still lingers among the English peasantry) is frequently due to circumstances of birth. Innate healing powers are attributed to the seventh son born in unbroken succession throughout the British Isles. Twins, considered unlucky and even killed in West Africa (M. H. Kingsley, *Travels*, 324), are called " children of the sky," and credited with rain-making powers by the Baronga of the eastern side of the continent (Junod, 412-16). In the Punjab, first-born sons are believed to have power over dust-storms and hail-storms (*FL*. xiii. 278).

Much attention has of late been directed to the idea of the magical virtue inherent in persons or things ; of which the New Guinea " charm-stone," so powerful that it had to be insulated from all contact, is our typical example. This " virtue " appears as *nkici* on the Loango Coast (Dennett, *FL. of the Fjort*, 135) ; as *baraka* in Morocco (*FL*. xvi. 28) ; as *gūn* in Hindustani. The Oceanic word *mana* has also been thought to be synonymous with *virtue*, and has been so used

by anthropologists ; but recent evidence shows that it is
an elastic term known over a very wide area, and has no one
English equivalent (*v.* Hocart in *Man,* vol. xiv., June, 1914).

Barkat, or magical power, says Major Aubrey O'Brien,
writing of the Punjâb, varies according to the rank, the
descent, or the personal qualities of the individual. He himself had considerable reputation as a rainmaker, and on one
occasion, during a severe drought, the opening of some badly-
needed irrigation-works was put off for some days until he
could accomplish a tedious and lengthy journey to cut the
dam in person and so secure a propitious beginning for the
undertaking. Mohammedan saints, "approved because of
their magical powers, not for their spiritual qualities," are
venerated in their lifetime, and form an important element
in the population. Sanctity of this kind is heritable property, but there is a constant battle among the saintly family
as to their inheritance. The eldest son tries to maintain
the rights of primogeniture, while the younger brethren argue
that sanctity is inherited by all the children alike, and that
they also are saints, competent to cure diseases, like their
father, and have a right to share in the profits of their common
inheritance (*J.R.A.I.* xli. 509 *sqq.*). As to the Hindoo population, the annoyance to which General Nicholson, of Delhi
fame, was subjected by the devotees who prostrated themselves before him, and welcomed blows from him, is a matter
of history ; and the following extract from the Calcutta
Sulabh Samachar, referring to the visit of King George V.
in 1911, shows the view which devout Hindoos take of the
royal dignity. "He who is a ruler of rulers on whose
dominions the sun never sets, under whose sway we enjoy
so much peace and happiness, from the sight of him will be
procured the fruit of beholding a Deva, who can doubt it ?
It is written in the Scripture that the King roams the earth
in the shape of a Deity. The Creator has made the King
out of the esssences of Indra, Varuna, the moon, the sun,
fire, air, Yama, and other deities. Therefore it is certain
that the sight of the King yields the same spiritual benefit

as the sight of a Deva, and by the attainment of this holiness, so difficult to procure, His Majesty's Indian subjects will be delighted, and will feel that their life's purpose is fulfilled."

From this it is but a step to the exaltation of a living man into a deity, as in the cases of the Roman emperors, the Dalai Lama, the Mikado of Japan, and others cited by Dr. J. G. Frazer. (*Hist. Kingship*, p. 142 ff.)

In the South Sea Islands, this mysterious property of sanctity is supposed to hurt, not to heal, and excites fear, not adoration. In Polynesia especially, the sanctity inherent in a chief or a priest was thought so powerful that it was held dangerous to touch him or his property or anything that had been in contact with his person. A slave in New Zealand is recorded to have died on learning that he had unwittingly eaten the remains of a chief's meal (*G.B.* i. 321).

On this idea of sanctity was based the famous Polynesian institution of the *Tapu* or *Tabu*, by which " the idols, temples, persons, and names of the King and members of the reigning family ; the persons of the priests ; canoes belonging to the gods ; houses, clothes, and mats of the King and priests ; and the heads of men who were the devotees of any particular idol, were always *tabu* or sacred. The flesh of hogs, fowls, turtle, and several other kinds of fish, coco-nuts, and almost everything offered in sacrifice, were *tabu* to the use of the gods, and the men ; hence the women were, except in cases of particular indulgence, restricted from using them. Particular places were also rendered permanently *tabu.*" (W. Ellis, iv. 387.) Sickness or misfortune would befall anyone who touched what was *tabu*. An incident occurring in New Zealand illustrates the working of these rules. Some blood from the wounded foot of a Maori chief fell on a canoe, which thereby became *tapu* to him, and the owner gave up possession without hesitation (*G.B.* i. 358). Again, in Fiji, Mr. Fison had a fine mat given to him by a man who durst not use it because the King's eldest son had sat upon it, and had thereby rendered it *tapu* (*G.B.* i. 318). Thus the *tabu* could be used as an engine of government and of political tyranny.

The word *tapu*, (in Melanesia *tambu*), corresponds to the Latin *sacer*, used to express both *holy* and *accursed*—a double meaning which is retained by the French derivative *sacré*, though it has been lost by the English *sacred*. Hence (*a*) things set apart, separated, not to be touched, because sacred, consecrated, dedicated, or devoted, and (*b*) things set apart because thought to be defiling, or contaminating, such as corpses, and, in some circumstances, women, are both said to be *tapu*. It is a distinct word from *rahui*, prohibited, forbidden. For instance, certain berries growing at Kirauea in the Sandwich Islands were said to be *rahui*, forbidden, because *tabu na Pélé*, sacred to Pélé, the goddess of the Volcano. Nevertheless, the Polynesian natives, according to Mr. Ellis, —writing in 1835 of the state of things he and his missionary companions had found existing in the early years of the century—were accustomed in speaking to Europeans to apply the word *tapu* or *tabu*, not (as originally) to the prohibited things, but to the prohibition itself (Ellis, *op. cit.* iv. 385). Hence we get the English substantive *taboo*, which has been defined as *a prohibition resting on a magico-religious sanction* (see Appendix A, p. 299).

To explain. Many things are forbidden merely by social convention, such as chaffing your paternal aunt in the Banks Islands, asking an Oriental after the health of his female relatives, wearing shoes in a Mohammedan mosque, or a hat in the presence of a European sovereign. Such *customary prohibitions*, whatever their several origins may have been, are not *now* taboos, strictly speaking. Disregard of them would be little more than " shocking bad form," entailing social ostracism, or possibly physical chastisement, on the offender, but not supernatural penalties nor even legal punishment. The *sanction* or force—legal, social, moral, or magico-religious —by which each prohibition is supported should always be carefully enquired into, and the expected consequences of disobedience noted ; and the term " taboo " should be confined to prohibitions the breach of which is believed to cause evil or disaster automatically, either (*a*) in the shape of sick-

ness, misfortune, or general " bad luck "—such as, to give
European parallels, may befall the man who grubs up the
fairy thorn, destroys the prehistoric monolith, or burns the
forbidden fuel—due to the inherent sanctity either of the
desecrated object or its owner, or the wrath of an offended
god ; or (*b*) by the defilement caused by the contaminating
evil of the tabooed object, which infects the taboo-breaker
by its contagion, imposes the like state of taboo upon him,
and generally necessitates ritual purification before he can
rejoin his fellows. For example, food-prohibitions rest on a
variety of bases. " Taboos of commensality " are usually
true taboos, entailing either a magico-religious penalty,
as in the case of the New Zealand slave already mentioned ;
or the penalty of defilement, as among the Hindus, where
caste is forfeited by taking food touched, cooked, or shared,
by one of lower caste. But prohibitions of particular articles
of diet have many sources. Some are totemic, based on
respect for the totem ; others are dictated by respect for
dead relatives. The English Gypsies often vow to abstain
from the favourite food of the deceased for this reason. Among
the Lushai of Assam, a man whose father has been killed
by a wild beast may never eat the flesh of that species (*FL.*
xx. 419). Other food-prohibitions depend on the principle
of sympathy, and others again seem to be merely precautionary
or prudential. Thus, Loango women married by the *lemba*
rite, which ties a particularly firm knot, may not eat the fish
xala, which is noted for struggling in the net when caught
(Dennett, *B.B.M.M.* p. 11). Young people in New Guinea
abstain from eating certain rough-skinned leaves lest their
own skins should become harsh and make them unattractive
to the opposite sex ; but when older they cease to be so
particular (C. G. S.). " Medicine-men " in India and Africa
frequently prescribe abstinence from certain articles of diet
to their patients, sometimes even for life. These are rather
magico-medical than magico-religious prohibitions.

Besides the things which were inherently *tapu*, the Polynesian priests could impose temporary taboos on things and

places, such as islands, districts, and the fruits growing on
them, which then might not be entered upon or eaten, under
pain of disaster or disease.   Such taboos were proclaimed
by setting up taboo-marks or signs on the spots in question.
Similar signs are used in other countries (*e.g.* Africa, Queensland, New Guinea) to mark grounds, crops, or personal possessions reserved for special uses either by public authority or
by the individual owner.   They are often enforced by a
spell or a curse laid on them by a wizard, in which case they
may rank as true taboos, otherwise they are merely equivalent to our " Trespassers beware ! "   *E.g.* the *giriba* sign of
New Guinea will bring pains and penalties even on the owner
himself, should he touch the fruit before the spell has been
removed by the wizard who laid it, but the *hata* sign only
indicates that the thief will have to reckon with the owner,
or with the village authorities, for his misdeeds (C. G. S.).
A prohibition enforced merely by legal sanction cannot be
ranked as a taboo.

The Polynesian priests could also proclaim seasons of *tapu*,
which produced a state of things something like a combination of a general fast and an interdict.   Such seasons, under
the name of *genna* (prohibition) are a regular part of the
social order among the Nagas of Manipur.   They occur both
periodically,—at the beginning and end of the two seasons
into which the climate divides the year, at certain stages
in the growth of the rice-crop, at the annual ear-piercing
of infants, the annual commemoration of the dead, and the
like—and occasionally, on events such as births, deaths,
epidemics, or hunting expeditions.   " The latter are as much
part and parcel of the village customary law as the former."
The length of the *genna* varies.   A household may be *genna*
for as much as a month after the birth of a child ; a village
for a single day only, before clearing a patch of jungle.   During the *genna* the village or household affected is cut off from
the outer world ; no one, whether an inhabitant or a stranger,
may go in or out.   Within, the men and women are rigidly
separated, each sex cooking its own food and eating apart ;

and various food and other prohibitions are observed until
the rites proper to the occasion are completed. A breach
of *genna* by one individual would bring disaster not only
on himself but on the whole of the social group involved
(Hodson, 164-180).

The word *tapu* as applied to anything separated, set apart,
is usually rendered in English by " tabooed " when speaking
of things, and " in a state of taboo " (viz. *separation of a
magico-religious character*) when referring to persons. Kings,
priests, warriors on the war-path, funeral parties, and women
in childbirth and other natural crises, are usually " in a state
of taboo," and are accordingly isolated from human contact
by minute and elaborate prohibitions, any breach of which
may lead to dire consequences. Thus, a whole Naga village
may be described as being " in a state of taboo " during a
genna. But when we enquire for whose sake the prohibition
is imposed, and which party, the taboo-breaker or the one who
is in a state of taboo, would be injured by its transgression,
a difference reveals itself. The warrior returning from
battle, or the mourner from the funeral rite, submits to
quarantine for the sake of those whom he might contaminate
by his " uncleanness," to adopt the expression used in the
Authorized Version of the Old Testament (Numbers xix. xxxi.)
in reference to these cases. And the innumerable restrictions
as to food, names, and occupations, imposed on women, the
secrets kept from them, the customs of avoidance between
the sexes, are not intended, or very rarely so, for the women's
own protection, but for the benefit of the other sex. It is
the man who breaks the taboo, not the woman who is in a
state of taboo, who will be injured by any transgression.
Fear of the contagion of feminine weakness is generally
assumed to be the cause of these prohibitions, but in view of
the extreme dread often evinced of a woman's curse, it is
equally probable that they are due to her supposed innate
magic power. At all events, an English Gypsy lad will not
eat food which has come in contact with a woman's garment
(*FL*. xxiv. 326), just as a Fijian will not venture to use a

mat which has been touched by a chief (*ante*, p. 54). In Oceania it is the ordinary man who is hurt by contact with the great personage. But in most other parts of the world the king, the priest, or the Brahman submits to a variety of troublesome restrictions for his own sake, to keep his own power or purity intact and uninjured. If any of the prohibitions are broken, it is he himself who is thereby hurt or weakened, and through him, possibly, the community ; but not the one who touched, spoke to, or looked at him. It is evident that the phrase " a state of taboo," as commonly used, does not always connote exactly the same thing, and that, to avoid any confusion of ideas, it is needful to ascertain in each case *for whose benefit* the separation is enjoined, and on whom, therefore, the penalty for infringing it would fall, as well as the nature of the penalty itself, which, as has been said, may either be misfortune and death to the offender or the community, or only the extension of the state of taboo to the taboo-breaker by contagion.

If we would survey the entire area of savage ideas about the human species, we must include the whole subject of the mutual relations of the sexes, the relation of the individual to the group, and the relations of one group or community to another. The *rationale* of tribal marks and ritual mutilations especially, is very obscure. It may be based on the familiar ideas of power, submission, mutual contract, unity, and sympathy, mingled in varying degrees, but it needs careful investigation. Photographs or drawings of the marks should be procured if possible, and care must be taken not to mistake mourning marks, individual peculiarities, or cuts made for therapeutic purposes, for tribal devices.

Methods of communication with outsiders should be noted, whether by speech, signal, or gesture (*v. A. N. and Q.*, p. 182). Many peoples,—for example, the North American Indians and the Queensland blackfellows—have regular codes of gestures. The African tribes signal to each other by " tuck of drum." In Europe, the Italians especially make plentiful use of significant gestures, and the Gypsies and other itinerant folk leave messages for each other by means of secret symbols. These things may seem somewhat outside our province, but they have a bearing on ritual and drama, and may eventually be found to throw much light on man's early attempts to communicate with the Unknown.

Many other points germane to the subject must, for lack of space, be left without comment.

The reader is referred to chapters xi. and xii., and also to the Questionary (p. 309), where an attempt has been made to cover the ground.

CHAPTER V.

THINGS MADE BY MAN.

> " His house, for so they say,
> Was haunted with a jolly ghost, that shook
> The curtains, whined in lobbies, tapt at doors,
> And rummaged like a rat : no servant stay'd :
> The farmer vext packs up his beds and chairs,
> And all his household stuff ; and with his boy
> Betwixt his knees, his wife upon the tilt,
> Sets out, and meets a friend who hails him, ' What !
> You're flitting ! ' ' Yes, we're flitting,' says the ghost
> (For they had pack'd the thing among the beds).
> ' Oh, well,' says he, ' you flitting with us too—
> Jack, turn the horses' heads and home again ! ' "
>
> Tennyson, *Walking to the Mail.*

SUCH is Tennyson's rendering of a tale common in both
Scandinavian and English country sides ; a homely version
of the belief which in more classic times took shape in the
cult of the Lar, or Hearth-spirit, who haunted the fireside
of the ancient Roman.   Nature has no monopoly of animism ;
for a house may have its *genius loci* as well as a grove or a
fountain, and most of the works of man are the subjects of
animistic, or at least animatistic, beliefs.

The simplest articles of daily use are held capable of giving
omens.   Knives falling, rings breaking, clocks stopping,
crockery rattling, furniture creaking, all are portents.   And
the uncanny powers of ordinary manufactured objects culminate in the vampire furniture recorded by Mrs. Trevelyan
in South Wales.   She tells of a handsome sixteenth-century
chair, guiltless of nails, which scratched the hands of every-

one who sat in it, and kept up the habit through several changes of ownership. Worse than this " Vampire chair " was a " Vampire bed " of the date of James I., which was bought at a sale by a resident at Cardiff. His wife and infant child had occasion to sleep in it during some repairs, and each night the child awoke screaming. On the fourth night it died in its mother's arms, and on its throat was found a red mark from which blood was oozing. Some time afterwards the owner himself slept in the bed, and was wakened every night by feeling something clutching at his throat. On the third night he sprang up and looked in the glass, and there saw that blood was oozing from the centre of a mark on his throat. A friend, who occupied the bed with the idea of investigating the matter, had a similar experience.

Another vampire bed and chair had a particular predilection for the clergy. " A very pious Dissenting minister " of the eighteenth century stayed at an old farmhouse in Glamorganshire, which had once been a mansion-house and still retained many pieces of the original furniture. He sat for some time in an old arm-chair beside his bedroom window, and when he rose to go, found his hand bleeding, with marks upon it like the marks of teeth. In the night he was wakened by a sharp pain in his side, and found blood flowing from it, and when he visited his grey mare in the stable, behold, she too had similar marks on her neck. On enquiry he found, said his great-grand-daughter, who told the tale, that other ministers had suffered the like in that room, and he attributed the matter to some former owner of the furniture haunting the house as a vampire. Other ministers after him had similar experiences, down to the year 1853, when the sufferer was no less a person than " a dignitary of the Church of England ! " (Trevelyan, 54 *sqq.*)

In the last story we see the mischief was ascribed, not to the furniture itself, but to the restless ghost of its deceased owner still clinging to it. And when the original makers or owners of remarkable implements, weapons, and the like have been persons of note, the occult powers of the objects may very well have been derived from them.　This is naturally the case with the amulets made by a skilled wizard, or the beads blessed by a saint, and it may also account for the special powers often ascribed to royal insignia.　The royal paraphernalia of the several Malay States are strictly tabooed from the touch of the vulgar herd.　To such a pitch does the poisonous force of the royal drums of the Sultan of Selangor extend that a Rajah who accidentally trod upon one of them died in consequence of his inadvertence !　A Chinaman who was ordered to remove a hornet's nest (!) from the inside of one of the drums also swelled up and died a few days later ; and, strange to say, Mr. Skeat himself, after seeing them and handling the silver trumpet, was seized with an attack of malarial influenza.　(*M.M.* p. 42.)　On his recovery he found himself obliged to attend a sacrificial feast given by a Malay friend in pursuance of a vow made to a local saint on condition of Mr. Skeat's restoration.

But the theory of supernormal qualities derived from ownership does not meet the case of veneration paid or powers ascribed to ordinary articles of household use.　Take the case of glass, a manufactured substance, and known to be such, which nevertheless, here in Great Britain, has attracted a whole string of superstitious observances.　The root-idea of them all seems to be a notion that glass and crystal have a mysterious prophetic power which enables them to create phantasms or spectres.　Hence the practice of " crystal-gazing " to procure visions of the future or the absent.　A girl who combs her hair and eats an apple before a mirror on the mystic night of Hallowe'en will see the face of her destined husband looking over her shoulder ; and if the mirrors be not covered in a death-chamber you may see the face of the dead in them. An infant is forbidden to see its face in the glass before it is a year old.　It is supposed that you cannot legally—at any rate not safely—take your oath as to the actual occurrence of anything you may have seen through glass.　It is an evil omen to see the new moon through glass, especially the first moon in the year.　It is also an evil omen to break a glass, and worse to break a mirror, which portends seven years' trouble, if not death.

> " The mirror cracked from side to side,
> ' The curse is come upon me ! ' cried
> The Lady of Shalott."

And finally, the sacred treasure, the Palladium, the family Life-Index, as we might call it, of the Musgraves of Edenhall, Cumberland, is a glass—

> " If this glass you do let fall
> Farewell the Luck of Edenhall."

It still exists, carefully kept in a leathern case for safe preservation (*Denham Tracts*, i. 184).

It may be that the act of manufacture, or transforming one article or substance into another, as in many primitive stories of Creation, was once held to be in itself mystical, uncanny ; especially when any chemical process was involved. It seems no more than likely that the process of fermentation, for instance, should excite wonder and admiration, particularly in the case of liquor, when the resulting effect of intoxication is taken into account. Nor would the witches' cauldron have acquired its reputation had not the idea of something uncanny been associated with the cookery of daily life. Countless little household rules point to this conclusion. In Shropshire and Staffordshire, one person only may stir a boiling pot or put dough into the baking oven. For two to share the work would cause strife. On the other hand, every member of the household must have a hand in stirring the Christmas pudding and the batter for the Shrovetide pancakes. A cross should be marked on every loaf, and on the bung-hole of every barrel, and a silver coin put into the churn, to keep off the witches (*Shr. FL.* 275 *sqq.*).

The churning charm,

> " Churn, butter, churn.
> Come, butter, come.
> Peter stands at our gate
> Waiting for a butter cake.
> Churn, butter, churn,
> Come, butter, come ! "

recorded by Aubrey in the seventeenth century, was heard in Berkshire so lately as A.D. 1900 (*FL.* xii. 330).

In the Hebrides, if you accidentally enter a byre at milking-time, or a dairy while churning is going on, you should say, " May God bless everything that my eye sees or that my hand touches." (Goodrich-Freer, p. 240.)

In the north-east of Scotland no baking must be done when there is a dead body in the house, and iron must be put into the meal chest lest the bread or meal turn mouldy. A woman must never sing while she is baking. The Yule Bread at Christmas must be baked during the night, and the cakes must not be counted. A cake must be named for each member of the family, and if one should break in the baking, the person who owned it will die before next Christmas. The May Day bannocks must be kneaded entirely in the hand, not set down except for baking, and must be lifted from the " girdle " into the hand of the recipient (Gregor, *Kilns, Mills,* 24, 35). The Dumb Cake, kneaded, turned, baked, and eaten in silence by a party of maidens, each contributing an equal share of material and labour, on a mystic night—Hallowe'en, St. Agnes' Eve, or even any Friday (Aubrey, p. 65)—will procure a dream or vision of the future husband.

In view of the possibility that an atmosphere of wonder hung about the mere act of making, it is worth while to investigate the folklore of ordinary domestic processes—boiling, baking, brewing, churning, and the like ; and of early arts, such as net-making, spinning, weaving, smelting and forging metals. Not every collector's notes will extend to arts and crafts in general (see chapter xiii.), so the present may often be found a suitable heading under which to record the infinity of bits of good and bad luck which attend the daily avocations of life in every European household. A little of the same kind of lore has been recorded in India, and much more might no doubt be gathered, both in the East and among the careful housewives of Africa. On the Loango coast no more apt simile for the devoted care of a statesman for his people can be found than " As a woman incessantly watches

her cooking-pots, so Mamboma watches over the Bavili." And
the feelings which prompt the housewife's labours may be
gathered from the prayer, pathetic in its naiveté, of the Nandi
women of East Africa, when they make pottery, " God, give
us strength, so that when we cook in the pots, men may like
them ! " (Hollis, *Trans. 3rd Int. Congr. Rel.* 1908, i. 90.)

Few things perhaps are better calculated to excite wonder
and religious awe than the art of fire-making. By it man
creates both his best friend and his possible destroyer. It
need hardly be repeated here, how in ancient Rome the
tending of a perpetually burning fire was a sacred duty, how
the yearly kindling of new fire is a religious rite performed
to this day at St. Peter's at Rome as well as universally in
the Greek Church—and how in important crises evil is averted
or success achieved by kindling ceremonial fires by the ancient
method of friction.

It is, however, not only the art of making, but the thing
made, or the instrument used, that may excite religious
veneration. In Bengal, so Mr. Crooke tells us (*Pop. Rel.*
ii. 185-187), on fixed days, the carpenters worship their adze,
chisel, and saw, the barbers their razors, scissors, and mirror,
the writers their books, pens, and inkstands. In Bombay, a
mill is the *devak* or guardian (tutelary genius) of the oil-makers ;
the dancing girls worship a musical instrument ; the jewellers
their pincers and blow-pipe ; the curriers an axe ; the market-
gardeners a pair of scales. " All these customs," he adds, " are
as old as the time of the Chaldeans," who " worship their net
and burn incense unto their drag, because by them their
portion is fat and their meat plenteous " (Hab. i. 16).

Perhaps with the " pious " regard for the bread-winning
tools there mingles here something of reverence for that
which, though man has made it, can do what man cannot,
something of the feeling which makes the sailor personify his
ship and the engine-driver his engine, and the fiddler " idolize "
his violin as a personal friend. Whatever be the cause, certain
it is that the most sacred objects of many peoples are things
made by the hand of man.

That mysterious instrument the Bull-roarer, whose weird cry scares women and children in nearly every quarter of the globe, and raises a thrill of awe even in the heart of the white man who chances to hear it, is no more than a thin pointed slat of wood, perforated at one end, and incised with markings either according to fancy or to prescribed patterns. A string is passed through the hole, and the little instrument held by it and whirled about the head gives rise to a thunderous booming sound, rising and falling like the wind. It is of incalculable antiquity, for bone bull-roarers have been discovered, dating from palæolithic times. It was used in the Dionysiac mysteries, where it was represented as being a toy of the child-god. In Europe it is now chiefly a child's toy ; also among the Eskimo, and sporadically in some North American tribes, some islands of Melanesia and the Torres Straits, in Sumatra, and in Ceylon, where Dr. Seligmann, in 1899, saw little Sinhalese children whirling bull-roarers at play, and also in a religious procession (*FL.* xi. 456). The bull-roarer—a Suffolk name, otherwise the buzzer, boomer, bummer, or thunder-spell—is known to have been also used in Scotland both as a charm against thunder, and as a means of driving cattle. The Kafirs too use it as a charm for the latter purpose, and the Bushmen for driving game. The Boloki of the Upper Congo know and make bull-roarers, but the elders do not like the lads to play with them, and give as their reason " You are calling the leopards." (Weeks, 157.) Among many of the tribes of both North and South America it is employed in weather-mysteries, and its sound is supposed to be the voice of the thunder-bird, or the prayer-stick of the thunder, or to prevail on the wind to bring fair weather. Other tribes, together with many of the Melanesian islanders, sound it to scare away evil spirits. Among the Yoruba of West Africa the Oro stick, as it is there called, is believed to be the voice of the god Oro, if not the god himself. At its sound the women hide themselves in their homes while the men parade the town dancing and singing, and criminals who disappear mysteriously under the auspices of the Ogboni

Secret Society are said to have been carried off by Oro. To the Australian blackfellows it is the very kernel of sanctity and mystery. Its sound is the voice of a god, and its existence is revealed to the boys in the rites of initiation into manhood as a sacred secret to be guarded from women, children, and the uninitiated. "You make him boy man?" asked Dr. Haddon confidentially of the Chief of Prince of Wales's Island. The old man assented. "You got thing, time you make him boy man?" Stolid silence was all the reply. "I savvy that thing," continued the visitor, imitating the action of whirling it, "you got him?" In extreme surprise the old man was obliged to admit the fact. Cautiously he whispered its name, "*waness*," and eventually, satisfied that the white man must be an initiate of some sort, he was even coaxed to make one for Dr. Haddon, which he gave to him privately in a secluded spot in the bush, making him promise not to show it to any woman. (Haddon, *Study of Man*, 277-327; cf. Lang, *Custom and Myth*, and *Encycl. Rel. s.v.* In this connection, the folklore of *sounds* should be investigated.)

The *churinga*, the sacred speciality of the Arunta tribe of Central Australia, are made of a micaceous stone, engraved with symbolical patterns, and often but not always, have the form of bull-roarers. Many of them are evidently very old. They are supposed to be the soul-caskets of dead ancestors, who are re-incarnated in their descendants. (See chaps. iv. and vi.) They are guarded in clefts and caves which no woman dare approach, carried in the private bags and pouches of the most grave and reverend seniors of the tribe, shown to youths who have "been made men" and have proved themselves worthy of trust, as the greatest privilege their manhood can bestow, and lent to allied tribes as the highest proof of confidence that can be given to friends. But when, on the birth of a child, a *churinga* of the right re-incarnation cannot be found on the right spot, the elders calmly proceed to make a new one, and, moreover, make it of wood! The *churinga* have excited widespread interest, but comparatively little attention has been paid to the fact that besides these *sacra* of individuals, the Arunta have other artificial sacred objects, the *nurtunja* and *waninga*, which are headdresses worn in the initiation mysteries, and which represent the collective totemic groups ; and, moreover, a mysterious pole, the *Kauaua*, " the most sacred ceremonial object of the tribe," which is common to the whole tribe. It is only used in the *Engwura*, or last and culminating ceremony of the initiation rites. It is made of a young gum-tree, cut down, stripped of its bark, and carried to the rendezvous without touching the ground, smeared all over with blood, and decorated at the top with the ornaments worn on the head by a man in full array (S. & G. *op. cit.* 627-630).

What the *meesham*, the secret treasure of the Musquakie or Fox Indians, may be, cannot be told. The prohibition to women to see it, extended even to Miss Owen, our authority for the traditions of the tribe, " What for you ask ? " said one of the men to her, " Him all same like your Ark to Covenant " (Owen, p. 40).

The *Kithathi* of the A-Kikuyu of East Africa is a small oddly-shaped hollow cylinder of burnt clay pierced with four holes, which is kept buried in the bush and is never carried into a dwelling or touched by human hands for fear of death or disaster. On it the accused in criminal trials makes oath of his innocence. The witnesses put sprays of a kind of creeping-grass round their necks to protect them from its power, and rub their feet in the contents of the stomach of a goat killed for the purpose to purify them before they go away. The Kithathi is rested in a fork of dead wood, and held steady by two twigs of certain trees passed through the holes ; the accused, naked, touches it with another twig, saying : " If I killed ——, may the Kithathi kill me," etc. Then he eats a little white clay and rubs some on his hands to purify himself from the contact sufficiently to enable him to eat, and goes away alone to lead a hermit-life for three months, during which he will die if guilty (Hobley, 139, 140).

Of the *Mayembe* fetishes of Uganda, Mr. Roscoe says

(*Baganda*, 271, 325-28), " Though they were made by men they were firmly believed to possess supernatural powers for averting evil and bringing good to their fortunate owners." Only highly skilled medicine-men were competent to make them. Herbs had to be carefully selected and other things, such as the hearts of lions or elephants, added to make the heart of the owner brave and strong. These ingredients were pounded together and stuffed into horns, or mixed with clay and formed into figures. One such fetish was animated by a spirit of the winds ; others were dedicated to gods, who " possessed " them accordingly. Mbajwe, the king's chief fetish, had its temple, its priest, and a female medium through whom it was supposed to give oracles. Prisoners were sent to it for trial, and were afterwards " sacrificed " outside the temple. Uganda possessed a whole Pantheon of gods who were held sacred and regarded with respect, yet the *Mayembe* fetishes, whether stationary figures or talismans worn about the person, were of more practical importance in emergencies.

The word *fetish* (Portuguese *fetiço*, from late Latin *facticius*, made by art) has been much overworked and abused. Originally applied by the early Portuguese navigators to the numerous small amulets and talismans which they saw the West African natives wearing, carrying, and treasuring, it has been extended to cover almost every kind of material object, movable or immovable, venerated in any part of the world. It is better, therefore, to restrict the use of the word as far as possible to western and equatorial Africa. It is there commonly applied by white men not only to amulets, natural and artificial, but to any movable object—a horn, a shell, a carved figure—which has been endued with magical power by the skill of the medicine-man. It is a strictly animistic form of belief. The fetish, whatever it be, is valued not for itself, but as the receptacle of some spirit, either a human soul or a wandering demon, which, spontaneously or by enchantment, has taken up its abode in it, like a hermit-crab in an empty whelk-shell. The fetishes act as guardians of life and property, give talismanic warning of misfortune, and bring down punishment on perjurers, trespassers, thieves, adulterers, and secret foes. Their energies require to be renovated and quickened from time to time by libations of blood, so that it becomes a very nice matter to distinguish, not only between the fetish and the idol—εἴδωλον, image, likeness (of a god)—but between the lustration and the sacrifice. Nowhere, perhaps, is it more necessary to discover and use the native words for the several acts and things, to prevent confusion between ideas actually distinct.

See Questionary, p. 313.

CHAPTER VI.

THE SOUL AND ANOTHER LIFE.

BELIEF in the soul as a separate entity having an existence independently of the body is found even in races very low in the scale of culture. Obviously, it lies at the root of belief in ghosts, *revenants*, or *gengängers*; and, *pari passu*, of belief in pre-existence and in a future life. And, furthermore, it leads on the one hand to exorcism and on the other to ancestor-worship.

"Language itself bears witness to the belief in the unsubstantial nature of the other self." Wellnigh universally, we find the name given to the soul derived from words for impalpable things, such as "breath" and "shadow." "The Tasmanian word for the shadow is also that for the spirit; the Algonquins describe a man's soul as *otahchuk*, 'his shadow;' the Quiché language uses *natub* for 'shadow, soul;' the Arawak *ueja* means 'shadow, soul, image;' the Abipones made the one word *loákal* serve for 'shadow, soul, echo, image.'... West Australians used one word, *wang*, for 'breath, spirit, soul;' in the Netela language of California *piuts* meant 'life, breath, soul.'... Hebrew shows *nephesh*, 'breath,' passing into all the meanings of 'life, soul, mind, animal'... the same is the history of Sanskrit, *âtman* and *prâna*; of Greek, *psyché* and *pneuma*; of Latin, *animus, anima, spiritus.*" (*Prim. Cult.* i. 430, 432, 433.) Again and again in folk-belief we find implied the conception of the soul as something invisible, impalpable, clinging, and difficult to be got rid of. In Uganda they think the soul of a dead man clings to his jawbone, which in the case of eminent men is preserved accordingly. The jawbone of Kibuka the War-God is in the Cambridge Museum. An English Gypsy (in 1911) gave as the reason for the destruction of his van after his child's death, that otherwise the ghost would cling to it (*FL.* xxiv. 353).

But "since the idea must incarnate itself," the soul is also often conceived as a visible object. The Chinese, among other nations, prosaically think of the soul as the very replica of the body, sharing even in its mutilations (*Prim. Cult.* i. 451). When the Macusis of Guiana "point out that the small human figure has disappeared from the pupil of a dead man's eye, they say that his spirit (or *emmawarri*) has gone." (im Thurn, 343.) St. Godric of Finchale watched all night by the dying hermit of Walsingham hoping to see the spirit depart, until, so he told his disciples in his old age, he was at length rewarded. Asked what it was like, the old man replied that "no man could perceive the substance of the spiritual soul." But being teased and pressed for an answer, he told how it was like a dry hot wind, rolled into a sphere and shining like the clearest glass, but what it was really like no one could express (C. Kingsley, *Hermits*, 322). Even in modern days thoughtful English peasantry have been heard to question whether such a sight might not be possible.

By the ancient Egyptians the soul was conceived not as a simple entity, but as a composite being of which the parts, united in life, were separated at death, each to find its own way to the gods. The principal soul, or element of the soul, was the *Ka*, a sort of wraith or "double ganger" of the man himself, the living principle which animated the body. To this were added the heart, the soul proper—often depicted as a bird perched on the coffin—the phantom form of the deceased, the shadow, the strength, and lastly the immortal part, called after Osiris the God of the Under-world (Wiedemann, 240-243). Some peoples even to this day hold that a man has many souls. The Fiote, Fjort, or Bavili, of the Loango coast, count four, viz. the *chidundu*, or shadow, which sleeps in the body of its owner and dies with him ; the *chimbindi*, or ghost, which wanders in the bush at the owner's death ; the *chilunzi*, or *ndunzi*, the intelligence, which dies with the man, so that a *chimbindi* has no *ndunzi*, or mind, of its own ; and the *nkulu*, the voice or soul of the dead, which after the funeral rites is transferred to the head of a near relation of the deceased, in order to inspire and guide him with the wisdom of the departed (Dennett, in *FL.* viii. 136 ; xvi. 372).

Not only men and beasts, but plants and even inanimate objects are often thought to have souls, shadowy semblances of themselves ; a belief distinct from that in spirits embodied in trees and rocks, or even of spirits introduced into artificial receptacles (pp. 73, 141). The Karens of Burmah, when the rice crop looks sickly, call back its *Kelah* or soul, saying, " O come, rice *kelah*, come ! Come to the field, come to the rice . . . come from the west, come from the east. . . . O rice *kelah*, come to the rice ! " (*Prim. Cult.* i. 475), etc., just as the medicine-men of many of the backward nations call back the soul of a sick man. The Malays, among whom the doctrine of souls is highly developed, say in such a case :

" Cluck, Cluck ! Soul of this sick man *So and so.*
  Return into the frame and body of *So and so.*
  To your own house and house-ladder, to your own ground and yard,
  To your own parents, to your own sheath," (*i.e.* the owner's body).

(*M.M.* 455.)

Fainting-fits, stupor, unconsciousness, or even ordinary sleep, are often explained by saying that a man's soul has left him. Sir John Rhŷs tells of a Welsh reaper whose soul was seen running about in the shape of a little black man while his body lay asleep in the harvest field (*Celtic FL.* ii. 601). The story is not uncommon among peoples more backward than the Welsh. Naturally the absence of the soul is dangerous to the man's life. It may be captured by a sorcerer and prevented from returning to the body. Certain medicine men among the Boloki profess actually to *see* the witches

running away with souls at night, which they then rescue
and restore to the owners. (*Congo Cannibals*, 285.) Mr. Gill
brought a soul-trap from Polynesia, which consisted of a
series of coco-nut rings in which the sorcerer made believe to
catch the soul of him who had offended him. Others brought
by the Rev. J. H. Weeks from the Congo may be seen in the
British Museum. Thus we arrive at the notion of the Separable Soul, the keeping of which in some external object for
safety forms the motive of so many folk-tales. It meets
us in real life in the *churinga* of the Arunta, the carven
soul-caskets of ancestors waiting to be reincarnated in their
descendants (cf. p. 71).

The lower races often account for dreams by supposing
that the absent soul really goes through its dreamland adventures while the body is asleep. So if they dream of the dead,
they have the best of evidence of their deceased friend's
continued existence, in that they themselves have actually
seen him.

Two lines of thought open out here. The soul is either
believed (1) to live on in some other body in this world, or
(2) to have travelled to another, or possibly to some undis-
covered country in this ; though, be it noted, in neither case
does continued existence necessarily, or even usually, imply
immortality. It may be said of many peoples as M. Casalis
says of the Basuto, " they have not given to their ideas on
this subject the settled form of a dogma," (Casalis, 243),
and the observer must be careful not to assume any such
belief without definite evidence.

In the first case, the deceased person may be transformed
into animal—or other—shape. Even in modern England the
restless ghosts of the countryside often appear in animal
form. When the " pius Æneas " had performed the funeral
rites of his father Anchises, had poured out the libations,
scattered flowers, and invoked his departed parent, from the
depths of the grave-mound there crawled out a huge serpent,
which glided between the altars, partook of the sacrifices,
and quietly returned whence it came. The amazed hero

doubted whether to recognize in the snake the tutelary genius of the place or an attendant slave of his late father. The modern Zulu experiences no such uncertainty. He knows that the snake which he sees on his father's grave is his father, and says on his return, " Oh, I have seen him to-day, basking in the sun on the top of the grave ! " (Callaway, 142.)

Or the departed soul may be re-born into another body, human or animal. Pythagoras and Buddha only systematized existing beliefs, such as are known from Greenland to Australia. The Yorubas of West Africa greet an infant on its birth with the words : " Thou art come ! " and enquire of the family god which of the departed ancestors has returned, in order to name it accordingly (Hartland, *P.P.* i. 199). At least one English family is known to the present writer in which a child is regarded more or less seriously by its parents as a deceased relative who has returned to this mortal life (E. S. H.). The Hurons of North America buried infant corpses in the roadway, so that their souls might enter into passing women and be born again (*Rep. Bur. Ethn.* v. iii.). Among the Arunta of Central Australia the belief has actually affected the structure of the social system. According to them, the souls of the departed haunt certain spots and spring thence into the bodies of convenient women ; and the totem of the child when born depends not on his natural descent, but on the totem of the soul reincarnated in him.

When the soul is supposed to leave this world for another, we find that it has " a journey to go," the typical feature of which is the crossing of a river, lake, or sea ; an idea deeply rooted in popular Protestant phraseology, though not found in either the Old or New Testament Scriptures. Bunyan's Pilgrims forded the River of Death : Roman shades were ferried across by Charon : faithful Mohammedans reach their Paradise by a bridge formed of a single hair. The wild tribes of the Malay Peninsula imagine a fallen tree-trunk bridging a boiling lake, and giving access to the Island of Fruits, the destined abode of the dead. It is not very long since, in our own country, the groat was put into the mouth of the dead man " to pay his footing " on the other side ; and the Yorkshire peasants of the seventeenth century used to sing a funeral dirge recounting the perils of the soul's journey over Whinny Muir (= the furzy moor) and across " the Brig o' Dread, nae brader than a thread," to its goal in Purgatory (Aubrey, 31).

Coast-dwelling peoples often picture the Land of the Dead as an island, perhaps one dimly visible in the far west, the land of the setting sun.　Even the very spot whence the souls set sail thither may be pointed out, as at the Baie des Tré-passés in the extreme west of Brittany, and at the north cape of the North Island of New Zealand.　Sometimes the dead are supposed to return to the country whence their forefathers, according to tradition, came.　Others place the Land of the Dead in the sun or the moon ; or yet above them—in the heavens of which the blue ether is the solid floor, and from which the birds bring messages and the storms come to declare the wrath of the gods.　Or, more prosaically, the Land of the Dead may be underground, beneath the earth to which the corpse has been committed ; or even in the very grave itself.

Whatever be the locality or character of the spirit land, whether it resembles the melancholy Hades of the classics or the joyous Magh Mell of ancient Ireland, the life lived there is pictured as simply a continuance of the present life.　" There," says Dr. Tylor (*Prim. Cult.* ii. 75, 76), " the soul of the dead Karen, with the souls of his axe and cleaver, builds his house and cuts his rice ; the shade of the Algonquin hunter hunts souls of beaver and elk, walking on the souls of his snow-shoes over the soul of the snow ; the fur-wrapped Kamchadal drives his dog-sledge ; the Zulu milks his cows and drives his cattle to kraal ; and the South American tribes live on as they left this world, whole or mutilated, healthy or sick, leading their old lives and having their wives with them again, though indeed, as the Araucanians said, ' they have no more children, for they are but souls.' "

Compare the following well-attested story from Lincoln-shire. An old woman who had forgotten to put her husband's drinking-mug and jug in his coffin according to custom, broke them and laid them on the grave. " I deads 'em both over his grave," she said, " and says I to mysen, My old man, he set a vast store, he did, by yon mug and jug, and when their ghoastes gets over on yon side, he'll holler out, ' Yon's mine, hand 'em o'er to me,' and I'd like to see them as would stop him a-having of them an 'all ! " (*County FL*. v. 241.)

In most cases the fate of all souls is the same, yet not invariably so. Character, rank, wealth, or circumstances of death sometimes affect it. Bad men (meaning thereby cowards) are by the Caribs doomed to become slaves to their enemies the Arawaks in a barren land beyond the mountains, while the brave feast in happy islands, served by Arawak slaves. Sometimes bad men are transformed into animals after death, while others retain their human form. The Gallinomero of California believe that bad men become coyotes ; at Ladak, on the borders of Tibet, they are turned into marmots. In the Tonga Islands, the souls of plebeians die with their bodies, while those of high rank live on in the island paradise of Bolotu. Ancient Scandinavian warriors killed in battle were privileged to fight by day and feast by night with the high gods in Valhalla, while the unfortunates who died " a straw-death, a cow-death," went below to the cheerless regions of the Underworld. Other souls find no resting-place, but return to terrify the living. Women dying in childbirth become in Northern India a peculiarly fearful kind of demon with feet turned backwards, known as a *churel* (Crooke, i. 269). In the Malay Peninsula, where the vampire belief flourishes, such women become a frightful kind of flying vampire called a *langsuir* (*M.M.* 325).

The wandering ghosts of Europe are usually the souls of suicides, murderers, and the victims of murderers ; or persons who have left worldly business unfinished—pledges unre-deemed, debts unpaid, heirs defrauded, treasure concealed ; things which prevent them from " resting quietly in their

graves," as the folk put it—albeit no form of creed known
to Christendom countenances belief in the residence of the
departed soul in the grave. But the cardinal reason for the
return of the ghost, all the world over, is the omission of
funeral rites. We are all familiar with the " Grecian ghosts,
that in battle were slain, and unburied remain " to return
again as Furies. Mr. Crooke narrates a story, told to him
quite seriously, of a man who on revisiting his wife after a
long absence found her and her family living in the house in
the form of *Bhūts* or malignant spirits. His father-in-law
had died first, and there being no one to perform his funeral
rites, he had become a Bhūt, and had killed the women one
by one, that they might wait upon him and prevent him
from having (as junior Bhūṭ) to serve the Bhūts senior to
himself. The only peculiarities about them were that they
spoke in nasal voices and avoided touching fire, metal, or
salt. They were about to kill him, but, advised by the
Bhūt of his wife, he escaped, carrying a brass cup of water
in his hand for protection. He then performed the funeral
rites, after which the *pīpal* (sacred fig) tree in the courtyard
fell down, by which he knew that the Bhūts had been released
and enabled to go to heaven (*FL*. xiii. 280).

These beliefs account for many funeral practices, such as
blocking up the door through which the corpse is removed,
carrying it away by a circuitous route, etc., and possibly also
for the custom to which prehistoric archæology owes so much,
of supplying the corpse with ornaments, weapons, food,
drinking vessels, even with wives and slaves, for his comfort
in the other world ; though indeed motives of family pride
and family affection, and also fear to make use of what belonged to the dead, may have had a share here.   Indeed, there
is reason to think—and the idea should be further investigated—that the original object of all funeral rites is to introduce and initiate the ghost, as it were, into the society of
the spirit-world, and that the malicious character so often
exhibited by the returning ghost is due either to its desire
for revenge on the living for their neglect or to its having

found itself " in the wrong Paradise," and in the society of evil demons. (Cf. ch. xii.)

A malignant ghost may either be propitiated or exorcised, or more rarely, destroyed. In the former case he acquires the position of a local godling. All over India, says Mr. Crooke (*Pop. Rel.* i. 96), may be seen shrines erected to appease some dangerous *Bhūt*. An Imperial trooper in the Punjâb was once burnt to death by an accidental fire in the shed in which he was sleeping. Though he was a Musâlman and not a Hindu by religion, a shrine was erected to him lest he might become troublesome as a *Bhūt*. On the Lower Congo this would not have been necessary, for there, burning the body which belonged to a malignant ghost is supposed to destroy the ghost itself and to put a stop to its ill-doings. Or the ghost may be shot by real or pretended guns, according to a prescribed ritual. (Weeks, *Prim. Bakongo*, 43, 44.)

Exorcism, or commanding an evil spirit to depart in the name of a higher power, generally divine but possibly human, needs expert knowledge. It is a function common to the priest and the wizard. In Addison's comedy of *The Drummer, or the Haunted House*, the " conjurer " is called in to lure the ghost into his magic circle, to " overpower him with his learning," and " lay " him in the Red Sea. At the same date, it was the common opinion in the north of England that " none can lay a spirit but a *Popish Priest*," (Bourne, chap. x.). The following is a form of ritual for exorcising a haunted house (*loc. cit.*). The priest must go to it on a Monday morning, and recite sundry versicles, the 24th Psalm, and an appropriate prayer, standing outside the closed gate. The next day he must do the same, but after the psalm the gate is to be opened, and he is to read a portion of Scripture and to recite a different prayer, standing on the threshold. On the third day he must go into the entry of the house ; on the fourth, into the middle of it ; on the fifth, go up and down the house ; and on the sixth, he must search through the whole house, each day saying the same psalm but a different lesson and prayer. On the seventh day—Sunday—he is to place himself in the best room, and there solemnly banish all demons by the most sacred names of his religion, to repeat another formula of exorcism for the whole house, and then solemnly bless it. Finally, he is to set up a crucifix in the chief room, to sprinkle the whole house with holy water, and to hang bunches of the herb *alyssum*, signed with a cross, at the four corners.

Rites of exorcism were frequently completed by summoning the spirit to appear and then setting him to perform an impossible task, banishing him to some remote spot for a term of years, or imprisoning him in some small receptacle, such as a bottle, a boot, or a snuffbox, which was then sealed up and thrown into water. Sometimes the ghost expands to huge proportions, and is tricked into entering the bottle by taunts and pretended incredulity, as in the Arabian Nights' story of the Fisherman and the Genie. " For," as an old Herefordshire man explained to Mrs. Leathe, " we have all got a sperrit something like a spark inside us, and a sperrit can go large or small, or down, down, quite small, even into a snuffbox ! " (Leather, 29.)

Instead of holding a religious service, the legal-minded Icelanders formally summoned the ghosts to appear before a special court (" door-doom ") and bound them over in legal form to cease from annoying the inmates of the haunted dwelling (*Eyrbyggia Saga*). But the *revenant* is not always malicious, nor is his return always a matter of dread. In New Guinea it would be thought very unlucky if all the ancestral ghosts deserted the settlement (C. G. S.). So also in India (Crooke, *Pop. Rel.* i. 182). If we meet with exorcism of malignant souls on the one hand, on the other we find food shared with the dead, libations poured out to them, portions set aside for them at meals or at in-gatherings ; feasts held, perhaps annually, in their honour, when they are welcomed and invited to share the family food and warm themselves at the family hearth. They are remembered ; their resting-places are visited and tended ; they are thought of as friendly, helpful, more powerful than in life. Prayers are addressed to them, offerings made to them; and so belief in the Separable Soul culminates in the Cult of the Dead.

" Black men do not worship all *Amatongo* [ancestral *manes*] indifferently," said one of Dr. Callaway's most intelligent witnesses : " that is, all the dead of their tribe. Speaking generally, the head of each house is worshipped by the children of that house ; for they do not know the ancients who are dead, nor their laud-giving names, nor their names. But their father whom they knew is the head by whom they begin and end in their prayer, for they know him best, and his love for his children ; they remember his kindness to them whilst he was living ; they compare his treatment of them while he was living, support themselves by it, and say, ' He will still treat us in the same way now that he is dead. We do not know why he should regard others besides us ; he will regard only us.' So it is then, although they worship the many Amatongo of their tribe, making a great fence round them for their protection ; yet their father is far before all others when they worship the Amatongo. Their father is a great treasure to them even when he is dead. And those of his children who are already grown up know him thoroughly, his gentleness and his bravery. And if there is illness in the village, the eldest son lauds him with the laud-giving names which he gained when fighting with the enemy, and at the same time lauds all the other Amatongo ; the son reproves the father, saying, ' We for our parts may just die. Whom are you looking after ? Let us die all of us, that we may see into whose house you will enter. You will eat grasshoppers, you will no longer be invited to go anywhere, if you destroy your own village,' [*i.e.* if you neglect us and let us die you will be the loser, for there will be no one to invite you or feed you with sacrificed meat]. After that, because they have worshipped, they take courage saying, ' He has heard, he will come and treat our diseases, and they will cease,' " (Callaway, 144-146).

Finally, we may cite two examples of ancestor-worship

drawn from peoples as widely removed as possible from each other in numbers, culture, and general importance.

I. The Veddas, the cave-dwelling aboriginal hunters of Ceylon, are perhaps the fewest and weakest of existing peoples. Sinhalese influence has caused the importation into the Vedda cult of many Sinhalese demons disguised as *Yaku*, or ghosts ; and Tamil influence leads to the *Yaku* being regarded simply as spirits or demons who live in rocks or trees, in pairs, male and female, who came from beyond seas, are dangerous, and send disease. They are now invoked and danced to as if they were proper Vedda *Yaku*, but the true basis of Vedda religion is the cult of the ordinary dead man—of their own dead, now become *Yaku* or ghosts. The jungle is haunted by them. They are regarded as friends and fellows. Food is shared with them. The charms which accompany ritual feasts are prayers asking them to come and share the meal, for " we also eat and drink " the same food. Women as well as men become *yaku*. The hill-tops where the rock-bee builds its comb are specially associated with them, and portions of honeycomb are left for them with whispered words by the women gathering honey. They are known as *kiriamma*, grandmothers (literally, " milky mothers "), and they some-times come back and lead children astray, for ghosts though they are, they are women still, and still love and long for children.

After a death, the spirit of the dead man stays by the corpse for a few days, and during that time would throw stones at anyone who came near (a common employment of ghosts, cf. the German *Poltergeist*). The *Dancing of the Nae Yaka* must then be performed. In each little community there is one man, the *Kapurale*, who has the power and knowledge needed to call the *yaku* (*pl.*). Food and drink (vege-table, and non-intoxicating), are prepared, and the officiant dances and sings, inviting the *Yaka* (*sing.*) of the deceased to come and take the offering. He imitates a *sambhar* hunt as he dances, and stirs the bowl of food with the ceremonial arrows which are the insignia of his office, and descend from *Kapu-*

rale to *Kapurale*. He invokes the chief of the *Yaku*, Kande Yaka, who was in life a mighty hunter named Kande Wanniya, and requests him to bring the *Nae Yaka*, or lately deceased person, along with him. Presently he becomes possessed by the *Nae Yaka*, who sometimes also possesses one or two of the relatives assisting. The *Nae Yaka* speaks through the *Kapurale*, promising help in hunting and the like. After the possession is over, all share the meal and the dogs' noses may be smeared with the drink.

The story told of Kande Yaka is that he killed his brother Bilinde; in one version, after his death, because he was lonely as a *Yaka* and desired his brother's company; in another, during his lifetime, because Bilinde worried him by continual whining. Another *Yaka*, Pannikia Yaka, is invoked in rites for obtaining prosperity. He is evidently the ghost of Pannikia, a Vedda who is historically recorded to have held office in the Sinhalese Court in 1506. But the wilder the group of Veddas, the fewer individual *yaku* they know. (Cf. Seligmann, *Veddas*, passim.)   C. G. S.

II. Ancestor-worship is the only form of Chinese popular religion which enjoys State recognition and regulation. It has profoundly modified the three great national religions of China, and has permeated, and perhaps paralysed, the most ancient of existing civilizations. If Chinese authorities are to be trusted, the earliest official religion of China was the veneration of Heaven and Earth as the two greatest of the three powers of Nature, and the progenitor of the third, which is Man. Even as late as the time of Confucius (5th-6th centuries B.C.), the elaborate ritual of the officially-prescribed services for the dead had hardly more than a commemorative character. But the idea that great men retained after death their interest in their own clans, and were still able from the Underworld to watch and influence the future of their descendants gradually gained force; hence reverence and affection for the departed developed into the worship of them, and into the offering of gifts intended to increase their power to grant favours. Even Heaven and Earth, nowadays, are often worshipped merely as the All-father and the All-mother.

As the Chinese in general consider the soul to be threefold, the rites of *manes*-worship are threefold also.

(1) The soul quartered in the ancestral tablet (*shên chu*) receives offerings of incense and lighted tapers on the first and fifteenth of each month, and on various other special days, with the occasional addition of food. No tablets are provided for children, whose ghosts are regarded as powerless. Ancestral tablets of important men (very rarely, those of women or of unmarried men) are stored in the *chia miao* or Ancestral Temple, where a full record of the family genealogy is often found. They are venerated every spring and autumn by the assembled kin.

(2) The soul resident in the family tomb is feasted there in spring and autumn, and receives an account of the year's events, with prayers for future help and protection.

(3) The soul dwelling in the Yellow Spring of the Under-world, and after a time reincarnated, is sustained by annual burnt-offerings of paper mock-money, food, clothing, houses, furniture, and all other necessaries ; and Chinese charity feasts and fees also the spirits who have no descendants to care for them, and might become desperate and malignant.

This cult has retained the family and not the individual as the social unit, and has contributed to stereotype the national social system to a very high degree. Marriage, the adoption of children, and the disposal of property, are still mainly family, and not merely personal, affairs. Early marriage, and polygamy if the first wife is childless, become imperative duties, in order to provide heirs to the family worship and property, and to supply spiritual necessaries to the family ancestors. Mencius writes, " of the three offences against filial piety, the greatest is to be childless." The ancestral tablet provides for only one " illustrious consort," who is scarcely less venerated than her husband ; hence other wives can only have the status of concubines. The bones of a dead Chinaman must be brought home from abroad to rest in the family graveyard, or a substitute soul-house must be provided, else the essential sacrificial rites cannot be performed, and his ghost will be a roving kinless spirit.

The cult of the dead has also given birth to the complicated system of fêng-shui (geomancy) which at times has led to the prohibition of telegraph lines, quarries, and roads, because they altered the lines of a district, and so were detrimental to the lucky influences of ancestral graves, and likely to bring ruin upon local families from the anger of the disturbed ancestral ghosts.

See De Groot, *Religious System of China*, vol. i. bk. i. p. xv ; Legge, *Chinese Classics*, iii. pp. 95, 100 ; and *Sacred Books of the East*, iii. p. xv. and xxvii. pp. 369, 370 for the historical evidence.

A. R. W.

See Questionary, p. 314.

CHAPTER VII.

SUPERHUMAN BEINGS.

Gods, Godlings, and Others.

I. Belief.

SETTING aside the great missionary religions of Europe and Asia, and making due allowance for racial idiosyncrasy, a more or less close correspondence is usually traceable between the theology of any given people and their social and political organization.

The Polynesians, with their aristocratic institutions and excessive regard for rank and family, venerated a divine hierarchy ; the medley of nationalities which make up the population of Hindostan is reflected (as we shall see later) in the heterogeneous multitude of their gods. Simple and uncultured peoples low in the scale of civilization usually know but few guardian deities. The more complex the civilization, the greater the tendency to polytheism. Different trades and industries come to have each its own patron deity or saint, women have their special goddesses. The same individual in different capacities worships different gods. As a warrior and a citizen, the Roman revered Jove or Mars ; as a house-father he worshipped his own household gods at his own hearth-fire. In public emergencies the Zulu joins in public sacrifices to the nameless Ruler of the Sky, but his real devotion is, as we have seen, to the *Amatongo*, the *Onkulunkulu* (*pl.*) of his own house (Callaway, 102), the spirits of his own known and remembered ancestors, who appear to their descendants in the form of snakes and send messages to them by omens, and who have power over death and can ward it from the living.

Political and commercial growth lead to contact of cultures, and thus make for polytheism. Princesses are influential missionaries. The Old Testament historians ascribe the introduction of the worship of the gods (or "abominations," *sacra*), of the Moabites, Ammonites, and Zidonians into Israel to the political marriages of Solomon, and in 2 Kings xvii. we have further an instructive story of the effect of conquest on creed and worship. When the King of Assyria deported the conquered Israelites wholesale to distant regions, and replaced them by Assyrians and Chaldeans, the newcomers became a prey to the lions that infested the desolated country. They took it as a judgment sent upon them by the wrathful "god of the land," whose rites they had neglected "because they know not the manner of the god of the land," so the king sent an Israelitish priest to instruct them. But side by side with the worship of Israel, each immigrant community carried on its own national worship ; "the men of Babylon made Succoth-benoth, and the men of Cuth made Nergal, and the men of Hannath made Ashima, and the Avites made Nibhaz and Tartak, and the Sepharvites burnt their children in fire to Adrammelech and Anammelech, the gods of Sepharvaim." Here the combination of the gods of the invading people and the god of the locality produces a polytheistic worship. The story, moreover, gives us a clue to the causes of the extraordinary persistence of magico-religious rites connected with the tilling of the soil, and to the prominent part often taken in them by aboriginal, low-caste, or peasant performers.

How a god may reflect the character of his people, and may develop with his people's growth, is well seen in the case of Mars. "There are two things," says Mr. Warde Fowler (*Roman Festivals*, p. 65), "which we may believe with certainty about the Roman people in the earliest times ;

(1) that their life and habits of thought were those of an agricultural race, and (2) that they continually increased their cultivateable land by taking forcible possession in war of that of their neighbours." Mars represented this double character. As the guardian god of the fields and herds of a small rustic community dwelling among hostile neighbours, he was naturally at the same time the ideal "strong man armed" keeping his palace. The first month of the old Roman year, dedicated to him and named after him, was the occasion of the yearly enrolment of the newly grown-up Roman youths in the military forces of the city. It was celebrated by well-known agricultural New Year rites, as well as by the ritual dances of the priests of Mars, who patrolled the city bearing the sacred armour of the god from station to station. And as the circle of the Roman territory spread outwards, and successive conquests gradually made Rome the centre of dominions which covered almost the whole area of the then-known world, the character of the patron-deity kept pace with the expansion of his people, and the rustic guardian of the ox and the plough was elevated into the god of battles of a world-empire.

It is hardly necessary to say that in enquiring into the theological beliefs of the lower races, we must put aside the conception of a supreme Creator Spirit, all-knowing and all-powerful, ruler of morals, wholly benevolent and wholly just, which constitutes the Christian's idea of Deity. The "gods of the heathen," whether they be personified natural objects, or animals, birds, or trees, or simply powerful unseen beings— super-men, in short—are seldom thought of as specially "spiritual," *i.e.* ethereal, non-material, or psychical. They have human—or perhaps animal—bodily forms, and very elemental human passions. Their powers transcend those of the ordinary man indeed, but hardly surpass those of the sorcerer. A supernatural animal or an anthropomorphic superior being may be credited with the creation—or rather the shaping—of the world in its present form, but the creation-story generally ends with the departure or disappearance of the creator, and has little or no concern with the life of the present day. It is, in fact, usually rather a matter of historical tradition than of theological belief. Even if the creative being is described as the father of mankind, it is often difficult to determine whether the first father of the tribe or nation is meant, or the tribal or national representative of Zeus, " Father of gods and men " ; to distinguish, in short, between the primal ancestor and the divine " All Father."

The Zulus supply a case in point. Captain Allen Gardiner, in 1835, declared that they acknowledged a Supreme Being, Creator of mankind, whom they called Ukulukulu the " Great-great " one (Callaway, p. 55), and Ukulukulu, or Unkulukulu, was accepted as the Zulu equivalent for *God* by a whole generation of missionaries. Bishop Callaway, dissatisfied with this, examined native witness after witness on the subject, and ascertained that Unkulukulu was not an epithet or a proper name at all, but a common noun signifying *forefather* or *remote ancestor*, and as such was used in speaking of the founders of tribes or clans, and, specifically, of the first man, the forefather of the human race. He, said the general Zulu tradition, came forth full-grown from a bed of reeds, and at his command animals, plants, weapons, tools, and all things needful for the conduct of life came into being. He had a wife ; he instituted marriage, circumcision, kingship, and warfare ; he gave instructions in fire-making, thrashing, and grinding, separated wild animals from tame and ordained what either should eat. But he is not supposed to have any present existence ; indeed, his name is used to hoax children, who are sent to call him when it is convenient to get them out of the way. He receives no worship, he has no restraining influence on conduct : on the contrary, his reputed work serves as an excuse for excess. "Since it was made by Unkulukulu, where is the evil of it ? " He is in fact an example of a well-known mythological personage, the Culture Hero of a Creation-Myth.

It may be taken as an axiom that a mythological story,

even a creation-story, is not sufficient by itself to constitute the hero a deity. Stories such as the above, *which have no practical concern with the life of the people*, should be classed as " stories told as true," (ch. xvi.), and not as matters of present day " belief and practice."

With the gods who are personified natural forces or objects, we are on firmer ground. The force or the object may be itself a deity, or it may be the abode or manifestation of a deity. Men may adore the sun as a god or adore the god of the sun ; may offer sacrifices to the river itself or to the god or goddess of the river. The myths told of them may be grossly material ; the separation between the original object of worship and the mythic divinity may become so entire that the Wind-god, the Rain-god, or the Thunder-god may preserve no trace of his origin beyond, perhaps, the meaning of his name. Yet such gods continue present forces affecting the actual life of mankind and arousing feelings of dread, awe, reverence, or gratitude, as the case may be. The Zulus again supply us with an example. They recognize the existence of a vague, nameless, apparently superhuman, being, who dwells above the earth, and whom they speak of as *Inkosi i pezulu,* " the chief who is above " (*Inkosi,* chief, or lord ; an honorific term of wide application, answering somewhat to the German word *Herr* or the Hindustani *Sahib*). No creative acts are ascribed to him, no stories (so far as appears) are told of him, but his existence is known to them through the thunderstorms, though it is not clear whether they think that the chief controls the lightning, or that the lightning itself is the chief. (Callaway p. 118.) When it thunders, they say, " The chief is playing." If anyone is afraid of the storm they ask, " Why are you afraid ? What thing belonging to the chief have you eaten ? " (*i.e.* destroyed or injured). If a man is struck by lightning, " The chief has found fault with him ; " if a cow, " The chief has killed food for himself." If rain is wanted, black cattle (as representing the rain-clouds) are collected, and one is killed with prescribed rites for a public sacrificial feast. The bones of the victim are burnt outside the village, and meaningless syllabic formulas are chanted, which are understood to be an appeal to *Inkosi i pezulu* to send rain on the earth. (*Ibid.* p. 92.) Here we have an undefined but practical belief in an existing being, " a magnified non-natural man," who, vague and shadowy though he be, can yet control the weather, can injure or benefit mankind, and can understand and reply to the requests made to him.

With the gods of the Sky and the Elements may be classed other personified Powers, the gods of the Sea and the Earth ; and more particular conceptions, such as the Wine-god, the Harvest-god, the War-god ;—" functional deities," as they have been called, who become (as already noted) more and more numerous and specialized as civilization progresses, as tribes amalgamate into nations, and the spheres of human activity are multiplied. Many of them are powers of evil, the gods of Fire and Famine and Pestilence, whose cult sometimes predominates so much over that of the benevolent beings that early voyagers were wont to pronounce that the gods of this or that nation were in reality devils. One reason of this predominance lies on the surface. The well-disposed beings may be neglected with comparative safety, but the evil must be actively propitiated for fear of harm. " Let us soothe his spirit with a sacrifice," says a character in a Lushai folktale (*FL.* xx. 402) of the demon who, he is persuaded, has maliciously enchanted his daughter's suitor ; and the proposal is typical.

Neither does the god of highest rank, any more than the most benevolent, always receive the greatest amount of adoration. Olorun, the " deified firmament," the Sky-god, who ranks first among the deities of the Yorubas, has neither temple nor priest, image nor symbol. He is held to be too remote from earth to concern himself with the ordinary affairs of men, and in ordinary circumstances neither prayer nor sacrifice is offered to him. Only in dire extremity, when other gods fail, does the Negro invoke his help (A. B. Ellis, *Yoruba,* 35). So it is also with his neighbour Mawu of the

Ewe-speaking tribes, and with many another. Whether they are all Sky-gods, as distinguished from Sun-gods or Storm-gods, there is not sufficient evidence to show.

Another class of gods consists of those who were originally not divine but human beings. Of the worship of men during their lifetime something has been said in chapter iv., and ancestor-worship has been noticed in chapter vi. But besides ancestors and evil ghosts, the cult of the dead includes the veneration of departed saints and heroes, whose super-human power is still active, especially in their bodily remains, and causes their protection to be invoked. And whereas ancestor-worship is necessarily a family, a tribal, or a national cult, these non-ancestral deifications or canonizations are local in their character, and the devotees are not necessarily mem-bers of any particular social group. The cult begins at a sacred place—a tomb, a well, or a shrine. It gives rise to pilgrimages in hopes of obtaining physical or spiritual benefit. It may be transported to other countries by grateful pilgrims, spreading the fame of benefits received and probably carrying away relics which may become the nucleus or *raison d'être* of daughter shrines elsewhere. Not only the tombs of saints and heroes, but of others, even malefactors, who have met with violent deaths, may be thus honoured (cf. p. 83). Edward II.'s tomb at Gloucester was formerly the resort of thousands of pilgrims. The Chapel of the *Decollati* at Palermo commemorates malefactors executed for brigandage and other crimes of violence, many of whom are buried in the adjoining graveyard. The church is full of votive offerings in the shape of effigies and pictures showing the many moving accidents from which the *Decollati*, who are depicted as roped, manacled, and up to their waists in the flames of Purgatory, have delivered their devotees (*FL.* xxi. 168).

The native *genius loci*, the local godling who haunts some uncanny, awe-inspiring, or sacred spot, and often receives offer-ing or tribute, be it only of flowers, from passers-by or visitors, scarcely attains to divine rank. Such vague anonymous beings are rather *numina* than *dei.* Sometimes they are merely the animating spirit of the crag or tree or river, inseparable from it and unable to move away from it. In other cases they have a quasi-independent existence and a human or partially human independent form, and so approach more nearly to the position of tutelary divinities. They seem usually to share the character of their abodes. The water-nymph is treacherous, the mountain-demon fearsome, the tree-spirit kindly, the household familiar homely and unpolished; and they are regarded and treated accordingly (cf. chaps. i. ii. v.). The *genius loci*, it need hardly be said, is largely represented in European folklore.

It yet remains to speak of the various races of beings, not human and yet not divine, who are supposed to share this lower earth, more or less invisibly, with mankind. In the earlier edition of this *Handbook* they were grouped to-gether under the heading of *Goblindom*, a word which has met with some acceptance as a convenient general term. Some of this camp-following crowd are distinctively *spirits*, properly so-called, not possessing any bodily shape peculiar to themselves, usually invisible, and appearing, if they do appear, now clothed in one form, now in another. They can contract themselves into the smallest crevices, or expand to gigantic proportions ; they are roving, powerful, and gener-ally dangerous, or at any rate mischievous. In fact, they differ from ghosts only in origin. The Land Dyaks of Borneo explicitly recognize this, and class both *umot*, or demons, and *mino*, or ghosts, together as *antus*, or spirits (Ling Roth, *Sarawak*, i. 165). The " spirits of Sasabonsum " are induced to animate the *suhman* of the Gold Coast native, just as the souls of magically-murdered men are inveigled into the nail-fetishes of the Loango Coast (see p. 141). The Malay *hantus*, the Burmese *nats*, the Arab *jinn*, the numerous " orders " of wandering " demons " who enter into and " possess " lunatics and sick persons, and whom Oriental and mediæval enchanters cajoled into tiny receptacles and compelled to their service, belong to the same group.

Other demons are goblins in the stricter sense of the word

—uncanny spectral creatures, but not spirits in need of a local habitation. Such a one is the Egyptian *afrît*, a being sprung from the blood of a murdered man spilt on the ground, who appears sometimes as a man, sometimes as a beast, but who cannot move far from the place of his origin (C. G. S., cf. p. 52). With him we may compare the various hobgoblins of the British Isles—the *barghaist*, the *boggart*, the *bogy*, the *buggan*, the *bocan*, the *pwca*, the *phooka*, who haunt dark and uncanny places and terrify belated wayfarers. Then there are the *Dogai* of the Torres Straits, female demons who carry off crying children, and who "lay their love on" mortals like the nymphs and fays of the northern hemisphere. The Dogai have ears so large that one serves as a bed and the other as a blanket. A human form with some distortion or peculiarity—such as half-headedness or back-footedness—which betrays their origin, is a common characteristic of the materialized type of goblin.

Other still further materialized beings form communities, are born, live, and marry, as do mortals. Of such are the giant Ogres of Southern Europe and the Elfin world of the north:—the British and Irish fairies, pixies, cluricauns, and leprechauns, the German dwarfs and kobolds, the Scandinavian trolls and huldre-folk. Without these the realms of imaginative literature would have been the poorer.

Of the other chief personages of European folk-belief, the Wild Huntsman seems to be a descendant of the Storm-god; the Enchanted Hero in the mountain cavern, who will one day return to save his country in its extremity, may stand for the legendary demigod; and the ancestral ghost—the Irish Banshee, the White Lady of the Hohenzollerns—whose appearance forebodes death to some member of her family, is doubtless a survival of ancestor-worship.

Animal goblins—kelpies and wish-hounds—must not be omitted from the catalogue of demons.

The mediæval conception of the Devil as a being with horns, hoofs, and a tail, whom the witches owned for their master and god, still, with his train of imps, lingers in popular imagination. But the idea of a stupid easily-outwitted being, the builder of Devil's Bridges and Devil's Dykes, the owner of Devil's Chairs and Devil's Punchbowls, akin to the giants to whom the like traits are attributed, is now rather a matter of legendary lore than of living belief.

II. Worship.

The same philosophy of Nature which governs the dealings of man with his fellow-man would, *prima facie*, also govern his intercourse with his gods. And in fact the power of the name, the restraints on using names, the secrecy observed with regard to names, the mystic properties of blood, the bond set up by sharing food, the sympathetic effect of the food on the eater, which we have had occasion to observe in considering the mutual relations of mankind with one another, all reappear in the worship of divine powers by prayer and sacrifice.

A sacrifice, for our present purpose, may be defined as something *devoted* to a god, and *consumed* either in his honour, or by him, or by him and his worshippers (but cf. Terminology, Appendix A, p. 299). It is thus distinguished from a simple offering, which may be anything dedicated to the service of a god, such as an altar, a slave, a garment, a jewel. It is further important to observe whether the deity alone is supposed to be the consumer of the sacrifice, or whether the worshippers share the feast. For if sharing food sets up a bond of union, food shared with a god sets up an alliance or fellowship with the god. But when there is no commensality, the ideas of communion and covenant cannot be present.

The mode by which an offering is supposed to be conveyed to the god varies much, either according to the residence of the deity in question or else to the conception of godhead entertained by the worshippers. Sacrifices to the earth-god or goddess may be buried in the fields or thrown down precipices into clefts or ravines. Those to ethereal and celestial gods may be burnt to ascend to the skies in smoke. Or the skin of the victim may be draped upon the image of the god ;

or the god's portion may be exposed, in the expectation that
he will come, as in the story of *Bel and the Dragon*, and devour
it secretly ; or he may simply partake of the spirit of it, as
the ancestral spirits of the Zulus were supposed to do by
licking it.

Some sacrifices seem to be intended rather for the direct
benefit of the human partakers than to do honour to or procure favour from any god, for no divine personage is definitely
mentioned in connection with the rites. Such are the famous
camel-sacrifices of the fourth-century Arabs (Robertson Smith,
p. 320), the bear-sacrifices of the Ainus of Japan (cf. chap. iii.),
and of the tribes of Northern Asia (*G.B.* ii. 374-388), and the
solemn kangaroo-feast which concludes the Intichiuma ceremonies of the Kangaroo clan of the Arunta (cf. chap. v.).
These, perhaps, are rather to be called ritual feasts than
sacrifices. Probably the partakers hope to acquire the superhuman qualities of the victim, such as endurance, strength,
or agility. In such cases the generally sacred or semi-divine
character of the species should be investigated, especially if
" possession " follows from drinking the blood of the slain.

A sacrifice may be offered as a voluntary gift, probably
with a lively sense of gratitude for favours to come and an
implied hint that it may be to the advantage of the god to
keep on good terms with his worshippers. Or it may be
offered more formally, as the customary and lawful tribute
of the subject to the prince, in which case it is apt to dwindle
into the substitution of the part for the whole, of the imitation
for the reality. Or again, the cost to the worshipper may
be the measure of the value of the sacrifice. Here comes
in the idea of affront and amends, of wrong done and atone-
ment offered, of doing something to appease the wrath of
a justly-offended god. " Shall I give my first-born for my
transgression, the fruit of my body for the sin of my soul ? "
Thus, in the horrible rite of child-sacrifice we seem to touch
the point where faith joins hands with practice and creed
unites with morality. The god here " makes for righteous-
ness "—of a sort !

Not that all human sacrifice was thus motived. Sometimes it was mere cannibalism, a meat-offering of such things as the worshipper's own soul loved ; sometimes it was a tribute, or a present of slaves, sent, as it were, by a sovereign to his brother monarch.

As an example of a private or friendly covenant-sacrifice, we may take the account given by Mr. and Mrs. W. S. Routledge (*Prehist. People*, pp. 229-234) of a sacrifice to *Ngai*, the Rain-god, among the A-Kikuyu, a Bantu tribe of East Africa. The *name* Ngai is borrowed from the Masai, but this does not affect the character of the rite. As to the A-Kikuyu conception of Godhead—they say the ghosts of the dead (*n'goma*) " can't be seen because they are like God," (*Ngai*). God, the sun, and the Kenya mountains are " all same thing." The sun, the moon, the lightning, the rain, all are worshipped, say our authors, " as manifestations of the [same ?] great Power." But Ngai, as will be seen, is sufficiently material to climb trees and to eat mutton.

A suitable site under a sacred fig-tree [1] having been chosen, and a number of branches from certain other trees selected and gathered, the party assembled at the homestead of a friendly chief named Mungé. The victim was produced—a ram with a white face whose ears had not been slit—and a calabash full of *njohi* (native beer) was brought. Each man drank in turn, and the victim was lustrated with beer and spittle, after which Mungé gravely murmured a prayer. They then set out in a carefully-ordered procession, the firewood and dried grass, the grid on which to roast the victim, and the calabash to contain the blood, carried immediately before the animal itself. The ground was cleared and the branches arranged on it—then all stood round the tree with their hands held aloft while Mungé uttered the following prayer verse by verse, pouring *njohi* down the trunk of the tree while the rest uttered responses.

" O God, accept this *njohi*, for the white man has come to

[1] For the Sacred Fig-tree of the A-Kikuyu, see M. W. H. Beech in *Man*, Jan. 1913, p. 4.

my homestead. If the white man becomes ill, let him not be very ill, nor his wife. The white man has come from his home through the waters ; he is a good man ; the people who work for him he treats well ; let them not argue with him. If the white man and his wife get ill, let them not be very ill, because I and the white man unite in a sacrifice to you. Let him not die, because to you we sacrifice an excellent fat ram. The white man has come from afar to us, and has made an agreement with me to sacrifice to you. Wherever he may go, let him not be very ill, because he is good and exceedingly well-off, and I also am good and rich, and I and the white man are even as of one mother. God, a big sheep have I dedicated. The white man and his wife and I and my people go to sacrifice a sheep at the foot of a tree—a most valuable sheep ! Let me not be very ill, for I have taught him to sacrifice to you even as a M'kikuyu."

The sheep was then slaughtered by being suffocated, its throat was cut, and Mungé stabbed it to the heart. The blood was caught in a calabash, and any that escaped was caused to drip on the bed of branches, not on the ground. When the carcase had been skinned and opened, the heart and kidneys were cut up, mixed with the blood, and made into black puddings. The meat was roasted on the grid over a fire which had been lighted—the head being cooked first —and the fat was put aside. The company was arranged in order of rank, and the cooked meat laid on the bed of branches. Mungé wound a long strip of the internal fat round the trunk of the tree, bit off some morsels of meat, spat on the ground, then into his own bosom, and placed a chunk of meat at the foot of the tree. The white man imitated him, and the party proceeded to eat the meat, adding bits to the pile under the tree from time to time. Lastly, they ate the black puddings, setting half of one aside. The meal ended, the head, the tail, the half-pudding, and some of the organs were placed in prescribed positions round the trunk of the tree ; the bones and the solid parts of the fat were added to the pile of meat. All then stood round the tree with hands aloft, while Mungé, offering another prayer, poured the remainder of the liquid fat down the tree-trunk. They lowered their hands and burst into song. At this moment a thunderstorm came on, bringing the much-needed rain! The little procession formed up in order and retired singing. In the night Ngai would descend the tree and eat of the sacrifice.

The whole affair was conducted with scrupulous regard for ritual, and with a reverence, order, and solemnity which causes Mr. Routledge to remark that " no religious service could well convey a more awe-inspiring sense of the nearness of the Creator." (p. 227.)

Two days later the rite was completed by the ceremonial drinking of *njohi* in Mungé's hut. Prayer was offered by each of the party in turn, the spokesman pouring a little beer on the ground at the end of each sentence, and the others responding *N'g'ana* (Amen) and *Sa-i, Sa-i* (hear, hear!) at the end of each sentence " exactly like a dissenting prayer-meeting." The petitions preferred were to the effect " ' that the clouds may give much rain, that our wives may be fruit-ful, and no sickness may come near our children, that our herds may grow fat and increase, and that our goods may be many,' " and also for the white man and his wife, adding " ' that the servants they shall take unto them may be filled with intelligence,' and God was reminded that he had been given a sheep two days ago, and was asked to grant these requests." (p. 236.)

With this sacrificial covenant with a friendly deity and the extempore addresses which accompanied it we may compare or contrast the forms of worship practised by the Todas, a Dravidian tribe of Southern India.

The Toda gods are anthropomorphic beings living on the peaks of the Nilgiris, who do not seem to have any great con-cern with the people's lives, but who yet may be offended and cause misfortune. Chief among offences to the gods are the disclosure of ritual mysteries and the infringement of ritual practices, and the sacrifices offered are expiatory and propitiatory. The proper sacrificial animal is an unblemished calf of fifteen days old, which is slain by the dairyman-priest of the community. Before killing it he recites a form of prayer, touching its head at every clause with the club, cut for the occasion, with which he is about to kill it. The prayer consists of a series of intercessions for the prosperity of the different villages of the clan, ending with " may the buffalo (calf) appear to Notirzi," a goddess who lives on the sacred hill known to Europeans as Snowdon, from whom the sacrificed calf is supposed to proceed to Kulinkars, her partner-god, who inhabits a hill so steep and rocky that "no man has ever climbed it." The priest then passes a small branch of a certain tree along the calf's back from head to tail, another from tail to head, a third from tail to head again, kills it by blows from the club without shedding blood, passes the club and the boughs thrice round its body, and flays and cuts it up in a special fashion. The blood is allowed to drip on to the skin, and each portion is smeared with it, spitted on stakes specially cut, and roasted at a fire which has been lighted meantime by friction. The ears and some other portions are burnt, the head is set up on a stake at one end of the fire, and the priest throws three charred sticks over it and the fire, saying, " May there be increase to Notirzi ! " He then eats his own allotted portion, and the people eat *ad libitum*. Whatever is left is carried to the village to be eaten, with this restriction, that the women may not eat the head and parts of the legs. The cattle are not eaten at any other time.

The Toda forms of prayer are peculiar. They make part of the daily ritual of the sacred dairies, and though the details vary in each dairy, the principle is the same in all. They begin with the recitation of a list of names of places or things, villages, buffaloes, dairies, dairy-vessels, and so on—which are not mentioned by their ordinary names but by secret and sacred names, called *Kwarzam*, and each of which Kwarzam is followed by the word *idith*, " for the sake of." Then comes the prayer proper, and at the end the names of

certain gods, adding " for their sake may it be well for us."
But there is no direct invocation of the gods, whether because
their names are too sacred for utterance, or because they
are beginning to lose individuality and the prayers are passing
into meaningless charm-formulas, it is impossible to say.
(Rivers, pp. 211-217.)

Among some peoples prayer takes the opposite form of
the recitation of a series of holy names, a string of invocations without petitions. Or the petitions preferred are not
for benefits, but for counsel, direction, revelation of the
future ; and a definite answer by word or sign is looked for :—
as when Amaziah enquired of Baal-zebub, the god of Ekron,
whether he should recover of his sickness (2 Kings i.), and
Ahab and Jehoshaphat assembled four hundred prophets and
enquired whether they should go up to battle against Ramoth-
gilead or forbear (2 Chron. xviii.).

This brings us to the consideration of the office of the
Priest. A Priest, typically, is an official guardian of sacred
things ; the warden of a temple (or dwelling-place of a god
or his idol) ; the keeper of a shrine (or sacred treasury) ;
the depositary of sacred traditions. As such, the priest
leads the ritual of worship, the details of which are often
known only to himself. When sacrifices are offered, it may
not be his part actually to deal the sacrificial blow, for
the prevalence of the rite of sacrifice is far wider than
that of the institution of priesthood, and the slaying of the
victim may be the duty of some other representative of the
community, or of the individual who offers the sacrifice.
But the priest communicates with the god ; he transmits
the requests and enquiries of the worshippers, interprets the
omens, and declares the will of the god to the people. Sometimes he is " possessed " by his god, who enters into him
as a demon enters into an empty vessel (in which case the
ordinary European visitor describes him as a " devil-priest ").
His god's power and influence are the measure of his own.
His person is sacred with a reflected sacredness, and he
is able to exorcise ghosts and demons by the god's superior

authority. These two functions, divination and exorcism, are common, as has been said, to the priest and the wizard— using the word *priest* to denote the man who acts by the power of the gods recognized by his people, and *wizard* to denote him who acts either by his own skill or by means of the spirits with whom he is in communication. (Cf. chap. viii.)

The duties of the priest may be illustrated from the institutions of the Skidi branch of the Pawnee Indians of the plains between the Missouri and the Rocky Mountains. They were organized in nineteen endogamous communities, known as " villages," under hereditary chiefs, each of whom was assisted by four braves. Next in rank were four priests (*Kurahoos*, literally " more than medicine-man ") ; distinct from and inferior to whom, were an unlimited number of medicine-men (*Kurna*). Each chief was the possessor of a sacred bundle which contained pipes, tobacco, paints, certain birds, and the " mother-corn," all wrapped in buffalo-hide. These bundles were the gift of ancestral gods, and were brought out at the annual religious festivals to which they respectively belonged and were present at the accompanying sacrifices. But the myths, songs, and ritual, connected with the bundles were only known to the priests, whose office was not hereditary but obtained by instruction in return for fees paid. The stories became part of the life of the priest who had learnt them, and were only disclosed to others when he found himself near death. There were also mystic dances, taught in the first place by the gods, which influenced the crops and the beasts of chase. These also had their sacred songs, myths, and ceremonial, known in detail only to the priests. In these dances the myths are dramatized. In the Skull-bundle ceremony the supreme god Tirawa is represented by the decorated skull of an ancestor ; the Buffalo dance seems to represent the story of the god of the North Wind, who in the guise of a " Wonderful Boy " knew how to call buffalo, while the Bear-dance was " the most sacred of all " (Dorsey, p. xxi.).

Such solemn mysterious sacred dances are found among nearly all the American tribes. The Sun-dance of the Black-feet has already been mentioned (p. 30). The old chief, Mad Wolf, whose wife organized it, described the effect on those who took part, as, " it does us all good "—" the old people feel better in their hearts " ; and the White friend who shared in it adds his testimony to " the religious dignity of the occasion . . . one never to be forgotten " (M'Clintock, 310, 322).

There is no more universal mode of expressing emotion than Dancing, and it forms part of religious and magico-religious functions in all stages of culture, from the Veddas (p. 86) and the Bushmen (p. 111) upwards. There is the solitary dance of the " possessed " devotee, of whom the Dancing Dervishes of Northern Africa may stand as a type : the processional dance, escorting a sacred object, as King David escorted the Ark to Jerusalem : the circular dance, surrounding a central object set up for veneration ; and the dramatic dance representing some desired event in pantomime is perhaps the most varied and the most widespread of all. On the Gold and Slave Coasts every god of note has his own dance, which is sacred to him and known only to the initiated (Ellis, *Yoruba*, p. 296). Dancing is, indeed, more than an expression of emotion ; it is a magico-religious act, a ritual solemnity, of serious and pro-found importance to the performers and to those on whose behalf it is executed.

It is obvious that there are very many solemnities of a magico-religious character in which no definite personal being appears to be invoked. To avoid the risk of conveying a false impression, such rites should not be recorded in con-nection with the Theology of the people, but under some other heading, such as Animals, Agriculture, or Annual Festivals, as to which there cannot be any question.

When an opportunity occurs of witnessing any important rite, it is advisable to learn as much as possible about it beforehand, so as to avoid missing important points when the time comes. It is not easy to observe, perhaps not even to see, all that is going on, especially if many performers are engaged ; so if a friend can accompany the principal spectator, so much the better. Particular attention should be paid to the details of the ritual, both the actions and the words or gestures used. So much ground has to be covered in this *Handbook* that it is impossible, for lack of space, to give more than a brief summary of any of the numerous rites mentioned in it, but the student must not therefore suppose that details are unimportant or superfluous and omit them accordingly from his record. Nothing so effectually shows the true import of a rite as the exact words spoken and the exact acts and gestures used ; and the spectator should remember that in these days of universal transition his own may, for aught he knows, be the last opportunity of seeing the rite in its entirety. The details should be recorded on the spot if practicable, for it is surprising how quickly such things fade from the memory. Afterwards, the affair should be discussed with the performers, and the words should be correctly ascertained and translated, rendering them first word for word, and then in their general import. An interview should be obtained with the leading performer, and the observer—always maintaining the attitude of a sympathetic enquirer and learner—should endeavour to ascertain from him not only why he did such and such things, but *what he did* on the whole. The spectator may see a man slaughter a sheep and hurry away, but the man himself may know that, urged by some compelling necessity, he has slain a divine being and is fleeing from the vengeance of the liberated spirit. Or the case may be reversed, and the visitor may have read into the affair more than was present to the consciousness of the performers themselves or warranted by the formulæ of the ritual.

All this may mean some days' work, but the collector will have the satisfaction of knowing that he has done a piece of good and thorough work and that his record will withstand criticism.

To arrive at some idea of the real hold of the gods on the

lives of individuals, the impulse of the people in emergencies or crises may be noted. In moments of distress or danger, when ordinary help is out of reach, to whom, or to what, do they instinctively turn for aid? And in rebutting accusations or giving important evidence, what is the most binding form of oath? From these two, the ultimate appeal and the ultimate sanction, we may gather an idea of what they think, or rather feel, to be the strongest forces outside themselves.

See Questionary, p. 316.

III. Divergent Types of Cult.

In view of the tendency in some quarters to class all cults of the Lower Culture together under the general term of Animistic Religions, it may be well to give three or four concrete examples, which, added to those appended to the preceding chapter, will serve to show what a variety of beliefs and worships is included under this comprehensive heading.

I. *Cult as a moral sanction.*

The political organization of the Australian Blackfellows is among the most loosely-compacted in the world (see p. 174). It is chiefly remarkable for the preponderating authority of the elder men, as such, and for the extreme severity of the initiatory rites by which the youths are introduced to manhood. For a long time the Australians were supposed to know no gods, but intimate and kindly acquaintance with them has disclosed the fact that many of the tribes, notably those of the south-east, severally recognise the existence of " a magnified non-natural man " (or sometimes two), living above the sky, to whom, in accordance with the actual language of the aboriginals, the name of "All-Father " has been given. The name " Father " is applied by the Blackfellows not only to a man's own father but to many or all of the men of his father's class or generation ; so the title "All-Fàther " seems to indicate an elder or superior who is entitled to respect from *all* the generations of men. The relations of the men with the god bear out this view. No worship is paid to him,—except so far as dancing round a figure of Daramulun, the deity of the Coast Murring group of tribes, and repeating his name the while, may be called worship—but his name and existence are disclosed in the initiation rites, and the final sanction of the code of morals then inculcated is the dread of incurring the god's wrath. To obey their elders, to observe the marriage regulations and the food taboos, to live peaceably, and to share their gains with their fellows, are the main points of the code, so far as we know them ; and it is noteworthy that the gods though not worshipped are nevertheless reputed to punish transgressions of it (Howitt, *Native Tribes*, pp. 488, 540, 553 ; cf. M. Czaplicka, in *The Fritillary*, No. 55, March, 1912).

The Andamanese in their wind-swept isles, exposed to all the fury of the tropical monsoons, are so low in the scale of civilization that, it is said, they do not even know how to make fire. They have, in fact, a tradition of a Flood, in which their fire was only saved by a woman who held it aloft in a platter above the reach of the waves. They believe in the existence of a gigantic anthropomorphic personage called in different dialects, Biliku, Bilik, Puluga, or Oluga, who lived on the earth in the time of their ancestors, and whose name is the same as that of the north-east wind. She, or in other accounts *he*, is generally associated with another being of less importance, Tarai or Deria, which is the name of the south-west wind. The pair are either husband and wife or two brothers. Biliku is sometimes said to have been the first human being and to have made the earth and the first Andamanese, but all the myths associate him (or her) with the weather. In the southern districts they say when it thunders that Puluga is snoring. Lightning is often explained as a firebrand thrown by Biliku across the sky. He or she is always described as being angry. In one story " the ancestors" drive him away because he destroys their huts and property ; in another she throws a pearl-shell (knife) which sinks their canoe. Another story goes that one day being very angry she began to throw fire about. The fire was *Purum-at*, that is, fire made from the wood of the (sacred ?) Purum-tree. One firebrand lodged in the tree and became the sun. Now the ancestors, who lived on the other side of the strait, had no fire, but the kingfisher stole fire for them from Biliku while she slept. When she awoke she was so much offended that she threw a firebrand ,or a pearl-shell knife) at the kingfisher and went away to the sky (or to some place towards the north-east).

No worship of any kind is paid to Biliku, and one would relegate these stories to the category of simple historical etiological myths, were it not that belief in Biliku does very practically affect the life of the people. For there are three things which " as every Andamanese child knows " are forbidden to be done, for fear of angering Biliku and causing her to send bad weather. They are (1) melting or burning beeswax; (2) digging up yams or cutting certain plants during the rainy season; (3) killing a cicada, or making a noise during the time when the cicadæ are singing at morning and evening.

The accounts current in the different little communities vary so much in detail that there is no agreement even as to the sex of the divinity. Other commands and causes of wrath may therefore be known in some places, and may have eluded the observation of our authority, but as to these three curious taboos, we are told, there is complete unanimity everywhere (A. R. Brown in *FL.* xx. 257-272; cf. *Man*, 1910, Nos. 2, 17, 30, 38, 47).

2. *Rudimentary Worship of Nature-powers.*

The Bushmen of to-day are the poor remnants of a race of hunters living in small groups scattered across the southern extremity of the African continent, having little intercourse with each other and enjoying no common action, even if they ever did so. The differences of dialect among them are so great that they are sometimes mutually unintelligible ; and naturally there has been much opportunity for varying

traditions to arise among them. Some think they may be
survivors of the prehistoric folk who once adorned the caves
of the Pyrenees with paintings, as they themselves within
recent times adorned the cliffs and bluffs of South Africa.

Dances formed a marked feature of their life, and are
depicted in several of their rock-paintings. They were dramatic in character and are still danced by some of the older
people. They are known as the Horse-dance, the Pot-dance,
and so on, but it is not easy without explanation to understand what they are intended to represent. Formerly they
were danced in masquerade as animals, and each dance had
its special song. There were the Baboon-dance, the Frog-
dance, the Bee-dance. One was more an acrobatic performance than a dance, and one was a general masquerade.
Some were distinctly licentious in character, and to most of
them some esoteric meaning, known only to the initiated,
was probably attached. The *Mo'koma* (a Basuto word), or
dance of blood, is a dance of men and women following each
other, and is danced all night in time of famine and before
going to war. Monsieur Arbousset, the French missionary,
who had seen it among the Eastern Bushmen, says that the
movements consisted of irregular jumps, like calves leaping.
The dancers exerted themselves so violently that occasionally
one would fall to the ground covered with the blood which
flowed from his nostrils. Then the women would gather
round him, put two bits of reed across each other on his back,
and, leaping backward and falling across his back, they would
wipe away the perspiration with ostrich feathers. Presently
he would revive and rise up again.

Of this dance, Qing, a young Bushman who in 1874 acted as
guide to Mr. J. M. Orpen, Chief Magistrate of Kaffraria (and
who had never seen a white man before, except in fighting),
said that *Cagn* gave them the song and told them to dance
it, and that people would die from it, and he would give
them charms to raise them again. "When a man is sick,"
said Qing, " this dance is danced round him, and the dancers
put both hands under their armpits and press their hands

on him, and when he coughs the initiated put out their hands and receive what has injured him—secret things. The initiated who know secret things are *Qognqe* ; the sick person is *hang cai.*"

Cagn, written by Dr. Bleek as ‖ Kaggen, and by Monsieur Arbousset as 'Kaang, is a principal figure of Bushman legend. He is identified by Dr. Bleek as the Mantis, and he appears in the stories of the Western Bushmen of the Kalikop Hills (south of the Orange River, where it falls into the Atlantic) as " a fellow full of tricks and continually getting into scrapes, and even doing purely mischievous things." Thus, he transforms himself into a dead hartebeest and frightens the children who cut up the carcase by re-uniting the joints and coming to life again. The hyrax is his wife, the porcupine his adopted daughter, and his grandson " the young ichneumon " is his constant adviser and admonisher. Among the material collected by Miss Lloyd after Dr. Bleek's lamented death are stories of the making of an eland by ‖ Kaggen, which is killed by his son-in-law ; of ‖ Kaggen's special protection of the elands, and of his relations with other kinds of game.

In the Maluti Mountains, five degrees of longitude eastward from the Kalikops, Qing, the young man already mentioned, knew many stories of " Cagn," in which he appeared as always fighting and often getting into ludicrous scrapes, which remind one of the adventures of " Mr. Ananci " the Spider, among the Negroes (see chap. xvi.). But in other cases he is represented in a more serious light ; sometimes as resuscitating the slain (cf. the *Mo'koma* dance, above) ; but also as the author of taboos, notably of the universal Bushman taboo against eating the back of the thigh of the hare " because it was human flesh " ; and particularly as a maker of things—snares, weapons, striped mice, partridges, and especially elands. His son Gowi " spoilt " the elands when half-made, so Cagn made them wild to punish him. It was an allusion to the elands that led Qing (voluntarily) to mention Cagn. Asked who Cagn was, he said, " Cagn made all things and we pray to him." Asked if he were good or

bad, he said, " at first he was very good and nice, but he got
spoilt through fighting so many things." [1] Asked how he
prayed to Cagn, he made answer, " in a low imploring tone,
' O Cagn ! O Cagn ! are we not your children ? do you not
see our hunger ? give us food ! ' And he gives us both hands
full ! "

Thirty years earlier, in the same region, M. Arbousset
learnt that 'Kaang, as he writes the name, was believed to
cause life and death, and to give or refuse rain ; that he gave
to beasts their several special markings, and that when game
was scarce the people said that 'Kaang refused it. A Bushman whom he asked whether his people did not pray to their
deceased fathers, as did their Bantu neighbours, said, No ;
that his father had taught him otherwise, and before his
death had solemnly enjoined him, when he went to hunt,
to seek carefully for the *Ngo*, and to ask him for food for
himself and his children. If the *Ngo* should move his head,
describing an angle (or a semicircle), the prayer has been
heard, and the hunter will that evening put a portion of
game in his mouth, hold it between his teeth, and cut it
with his knife, with his arm bent to describe an elbow like
the *Ngo*. M. Arbousset gives the prayer in the Bushman
tongue, translating it " word for word " as follows :—" Lord,
is it that thou dost not like me ? Lord, lead me to a male
gnu. I like much to have my belly filled. My oldest son,
my oldest daughter, like much to have their bellies filled.
Lord, bring a male gnu under my darts." The word translated " Lord " is *'Kaang*, and it is perplexing therefore to
find Mons. Arbousset identifying the *ngo*, not with the Mantis,
but with the caddis-worm. That carnivorous insect, the
Mantis, is far from an inappropriate divinity for a race of
primitive hunters. " Voracious as a wolf, combative as
a game-cock," as the Rev. J. G. Wood says of him, and

---

[1] Miss D. Bleek, on whom the mantle of her late father has happily
fallen, allows us to quote her explanation of this phrase ; viz. that by
" good and nice," Qing would mean " whole, perfect, sound," in contrast to " spoilt," which in other contexts he is represented as using
in the sense of " marred, damaged, ruined."

holding himself erect in human fashion, he remains for hours motionless on a leaf or a twig till his prey comes within his reach : then suddenly unfolding his long angular spine-armed forelegs, he seizes and cuts up the unhappy insect.

No trace of any worship of Cagn has been found among the Western Bushmen. Qing, on the other hand, could not relate any astronomical stories. To a question about a sun-myth he replied, " Now you are asking me about the things that are not spoken of," adding that " only the initiated men of that dance " (of whom he was not one) " know those things." But the old men from the Kalikop Hills, whose evidence was so carefully gleaned and recorded by Dr. Bleek and Miss Lloyd, observed the stars and personified the heavenly bodies. They prayed to the Moon for renewed life. " Take my face yonder . . . give me thy face, with which when thou hast died thou dost again return . . . that I may also resemble thee." When Sirius and Canopus came out in winter, they had been accustomed to wave burning sticks towards them to warm them. They addressed them as " Grandmother," they sang to welcome them. They hailed Canopus as the bringer of plenty and prayed to her (for both these were female stars) for success in hunting. " Thou shalt give me thy heart with which thou dost sit in plenty, and thou shalt take my heart with which I am desperately hungry, that I also might be full like thee. . . . Thou shalt give me thy stomach with which thou art satisfied, thou shalt take my stomach that thou mayest also hunger. Give me also thy arm, thou shalt take my arm, for I miss my aim with it ! " (See Arbousset, *tr.* Brown, 1846, p. 253 ; J. M. Orpen in *Cape Monthly Magazine*, July 1874 ; L. C. Lloyd, *Acc. Further Bushman Material*, p. 21 ; Bleek and Lloyd, *Bushman FL.* pp. 338, 83, 57 ; and Sharp, *Camb. Nat. Hist.* chap. x. *Mantidæ, Soothsayers.*)

3. *The Cult of Mystic Power.*

The religious system of the North American Indians has been developed so independently and withal so elaborately that it demands a brief separate resumé on its own merits. While it presents a great variety in the way of local development and specialization, it is possible to trace in it certain constant elements.

There is a very widespread cult of the Sun, to whom prayer and offering are almost everywhere addressed, and, to a less degree, of the morning-star. Associated with this, and perhaps arising out of it, are local cults of mythical persons more or less consciously associated with the sun or the east. These persons are sometimes culture-heroes, credited with the invention of arts and institutions ; and there is a strong tendency (at least in the historical period) to look for their return as deliverers of the Indian race and restorers of the old order. A cult of the dead appears sporadically in the South-west.

There is an almost universal cult of the larger game animals, and of beasts and birds of prey, and a widespread cult of thunder, which is more or less identified with the eagle. In arid regions, there are specialised cults of rain, clouds, etc.

To all these, mystic power of a high order is attributed ; but not to them alone, for it seems that everything in nature is credited with this power or quality, as well as consecrated objects, human beings, and names. This belief is expressed in the Iroquois word " orenda," the Algonquian " manito," the " wakan " and " wakonda " of the Dakota, Omaha, Ponca, and other tribes of the Siouan family, and in the popular translations " medicine " and " mystery." The Siouan conception of " wakonda " is certainly made personal, if not anthropomorphic, as a conscious, intelligent, and possibly moral power which " moves " all things, " causes to move " (*i.e.* gives life), and hears prayer. The Algonquian " manito " was also personalized, especially in the idea of mystic personal guardians : but it seems that the use of " manito " or " good manito " for Good or Great Spirit, and " evil manito " for devil, was developed under European influence.

Prayer is highly developed in American religion. It is often accompanied by offerings. A mental attitude of humility

and confessed need is very generally required, as appealing
to the compassion of the power addressed ; in many cases
other conditions are recognized, moral and ritual, such as
" cleanness of heart," " a straight path of life," continence
(temporary), married fidelity, penance, fasting, sweating or
smoking.

In Mexico and Central America, with an unusually complicated social and political life, appears a corresponding local
elaboration of mythology and ritual (including the rite of
human sacrifice) with a specialised priesthood and permanent
places of worship. Human sacrifice was formerly associated
with sun and star cults in the South-west. But, generally
speaking, the apparatus of American religion is simple.

Tribal rites of wholesale initiation, such as are found in
Africa and Australia, are almost unknown in America, the
nearest approach being the initiation of warriors. On the
contrary, almost all American peoples lay great stress on
individual initiation of a solitary, mystic, and ecstatic kind,
connected with the acquisition of a mystic patron, a guardian
animal or person. Starting from this common ground, we
find developments of two kinds ; on the one hand, the high
social importance of individual shamans (" medicine-men ")
qualified by personal experiences of ecstatic and even morbid
type, especially among tribes whose social organization is
slight ; and, in the more closely organized tribes, a corresponding importance of esoteric religious societies (" medicine
societies "), which ensure and utilize religious experiences in
their members. Both institutions preserve the idea of mystic
patrons—guardian-animals or persons—whether of individuals
or of societies.

In American mythology creation-myths, stories of culture-
heroes, and stories of revelations and dream-journeys play a
large part.   B. F.-M.

4. *Systematic Polytheism without Idolatry.*

Uganda was a powerful state whose kings claimed to be
able to reckon their matrilineal ancestry back for some twenty

generations (see p. 165). It possessed a definite political constitution, of a much more despotic character than that of the Bushongo (p. 180).

Society was organized in exogamous patrilineal clans, each of which possessed two totems, the one of greater importance giving a name to the clan. Branches or sub-divisions of these clans formed local settlements, each under its own chief, living on its own freehold land. Most of the clans had special hereditary occupations—hunters, cattle-herds, smiths, boat-builders, bark-cloth makers, and the like ; and each had its special office in the service of the state, or rather of the sovereign. Each clan worshipped its own god, who lived in his own local temple among them, and was never identical with either of the clan-totems. Some chiefs also had the guardianship of one of the national gods committed to them, for the ecclesiastical organization was as complete and homogeneous as the political.

The god of highest rank was named Mukasa. He was a benevolent deity, inasmuch as he never required *human* sacrifice. He was the god of plenty ; he gave increase of food, cattle, and children. From him came the great blessing of twins, which he gave to women whom he specially esteemed. He was also the god of the great Nyanza Lake and gave the increase of fish. He controlled the storms and gave good passages to voyagers ; the boatmen sought his blessing before setting out and called to him when in danger. His chief temple was in the island of Bubembe, at which only the king might worship, but he had numerous lesser temples on the mainland in each of which was his sacred emblem, a paddle. Every year he sent an offering of fish to the king, which was presented by selected messengers marching in procession, singing and moving their arms as if paddling a canoe. Every year the king also sent Mukasa an offering consisting of nine men, nine women, nine white cows, nine white goats, nine white fowls, nine loads of bark-cloths, and nine loads of cowry-shells. This was the occasion of a great annual festival lasting twenty days, during which separation of the sexes was observed, and at the end of which the priest gave the blessing of Mukasa to the attendant crowds, their wives, children, cattle, and crops. Mukasa had family connections among the gods. His father Wanema, or Musisi, was god of earthquakes; his grandfather Wanga, the oldest of the gods, put back the sun when it fell from its place in the heavens. Wamala, another son of Musisi, formed Lake Wamala. Mukasa's chief wife Nalwanga was a python. Her temple stood beside his, and she was invoked by barren women. His sons Nende and Kirabira were war-gods, and Mirimu, another son, had the special office of helping men to take their enemies' weapons in battle. But the principal war-god was Mukasa's brother Kibuka, who was said to have been killed in battle against the Banyoro, and whose emblems were carried to war by his priest and medium. Both Mukasa and Kibuka, if not the whole family of gods from the Sese Islands in the Victoria Nyanza, are suspected by Mr. Roscoe, to whom we owe our knowledge of Baganda theology, to have been deified human beings. It is thought some confirmation of this opinion in the case of Kibuka, in spite of his habit of hovering over the battlefield in a cloud, that when the god, which was kept carefully concealed from the people under a drapery of bark-cloth, was brought to England and examined, the conical bundle was found to contain a stool with a hollow top, in which was a bag containing portions of a male human body. Other relics attributed to the warrior were brought with it, and all are now in the Museum of Ethnology at Cambridge.

Besides this divine family there were the Plague-god, who was kept covered up on the frontier lest he should get out and destroy the people; his nurse, whose temple was near his, and who protected women in childbirth; the Creator-god, who was little regarded; the Earth-god, who destroyed ghosts and made the crops grow; the gods of the chase and forest, the chief of whom, Dungu, had a magic drum containing parts of every animal and bird hunted; the gods Nkulu and Mbale who gave children; and Nagawonyi, the goddess of Hunger, to whose temple, in time of drought, women were wont to take specimens of withered fruits to show her their distress, and induce her to use her influence with Musoke and Gulu, the gods of the elements, to put an end to the drought and consequent famine. Nagadya, the mother of Kibuka the War-god, was also expected to intercede with the gods to send rain, and her temple at Entebbe was resorted to in times of scarcity.

Gulu was a very ancient and important god. He lived in the sky and controlled the storms. When these were very heavy, the people beat drums to let him know where they were, that he might not hurt them with the lightning ; and they made fires that the smoke might keep the clouds from falling. Gulu's son, Walumbe, was the god of death, who had to be propitiated by the king on his accession, to prevent him from killing the people wholesale. Lastly, there was Namulere, who was the servant of the other gods, and whose " medium " was sent for to help woodcutters in difficulties. Each of these *Balubare*, or gods, had one or more temples on the hill-tops in the midst of their own estates, which the king sometimes looted if the god displeased him. The temples were thatched huts like the dwellings, and great ceremony was observed when from time to time they needed rebuilding. There were no idols, but various sacred objects were kept in the temples, and in every temple there was a sacred fire, which was never allowed to go out, and was tended by young girls not come to womanhood. One or more priests acted as guardians of the temple, received visitors, and transacted their business with the god. The gods were supposed to foretell events and to give advice, as well as to confer benefits. Those who applied to them presented their offerings and explained their wants to the priest, who announced them to the god, and the latter gave his answer through his " medium." This was generally a man, but sometimes a woman, devoted to the service of the temple, who became " possessed " by the god, and in that state gave oracles, which the priest interpreted to the worshippers. The human sacrifices, which at times amounted to almost wholesale slaughter, were not offered at the temples, but at certain fixed sacrificial places, some of which, however, had special temples attached to them. This elaborate system of deity-worship did not preclude the veneration of a sacred python which had a temple on the borders of the Lake, nor the respect paid to the places haunted by lion and leopard-spirits, nor the dread of evil ghosts of human beings. And though everything about a temple,—the objects kept in it, the persons of the priests, the mediums, and the virgins,—was held sacred and treated with respect, yet the gods were not so much relied on, or so important, as the *Mayembe* fetishes (Roscoe, pp. 271-345).

5. *Heterogeneous Polytheism with Idolatry.*

India is *par excellence* the land of polytheism, which is there carried to an extreme degree. With the *Deva*, or High Gods of the Hindu official pantheon—Brahma, Vishnu, Siva, and their kindred—the ordinary peasant has little to do. They are the gods of the wealthy classes, and to him are little more than names. His worship is paid to the *Devata*, or godlings :—the powers of Nature, Sun, Moon, Earth, Rivers, and Waters, all personified and deified ; the multitude of local village godlings ; the godlings of disease ; the sainted dead ; the evil and malicious dead—a " mob of divinities," as Mr. Crooke styles them.

" The number of these godlings," he says, " is immense, and their functions and attributes so varied that it is extremely difficult to classify them on any intelligible principle. Some of them are pure village godlings, of whom the last census has unearthed an enormous number. . . . Some of them, like Hanumān or Bhīmsen, are survivals in a somewhat debased form of some of the second-rate deities or heroes of the older mythology. Some have risen to the rank, or are being gradually elevated to the status, of tribal deities. Some are in all probability the local gods of the degraded races whom we may tentatively assume to be autochthonous. Many of these have almost certainly been absorbed into Brahmanism at a comparatively recent period. Some are even now on their promotion for elevation into the orthodox pantheon. . . . The deities of the heroic class are as a rule benignant, and are generally worshipped by most Hindus. Those that have been definitely promoted into the respectable divine cabinet, like Hanumān, have Brāhmans or members of the ascetic orders as their priests, and their images if not exactly admitted into the holy of holies of the greater shrines, are still allotted a respectable position in the neighbourhood, and receive a share in the offerings of the faithful. The local position of the shrine very often defines the status of the deity. To many godlings of this class is allotted the duty of acting as warders (*dwārapāla*) to the temples of the great gods. Thus at the Ashtbhuja Hill in Mirzapur the pilgrim to the shrine of the eight-armed Devi meets first on the road an image of the monkey-god, Hanumān, before he comes into the immediate presence of the goddess. So at Benares, Bhaironnāth is chief police officer (*Kotwāl*) or guardian of all the Saiva temples. Similarly at Jageswar beyond Almora we have Kshetrpāl, at Bhadrināth Ghantakaran, at Kedarnāth Bhairava, and at Tungnāth Kāl Bhairon. In many places, as the pilgrim ascends to the greater temples, he comes to a place whence the first view of the shrine is obtained. This is known as the *devadekhni* or spot from which the deity is viewed. This is generally occupied by some lower-class deity who is just beginning to be considered respectable. Then comes the temple dedicated to the warden, and lastly the real shrine itself. There can be little doubt that this represents the process by which gods which are now admittedly within the circle of the deities of the first class, such as the beast-incarnations of Vishnu, the elephant-headed Ganesa, and the Saktis or impersonations of the female energies of nature, underwent a gradual elevation. This process is still going on before our eyes. Thus the familiar Gor Bāba, a deified ghost of the aboriginal races, has in many places become a new manifestation of Siva as Goreswara. Similarly the powerful and malignant goddesses, who were by ruder tribes propitiated by the sacrifice of a buffalo or a goat, have been annexed to Brahmanism as two of the numerous forms of Durgā Devi by the transparent fiction of a Bhainsāsuri and Kāli Devi.   In the case of the former her origin is clearly proved by the fact that she is regarded as a sort of tribal deity of the mixed class of Kānhpuriya Rājputs in Oudh. Similarly Mahāmāi, or the ' Great Mother,' a distinctively aboriginal goddess, whose shrine consists of a low, flat mound of earth, with seven knobs of coloured clay in a single row at the head or west side, has been promoted into the higher pantheon as Jagadamba Devi, or ' Mother of the World.' " (Crooke, *Pop. Rel.* i. 83-85.)

CHAPTER VIII.

OMENS AND DIVINATION.

CURIOSITY, the desire for knowledge, and the craving to penetrate mysteries and to know what the future holds in store, are feelings natural to mankind. Add to them an animistic attitude of mind, a vague sentiment of awe towards uncomprehended things, and the habit of reasoning *post hoc, propter hoc*, and we have the basis of belief in *Omens*. Out of this belief arise *Divination*, or the performance of rites for the express purpose of discovering mysteries, past, present, or future, and *Augury*, or the pseudo-science of observation and interpretation of omens.

No unexpected or unusual occurrence is too trivial to be the subject of an Omen. Mysterious sounds, knocks, bells ; accidents to inanimate objects, as implements, tools, pictures (cf. the fall of the sword in the *Lady of the Lake*) ; personal accidents or sensations, shivering, tingling, stumbling (cf. the Conqueror at Pevensey) ; the movements, cries, or actions of birds and beasts, wild or domestic ; dreams ; unusual appearances in the fire or the heavens (cf. the " star Cometa " of the Bayeux tapestry) ; unaccountable events, such as flowers or fruit-trees blossoming out of season, or a space omitted in sowing a crop ; any thing, person, or animal, seen or encountered at the New Year, or on beginning a journey or any other enterprise ; all these are everywhere liable to be taken as Omens.

Omens, it has been said, indicate the fate, luck influences

it ; but it is often difficult for the collector to distinguish between the two. When (*e.g.*) the English peasantry speak of " signs," or " tokens," or " warnings," it is clear that only a presage or portent of future events is meant, not a cause ; but other cases are more doubtful. The late Mr. Charles St. John, setting out on his first deer-stalking expedition, met " one of the prettiest girls in the country " not half a mile from the house. " Deed, sir, that's a bonny lass," said Donald the keeper. " It's just gude luck our meeting her ; if we had met that auld witch her mother, not a beast would we have seen the day." " I have heard," adds his master, " of Donald turning home again if he met an old woman when starting on any deer-stalking excursion," (*Wild Sports of the Highlands*, p. 171). When C. N. was about to set out to enter a new place of service (Nov. 24th, 1891), her mother went to look whether any woman was in sight, and seeing one, made the daughter wait till she had passed by. " There now, if I hadn't gone out, you'd have met that woman," said she ; for *all* women and not only old ones are generally unlucky omens in England (*FL.* xx. 321). Particular persons are often engaged to be the " first foot " in the house on New Year's Day, to ensure good luck for the year, and hawkers think that their day's takings are affected by the first customer. In such cases as these, perhaps the folk themselves hardly know exactly what they believe as to cause and effect. For this and other reasons it is better not to record all omens together in one miscellaneous heap, but to distribute them under the heading of plants, animals, persons, etc., according to their nature ; when they will not infrequently be found to explain themselves.

We are accustomed to think of Divination as a practice resorted to by individuals, especially by young women, desirous of knowing their future lot in life. A pod with nine peas is placed over the door, the first bachelor who enters is the destined husband. The girl washes her linen in her bedchamber at midnight, or the young man walks three times round the church at the same " witching hour " ; they accompany the act with prescribed words and gestures, and the future partner for life appears as in a vision. But in uncivilized nations divination plays an important part in public as well as private life, and no serious enterprise is set on foot without it. The Sea Dyaks of Borneo begin no undertaking—house-building, farming operations, warlike expeditions—without consulting the seven species of Omen Birds. There is a regular signalling code of interpretation ; the birds must be heard in such a position—right or left, in front or behind—and in such an order ; and the business in hand may get hung up for days, waiting for favourable omens. Omens are derived from many other creatures, but only the Seven Birds are held sacred or used in formal augury. These birds are believed to be the sons-in-law of Singalang Burong, the Bird-god of War, patron of head-hunting, who lives in the sky and is visible as a large kind of hawk. Legend relates that the Bird-god's daughter married a mortal, and forsaking him returned to her home by way of the sea. Her husband and son followed her and were received at the Bird-god's palace in the skies, where the boy soon gave proof of his parentage and divine descent. There they learnt how to catch fish, to trap game, and to grow paddy, and were commanded to obey in everything the warnings and directions of the Seven Omen-birds, the boy's maternal kindred. Thus instructed they returned home to become the Culture-Heroes of their race (Ling-Roth, i. 19 *sqq.*).

Among the Yoruba of West Africa there is a special god of divination, Ifa, who is consulted by his priests on the first day of every (five-day) week by casting lots, or rather throwing dice, with sixteen kernels of the sacred palm-tree, called *ikins*. They are gathered up in the right hand and let fall repeatedly through the fingers into the left. Marks are then made on a whitened tablet corresponding with the kernels left, and on these the interpretation is based. The palm-kernels are solemnly consecrated to their sacred use by elaborate rites, and are supposed collectively to represent the god. Each of them has a distinctive name, and by itself represents a pair of *odùs*, or subordinate godlings. Behind each of them are sixteen other *odùs*, making the whole number 256, which may again be multiplied by 16 or even by 32. With each *odù* is connected a number of stories, parables, or sayings, which the *babalawo* or priest is supposed to commit to memory and to apply to the case in point, according to the position of the *ikins* in the divining-bowl or the tablet. Ifa has also a servant-god named Opele, who is consulted every morning by means of eight flat slips of wood strung together and thrown on the ground. (A. B. Ellis, *Yoruba*, 56-64; Bishop J. Johnson (native) in Dennett, *B.B.M.M.* 246. The use of a species of dice in divination is very common throughout Africa, *infra*, p. 131.)

Enquiry of the gods, as distinguished from prayer to them, is a marked feature of early religious practice, and hence Divination is often closely connected with Sacrifice. The movements of any birds or beasts seen immediately after the rite may indicate the will of the gods; or the entrails of the victim may be examined by skilled persons and the future prognosticated from their appearance, as was done by the College of Augurs in Ancient Rome. Divination by the blade-bone seems to be a survival of sacrificial augury. Or the god may enter into and "possess" the priest or priestess subsequently to the sacrifice, and declare his will through them. Or another attendant at the temple may be the medium of inspiration and deliver the Oracle, as in the case of the Pythonesses of ancient Greece and in modern times of the temple-mediums of Uganda.

Divination, or "soothsaying," like exorcism, is a function common to the priest and the wizard (cf. chap. vii.). The *shaman* of Central Asia unites the offices of priest and wizard (and it may be added, of leech) in his own person. On the one hand he leads and directs the worship of the gods of his people, and on the other he performs feats of jugglery, such as swallowing live embers, being imprisoned, bound hand and foot, and then reappearing free. But above all things he practises divination. He predicts coming events, directs courses of action, discovers the cause of sicknesses, and communicates with the gods whom he venerates by the aid of the spirits or demons whom he controls.

His characteristic methods are beating his tambourine, singing, dancing, ventriloquism, and cataleptic trances. Richard Johnson, an English traveller, who visited the Samoyedes of Northern Siberia in 1556, witnessed the performance of the rites preliminary to the migration of a tribe at the mouth of the river Pechora. The shaman first beat his tambourine and sang with wild cries, the company responding loudly. He seemed to become delirious, then fell on his back and lay like a corpse. The people said the deity was now telling him what they were to do and whither they should go. They cried " Ogu ! " thrice, and the wizard rose, continued his chant, and ordered five reindeer to be killed, which was done. He then began to perform juggling tricks ; stabbed himself with a sword and remained unwounded ; twisted a rope round his neck, was concealed by a long robe thrown over him, and made his assistants pull the ends of the rope till his severed head was heard to fall into a kettle of boiling water, and the Samoyedes said he was dead, after which he appeared unhurt (*J.A.I.* xxiv. 140).

The functions of the shaman as an intermediary between man and the spirit-world throw so much light on the whole subject that it seems desirable to devote some space to them.

The following is in brief the ritual of a festival in honour of Bai-Yulgen, the Sky-god, held from time to time (? annually) in every family among the Tartar tribes in the Altaian mountains of Central Asia, as recorded 1850-60 by a Russian mission priest, Father Wierbicki. On the first day a new *yourta* (hut) is built and decorated under the superintendence of the *Kam* or shaman. A birch-tree with leaves and bark is set up in the middle, and nine steps are cut in the trunk ; a courtyard is enclosed round the *yourta* and a birch stick with a horsehair halter is set up to hold the soul of the horse that is to be sacrificed. The horse is then chosen, and a man is selected to hold it. The shaman waves a birch-twig over the horse's back, to send its soul to Yulgen, whither the soul of the horse-holder is to accompany it. The shaman summons his familiar spirits one by one, each replying to his call, and he collects them in his tambourine. Then he goes outside the *yourta*, seats himself on the effigy of a wild goose placed there, sings and acts the scene of pursuing the soul of the sacrificed horse. The soul neighs, kicks, and runs away, but is finally caught and secured to the birch-stick in the courtyard. The real horse is then brought, and the shaman having blessed it slaughters it with the aid of the bystanders, in a peculiarly cruel manner. "The bones and skin become the sacrifice, and the flesh is eaten up with various ceremonies, the *Kam* receiving the choicest portion." (*J.A.I.* xxiv. p. 75.)

On the second day, after sunset, a fire is lighted in the *yourta*, and the shaman feeds first the "lords" (*i.e.* spirits) of the tambourine—who represent the "power" of his own family—with the sacrificial meat, and then feeds the "master" of the fire, who represents the "power" of the family of the owner, the founder of the feast. He also gives them drink, and then feeds the bystanders. He next fumigates with juniper nine garments which are offerings by the master of the house to Yulgen, puts on his official dress, fumigates his tambourine, and summons the spirits one by one as before. Lastly, he calls on "Merkyut the bird of heaven" to sit on his right shoulder, and bows under the weight of the spirit burden. He goes round the birch and the fire, kneels before the door and asks the porter-spirit (elsewhere called the porter-god) to grant him a guide. He beats the tambourine and shakes convulsively. Then with his drumstick he sweeps all uncleanness from the back of the master of the house— among these tribes the back is accounted the seat of the soul—and embraces each of the party in turn, holding his tambourine against their breasts, his drumstick against their backs. Thus he frees them from the dominion of the evil Erlik, god of the Underworld, and from all the ills and misfortunes Erlik could bring upon them, and finally he drives the misfortunes out of doors. After this he drives the spirit and power of the host's forefathers into their descendant by blows on the tambourine held close to his ear.

The shaman then begins his spirit-journey to the heavens. He passes into a state of ecstasy, jumps, runs about, mounts on the first step in the tree-trunk, then seats himself on a bench covered with a horse-cloth, which represents the soul of the sacrificed horse. He sings, he narrates his experiences, accompanying his chant with dramatic action. He ascends from one zone of heaven to another. At every stage he mounts a step of the birch-tree. The spirit-horse is tired out, the horse-holder laments. The rider mounts the wild goose, he hurries on, he meets birds and converses with them. In the third zone there is a halt, and he learns of coming changes of weather, impending sickness, misfortunes *to neighbours* (!), sacrifices that must be offered. In the sixth zone he bows before the moon, in the seventh before the sun. The more powerful the individual shaman is, the higher he is able to ascend. Arrived at the limit of his power, he addresses a humble prayer to Bai-Yulgen, dweller in the blue sky. Then he is definitely informed by Yulgen whether the sacrifice is accepted, what the weather will be, and what the coming harvest, and also more particularly what further sacrifices are expected. This done, he falls exhausted, and lies silent and motionless on the ground. The *scena* is over, the vision past. A third day's festivity may follow, but it is devoted to feasting without special significance (*J.A.I.* xxiv. 74-78).

So much for Divination in its religious aspect. Its use in Medicine will be dealt with later. The part it plays in judicial procedure is equally important, especially in Africa, where it is the recognized mode of detection of criminals, especially witches. The wizard, medicine-man, or witch-finder (often absurdly called the "witch-doctor") decks himself with the skins and entrails of animals, and dances, a ghastly figure, before the assembled people. He gradually excites their feelings by a series of statements and questions to which they reply by a common shout of assent. Then, working himself up into a frenzy, he denounces the person on whom he has fixed the guilt as a witch, the enemy of the whole community, and incites the crowd to fall upon him. The victim may even be lynched and executed at once (Matabeleland, *v. J.R.A.I.* xxxix. 537-541), or a chance of escape may be afforded by the further test of the Ordeal. This in witch-craft or other serious cases throughout Africa is usually a draught of a nauseous and semi-poisonous decoction either of a species of bean or of casca or *nka* (*nkasa*, Loango) bark, which only a guilty stomach can retain. In less important matters—such as thieving, lying, adultery—the *nganga* (Congo medicine-man) produces a magic box, which can only be opened by an innocent person, or a hot knife, which will not burn the guiltless. Or the accused may dip his or her arm into a vessel of boiling water or oil—or may be made to lick the hot iron blade of a hoe. This is a Mashonaland test of an adulteress, which reminds us of our own early judicial pro-cedure, when an accused woman had to prove her innocence by walking over hot ploughshares. The belief that a corpse will bleed at the touch of a murderer is said to have been (unsuccessfully) put to the proof as an ordeal in a Shropshire village in the nineteenth century.

There is this distinction between divinations and ordeals ; that while both are methods resorted to for discovering the truth, Divination is practised by third parties to fix the guilt of a crime on a particular person, but the Ordeal is undergone by the person accused to vindicate his innocence. A striking example of an ordeal is that of the *Kithathi, ante,* p. 72.

A totally different mode of divination from any of the preceding is that of " throwing the bones," which is practised by the Basuto, Bathonga, Baronga, Matabele, and other tribes of South Africa, not only to identify thieves, to find strayed cattle, or to determine the site of a homestead, but to learn the situation of absent friends and to predict future events, such as the fate of an individual, the success of a journey, a war, or a hunting expedition, much as cards are used by fortune-tellers in England. It involves a regular system of augury. A set of bones consists of a number of the astragalus bones of domestic animals to represent the villagers themselves, similar bones of wild animals to represent the spirits which dwell in the bush, sundry shells, which signify great powers, good or evil, such as the waves of the sea, some bits of tortoise-shell, the claw of an ant-bear, which stands for death, one or more stones, which, if black, mean mourning, perhaps some seeds or other miscellanea, and, in one recorded case, a clinical thermometer! The position of the various articles when thrown like dice and interpreted by a skilled professional diviner gives the information desired. A variety of " the bones " in use in Matabeleland, Mashonaland, and North-Western Rhodesia still more resembles our cards. It consists of four or six large teeth of wild animals, or four slips of wood, carved and marked with patterns, each of which has its special name and significance, but the method of interpreting the combinations of them when thrown varies in different districts (*J.R.A.I.* xxxix. 537-541, *FL.* xiv. 122-3 ; cf. Junod, *Les Baronga,* and *Life of a South African Tribe*). The Khasis do nothing that they consider of even the least importance without previously breaking eggs. They throw an egg, with muttered formulæ, on a board made for the purpose, and augur, according to fixed rules, from the position of the fragments of egg-shell (Gurdon, 119, 221).

Augury as concerned with the private affairs of individuals lingers far into civilization. It has given rise to the pseudo-sciences of palmistry and astrology, which still flourish even in London. The latter, under the name of " casting " (or " reading ") " the planets," has not yet died out among the folk in English and Welsh villages and back streets. The supposed works of Albertus Magnus, the famous mediæval astrologer are still consulted in Guernsey. The interpretation of dreams and the " laying out " of playing-cards are other surviving branches of augury.

It is impossible to enumerate all the modes of divination known. Some, like the visions of the shaman, depend mainly on the inherent powers of the diviner. Of such are the hypnotic trance of the spiritualist percipient, the spectral procession witnessed by the watcher at the church-door on fateful nights, the visions of the crystal-gazer, the prophetic dreams of the ancient seer, sleeping on the hill-side " wrapped in his tough bull's hide." Some are supposed to act independently of human agency, like the Divining Rod, the representative of the magician's wand, perhaps the most ancient magical instrument in the world, which is still in use to discover springs of water, and even, it seems, veins of ore and hidden treasures. Others again are rites which may be performed by anyone, and the result of which affords the desired information automatically, without the need of an interpreter. Any game of chance or trial of skill may thus be used for divination. The Lapp women used to shoot blindfold at the skin of the first bear killed in the season, and the first whose arrow hit it took her success as a presage that her husband would kill another bear (Scheffer, 272). Other typical methods are spinning a coco-nut, a teetotum, or a knife, striving who can shoot farthest, throwing at a mark, throwing chips, stones, or melted lead into water ; grasping symbolic articles blindfold ; procuring significant dreams by inducing thirst, repeating charms, and so on ; performing rites with plants and herbs, such as sage, hempseed, peas, nuts, ash-leaves, or apple-parings ; swinging a pendulum, or a lemon (as in the Malay Peninsula), or a key tied to a Bible (as in England) while reciting a list of names ; counting the petals of a flower with some similar formula ; trying the *sortes Virgilianae.* In Persia a volume of the poet Hafiz is used for this. A dervish sticks a knife at random between the leaves, and the words at the top of the right-hand page give the omen. In England the book used is the Bible—cf. *Enoch Arden.*

See Questionary, p. 320.

CHAPTER IX.

THE MAGIC ART.

Sorcery, Witchcraft, and Charming.

STUDY of the mental attitude of uncultured man towards his surroundings affords a clue to the processes by which he endeavours to control circumstances and events.

The widespread belief in inherent magical virtue has been already noted (chap. iv.). There is hardly anything in the universe, be it man or beast or bird, " rock or tree or falling water," to which some amount of this mysterious property is not somewhere attributed. Every human being is tacitly credited with the possession of enough of it for the purpose of ordinary blessing and cursing, though some may have more than others. That the power of spirits or demons surpasses that of mankind goes without saying. Sounds, words, gestures, actions, processes, places, times, numbers, figures, colours, odours, all may have a certain amount of magical power. And as the main object of the wizard and of those who resort to his aid is to gain power, whether over the forces of nature, over spirits, over diseases, enemies, thieves, sweethearts, beasts of prey or of the chase, we find all the above influences made use of in the Magic Art. For the greatest wizard is he who has inherited or acquired the greatest amount of personal power, who has brought into subjection the most powerful spirits or forces, who is acquainted with the most potent rites and spells.

The power of the wizard is sometimes hereditary—that is

to say, inborn, innate—especially in the case of healing, divinatory, or prophetic powers ; but heredity does not go very far. " On est né brahmane," says M. van Gennep, " mais il faut apprendre pour agir en brahmane." The skilled wizard undergoes training and initiation, often lasting for several years, and usually involving more or less of hardship. Sometimes an omen indicates the future sorcerer, sometimes the elders of the craft pitch upon a suitable neophyte. If divination or communication with the spirit-world is the main object, an unhealthy, nervous, or even epileptic subject is selected ; in other cases strength of mind and body is usually necessary. The training consists, normally, on the one hand, of enduring hardships, such as solitude, fasting, living on nauseous and unnatural food, till a condition of over-strained nervous excitement is produced ; on the other, of direct instruction imparted by past masters in the craft. Often the power of the teacher must be communicated to the scholar by blows or other actual contact, by inheritance of the master's magical apparatus, or the like. Sometimes (as among the Lapps) magic power is conceived as so definite, though immaterial, an object, that it can be conveyed as a death-bed legacy to a child or friend.

The combined elements of natural faculty, communicated power, and acquired skill, meet us everywhere in varying degrees. Among the Altaian Tartars the ability to " shamanize " is inborn, only the knowledge of chants, prayers, and rites must be taught (*J.A.I.* xxiv. 90). Among the Yakuts of Siberia the guardian spirit of a dead shaman ancestor endeavours to enter the youth, who raves, falls unconscious, retires to the woods, and the like, till his family, recognizing the symptoms, call in an old shaman to instruct and consecrate him for his office (*J.A.I.* xxiv. 85). The *nganga ngombo*, or witch-finder, of the Congo—who to be successful must be by nature an active, energetic, resourceful man with all his wits about him—gets his power, after a lengthy pupilage, by the beating of his master's drum and the shaking of his rattle close to his ear till he becomes dizzy, excited, and apparently " possessed " by his master's fetish-power (*FL*. xx. 183). Or he may receive the power without any period of pupilage, during a night-long dance called *ekinu*, held to cure him of insanity or to purify him from homicide. Passing the ordeal for witchcraft successfully may also qualify a Congo native to set up as a witch-finder. Or again, a man who has recovered from disease by means of a particular wonder-working fetish, may pay the *nganga* who treated him a fee for instruction in the methods and medicines used, after which he is entitled to set up as a *nganga* in his turn (*FL*. xxi. 448). The Arabian or the mediæval magician would serve a master for years to learn the secret of a single spell ; *cf.* the story of the Magician's Apprentice who—half-taught—raises the Devil but cannot lay him again, which is known throughout Christendom. The European peasant who would be initiated into the mystery of witch-craft seeks no human teacher, but profanes the sacraments —the details of the ceremony are still known in many English villages—repeats the Lord's Prayer backwards, or in some other way abjures the Christian faith and enters the service of the Devil, by whose power his—or usually her—feats are performed. So also the witches of North Africa abjure Islam and engage in unholy practices (Doutté, p. 51).

Sometimes a formal ceremony of admission completes the novice's training. Among the Buryats of Southern Siberia the rites of consecration of a shaman are very elaborate. There is first a preliminary ceremony of purification. An old shaman officiates, assisted by nine youths. A goat is sacrificed and its blood mixed with water. Birch-brooms are dipped in the mixture, and the candidate is beaten with them on the bare back and enjoined to be merciful to the poor : libations are poured out and prayer is made. The dedication itself does not take place till some time later. The cost is provided by a begging expedition. The " Father-shaman " and his assembled colleagues then set up a thick birch-tree, cut from a burial-place with prayers and offerings, in the house of the new shaman, where its top projects from the

smoke-hole. This symbolises the porter-god who gives access
to heaven, and is left permanently to denote a shaman's
abode. They further erect in some convenient spot a birch
decorated with symbolically-coloured ribbons, under which
a drink-offering is placed on a piece of white felt ; another
birch to which the sacrificial horse is tied ; a third, which
the new shaman must climb ; and nine others, decorated
with ribbons and hung with nine beast-skins and a vessel
of food. All these are tied to the house-birch with red and
blue tapes, as roads for the shaman's soul to travel on ; and
besides all these, nine posts are provided with victims tied to
them, nine kettles to cook the sacrifice, and some thick birch-
sticks to which to tie the bones. From early morning the
shamans are busy " shamanizing " in the *yourta, i.e.* singing,
dancing, praying, and falling into trances. They purify themselves and the contents of the *yourta* with aspersions of *tarasun.*
The insignia of the shaman's office are then consecrated, and
especially the horse-staves, which are the most important
instruments of the Buryat shaman. They must be cut from
a birch-tree growing in a shamans' burial-ground, without,
if possible, killing the tree, as its death would be a bad omen
for the shaman. A horse's head is carved at one end and
the other is formed like a hoof. Bells, ribbons, and small
stirrups are fastened to them. The consecration endues them
with life ; they become living horses, fit to carry the shaman's
soul on its spirit journey. The father-shaman summons the
protecting gods, the candidate repeats the prayer after him,
and climbs the birch-tree to the house-top, where he calls
on the gods. The rest of the account is somewhat obscure,
but it would seem that when the time for issuing from the
yourta is come, a fire is kindled outside the entrance, purify-
ing wild thyme is thrown upon it, and every one passes through
it. They go in procession to the place prepared ; the candidate, anointed with kid's blood, is carried on the felt carpet
by his comrades ; and finally climbs the principal birch-tree,
and there calls on the gods and on the spirits of his dead
shaman-kinsmen. The day is concluded by sacrifices and

public games. Repeated ceremonies enable the shaman to attain higher degrees in the hierarchy (*J.A.I.* xxiv. 86-90).

The position of the shaman is thus that of the recognized go-between of the visible and invisible worlds. He is, in fact, a public functionary whose services are in request by the community on all important occasions, public as well as private. He drives away disease and performs rites to obtain good harvests or successful hunting-seasons. The Malay *Pawang* is also " the accredited intermediary between men and spirits . . . without whom no village community would be complete." (*M.M.* 57.) In marriage rites he has been superseded by the official Imam of the Mohammedan mosque, but he officiates at tooth-filing, he is called in in cases of sickness, and it is he who directs agricultural operations, wood-cutting and fishing expeditions, and prospecting for minerals. He has a vast store of rhythmical charms with which he summons or banishes spirits, both souls and demons, with confident authority. The functions of the *Peai*-man of British Guiana are also concerned with spirits, and also exercised for the common weal. He communicates with the souls of absent members of the tribe ; he advises where game is to be found ; he is called in in sickness to summon, banish, and correct the demon *kenaima*, or avenger of blood, who is afflicting the sufferer. All these stand on the boundary-line between the priest and the sorcerer, and it will be wise not to insist too strongly on placing them in either category. The North American " medicine-man " is a personage of the same type, and the name of *shaman* is often applied to him by American writers.

The word *shaman* belongs to the Tunguz dialect, but is used by other Siberian tribes, and the type of soothsayer or wizard denoted by it is general throughout Northern and Central Asia. How the shaman may degenerate into the mere sorcerer is seen in Tibet, where the " black-hatted devil-dancers " attached to the Buddhist monasteries are, says Colonel Waddell, " survivals of the old pre-Buddhist religion of the country." (*Lhasa*, pp. 229, 381.)

The Naga tribes of Assam exhibit the three types of priest, wizard, and witch, clearly marked. There are in each village both the *Khullakpa*, the religious head-man of the community, whose office is hereditary, whose sanctity is protected by taboos, and who ordains and regulates the village *gennas*; and the *maiba*, who is " doctor and magician in one," whose power is merely a matter of individual skill, and who is an independent private practitioner. And finally, " in the next village, or a day's journey away, or over the next range of hills " live " the old women who can detect thieves, and the magicians who cause sickness "—" people who practise the black art and whose rites are secret, private, disreputable." (Hodson, 142.)

The Todas carry the differentiation of functions still further. There are among them, first, the Priests (*palikartmokh, wursol,* and *palol*), who live under a perpetual burden of taboos, and who are responsible for the charge of the sacred buffaloes and the performance of the ritual of the sacred dairies. Next come the *teuodipol* (" god-gesticulating men "), diviners or Soothsayers, who discover secret things. They dance till they become possessed by the gods, and in that state utter their oracles or prophecies in strange tongues. Thirdly, there are the *piliutpol* (" sorcery-praying people "), or Sorcerers, who cast spells on their private enemies and remove them when satisfaction or submission is made; and, lastly, the *utkoren* or *utpol* (" praying people "), or Charmers, who counteract or remedy the ill-effects of the Evil Eye. (*Todas,* 42, 249, 255, 263.)

In Africa, the *nganga* of the Congo basin is a private practitioner. He may be required to administer the ordeal for witchcraft to some accused person, and in so far to act as a public functionary, but he has no definite official position in the community, and his powers are often limited to special methods of treatment or special classes of cases. He is called in by individuals for their private purposes, to cure diseases, supply amulets and fetishes, and procure revenge on private foes. For the latter purpose he must use his knowledge of

" black " magic, but he is not therefore a witch, and his
doings must not be confused with witchcraft. The witch
everywhere is the enemy of society, leagued with other
witches to work evil out of pure malice ; and the witch-finder
or diviner is opposed to him, as noted in the last chapter.
The African witch keeps animal-familiars, transforms himself
—or herself—into animal shapes, and rides through the air
to the rendezvous of the " craft," like the witches of Europe.
But the alienation from the authorized religion of the country
and the contrary cult of the powers of evil, which characterize
European witchcraft, naturally do not obtain in Africa, so
far as has been ascertained.

The word *witch* was in Anglo-Saxon times and much later
applied to both men and women. Bunyan so uses it, and it
is far from obsolete in English country places, where witches
are still believed to " lay spells " on man and beast. And
just as the *nganga* is opposed to the African witch (*ndoxi*),
so the " charmer " or " white witch," otherwise the " wise
man " or " cunning man," is called upon to counteract the
spells of the English witch. Sometimes the " white witch's "
powers are limited to healing diseases, or even to giving
charms against some particular disease, but as a rule they
include discovering thieves and witches, remedying the effects
of witchcraft, and wreaking vengeance on the evildoers, so
that the " white witch," too, is often regarded with some
amount of dread.

The Oriental magician was distinctly a private practitioner
unconnected with religion or office, but working on his own
account, for his own benefit or that of his private clients.
Much false science—*e.g.* astrology, palmistry, geomancy—and
some real scientific knowledge have resulted from his studies,
which influenced and still influence the practice of the Magic
Art wherever Chaldean or Arabian culture has penetrated.
In the East the Malay *pawang* issues his commands to the
spirits in the name of King Solomon, chief of magicians, and
in the West the mystic sign of the pentacle, or Solomon's seal,
is in use to ward off evil spirits in Portugal and even in Wales.

To turn from the wizard himself to his methods of working, it may be noted that the African wizard acts mainly through the medium of material objects, which he treats, medicates, and endues with spiritual or magical power ; the Asiatic works rather by the direct agency of the spirits by whom he is possessed, with whom he is in communication, or whom he has compelled to his service. These two strains of thought and practice pervade the Magic Art everywhere, in relative proportions varying with the ideas of different races as to the relations of the material and spiritual worlds. But whatever be the source of the wizard's power, it is brought to bear on his subject by the application of the principles of Sympathy and Symbolism to the person or thing in question.

By " person " we must here understand that enlarged idea of personality which treats the name, the shadow, the effigy, or the portrait, as integral, almost substantive, parts of the individual himself. The following example both exemplifies this idea of personality and illustrates the relations of the African sorcerer with the spirit-world.

On the Loango coast, when a new fetish-figure is wanted for judicial purposes, it must be determined whose life shall be taken to animate or preside over the image. " A boy of great spirit, or else, above all, a great and daring hunter, is chosen." Then the party go into the bush accompanied by a *nganga* whose special department is this kind of fetish, and *call the victim's name*. The *nganga* cuts down a muamba-tree, from which (they say) blood gushes forth, which is mingled with the blood of a fowl killed for the purpose. No one may call another by name during the expedition, as the man named would die, and his spirit would enter into the tree instead of that of the selected victim (note the taboo accompanying the rite). The figure of a man, or perhaps of a dog, is made from the wood of the tree. If such a fetish-figure is knocked in a lawsuit, anyone bearing false witness will die. Accused persons pass before the fetish, calling on it to kill them if they do, or have done, such and such a thing. Others drive nails into it, calling on it to kill their enemies, and the *nkulu* (soul) of the man whose life entered into the tree carries out their demands. (*FL.* xvi. 383. Specimens of these nail-fetishes may be seen in many European museums.)

Or, conversely, the "enlarged personality" of the wizard or his colleague may be applied to the actual subject to be affected. Thus, in Japan, the picture of two wild dogs, the attendants of a particular deity, is used to guard the house from thieves, the picture of a powerful demon-killer to protect it from the attacks of demons (Hildb. pp. 142, 143).

Something has already been said of the doctrine of *Sympathy* (cf. chap. iv.). It has two forms. First, (*a*) there is the continued sympathy attributed to the severed parts of a single whole, such, for example, as the hair and the person. This affords a world-wide field for magical practice. If a Japanese youth can obtain a hair from the head of an obdurate fair one, knot it with one of his own, and carry it about with him, the lady should listen to him within a week. And on the theory that the portrait is a part of the person, a woman may boil the photograph of her rival in oil to injure the original (Hildb. pp. 152, 156). (*b*) The second form of sympathy is that supposed to be set up between two separate persons or things which have once been in contact, such as the weapon and the wound. If the former be kept bright, the latter will heal. It is not always easy to distinguish this from simple *contagion*, by which some property of the one object is communicated to the other. A goître touched by a dead man's hand will moulder with the corpse; a wart rubbed with a bean-pod or a piece of meat will disappear as the pod or the meat decays. These may be effects of sympathy. But when disease is cured by the touch or the breath of a living man, when an English girl rubs against a bride to catch the infection of matrimony, or a Basuto child wears a kite's foot to acquire speed, or a sheep's bone to gain strength, then we seem to have to do with contagion pure and simple.

Symbolism is often known as "mimetic" or "imitative" magic. It also has two forms : (*a*) *like causes like*; as when by tying knots the winds may be arrested, or the bodily functions impeded, and by loosening them may be set free ; by reversing some ordinary action—turning a chair round, wearing a garment wrong-side-out, throwing salt over the left shoulder, moving contrary to the sun, repeating a formula backwards—the *luck* may be changed and the course of events altered ; or by piercing the representation of a heart, the heart of a lover or an enemy may be wounded ; and so on. These things seem *to us* symbolic, but it should be noted that to the uncultured mind the dramatic action probably represents actual fact. (*b*) *Like cures like* ; on which homeopathic principle thorns are hung up to protect from lightning, artificial eyes are worn to ward off the glance of the Evil Eye, and an old remedy for hydrophobia is recorded in the saying, " to take a hair of the dog that bit you."

Some would add *Antipathy* to this list, as the basis of Charming, or " benevolent magic." " Bell makee sing, debbil no come," said a man to Dr. Hildburgh in Shanghai (*op. cit.* p. 146). " To hate—as the devil hates holy water," is an Irish saying ; " Rowan-tree and red threed Put the witches to their speed," a Scottish one (Gregor, *N.E. Scotland*, 188). But these things may equally well be interpreted merely as overcoming the enemy by the exhibition of superior magical force, as the rival magicians of folk-tales vie with one another and outwit one another. The sounding bell, the holy water, possess power superior to that of the demon ; the sacrificial hue of the red berries and the red thread surpasses the resources of witchcraft ; and the silver bullet that slays the witch probably exhibits the superiority of " white " to " black " magic (*cf.* W. R. Halliday in *FL.* xxi. 147-167).

In important rites the operator gets together all the magic forces at his command, human, spiritual, and material, chooses an auspicious time and place, and then proceeeds to put these principles into practice. Here for instance is a Malay recipe for causing dissension between a husband and wife. Make two wax figures resembling the persons and hold them face to face while you repeat three times a formula to the effect that the female figure is as a goat facing a tiger. Breathe on their heads after each repetition. Lay them one on each side of you back to back, burn incense, and repeat the formula twenty-two times over each. Put them together back to back, wrap them in seven thicknesses of certain leaves, tie them with threads of seven colours wrapped round them seven times, repeat the words again, and bury them. After seven days, dig on the spot, and if the figures have disappeared the couple will certainly be divorced (*M.M.* p. 573).

Miss Mary Owen's negro instructors in Voodooism classified their processes as follows: (1) Good "tricks"; (2) Bad "tricks"; (3) Magical treatment of a person or any part of him; (4) "Commanded" things, such as sticks, thorns, or beeswax, harmless in themselves, but commanded to injure some person indicated.

This attempt of the experts themselves to systematize their science is very interesting. The "good tricks" were said to be the hardest to perform, because "it is always harder to do good than evil." Talismans or luck-bringers, "endowed with a familiar or attendant spirit in the name of the Lord" belonged to this class. The "luck-balls" made by "King Alexander" consisted of articles—bits of red clover or any trifles connected with the future owner—to represent the recipient, bits of tinfoil to represent the inhabiting spirit, and pinches of dust to blind the eyes of enemies, all knotted up ceremonially in skeins (four of each) of *white* silk and yarn to the accompaniment of murmured repetitions of a charm desiring all sorts of blessings for the owner of the ball and concluding, "I call for it in the Name of God." The ball was energized by the conjuror's "own strong spirit" imparted to it by his saliva, by breathing on it, and, most powerful of all, by a tear; and it was to be reinvigorated by a bath of whiskey once a week! In his ancestral land of Guinea this would, no doubt, have been a bath of goat's or fowl's blood.

"Bad tricks" were made of evil things, combined in the name of the Devil. Miss Owen learnt how to make "a trick of stump-water, grave-dust, jay-feathers, and baby-fingers, that can strike like lightning!" Such as these are the fetish-protectors of property in Africa and the *giriba* of the New Guinea gardens—spring-guns ready charged, as it were, to injure meddlers automatically.

Magical treatment of persons or their property—an almost world-wide practice—was thus exemplified by " King " Alexander. In the old slave days, in Southern Missouri, he and a rival conjurer, his enemy, spent a night in the same cabin. Both feigned sleep, each meanwhile *willing* the other to slumber with all the strength that was in him, " but," said the narrator, " I'd been a conjurer longer than he had, and my will was made up strong." At length the host slept. The guest arose softly ; scraped the inside of the other's shoes and the collar of his coat, put the scrapings into a gourd with some alum, red clover leaves, " snake-root," and the leaves and stalks of a " may-apple," and threw the gourd with its contents into the river with the command, " In the Devil's name, go ! and may he whose life is in you follow you ! " And the next week his enemy was sold, and sent down the river (*Trans. FL. Cong.* 1891, p. 235).

The fourth method, that by " commanded things," is prominent in Australian magic in the form of " pointing " or " singing the bone." A human, or sometimes a kangaroo, bone is sharpened to a point, and " magic is sung into it," then it is pointed in the direction of an absent foe, after which the victim invariably dies. Or it may suffice merely to mention the name of the victim and the death he is to die (Howitt, *Native Tribes*, pp. 359-361). In the Malay form of *tuju*, or pointing, the sorcerer points a magic dagger or other weapon, with the proper formula, in the direction of an enemy, who forthwith falls sick and dies. Or he commands a demon-caterpillar or other insect to enter into the victim's body and devour his internal organs (*P.R.* ii. 199). A witch in Gaelic-speaking Ireland, angry with a cowherd, " by simply pointing her finger at him took an eye out of him." (Deeney, p. 78.)

But the Voodoo sorcerers also reckoned as " commanded " things the thorns or nails used to pierce the effigies of persons to be killed or injured. Where the thorn pierces, there will the original be affected. This bewitching by effigy is a world-wide process. The figure is *named* for the person it is supposed to represent, and is sometimes burnt, drowned, or buried, when the like death will befall the victim. Even in the islands of the Torres Straits we find several varieties of this practice, and the figures are often made of beeswax, or of wood covered with beeswax, just as by the American negroes. Or the *maidelaig* may take the dried joints of a vine-like plant, which resemble human bones, place them together in human form, and name each segment, a piece for a limb. " Then," says Dr. Haddon, " he crouched like a fish-eagle, and imitating the way that birds tear flesh off bones, threw them behind him without looking round, then left the spot." The patient dies, unless the wizard relents, turns, and looks at the dried sticks ; then afterwards undoes the spell by returning, picking them up, placing them together, and putting " medicine " upon them (*Torres Straits*, v. 325).

The following further examples of the working of these magical methods are singularly complete, inasmuch as the several elements of (*a*) the magical force itself, (*b*) the instrument through which it works, and (*c*) the means by which it is brought into play, are clearly distinguishable in them.

(i) The ancient Peruvians before entering on a campaign were wont to starve black sheep (llamas ?) for some days and then to kill them, saying, " As the hearts of these beasts are weakened, so may our enemies be weakened." (*FL.* xv. 151.)

(ii) The Arunta tribesman charges a bone or a slip of wood with *arunquiltha* or magical poisonous properties, cursing it with the words, " May your heart be rent asunder, may your backbone be split open and your ribs torn asunder." Then he chooses a convenient opportunity, and standing with his back to the destined victim secretly points the deadly weapon at him, repeating the same words. The man inevitably sickens and unless " saved by the magic of a medicine-man," dies within a short time (S. and G. 534, 536).

(iii) The practice of making a *Corp Chre* or *Chreadh* (a " clay body ") to injure an enemy lingered in the Hebrides within recent years. The effigy was stuck with pins, each of which would cause pain to the person represented in the corresponding part of his body. Spells were muttered over each pin. If he were intended to die speedily, a pin was thrust into the region of the heart ; if he were intended to linger the heart was avoided. When the whole was finished, it was placed in running water, and as it crumbled so would the original waste away. In Islay, when the *Corp Chre* was made ready for the pins, the operator addressed it with the words, " From behind you are like a ram with an old fleece " ; and as the pins were put in a long incantation was repeated, beginning " As you waste away, may she waste away ; as this wounds you, may it wound her." A *Corp Chre* from Islay, made thus, is in the Folklore Society's collection in the Museum of Archæology and Ethnology at Cambridge. One from Inverness-shire made for actual use so lately as 1889 is in the Pitt-Rivers Museum at Oxford, beside another from the Straits Settlements.

The first of these cases exemplifies the sympathetic method in an extreme form, for there is in it no sort of physical contact between subject and object ; the second case is symbolic, mimetic, or dramatic ; and the third combines the two. But whatever be the method adopted, whether the aid of spirits is employed or not, whether the object of the rite is distant or near at hand, it is evident that the will and intention of the operator, expressed or implied, is at the back of it all. It is this which touches the electric button, fires the powder-magazine, explodes the dynamite, liberates and directs the magical forces.

> " It is not earth that I switch,
> But the heart of So-and-so,"

says the Malay, in the process of abducting his victim's soul (*M.M.* p. 569).

> " 'Tis not this bone I mean to stick
> But my love's heart I mean to prick.
> May he have neither rest nor sleep
> Until he comes with me to speak,"

says the English girl, stabbing a blade-bone of mutton. And the Psalmist compares an obstinate man to the deaf adder " which refuseth to *hear the voice* of the charmer, charm he never so wisely." The magical treatise of Abbot Trithenius of Spanheim, published at Frankfort in 1606, gives the operative clause of each recipe in cipher. When these potent words were deciphered, which was not accomplished till 1721, they proved to be merely a *command* to a particular spirit to appear visibly and perform certain confidential duties entrusted to him.

The importance of the *words* used in each case is obvious. They may be, as above, only a simple extempore command, but more frequently they consist of a prescribed formula, which is sometimes sung to a special chant, whence the words *charm, enchantment, incantation*. (The magic song of the Sirens will occur to everyone.) The formulas are usually a carefully-guarded secret, and if not sung are muttered hurriedly and inaudibly. Even in England the words of healing charms are kept secret, the power of giving them is a special one, and their efficacy is lost if they are divulged.

The formulas usually consist of one or more of the following elements : (*a*) sacred or powerful names ; (*b*) invocations, threats, or entreaties ; (*c*) expressions of the commands, wishes, or intentions of the operator ; (*d*) sacred narratives of events similar to that which it is desired to effect. In dealing with spirits, *names* are especially essential, for, naturally, power over the personality of a bodiless being can only be obtained by his name. Many charms include the recitations of a long string of names, and invocations of greater superhuman beings to control lesser ones. Others begin by rehearsing the origin of the enemy as an assertion of power. The words of charms, however, are often not very intelligible, whether from long passage from mouth to mouth or owing to borrowing from foreign languages. Some apparently meaningless words may perhaps be undeciphered ciphers. Where writing is in use, the words of the charm are often written, and carried about the person or hidden in the house, either as a protective amulet or a " luck-bringer." Or the amulet may be eaten ! or the words washed off, and the inky water drunk for curative purposes.

Amulets, protective and prophylactic, and talismans (luck-bringers) constitute a *multum in parvo* of magical art. They may be effectual by their own innate powers, as coral, amber, holed stones, and the like ; or because they are parts of powerful beings, such as relics of saints, teeth and claws of certain animals, twigs and berries of certain trees, and so forth, or they may be figures or representations of such beings. Or they may owe their power to the skill of the wizard, as do the written charms and " King Alexander's " luck-balls. Their qualities may be communicated by contagion—the elephant's hairs may be carried to promote strength, the tiger's claws to give courage. They may have power to bring good fortune and prosperity, as *e.g.* a crooked sixpence or a four-leaved shamrock. Or they may be simply protective ; the cross may guard the owner from witchcraft, the " horns " from the Evil Eye. As a rule, they are worn secretly for good luck, openly to avert evil. And the anxiety to " make assurance doubly sure " which shows itself in the elaboration of complicated rites, appears also in complicated amulets like the Italian *cimaruta* and the Portuguese *cinco seimão* (from *senăl de Solomăo*, or Solomon's Seal).

It has already become obvious that very many magical acts are independent of expert aid. Anyone can make " the horns " against the Evil Eye, can put a silver coin in the churn to guard the cream from witchcraft, can steal a potato to cure rheumatism, can strew broken glass in an enemy's footmarks, can call up the phantom of a lover by sowing hempseed with the words,

> " Hempseed I sow, hempseed I grow,
> Let him that is my true love come after me and mow " ;

and the act will be efficacious. Anyone can do it, as Professor Haddon says, if only he knows what to do. The magic power in such cases resides in the gesture, the matter, the act, or the word-formula itself, not in the person of the performer, though, of course, its action is directed by his intention. And it is a nice question whether all this " household magic " was originally the sole property of the expert, gradually made public and perhaps only imperfectly divulged, or whether it consists of the simple elements from which the more elaborate rites of the professional wizard have been built up; whether, in fact, it represents degeneration or early stages of evolution. Be this as it may, there is hardly any event in human life, or any occupation known to man, which, in the lower cultures, has not its own magical accompaniments. Birth, maturity, marriage, and death, warfare, hunting, fishing, cattle-herding, husbandry, spinning and weaving, cookery, building, smith's work, and to crown all, thievery, all need the assistance of magic art, often on the part of experts, but also on the part of the workers themselves. For instance, the Rev. R. M. Heanley, watching the building of a churchyard wall in Hampshire, expressed some doubt of its stability. " Never fear ! " said the mason, " he'll stand right enow, for *I built your shadow into him* yesterday when you wasn't looking." But the collector of folklore will find it best to inquire for and record such acts or rites in connection with the particular activities they concern, rather than to heap them all together under the general heading of Magic.

It is advisable always to use the native terms if possible. On no account should the technical names of one area or culture be transplanted into another. When translation is needed, translate into English. *Wizard* (from M.E. *wisard*, O.F. *guischard*, knowing one, sagacious man) is, perhaps, the least specialized generic term for the expert in magic arts, and as such it has been used here. The idea that it is the masculine form of *witch* is a vulgar error. The word *magician* recalls the Arabian Nights, and *sorcerer* has evil associations. *Medicine-man* is a much overworked word. It is not an unsuitable name for one who uses charmed or medicated materials with intent to benefit persons or things, but should not be used indiscriminately. *Witch-doctor* is a contradiction in terms, and so is *counter-charmer*. The words in ordinary use by the English peasantry may be found useful elsewhere ; *witch* for the malicious evildoer and *spell* for his deeds of darkness ; *white witch* and *charmer* for his opponent. *Wise man* and *cunning man* literally translate both *wizard* and *nganga* (" knowing one," *FL.* xx. 189). *Conjurer,* a word in frequent use in the Welsh Marches among other places, generally denotes a man of some pretensions to learning, who is supposed to own magical books, to know how to " cast the planets," and to be able to call up and banish spirits. Such men inherit a different stream of traditions from the witch and the charmer, and are in fact the degenerate representatives of the mediæval magician.

Does the sorcerer believe in his own sorcery ? Authorities differ.

" Many things have been done by scholarship, but as for me, I have had dealings with the Devil," was the statement ascribed to a certain Berkshire man on his deathbed (*FL.* xiii. 428). The Buryat shamans when attacked by sickness call in their colleagues to treat them (*J.A.I.* xxiv. 139). But the Barolong rain-maker said confidentially to Dr. Moffat the missionary, " It requires very great wisdom to deceive so many. *You and I know that !* " (Moffat, p. 314.)

See Questionary, p. 320.

CHAPTER X.

DISEASE AND LEECHCRAFT.

" Le médecin n'est à l'origine qu'un contre-sorcier . . . la pharmacie n'est qu'une specialité de la magie." So writes M. Doutté (*Magie et Réligion*, 36, 37), and the fact is as he states it. Folk-medicine is simply " applied magic "—charming directed against a special foe, namely Disease. But it is convenient for many reasons to consider it separately. It is only in modern times that medical science has disentangled itself from magic and empiricism, and the history of folk-medicine should to some extent enable us to trace the steps in the process of emancipation. Moreover, absurd and irrational though its methods be, they yet exhibit the natural workings of the untutored mind, and thus are not without importance in the study of psychology.

Nearly all, if not all, unscientific peoples appear to view disease as a living entity capable of being passed from one to another like a cast-off garment. Some seem actually to regard it as a personality, a self-acting conscious being, whose attacks are voluntary and intentional. Thus in India small-pox and cholera are regarded as goddesses, and are venerated and propitiated accordingly. In the South Sea Islands illness is usually ascribed to the breach of a taboo. In this case help is generally useless; the victim is doomed, and dies accordingly. Other more common theories are that it is the effect of possession by demons, that it is due to the wrath of an offended deity or the displeasure of deceased relatives, or, again, that it is the work of a human enemy, a sorcerer.

In such cases the first task of the medicine-man is to discover the cause of the trouble, so that the deity may be propitiated, the *manes* appeased, the demons expelled, or the witch identified and punished. It is a point of honour with him, as it is with the English " charmer," not to enquire into symptoms. He must appear to know them intuitively. The Rev. J. H. Weeks gives a droll account, too long to quote, of the process of suggestion and exhaustion by which the Congo medicine-man arrives at a diagnosis without appearing to his simple audience to seek information (*FL.* xxi 448 *sqq.*).

The usual methods of divination are brought into play, and in the case of sickness are generally accompanied by much noise, drumming, and rattling, to scare any evil spirits which may be about. Sometimes the sick man is thrown into a sort of trance or stupor, and in that condition interrogated, when the enemy replies by his mouth. The duties of the Siberian shaman are greatly concerned with the treatment of disease. In his accustomed manner he sings, dances, and summons the spirits to his assistance. Perhaps the sick man's soul is absent from his body (a not uncommon theory of disease) and must be sought and replaced. The shaman undertakes the spirit-journey. The soul eludes his pursuit, it travels by ways which sheep have trodden and where its traces are indistinguishable. The shaman, so he sings, searches the woods, the steppes, the seas, to find it. It has quitted this earth for the realm of the gloomy Erlik, ruler of the Under-World. This entails on the shaman a toilsome and expensive journey, and the patient must offer heavy sacrifices. Perhaps Erlik demands another soul in exchange. The dearest friend of the sufferer is fixed upon, and the shaman ensnares his soul while he is asleep. It turns into a lark, the shaman becomes a hawk, catches it, and gives it over to Erlik, who thereupon respites his original captive for a term of years. The sick man recovers, but his friend is taken ill and dies (Buryats: *J.A.I.* xxiv. 69, 70).

Should the disease be due to spiritual agency, exorcism is indicated. Sir Everard im Thurn submitted to treatment for headache and fever at the hands of a *peai*-man in British Guiana. The patient and the practitioner spent the night in a dark hut, the former lying in a hammock, the latter crazing himself with draughts of tobacco-juice, working himself up apparently into a state of frenzy, and keeping up an incessant ventriloquial conversation with the *kenaimas* or avenging spirits which were supposed to be tormenting the sufferer. In the morning he produced a caterpillar which he professed to have extracted from his patient's body, and which he declared was the bodily form of the *kenaima* which had caused all the trouble (*Indians of Guiana*, p. 335-338).

Sometimes the disease-demon must be provided with a substitute for his victim, a new body for his habitation. Mr. Skeat describes a rite for expelling disease in which this is the main point (*M.M.* p. 432). The charmer sets little dough images of all kinds of beasts, birds, fishes, etc., on a tray, and, with other ceremonies, coaxes the evil spirit to leave the sick man, as follows :

> " I have made a substitute for you
> And engage you for hire.
> .   .   .   .
> As for your wish to eat, I give you food,
> As for your wish to drink, I give you drink,
> So, I give you good measure whether of sharks,
> Skates, lobster, crabs, shellfish (both of land and sea)—
> Every kind of substitute I give you,
> Good measure whether of flesh, or of blood, both cooked and raw.
> Accept, accept duly, this banquet of mine. . . ."

A curious belief, of which examples might be adduced from America, Asia, and the Southern Seas, as well as from all parts of Europe, is that a serpent, lizard, or other animal may be swallowed or be generated inside the patient. Dr. Hyde (*Beside the Fire*, p. 46) tells the story of a Connaught man who slept in the hayfield and there got thirteen specimens of a creature called an *alp-luachra* (a newt) housed in his body. These creatures fed on whatever he ate, and he obtained no benefit from it. He was cured at last by being made to eat a quantity of salt beef without drinking, and then to lie down on the ground and hold his mouth open over a stream. His uncomfortable tenants being made excessively thirsty by the salt beef, one by one found their way out of his mouth and into the water.

Other curative rites in actual use seem to aim at getting quit of some physical or spiritual incubus and beginning life again as a new man. Such are mock-birth, mock-burial, and even mock-cremation, which sometimes ends disastrously! Change of name is another resource ; but this, perhaps, does not mean change of nature so much as escape from the power of the malicious demon or witch who has sent the disease.

A crude and practical method of freeing oneself from disease is by simply transferring it to some other person or thing. Pliny reprobates this unfriendly act, which survived as a serious prescription down to the seventeenth century. Beckturius, a medical man of that day, recommends as a remedy for fever, that the patient's nail-clippings should be put in a piece of rag and tied to the door of a neighbouring house (cf. *FL.* xxiii. 236). The present writer knew an old woman in Kent who believed herself to have contracted ague as a child by taking a ribbon which some passing sufferer from the same complaint had tied to the gate of her parents' garden. (She was cured on the advice of a Gypsy woman, by being chased up a hill by some boys with sticks till she sank down exhausted.) Or the disease may be transferred, not to another sufferer, but to some dead or decaying substance, together with which it perishes. Most of the common wart- and wen-cures are based on this sympathetic principle. So is the well-known " split-ash " cure for infantile hernia. Here growth and healing, not decay, are the objects aimed at, and the ceremony seems also to be connected with the idea of re-birth. The child is passed through the opening in the split tree, the tree-trunk is bound up, and often plastered, and as it heals, so will the child. This remedy, mentioned by Marcellus of Bordeaux, physician to the Emperor Theodosius I., was pronounced obsolete by White of Selborne in the eighteenth century. Yet in the year 1910 Mr. Crooke, remarking on the sickly looks of a child in the Cotswold Hills, was told by the mother in a self-defensive tone that she had done all she could for it, she had had it passed through an ash-tree !

All these methods really aim at getting rid of disease, not at healing it. The simplest possible method of healing, namely, by application of remedies to the diseased part, may be noted first in connection with sacred persons, things, or places. The royal touch for scrofula, the draught or the bath in the holy well or the sacred stream, the pilgrimage to the sacred shrine, all aim at *cure*, at overcoming the disease by the " virtue " residing in the beneficent power resorted to. Mr. H. A. Rose has collected a valuable group of evidence in the Punjab on this head (*FL.* xxi. 313-335). His information reveals the existence of whole families in whom the power of healing diseases—chiefly sores, wounds, and swellings—by touch, is hereditary, and whose mystic power is so great that food cooked, or a string knotted, by one of them, has all the virtue of the touch, the breath, or the spittle. In one case, even rubbing against the wall of the healer's shop will suffice, should all the owner's family be absent. As for departed saints and *fakirs*, the mould from their graves, the wells from which they drew water, the very guardians of their shrines, exercise the same healing power which they themselves possessed in their lifetime, and the words they spoke are still potent charms in the mouths of others (p. 328). Certain conditions may have to be observed—the remedy must be tried on a certain day, the patient must submit to restrictions in the matter of diet—but it is the vicarious contact with the holy man that effects the cure.

Charms and amulets have been already referred to. Here are some further specimens of the former. The first is from the *Anglo-Saxon Leechdoms* (i. 393 *n*). " For a stitch in the side let a cross be made and a Paternoster sung over the place, together with the words, ' *Longinus miles lancea punxit Dominum, et restitit sanguis et recessit dolor.*' " To recover a

man from an epileptic fit an old Welsh book of folk-medicine
prescribes as follows : " Set thy mind well upon God and
say these words thrice in his ear—Anamzapta." Mr. G. F.
Abbott gives the following from a MS., apparently of the
eighteenth century, procured by him in Macedonia : " For
pain in the breast say this prayer—' St. Kosmas and Damian,
St. Cyrus and St. John, St. Nicholas and St. Akindynos, who
hold the scythes and cut the pain, cut also the pain of the
servant of God, so-and-so.' " (Abbott, p. 235.) The same
MS. prescribes for ague and for tertian and quotidian fever,
charms to be written on apples and pears and eaten. In the
Saga of Egil Skallagrimson a sick woman is made worse by a
piece of whalebone carved with runes placed in her bed. The
hero declares that they are the wrong runes, cuts them out,
scrapes them off into the fire, and cuts others, which, placed
under the patient's bolster, bring immediate relief.

Besides exorcism, charming, and symbolic rites, folk-medicine includes to some extent the administration of drugs
which among both white and coloured races are sometimes
of the nastiest and most disgusting kind (cf. *FL.* xiii. 69-75).
The selection of the drugs used is often determined by super-
ficial resemblances only, on the axiom that " like cures like "
(cf. chap. ix.). The old medical theory known as " the doctrine of signatures " held its ground among the Faculty till
comparatively modern times. " It supposed," writes Dr.
Tylor (*Early Hist.* p. 122), " that plants and minerals indicated
by their external characteristics the diseases for which Nature
had intended them as remedies. Thus the Euphrasia or eye-
bright was, and is, supposed to be good for the eyes, on the
strength of a black pupil-like spot in its corolla, the yellow
turmeric was thought good for jaundice, and the bloodstone
is . . . used to this day (Plowden, 124) for stopping blood."
There can, however, be no doubt that the medicine-men of
all the continents do acquire a certain amount of real knowledge of the properties of herbs, even if only of poisonous
and narcotic herbs. But the healing powers of plants are
rarely supposed to be effectual unless they are gathered at

certain times and with prescribed rites. The *Pœnitentiale*
of Egbert, Archbishop of York in the tenth century, forbids
the gathering of herbs with any incantation other than
Christian prayers. A famous passage in Pliny's *Natural
History* details the mode of gathering mandragora. The
ginseng plant which the Cherokee Indians use in their medical
practice also has a root resembling the human form. " The
Doctor speaks constantly of it as of a sentient being, and it
is believed to be able to make itself invisible to those unworthy
to gather it. In hunting it, the first three plants found are
passed by. The fourth is taken "—four is a sacred number
throughout North America—" after a preliminary speech, in
which the Doctor addresses it as the ' Great Adawehi '
(magician), and humbly asks permission to take a small piece
of its flesh. On digging it from the ground he drops into
the hole a bead, and covers it over, leaving it there by way
of payment to the plant-spirit. After that he takes them
as they come without further ceremony," (xix. *Rep. Bur.
Amer. Eth.* 425.)

The following are some of the principal maladies for which
medico-magical remedies are employed in different countries,
viz. ague, bites of animals, bleeding, burns, boils, colds,
coughs, cramp, diarrhœa, epilepsy or " falling sickness,"
eye-troubles, fevers and pestilences ; female complaints, difficult child-birth, barrenness ; "fright," or nervous shock ; head-
aches, hæmorrhages, infantile convulsions, hernia, teething
troubles, jaundice, kidney disorders, nightmare and sleepless-
ness, rheumatism, rickets, scrofula, shingles, skin-diseases,
sprains, " stitch," swellings and tumours, toothache, warts,
wounds, wasting debility, whooping-cough, and other zymotic
complaints.

In making enquiries, the collector will probably ask how
such and such a disease should be treated ; but in arranging
his notes afterwards it will be advisable to classify them
according to the kind of remedy used. The local or native
names of the various diseases should be stated.

See Questionary, p. 323.

PART II.

CUSTOMS.

"Let us all act according to our national customs!"

SIR CHARLES NAPIER (*Life*, p. 249).

CHAPTER XI.

SOCIAL AND POLITICAL INSTITUTIONS.

EXAMINATION of the ideas which give birth to folklore practice has shown us the similarity, nay, the identity, of the early workings of the human mind throughout the world. But something more than this is demanded of the folklorist, namely, to study the development and differentiation of custom in different parts of the world, and to gauge the parts played respectively by race, by environment, and by contact with foreigners, in the evolution of these different forms of culture. To this we must now turn.

It may be asked, why we include custom—in the sense of social institutions—in the category of folklore. The answer is mainly this : that institutions, like beliefs and stories, are the product of human mentality conditioned by environment, and like them, too, are immaterial, invisible, intangible. They are thus distinguished from arts and crafts (technology), the material product of human ingenuity and industry. Institutions form the framework within which beliefs and stories exist, and from which they take form and colour. How institution may be bound up with belief and belief with institution, and how both may give rise to myth, may be perceived at once by reference to the cardinal cases of Totemism and Caste. And when any social system decays or is swept away, the process of decay may be observed to extend to other phases of folklore also. The rites become meaningless ceremonies, the beliefs lose their *raison d'être*, the stories are

forgotten or sink into children's tales. All are subject to
the same laws and affected by the same influences. Thus
no record of the folklore of any people can be complete
which does not take their social organization into
account.

After accurate observation, the next requisite for accurate
record is accurate terminology ; and, moreover, the use of
a common terminology, without which one man's record
cannot be compared or equated with another's.

A frequent source of confusion is the loose use of the words
tribe and *clan*, which are often treated as if they were synonymous. Properly speaking, a tribe is a loosely-compacted
political unit, which may be either indigenous or immigrant,
either free or in subjection to another tribe or a nation, either
of pure ethnic descent or formed by the coalescing of several
tribes, which may either amalgamate or preserve their identity
as sub-tribes ; while clans are social units contained within
the tribe. The definitions agreed upon by the Joint Com-
mittee on Terminology for the common use of this work and
of the new (1912) edition of *Anthropological Notes and Queries*,
give, " *Tribe*, a group of a simple kind, nomadic, or settled
within a more or less definite locality, speaking a common
dialect, with a rude form of [common] government, and
capable of uniting for common action, as in warfare ; " and
" *Clan*, an exogamous division of a tribe," adding the quali-
fying particulars presently to be noted. The words Sept,
Gens, and Totem-kin have been used synonymously with Clan,
but the latter is recommended. Some American authors
use Gens only when there is patrilineal descent ; Clan, where
there is matrilineal descent.

The clan system is generally, but by no means invariably,
totemic, (see *Totemism* in chap. iii. pp. 41–43). The members
of each clan usually believe themselves to be of one blood,
descended from a common ancestor, generally eponymous.
But as this ancestor usually bears marks of mythical origin,
even if he be not actually one of the lower animals, the use
of all words implying blood-relationship is best reserved for

cases of real consanguinity ; *i.e.* for " such relationship as can be genealogically proven." The words *clanship* and *clansman* will sufficiently indicate the mutual relationship of the several members of a clan.

The clans contained in a tribe are sometimes grouped together in two or more exogamous parties, which have been conveniently termed *phratries,* or, if only two, *moieties.* These are in Australia still further divided into two, four, or even eight, *classes,* as to which complicated rules of exogamy prevail. For details of these the student must be referred to the works of Australian anthropological explorers, Fison, Howitt, Spencer and Gillen, John Mathew, and others ; and to those of their English commentators and critics, J. G. Frazer, Andrew Lang, and N. W. Thomas.

Sometimes the whole population is divided into two exogamous *moieties* only, without any clans. Where this dual organization is found, matrilineal descent invariably prevails also, so that a man's children always belong to the opposite moiety from himself.

The *Caste* is easily distinguished from the clan by the fact that it is endogamous instead of exogamous ; *i.e.* that marriage takes place within the social group instead of outside of it. The word *caste* is derived from the Portuguese *casta,* pure, and the great aim of the higher and more important Hindoo castes is to preserve themselves from defilement by contact, even of the slightest kind, with outsiders. But among the lower and minor castes and sub-castes, who are engaged in carrying on special avocations peculiar to themselves, it may be surmised that the rule of endogamy is largely kept up by the desire to keep trade secrets within the charmed circle. To these two characteristic marks of the caste, endogamy and hereditary occupation, M. Bouglé (iv. *Ann. Soc.* 1901) would add a third, the practice of hereditary religious rites. The caste thus forms a close corporation, and the social system founded on it is based on a principle of " *répulsion réciproque* " which has a natural tendency to constant sub-division and resulting weakness, absolutely opposite to the aggregating mutually-attractive influence of the exogamous organization of the clans. To frame a definition which should successfully distinguish the caste from the Tribe is more difficult, but in practice, says Mr. H. A. Rose (*Man*, 1908, 52), " it is as a rule easy to distinguish caste from tribe in India," and the use of the word *caste* should properly be limited to the institution as it exists in India, and to similar institutions which may be found elsewhere.[1]

The next point is to discriminate between *Clanship* and *Kinship* ; between common membership of an intimately-connected social group and actual blood-relationship such as can be genealogically demonstrated. The *Clan* must be distinguished from the *Kin*. To this end the customary ambiguous use of the word Family to denote a whole kindred or a whole household (*familia*) must be avoided. The term *Family* should be limited to the group consisting of parents and children, including adopted children, that is to say, " all children, adopted or other, who are treated by law and custom as descendants from the person, whether father or mother, through whom descent is traced." The larger group consisting of the descendants of common grandparents or great-grandparents—the German *Grossefamilie*—may conveniently be styled the *Kindred*. When living under one roof, they may be known as the *Undivided Household*. And the whole circle of relations, real or conventional (excluding relations by marriage), to the utmost limit of genealogical demonstration, may be described as the *Kin*.

When Sir Henry Maine brought the study of early institutions into prominence, he began with the Patriarchal Family, then supposed to be the most primitive social institution in existence. Later research has shown that far behind the

---

[1] The subject may be studied in Risley, H. H., *Tribes and Castes of Bengal*, 1891 : Crooke, W., *Tribes and Castes of the North-West Provinces and Oudh*, 1896 : Thurston, E., *Castes and Tribes of Southern India*, 1909 : Lyall, Sir A. C., *Asiatic Studies*, 1899 : the *Imperial Gazetteer of India*, 1907, vol. i. : Hastings' *Encyclopædia of Religion and Ethics*, 1910, art. " Caste " : and Gait, E. A., *Indian Census Report*, 1911, vol. i.

patriarchal system there lies a stage in which the fabric of society is built upon the relationship between the child and the mother and her clan or kin, to the exclusion, or comparative exclusion, of the father. Where such a system prevails no man is heir to his own father, but to his mother's brother. No king even,—as in Barotseland and elsewhere in Africa at the present day—can transmit his lineage, or hope to leave his throne to his posterity. His brother if living—if not, his royal sister's son—must succeed him. The princess-mother never becomes queen-regnant, her husband may never aspire to the throne. But, low-born though he may be, he is nevertheless the "noble father of kings-to-be," and his daughter by his princess-wife is destined to carry on the royal line to another generation.

Matrilineal succession is very common, but it is sometimes—as in several African cases—confined to the royal house only, while the rest of the nation uses the patrilineal reckoning, or *vice versa.*

An intermediate stage seems indicated in the Old Testament history, where the kings of Judah and Israel succeed to their fathers, but the name of each king's mother is carefully recorded ; and where marriage between the children of one father by different mothers seems to have been permissible (2 Sam. xiii. 13).

Matrilineal descent is often found in conjunction with *matrilocal marriage, i.e.* the custom by which the man "leaves his father and mother," not the woman hers, and takes up his abode temporarily or permanently, with his wife's family— a practice found, for example, in Ceylon, and among various Bengali tribes. And, further, there are cases—of which North America supplies many examples—in which the mother not only transmits the right of inheritance, but wields supreme authority over the children and grandchildren, either personally, or by her brothers, their maternal uncles ; or else the mother's kin as a whole exercises dominion over her descendants. A state of society characterized by two or all of these three conditions—*matrilineal descent, matrilocal marriage,* and *matripotestal family*, is known to students as the system of *Mother-right*, German *Mutter-recht*.

There are other peoples again, including some very low in the scale of civilization, as the Andamanese and many of the Eskimo, who reckon descent as we do, on both sides of the house. In fact, the system of " counting kin " varies very much in different countries, and in every locality it demands careful examination, for on this depends the local law of inheritance, with all that it involves. Much good ethnographical work has been spoilt (and, we may add, many political mistakes have been made and political disasters caused) by the omission to note such seeming trifles as whether by " aunt " and " uncle " paternal or maternal relatives are meant, or whether " cousins " are the children of two brothers, two sisters, or a brother and sister. As these and other such distinctions are usually denoted by different words, a competent knowledge of the language should prevent such blunders.

Reliable information on such points cannot easily be obtained by asking abstract questions as to heirship, relationship, etc. The uncultured native is not accustomed to deal with things in the abstract, and his mind does not readily grasp them. He cannot generalize from details. The matter is further complicated in many countries—viz. Australia, Oceania, India, and probably other parts of Asia, Africa (excepting North Africa), and America (except among the Eskimo), by the existence of the " classificatory " system, under which the people are accustomed to address all the men or women of their social group who belong to the same generation as their parents, as " father " or " mother," and all those of their own generation whom they cannot marry as " brother " or " sister." In spite of this, the blackfellow knows perfectly well who is his actual mother, and distinguishes her from other women, and it is the same, except in very abnormal systems, with his putative father. But to the European mind these " classificatory " relationships are as great a stumbling-block as our systematic and generalizing modes of thought are to the natives.

The fact is that, while the "consanguineous" system of relationship to which we are accustomed is based on the institution of the Family, the "classificatory" system is based on that of the Clan. And when it is found apart from the Clan system, it affords presumptive evidence of former clan organization among the people in question. But it does not obtrude itself on European notice, and frequently therefore escapes observation. There is the more need, then, to draw attention to it.

In the Classificatory system :

(i) all members of a given social group and certain other relatives who belong to the same generation are counted as brothers and sisters to each other ; all those of the previous generation as their fathers and mothers ; and all those of the succeeding generation as their children :

(ii) two reciprocal relationships, such as grandfather and grandson, uncle and nephew, are often known only by a common term (as if we had but the one term " spouse " for both husband and wife) :

(iii) different terms are used : (*a*) for relatives on the father's and the mother's side—whereas we speak of both indifferently as uncle and aunt, grandfather and grandmother, etc.—(*b*) for relatives by marriage on a man's or woman's own side of the house or on his wife's or her husband's—whereas with us a man calls both his sister's husband and his wife's brother, his brother-in-law ; his brother's wife and his wife's sister, his sister-in-law ; and the same with a woman. The differing nomenclature of the classificatory system obviously denotes different footings of relationship in each case :

(iv) different terms are often used for relatives (especially brothers, sisters, and cousins) according as they are older or younger, actually or conventionally, than the speaker :

(v) different terms are often used for the relationship between two individuals of the same sex, and the same relationship between two individuals of the opposite sexes (as if, with us, a son should call the father " Pater," and a daughter address him as " Daddy " ; or a mother be " Mater " to her son and " Mummy " to her daughter). Sometimes the father uses a different word for children from that used by the mother. Not unfrequently there is one word for a brother meaning one of two brethren, and another for a brother in relation to his sister ; one word for *sister* as one of two sisters and another for a sister in relation to her brothers. The explanation of this is that brothers and. sisters may belong to, or become members of, different clans, and that consequently they stand in different relations to each other from those of the brother to his brother or the sister to her sister.

Now as, in the lower culture as well as, or even more than, in the higher, sundry degrees of relationship involve special duties, privileges, and restrictions—matters as to which the student desires to inform himself—it is important to understand what is the system, consanguineous or classificatory, on which they are based. And it is obvious that the English terms of consanguinity cannot be used as equivalents for the terms of classification. It is therefore advisable, having learnt the native terms for the simple basal relationships of *father*, *mother*, *child*, *husband*, and *wife*, to ascertain from an individual native the personal names of those who stand in these relations to himself individually and to set down the information in the form of a tabular pedigree ; then to enquire the personal names of those who stand or stood in similar relations to those already noted and add them to the table, and so on. As savages frequently preserve the names of their ancestry very carefully, several generations can be recorded in this way, and a circle of relations to the third or fourth degree of kindred ascertained.

Next, ask your informant what he calls each of the several persons entered in the pedigree when he speaks to them, and what each calls him, and thus learn the native terms of relationship, the system of classification of kindred, etc. " In the case of many relationships two forms are used, one in addressing a relative and one in speaking of him, and both of these should be obtained. In many parts of the world different terms of relationship are used by people of different sexes " ; (these should be marked " man speaking "—m.s., and " woman speaking "—w.s.—respectively) ; " and the terms are also " (as already said) " affected by the respective ages of the two parties to the relationship," such as elder or younger brothers, etc. (W. H. R. Rivers, in *Soc. Rev.* Jan. 1910). On the Congo, different terms of relationship are used in speaking to acquaintances and to strangers.

It is advisable to get lists of kinship terms from several different pedigrees, or else to put the list by for a time and then ask your informant again. It is also well to supplement the genealogical tree by asking for a list of all the people to whom a given man applies a term of relationship, such as kinsmen too distant to appear in the pedigree, fellow clansmen, relatives by adoption, etc. And endeavour should be made to ascertain whether any special rights or functions belong to particular relatives in the case, *e.g.*, of marriage or funeral rites. It is probable that this occurs to a much greater extent than has hitherto been supposed. The tree should be filled in by adding the residence, the clan or other social group, and the rank or status, if any, of each individual entered. (To give it any *statistical* value the names of infants or others dying without issue should be included.) The information can be verified by comparison with the genealogies of others, for some of the same individuals will probably recur in different relations in other pedigrees.

Among most peoples of low culture the older men preserve a knowledge of their collateral relationships as well as their lineal descent, so the needful information can be readily obtained. Difficulties when they arise occur either through the common taboo on the names of the dead—a taboo, however, which often affects only the members of their own kin ; through the practice of adoption, by which an adopted child

is counted precisely as a real child ; or through the habit of
exchanging names, which naturally gives rise to a good deal
of confusion.

" Having obtained a sufficient number of pedigrees to enable
him to form a reliable induction, and having supplemented
them by general questions in the ordinary way, the enquirer
may codify his evidence, secure that he is in a position to
give a demonstrably true account of the system of relationship, the marriage laws, and the laws of inheritance of the
people among whom he has been enquiring, as well as a good
deal of local history, such as the date and progress of war
and migrations ; " not to speak of facts of biology and physical
anthropology which do not concern us here.

" The genealogical method," adds Dr. Rivers (*op. cit.*), " is
especially important in the study of the inheritance of property.   Thus, it is possible to take a given piece of land and
enquire into its history, perhaps from the time when it was
first cultivated.   The history of its divisions and sub-divisions
on various occasions may be minutely followed, and a case
of ownership which would seem hopelessly complicated becomes perfectly simple and intelligible in the light of its
history, and an insight is given into the real working of the
laws concerning property which could never be obtained by
any less concrete method."

In the comparatively rare cases in which the system of
Mother-right (p. 166) reaches the point of actual *matriarchy*—
i.e. maternal *rule*—the women exclusively own the houses
and their contents, and transmit the inheritance to their
daughters, while the men own merely their tools, weapons,
and other personal belongings.   The Khasis afford a notable
example of this.   With them, on the death of the mother, all
the daughters are portioned, and the *youngest* daughter
inherits the maternal dwelling, and with it the responsibility
for the performance of the religious rites of the household.
" The man is nobody."   He does not always even live or eat
in his mother-in-law's house, but merely visits his wife there.
The proceeds of his labour will be inherited by his wife,

or, if he die a bachelor, by his mother (Gurdon, 82, 83). But more commonly the ownership is vested in the men, and their succession to property is regulated by maternal descent. A man's heir is either his brother by the same mother, or else his sister's son. Failing him, the sister herself inherits. On the Lower Congo a chief's brother by the same mother succeeds to his position, and his eldest sister's eldest son to his goods (J. H. Weeks, MS. note).

Where Father-right prevails the law of property naturally accords with it, but it is not always the first-born son who inherits. Sometimes all the children share alike, sometimes the sons divide the property among them. On the Upper Congo the eldest son takes half, the second two-thirds of the remaining half, and so on in diminishing proportions (J. H. W.). In other cases the elder sons are successively portioned in the father's lifetime and the youngest falls heir to the family hearth—a custom which, under the name of Borough-English, lingers in cases of intestacy in not a few scattered manors and boroughs in our own country. Failing sons, sometimes the daughters inherit, sometimes more distant kinsmen in the male line ; and, in default of other heirs, even slaves. We see this in the case of Abraham, and the custom must have lingered, at least in memory, among the peasantry of Palestine, judging from the proposal of the Wicked Husbandmen (St. Luke xx. 14) to kill the son in order to obtain his inheritance. On the Lower Congo, should there be no heir by blood, the eldest slave (*i.e.* the slave bought first by the deceased man) becomes the heir. " I knew a case," writes Mr. Weeks, " where a boy of about twelve inherited his master's wealth because he was bought first, but an adult slave, bought later, looked after the goods till the boy was old enough to do so himself."

Among nomadic peoples, individual ownership is naturally limited to a man's personal belongings, and there is no private property in land. But even nomadic tribes have a certain sense of collective property in the area of the customary tribal wanderings, and resent the intrusion of another tribe into their territory. And the idea of collective ownership of land seems to survive very far into civilization. M. de Laveleye, in his work on *Primitive Property*, quotes an ancient Czech poem on a quarrel between two brothers as to their inheritance, in which the queen Libusa gives judgment thus : " You should agree as brothers on the subject of your inheritance, and you shall hold it in common according to the sacred traditions of our ancient law. The father of the family governs the house, the men till the ground, the women make the garments. If the head of the house dies, the children retain the property in common and choose a new chief." This is still the rule among the Southern Slavs, from the banks of the Danube to beyond the Balkans (E. S. H.).

Among the Southern Bantu peoples, the whole of the tribal territory belongs in theory to the supreme chief, who parcels out so much as is necessary to the several heads of families among his people. The grantee cannot dispose of the land, it must descend in his family after his death. He has thus no more than the usufruct. Nor can the chief resume any land once granted, unless the grantee flee the country, or be put to death for some crime, such as rebellion or witchcraft. His land is then granted out again to another. In the words of the Cape Government Commission on Native Laws and Customs, the chief may be considered as " a Trustee holding the land for the people, who occupy and use it in subordination to him, on communistic principles." (E. S. H.)

Another type of land-tenure is exhibited in the Village Community, which combines "several" and common ownership with a nicety of adjustment peculiar to itself. It is a self-governing local agricultural unit, either directly subordinate to the national government or mediately subject to it through a headman or overlord. For living examples of the system the student must look to India, to Russia, or to remote corners of Northern and Central Europe. Relics of its existence may still be traced on the surface of Great Britain, and in many of the customs of the folk. And it is not too much to say that the folklore of Great Britain cannot properly be appreciated or understood without reference to the Village Community (see *infra*, p. 188).

Inheritance and land tenure are far from being the only subjects of customary law. There is perhaps no people so uncivilized that it does not possess some accepted standard of morals, some criminal code, and some kind of judicial procedure. And in civilized countries the folk often have a code of their own, differing from the official standard on such subjects as the relations of the sexes, the duty of vengeance, the law of contract, the law of inheritance, and the proprieties of social life. They have, too, traditionally-prescribed methods of exhibiting their indignation at any breach of their own code. Acquaintance with the local code of law and morals is naturally very important to good governance and good understanding. Mr. C. H. Hobley points out (*J.R.A.I.* xli. 456) that the apparently unaccountable desertions by which the A-Kikuyu of British East Africa break their contracts of service are often necessitated, in their idea, by the need of obtaining ceremonial purification after some breach of native law or custom, or of going through the formalities necessary before taking possession of an inheritance. The men are compelled to go by fear of the consequences of omitting the rites in question, and dare not return for fear of punishment for absence without leave. But if they know that their employer will understand the position, they are not afraid to ask for leave of absence, and they then usually return in a few days, thus reducing the inconvenience to a minimum. Among their neighbours the A-Kamba, it has been found difficult to get dwellings erected for the single men in Government employ. The explanation is that only married men are qualified to act as builders (*J.R.A.I.*, xliii. 538).

Naturally, the native codes do not coincide with those of civilization. They are apt to make little or no distinction between ritual, moral, and criminal offences. As in the stories of Jephthah and of Herod, the sanctity of human life generally ranks far below the sanctity of an oath. Defrauding a fellow-tribesman may be a crime, but stealing from or cheating an outsider may more probably be reckoned a virtue. The laws of hospitality may be extravagant in one direction and strictly limited in another. But it is impossible to do more than glance at the subject here. Savage ethics may be studied at length in Dr. Westermarck's *Origin and Development of the Moral Ideas* ; and Sir Henry Maine's *Ancient Law*, though a pioneer work, has not yet been superseded as an introduction to the study of early legal and judicial practice. A few hints on the subject will be found in the Questionary, p. 327. A good deal of African native law has been recorded in the *Journal of the African Society* and other recent ethnographical studies (*v.* POST, in Appendix D.).

Turning now to early forms of Political Organization, the following examples exhibit well-marked and contrasted types, and may be found suggestive.

I. *The Tribe in Australia.*

The Australian tribe possesses a common name, a common dialect, and a well-known and recognized tribal territory, which other tribes may invade indeed, but which they never attempt to conquer. But it has no common government and takes no common action, except by assembling at the *bora* or initiation rites, held from time to time at the instance of some local sub-division and often attended by other invited tribes. The different tribes intermarry, always, however, observing the matrimonial class-regulations. Each tribe contains an elaborate system of exogamic classes and clans, often matrilineal but not matripotestal. This system, however, only affects the marriage system and has no political significance. The real political unit is the small local group, which occupies a certain well-defined area of the tribal land, and which may include members of several clans. An elaborate code of procedure regulates the mutual intercourse of the groups, and the office of messenger, whether professional or specially-accredited, is an important one. Each group is practically autonomous. The supreme authority is vested in the council of old men, led by the headman, who has considerable power in his own group, but no position or authority outside it. The council takes independent action, administers justice according to a well-understood code, punishes breaches of tribal law, and resents injuries by other groups either within or without the tribe. (See G. C. Wheeler, *The Tribe in Australia.*)

II. *Mother-Right in a North American Tribe.*

Among the Indian tribes of North America the clan (where it exists) is the smallest organized unit, and the tribe is a corporate body with a strong central government. The Wyandot tribe of Kansas affords in addition an excellent example of Matriarchy in the true sense of that often-misused word. This tribe consists of eleven *gentes* or clans, which are grouped in four phratries, and each has its own place on the march and in the tribal camp. The tribe is strictly endogamous, and a stranger wishing to marry into it must first be adopted into some family of a suitable clan. But the clan is exogamous ; and though a man may have several wives they must all belong to different clans.

The right to dispose of a girl in marriage belongs to her mother, in whose "lodge" the young couple begin their married life. Later, they set up a separate household among her clan, to which their children will belong, but the husband continues to enjoy all the rights of membership of his own clan. The lodge and the household goods belong to the wife and descend to her eldest daughter ; the husband's personal possessions—clothing, weapons, fishing-tackle, and tools—are his own, and such of them as are not buried with him are inherited by his brother or his sister's son.

The land is the common property of the tribe. The Tribal Council decides what part of it is to be cultivated, and allots a portion to each clan, and a clan cannot change its portion without permission. The women-members of the clan-council allot a patch of ground to each household, and mark it distinctly. The ground is re-partitioned every two years, and is tilled by the able-bodied women, each householder getting her fellow clanswomen to help her to work her patch.

Each clan is governed by a council consisting of four women-householders chosen by the other female householders of the clan, who hold office for life ; and of a Chief who is chosen by them from among their brothers and sons.   The councils of the eleven clans make up the Tribal Council, for which the male members choose a Sachem or Tribal Chief from among the men of the Deer Clan.   The subordination of the Clan Council is formally acknowledged by the ceremonial installation of each new councillor or chief, when the clan gives a feast to the tribe and the Sachem himself announces the new councillor's election and puts the official chaplet of feathers on her head.   The meetings of the Clan Councils are frequent and informal ; the Tribal Council meets regularly at every full moon, summoned by the chief of the Wolf Clan, whose duty it is to superintend the building of the Council-house, to announce the decisions of the Sachem to the tribe, and to execute the directions of the Sachem and Council.   The meetings are opened with ceremonial tobacco-smoking, and the procedure throughout is strictly formal.   Any flaw in the procedure of judicial business is looked upon as super-natural evidence in favour of the accused.   There is a definite division of business between the tribal and clan councils, and unusually important matters may be decided by calling a General Council of the tribe or clan.   This is the " civil " constitution.   The military council consists of all the able-bodied men of the tribe, who choose the military chief from the Porcupine Clan.   He usually has one or more chosen comrades who adhere closely to him and who are ready to take his place if he should be killed in battle (*Rep. Bur. Amer. Ethn.* 1879-80, p. 68).

III. The Tribe in Europe.

The tribal system of Albania resembles a clan-organization on an extensive scale.   The tribe or *fis* contains one or more *bariaks*, or groups of men who fight under one standard, and the *bariaktar*, or hereditary standard-bearer, is the head of the group. The whole *fis* traces its descent from a common ancestor in the male line, and the unit is the kindred dwelling together (in the less sophisticated tribes) as an undivided household. The head of the household has absolute authority over all the members of the " house," even where they do not actually dwell under his roof. A group of closely-related " houses " forms a *mehala*. The government is by the *medjliss* or council of elders, and a full council of all the heads of households and *bariaktars* is assembled to decide matters which affect the whole tribe. Marriage with kindred on the father's side is strictly forbidden to an apparently limitless degree of relationship. The *fis* is, therefore, strictly exogamous ; but as consanguinity is reckoned in the male line only, and as the same neighbouring tribes exchange daughters in every generation, it follows that they must be very closely inter-related, though they themselves are not aware of the fact. The women are kept in great subjection, and have no voice in their own matrimonial affairs. The tribes are nominally either Christian or Moslem, but they retain their own standard of conduct in spite of either religion. In most tribes a man, whether married or single, takes his brother's widow to wife notwithstanding the anger of the Church. Blood-brotherhood, made by each party swallowing a few drops of the other's blood, conveys all the privileges, and also the disabilities, of consanguinity. Blood-feuds are rampant. A squabble between neighbours, a blow, a disrespectful word, an unimportant breach of contract, " blackens a man's honour," and is sufficient to start a feud that will rage backwards and forwards, a life for a life, male blood of the one house or tribe for male blood of the other, for an indefinite number of years. Women and guests are sacred, and no fighting takes place in their presence ; but with this restriction the feud goes on till the one side is willing to give, and the other to accept, the *blood-geld* prescribed by the " Law of Lek." This is the traditional code of the mountaineers, attributed to a chieftain named Lek, a member of a family which held sway over the greater part of High Albania down to the conquest by the Turks in 1479 (M. E. Durham, *High Albania, passim*).

IV. Aristocracy.

In contrast to these free democratic tribal systems, Polynesian society was organized on a strictly aristocratic basis. The political power was in the hands of the chiefs, and noble birth was of the first importance ; so much so that the child of a noble family was considered higher in rank than his parents, from the fact that he is a step higher in the patrician genealogy (Polack, i. 27). This, although the father was magistrate in his own family, and his authority apparently extended to life and death over his children and slaves (Ellis, *Poly. Res.* iii. chap. iv. v.).

The *Manahune* or common people formed the lowest grade of society. Among them seem to have been reckoned all landless men, fishermen, artizans, dependents, personal attendants of the chiefs, and slaves. The next rank was that of the *Bue Raatira*, the landed proprietors, gentry and farmers, including all priests who were not by birth of the *Hui Arii* or nobility, the highest rank.

Polynesia is the home of *tabu*. The separation of ranks is secured and the power of the chiefs supported, by a multitude of prohibitions to touch, taste, or handle anything appertaining to a chief. A breach of any of these prohibitions is practically sacrilege and automatically brings down death or disease upon the offender (see *ante*, chap. iv.). In New Zealand especially, every chief was sacred, even to the cuttings of his hair; and the barber who trimmed it was required to undergo purification before he was freed from the contagion of *tabu* consequent on the operation (Polack, i. 36 *seq.*). In New Zealand and the Marquesas there was no supreme king, but in the other groups there was a king, or sometimes a queen, who ruled by hereditary right, who was treated with extravagant reverence and ceremony, and whose government was, in theory at least, despotic. But every chief was the sovereign of his own district, though he acknowledged the supremacy of the king and was accountable for the conduct of the people under his jurisdiction. The royal family belonged to the *Hui Arii*, and any children the king might have by a woman of either of the other ranks were put to death. The king was sacred; all his personal belongings were sacred; his name and—by a custom equivalent to that called *Hlonipa* by the Kaffirs of South Africa —all sounds resembling it were forbidden to be uttered. The ground he trod on even accidentally became sacred: hence, when he went out of doors he was carried on the shoulders of men set apart for the purpose, who thus themselves became sacred (*tabu*). Any house he entered at once became his, and sacred from all others. To touch him was not permitted, and to stand over him, or even to pass the hand over his head, entailed the penalty of death. The rites by which he was invested with the royal dignity were most elaborate, and the sacred girdle, formally put on him, identified him with the gods.   E. S. H.

V. Barbarian Monarchy.

The functions of a sovereign in the lower culture often include matters not expected of him among more " advanced " nations. Even if he be not, as noted in ch. iv. (p. 56), reckoned among divinities himself, he is often expected to be in confidential communication with Divine Powers. He is apt to be held responsible for the weather and the crops, for the health of his subjects and the fertility of their herds. Naturally, therefore, his own health and soundness are of vital importance to the community. For their sake he must observe many irksome rules of conduct, and bodily weakness may render him liable to deposition or even death (see Frazer, *G.B.*, vols. i. ii. and cf. Seligmann in *J.R.A.I.*, xliii. 664; Questionary, p. 327).

The choice of the right man for the kingly office is therefore a matter of the first importance. Hereditary succession is by no means a universal rule. Even the English crown was originally " hereditary in the family but elective in the person," and during the Middle Ages it often fell to the ablest claimant. In fact, the rule of hereditary succession did not become a matter of statute-law till after the Revolution. In ancient Ireland, according to tradition, the rightful successor to the throne of Leinster was identified by the " roaring " of the Stone of Destiny under his feet (p. 25). The selection of a king by divination, and his recognition by sagacious animals, by the royal insignia, or by the late king's wives, are common incidents of folk-tales (*FL.* xiv. 28) and probably represent actual facts. It is related that the inhabitants of a district in the Island of Upolu, being in want of a " king," stole a baby of high rank from a distant village and brought him up as their king (Turner, p. 247).

We may take the empire of the Bushongo as an example of a constitutional monarchy of a barbarian type. They are a relatively-advanced people in the region of the Upper Congo, who dominate several sub-tribes. There is no clan-organization ; the people live in settled villages, each governed by a chief, with a body of councillors modelled on that of the royal court. The land belongs to the local sub-tribe, and is inalienable, but may be leased to outsiders : the crops belong to him or her who sowed them. Consanguinity is reckoned on both sides of the house ; nevertheless, the inheritance does not fall to the son but to the full brother, and, failing him, to the full sister's son. Failing full blood, relations on the father's side have the preference. But the succession to the kingship is hereditary in matrilineal descent, and the king's mother is held in great respect. The sovereign, or Nyimi, usually nominates his successor from among his relatives on the mother's side, and confides his wishes to his son, who after his decease announces his choice to the people and despatches the official heralds to inform the chosen heir. The new Nyimi puts on his royal robes, the vassal Pygmies arrive to act as his guard. On the third day all put on their official garments, and the new Nyimi, when called upon by the heralds, publicly recites the list of his predecessors and exhibits the royal family to the people. Then those present acknowledge him as their sovereign ; he is placed in a litter and carried to the capital. He takes possession of his predecessor's goods, and the people build him a new capital, which becomes his permanent residence.

Although monogamy is the custom of the country, the Nyimi has numerous wives, including those of his predecessor. If he sneezes, everyone must clap hands three times ; if he spits, the man nearest him receives his expectorations in a kerchief. A subject may not speak to him till addressed.

He himself is subject to sundry prohibitions of a precautionary character. He must never shed human blood. He must not speak with a knife in his hand, nor may anyone holding a knife speak to him. Neither he nor any other man of royal blood may eat in the presence of women, nor may he touch the bare earth. To avoid this, the Nyimi himself travels in a litter and is seated on the back of a slave crouching on all fours ; the rest of the royal family are carried on men's backs and seated on skins or chairs.

The title of *Chembe Kunji* (God upon earth) was formerly applied to the Nyimi. Sick persons are spoken of as being healed by " his divine influence." But rain-making, so often an attribute of kings, especially African kings, is not needed in the climate of Bushongo, and for rain-stopping recourse is had to a professional expert.

The Nyimi's court consists of the following officials : the three princes next in succession ; the two heralds already mentioned ; the keeper of the traditions (who must be a son of a former Nyimi) ; the relater of the traditions ; an official who introduces convalescents into the Nyimi's presence and receives fees from them ; three sinecurists, of whom one is privileged to pick up and appropriate any presents made to the Nyimi which the donor in his excessive emotion may let fall ! the second, to appropriate the lower jaw and breast of all animals offered to the Nyimi, and the third, to receive presents from the fathers of twins ; the guardian-attendants of the heir-presumptive, of the Nyimi's children, his wives, and his tame birds and beasts, especially of the crested eagles kept in the palace courtyard ; a doorkeeper, bellringer, mat-spreader, running-footman to clear the Nyimi's way, chief huntsman, drummers, *marimba*-players, the " superintendent of works," the town-crier (who must be a twin), and, finally, sixteen courtiers without special office, and a number of assistant officials. All these people are *Kolomo*, or councillors, and form part of the royal council. They rank below the six chief councillors—namely, the Prime Minister, the Commander-in-Chief, and the representatives of the four chief provinces of the empire—but are on an equality with the judges, commanders, and lesser representatives. Of these latter there are eleven for the sub-tribes, sixteen for the trades, and one for the *fathers of twins*—for among the Bushongo twins are not feared or despised, but honoured. There are nine Military officials ; namely, the Commander-in-Chief already mentioned, his second in command, another who invests the village chiefs with their insignia, two assistants, and three treasurers with special duties. The Judicial functionaries are, besides the Prime Minister and the Commander-in-Chief, who judges offences committed with sharp weapons, five judges for injuries with other instruments, suicides, thefts, witchcraft, and matrimonial cases respectively, five subordinate judges, the administrator of the ordeal poison and his assistant, and a beadle to arrest fugitives from justice, with two assistants.

All these *Kolomo* hold office for life. Their appointment nominally rests entirely with the Nyimi, but he is obliged to make the selection in accordance with public opinion, and it will easily be guessed that with so large an assembly to consult he is far from being the absolute monarch in reality that he is in theory. Nevertheless, he has not sunk into a *roi fainéant*, and his kingdom, if tradition may be trusted (and it is to some slight extent corroborated by astronomical calculations), must have endured for a length of time which contrasts forcibly with the duration of the empires of conqueror-despots, in Africa and elsewhere, which usually fall to pieces after the death of the founder (Torday and Joyce, *Les Bushongo, passim*).

VI. *Secret Societies.*

We have not come thus far without discovering that almost every community has its own secrets, jealously guarded from the knowledge of women, children, and strangers. The secret thing may be a talisman on which the welfare of the community depends; it may be a sacred myth, or a magico-religious rite. Sometimes the whole body of the adult male members of the community are the guardians of the mystery; in other cases the warriors, the priests, or the innermost circle of initiated men form a close corporation, and are, as it were, the trustees of the people as a whole. And sometimes a voluntary society of initiated members makes the mysteries its own, and the " men's house " or common dwelling of the men of the community, where it exists, may become the rendezvous of the fraternity and the scene of the esoteric rites.

These societies are found in North America, West Africa, Polynesia, Melanesia, and other countries. Initiation, secrecy, a generally magico-religious character, and the practice of appearing in public masked or disguised, are characteristics common to them all, but beyond this their functions differ. So also does the degree of secrecy observed. In some cases —*e.g.* in West Africa—no one knows whether his neighbour is a member of a society or not; in others—as in North America—everybody must be a member of some society: the performances are public, and it is well known to what society each person belongs.

In North America the societies seem to be gradually breaking down the old clan-system. Women are now admitted to them, though in subordination only. In the Kwakiutl tribe of the North-West the tribesmen are grouped as members of clans in the summer, and as members of the societies in the winter; in the tribes of the Central Plains the societies are recruited from the various clans indifferently, and in the South-West the clans have disappeared altogether, while the societies are flourishing. The choice of the society to which each individual will belong is determined by the dreams of the fasting candidate. In those dreams an ancestral spirit, the patron of some particular society, is supposed to appear to him and instruct him in the ritual of the dances which are the great and special function of the American societies, and in which their sacred traditions are enshrined. They are dramatic in form, and are executed by masked and disguised dancers, who personate supernatural characters, enact myths of origin, and the like. The dances are publicly performed on stated occasions, and are regarded as being of vast importance to the prosperity of the people as a whole, in such matters as war, hunting, agriculture, and the weather.

Membership of the West African societies is voluntary. It is often not confined to a single tribe, nor even to one sex, and in the latter case the secret rites are reported to be of a licentious character. But the principal function of the more important societies is that of guardians of public order. " They punish criminals, act as the native police, collect debts, protect private property, and, where they extend over a wide area, help to maintain inter-tribal amity." The famous " Mumbo Jumbo " of Mungo Park was an institution of this kind. There are many grades in each society, each of which has its own office in the execution of the law, and as the initiate " passes from grade to grade, the secrets of the society are gradually revealed to him." (H. W., p. 115). The method of procedure is to appear in the streets masked and disguised, and there deal summary justice. " The belief is assiduously cultivated among outsiders that the initiated members are in constant association with spirits, with evil spirits especially, and with the ghosts of the dead," (H. W., p. 104), and their appearance excites a magico-religious dread. Uninitiated men of Old Calabar may not be seen in the streets during a visitation of *Egbo*, and Yoruba women must remain in seclusion from evening till morning when the Ogboni Society bring *Oro*, the bull-roarer, the voice of Oro the god, into their town. The misdeeds of women are part of the special province of these societies, and the women of the Guinea Coast have in some cases succeeded in forming secret societies of their own to combat them.

The secret societies of the South Sea Islands are organised in grades, " through which candidates able to pay the cost of successive initiations," which may be considerable, " may progress to the highest and innermost circle." (H. W., p. 76). The Areoi Society of Polynesia, which extended from Tahiti to Hawaii was reputed in Tahiti to be of divine foundation, and its members were regarded as representatives of the gods on earth, and as destined to the highest places in the Tahitian heaven. A candidate for membership had to show evidence of inspiration by the gods, and might be kept for months and even years on probation before being initiated. He must then remain in the lower grades until he had mastered the songs and dances and dramatic performances which constituted the main function of the guild—the " mysteries " in which they celebrated the deeds of the god Oro (not, of course, the same as the Yoruba divinity just mentioned), and annually offered to him the firstfruits of the harvest. Human sacrifices, too, were offered in the *maraes* or lodges which were the exclusive property of the society. Parties of *Areoi* travelled from island to island and obtained an easy livelihood by giving their magico-religious performances, occupying the *maraes* or men's houses, and subsisting on the contribution exacted from the inhabitants. The Dukduk Society of the Bismarck Archipelago (Melanesia) has been described as " judge, policeman and hangman all in one." Where it prevails, " the natives are afraid to commit any serious felony." (H. W., p. 110). But, on the other hand, it is worked as an instrument of oppression and pillage, and the arrival, at the new moon, of the two weird figures of the duk-duk and his wife, in shape like gigantic cassowaries, on the sea-beach at dawn, is the signal for the extortion of tribute and the infliction of painful ordeals on the uninitiated. The masked and disguised figures sometimes also parade the island performing dramatic dances, which are supposed to benefit sick persons.

The secret societies of the Banks Islands form a peculiar double organization, consisting of the *Tamate* societies which meet at private rendezvous in the bush, and the *Sukwe*, which inhabit the men's houses, or *gamal*, in the villages. A man who does not belong to the *Sukwe* may not enter the *gamal*, but must live and eat with the women. The *gamal* is divided into compartments severally appropriated to the different grades of membership, and no man may enter that of a grade higher than his own. There are no ordeals to be passed or mysteries to be revealed in initiation; the rites consist chiefly of singing, dancing, and feasting. A man's social position both in this world and the next depends on membership of the *Sukwe*, for, as a native explained to Dr. Codrington, " if anyone should die who has not killed a pig " (for the admission feast), " his soul will just stay on a tree, hanging for ever on it like a flying fox," but the soul of a member of *Sukwe* will remain in *Panoi*, the land of the dead (p. 129). To get beyond a certain stage of rank in the *Sukwe*, it is necessary to belong to the *Tamate liwoa*, the largest and most important of the numerous *Tamate* societies. The word *tamate* is used in many senses; it may mean a ghost, a member of a society, the hat or mask worn by the members, or the society itself. The initiation rites vary much. In those of the *Tamate liwoa* the candidate is beaten, taken to the *salagoro*, and kept there for a hundred days or more, until he has paid the necessary fines. Meanwhile he must wait on the members and bear taunts and trials of temper. The secret of producing the sacred sounds (*were-were*) which accompany all solemn rites is revealed to him, and finally he is decorated and led out in procession, but he is not allowed to *were-were* until he has belonged to the society for some years. Each *Tamate* society has besides its special hat, a badge, which, affixed to any kind of property, protects it from depredation by outsiders but not from fellow-members. Hence, from one point of view, it is an advantage to belong to a small *Tamate*.

Further, none but members of certain *Tamate* societies may perform certain portions of the *Kolekole* rites, which are rites performed in connection with houses, hats, and other articles of human manufacture. Their significance is obscure, but they hold an important position in the lives of the islanders (see Dr. W. H. R. Rivers, *The History of Melanesian Society*, now in the press).

The origin or origins of these and other such secret societies is an important and difficult problem. It is impossible not to be reminded by them of the Mysteries of Ancient Greece, of the Vehmgericht of mediæval Germany, and of the Free-masonry of modern Europe. Their initiation rites, the mutual obligations of their members, and their functions towards the community, bear a marked resemblance to the organiza-tion of totemic clans, from which they may have developed, for they seem to be most flourishing where the clan system is in decay. But they cut right athwart all co-existing political or social institutions, they are independent of the general scheme of things, and they possess tremendous power. The suggestion has been made (by Dr. Rivers, addressing Section H. of the British Association in 1912) that they are the product of the contact of an intrusive culture with the indi-genous culture ; the invaders continuing the performance of their own traditional rites in secret, and admitting the native inhabitants to participation in them by degrees, as the two peoples gradually fused into one community. They would thus afford evidence of past history, of former cultural contact, which would be of the first importance in the analytical study of folklore. Grimm advanced a somewhat analogous proposition with regard to the witchcraft of mediæval Europe, its secret rendezvous and its unholy alliance with evil spirits. He believed it to be a survival of indigenous Paganism, crushed by Christianity and lurking in secret places. But whether either of these hypotheses prove tenable or not, the secret societies, their constitution, functions, rites, and their relation to other institutions demand minute and exact investigation by all who have the opportunity of studying them at first hand. (Cf. Hutton Webster, *Primitive Secret Societies*, from which the above quotations are taken ; and Questionary, p. 328.)

VII. *The Village Community in England.*

It would be a hopeless task to consider here in any detail an institution which is found in lands so far apart as India and Scandinavia, and has assumed great varieties of form during the many centuries of its life. The utmost that can be attempted is to indicate the outlines of the system as they are revealed in the ancient villages of England.

At every period of English history, from the Anglo-Saxon Conquest to the agrarian revolution which marks the close of the eighteenth century, the basis of the national life was supplied by the village community, and the agricultural system of which it was the expression. The normal village was planted at a junction of roads, towards the centre of a wide expanse of arable land ; and it was in the treatment of the arable that the features characteristic of early methods of cultivation were most clearly manifested. The rudimentary nature of current agricultural practices rendered it necessary that no portion of the arable land should bear crops for more than two years in succession ; and in the larger part of England a traditional rotation was established by which, in each year, one-third of the arable lay fallow. In the following season, the same tract of land would be sown with wheat, a year later it would bear peas or beans. The result of this custom was that the whole of the arable land within the village territory in due course underwent a period of fallow ; and, upon the fallow, the cattle within the village were depastured according to rules determined by the common consent of the whole community.

Each of the three large " fields " into which the village land thus fell was divided into a vast number of strips or

" lands " of unequal area, defined either by a balk of un-
ploughed turf or by a vacant furrow. Within the same field,
single strips might well vary from half a rood to an entire
acre or more. The plotting of these strips, a work accomplished in an age of incalculable antiquity, was determined
by the natural drainage of the soil ; the complex plan of an
open field can only be understood in relation to the contour
of the ground. Groups of strips naturally connected were
known as furlongs, and frequently bore the name of some
early settler of local prominence. Along the heads of the
strips ran vacant " lands " used for turning the plough ;
they were called " headlands," and their direction is marked,
even at the present day, by the irregular course of countless
English lanes.

There is much to suggest that at the beginning of things
the arable strips were distributed among the settlers according
to a regular sequence followed consistently throughout the
village territory. Godric was followed by Wulfnoth ; he,
by Sigeberht ; he, by Ethelred ; and he, by Herewulf, wherever there were lands to be divided. Upon the Conversion,
the village priest was fitted into the scheme ; the strips of
glebe recur at regular intervals. But the most significant
fact in this connexion is that the lord of the village himself
frequently took up his holding, not in a compact block
around his residence, but as a participant in the regular
distribution of strips. Even in the thirteenth century, the
lord's land may still be discerned lying disconnected all over
the village fields ; and this although the traditional system
had been distorted during the passage of centuries by purchase or inheritance.

Over the central parts of England, the holding of a representative villager consisted of some thirty acres, distributed
equally between the three arable fields. Such an arable
holding carried with it the possession of strips of meadow,
and the enjoyment of rights of common over waste lands,
determined by the extent of the village territory. Already
by the date of *Domesday Book* (1086) there was much diver-

gence from this average, and among the Scandinavian settlers beyond the Welland a normal tenement of fifteen or twenty acres seems to have prevailed from early times. But whatever its extent, it was the arable holding of the villager which determined his economic place in the community. If a man of thirty acres furnished his two oxen to the great co-operative plough of eight oxen which went over the village lands, a man of fifteen acres need only furnish one ox, but his interest in the common pasture would be stinted in proportion. Nor should the existence be ignored of the quite ubiquitous class of cottagers ; men without a stake in the common fields, who furnished the incidental labour required by the community for which its customs did not provide.

The men of the community were bound to each other by participation in the common agricultural life of the village ; they were bound to their lord, in historic times, by customary services rendered upon his land. From all alike, whether free or unfree, labour was demanded proportionate to each man's share in the open fields. Innumerable local surveys show the serf working for two or three days a week upon the lord's demesne, furnishing additional labour at the busy seasons of haytime and harvest, making customary payments in kind or in money. But they also show that the same services were demanded from men who were personally free ; there is no kind of labour, and no form of money payment, restricted exclusively to the servile population. Even the famous payment of *merchet*, the fine paid to a lord by a serf upon the marriage of his daughter, undoubtedly descends from similar payments made by free men in early days to their lords. It is very true that heavy disabilities lay upon the serf of the thirteenth century. He might not leave the manor to which he was bound. He could be given or sold with it or, together with his land, away from it ; and the king's courts would not enter into any dispute between him and his lord, save as to a matter of life and limb. So, too, less labour would usually be demanded from the freeman than from the serf ; the former might depart at will from the community, he might sell or give his lands to whom he wished. But the trend of all our evidence is to show that he was separated by no fundamental distinction of origin from his servile neighbour.

Above all members of the community, lord, freeman, or serf, there rose the Custom of the Manor, expressed in the judgments of its court. To this court all within the community owed suit and service, by its authority the agricultural routine of the village was maintained, within its precincts the unfree conveyed their lands by surrendering them into the lord's hands, with the prayer that he would grant them out again to their destined possessor. The court was the lord's, but it was by no means the instrument of his arbitrary will ; if he neglected to scour his drains he must be prepared for the animadversions of his own men. The custom of the manor, the accepted scheme of rule and service, was binding on lord as well as man. To change the traditional agricultural order was a task beyond the lord's ability ; its abolition was never desired until the Middle Ages were nearing their end. To the villager, the custom gave substantial security of tenure ; and serfdom in England ended when the lawyers of the king's court ruled that he who held land by unfree tenure might not be dispossessed of his tenement so long as he performed the services due therefrom.

The opposition of free and unfree gradually fades as the village community is traced back into the obscurity of the age beyond the Conquest, when the lordless village becomes a social fact of high significance. Yet it would be an error to regard the lord as a late or unsuccessful element in the life of the village community. Local nomenclature may not safely be ignored ; the names Alfriston, Chellaston, Hunstanton, suggest with some emphasis that Aelfric, Ceolheard, and Hunstan possessed an original superiority over these places and their inhabitants. Thrown back to a date sufficiently remote, the village community seems to resolve itself into a group of settlers, varying in wealth and status, but united in the cultivation of the lands they occupied with the leader to whom they owed their obedience and personal service. From some such form as this, the unrecorded processes of social and economic development are sufficient to produce the village community as it is revealed to us at last in the writings of the eleventh century.　　　F. M. STENTON.

See Questionary, pp. 324-329. (Social groups, p. 325. Marriage System, *ibid.* Property, p. 326. Law, p. 327. Rulers, *ibid.* The Village Community, p. 328.)

CHAPTER XII.

RITES OF INDIVIDUAL LIFE.

Birth, Maturity, Marriage, and Death.

IN early states of society Ceremonial has both a utilitarian and a magico-religious aspect ; the one in regard to society, the other in regard to the individual. There can be no doubt or dispute about the validity of a contract or the right to an office when the agreement has been ceremonially ratified, the official ceremonially installed. Among unlettered peoples the performance of a ceremony before witnesses is, in fact, the only method of attesting the actual occurrence of any important transaction, and its use for this purpose persists long after the invention of the art of writing. The Hebrew kinsman publicly drew off his shoe " for to confirm all things " (Ruth iv. 7), in testimony that he renounced his rights over his kinsman's inheritance, and the mediæval lord of the manor gave " seisin " to a new tenant by the delivery of a rod or a sod of turf in the presence of the assembled court of the manor—a ceremony which has lingered, with regard to copyhold lands, almost if not quite down to our own day.

It is obviously of first-rate importance to any community, civilized or uncivilized, to be certified who is born into its midst, who has taken whom to wife, who has gone to " join the majority." And the ceremonies which mark the transition from one state of existence or condition of life to another are naturally of double importance in the lower culture.

These rites of Birth, Initiation, Marriage, and Death are often very elaborate, and though everywhere much the same in principle they vary greatly in detail. The most convenient way of treating them is that of M. van Gennep, who considers *Rites de Passage* (as he terms them) as a homogeneous series or sequence of ceremonies extending over a length of time ; and classifies them as (1) rites of gradual *separation* from a previous state of existence ; (2) rites belonging to a *marginal period*, when the subject of them is in a transitional state, separated from his former condition and not yet admitted to another, and living meantime under restrictions which are only gradually removed ; (3) the ceremonial *incorporation* of the individual into a new community. During all these three periods, divinations and charms may be resorted to and other attendant ceremonies performed, side by side with the operative and essential ritual acts.

To take BIRTH first. A woman before the birth of her child passes through (1) a preliminary period of partial separation from society. Certain kinds of women's customary work are forbidden to her, certain articles of food prohibited. Sometimes her husband shares the prohibitions with her, sometimes he observes analogous rules himself, sometimes the pair live apart. (2) As the birth approaches her separation from ordinary life becomes more complete. A place apart is generally provided for her habitation, special persons attend upon her there. This " marginal period " continues for some time after the crisis, and is brought to an end by rites of purification, after which she is (3) readmitted to society, perhaps with a ceremonial meal. But her re-integration is very gradual, for she frequently does not return to conjugal life until her child is weaned.

Some examples may be cited. The Toda woman gives birth to her child in her ordinary dwelling, but she goes through two (on the first occasion, three) sojourns in a separate hut, one before and one after the birth. Her husband and any one else who accompanies her the second time become " unclean " thereby, and have to share her isolation. She enters the hut after the birth with her back to the sun for fear the evil demon Keirt, who lives near it, should injure herself or her child, but comes out facing it. While in the hut she is forbidden to drink the sacred milk, and each return home is marked by swallowing draughts of it (or of a ceremonial representation of it), after bathing and putting on a new mantle (*Todas*, 313). " It will be seen," says M. van Gennep, " that the object of these rites is to separate the woman from her surroundings, to keep her for a longer or shorter period in a borderland divided into three portions, and only to replace her in her ordinary surroundings by stages." (v. Gennep, p. 60).

Among the Musquakie Indians, the woman builds a little hut, and retires there when the birth approaches. If by mischance the " birth-house " is not ready, her family leave her alone in the wigwam, but this is a most unlucky *contretemps*, for the baby will die before its parents if it has no house of its own, and to be born out-of-doors would be a disgrace. Neighbour women attend the mother, and when the birth has taken place the medicine-woman comes, summons the neighbours, exhibits the child to its father through a hole in the back of the hut, and loudly proclaims its name. Afterwards the mother goes to the river and bathes herself and her baby. The men keep out of her way, else they also would have to seclude themselves. The mother remains thirty or forty days in the birth-house, visited by one woman only. After this she bathes again, sets fire to the birth-house and its contents, sprinkles herself and her child with the ashes, and goes back to her husband (Owen, 63-65).

The expectant mother in Pahang (Malay Peninsula) may not sleep in the daytime, or her child will be carried off by evil demons. She may not blame any one, else it will have the very qualities she censures. Her husband may not shave nor cut his hair, he may not kill fowls nor shed the blood of any creature, nor may he sit in the doorway of his house, till the child is born (*M.M.* 344-5). These are evidently " sympathetic " prohibitions. They are not restrictions for the purpose of preserving the parents in a state of taboo for the sake of the community, but precautions against injury to the unborn child. Akin to them is the curious custom of the *couvade*, found in South America and elsewhere, by which the father takes to his bed while the newly-made mother goes about her duties as usual. Neither, apparently, is separated from contact with society.

The birth-rites specially connected with the infant begin with its separation from that Other World whence, in many philosophies, it is regarded as having come ; include the " marginal period " of the interval between the birth and the name-giving, or other form of reception into the world of human life ; and are protracted during the first year or so of life, during which the child is subjected to sundry pro-hibitions and restrictions. It is sometimes the duty of some particular relative—in the Banks' Islands, of the father's sister—to play the part of midwife ; sometimes delivery is treated as a magico-religious function of a sympathetic char-acter, and the " how " is as important as " by whom." In the interval after birth and before its ceremonial reception into the world, the child is supposed to be peculiarly liable to evil influences. The Todas keep its face covered as long as it is in the seclusion-hut with its mother, and for some time afterwards. On the fortieth day, or at the end of the third month, the baby-boy is taken by its father to the dairy in the early morning and laid on the ground with its forehead touching the threshold. It is then taken to the place where the buffaloes are standing, where it is held facing the sun, and the covering is removed from its face. A girl is taken by her mother to the nearest point at which women are allowed to approach the dairy (*Todas*, 331). Immediately, or shortly, after this, the name is given. The boy's father, in front of the house, shaves the middle of the child's head, and an amulet against the evil eye is put round its wrist ; the maternal uncle gives the name, promises to endow the child with a calf, and then touches its head with each of his feet. Three grains of barley are put into the boy's mouth and three into his back-hair, and are then thrown away. The child, which has hitherto been suckled, is then fed for the first time, and the parents, if rich, may give a feast (*ibid.* 332). Thus the infant is formally introduced to life and admitted to membership in the community.

The *rites d'agrégation* of infants often include physical operations, such as ear-piercing or circumcision. Among the Kabui Nagas the ears of all the infants born within the year are pierced on the same day, and the whole community observes a three days' *genna*, or separation from the outer world (Hodson, p. 175).

It may be worth while to recall the analogous rites of Great Britain. An old-fashioned Welshwoman might not spin during pregnancy ; if she did so, her child would be hanged with a flaxen or hempen rope. She might not even tie a cord round her waist, or the child would be unlucky. She might not step over a grave, or it would die. In connection with another set of ideas she is forbidden, even at the present day, to make up butter or do any work in the dairy, to salt bacon, or to touch any part of a slaughtered pig, " for the touch of such a woman is regarded as very pernicious." (Trevelyan, 266.) If the husband does not share his wife's restrictions, he shares her sufferings. (See Mrs. Leather's *Herefordshire*, p. 111. The belief though seldom recorded is very common.) A Scottish mother is peculiarly liable to be carried off by the fairies during her seclusion after the birth has taken place. Neither she nor her unchristened babe must be left alone without some guardian talisman : a sharp tool, a piece of " cold iron," a holy book, part of her husband's clothing, or a " witch-brooch " pinned in the baby's under-garments. Everywhere the mother's first exit from her own house must be to visit the church. In Aberdeenshire she would be liable to be forcibly put out of any house she attempted to enter before going to church, and in the north of England it is believed, says Mr. Henderson (*Northern Counties*, p. 16), that she would have no remedy at law for any insults or blows she might receive if she were seen out-of-doors " unchurched."

The infant, too, should not go out till it is taken to be christened and it is held very unlucky to call it by its intended name before it has been formally bestowed upon it. The christening-cake and feast usual in England are replaced in the Northern Counties by the cake and cheese with which the neighbours are regaled immediately after the birth. A piece of this is carried by the nurse on the christening day, and bestowed on the first person of the opposite sex to the baby who may be met on the way to church. On its first entry into any house, after the christening, the child must receive a present —an egg, salt, cake or white bread, sometimes a few matches. (*County FL.* ii. 287.) An auspicious day must be chosen for discarding the baby-clothes. Throughout the country the infant must not be weighed, it must not see its face in a mirror, its hair and nails must not be cut, nor, in some places may its hands (or its right hand) be washed, though it may dabble them in water or they may be wiped with a damp cloth. Most of these taboos continue in force for twelve months, by which time the child has usually been weaned, and its independent existence is complete.

ADOPTION is among some peoples a custom sufficiently established to possess a recognized ceremonial. The ancient Greeks and the Balkan peoples effected adoption by a ceremony of mock-birth ; the Abyssinians by pretended suckling. In the Roman ceremony the person adopted first relinquished his original household by a solemn *detestatio sacrorum*, or renunciation of the domestic worship, and then underwent a *transitio in sacra*, or initiation into the cults of his new household. Here we see the characteristic features of a *rite de passage* clearly marked.

When Mr. Walter M'Clintock was to be adopted by the Blackfoot chief, Mad Wolf, he came by appointment to the wigwam of the chief, who was seated in the midst of his family and friends, the men on the left, the women on the right. The whole of the rites were of a highly religious character. They smoked awhile in silence, and then Mad Wolf having purified himself with the smoke of a kind of incense, chanted prayers to the Sun, Moon, and Earth, including intercessions for him who was to be adopted. Next, Mad Wolf painted the young man's face with red paint, symbolizing the course of the Sun, and solemnly blessed him as he knelt before him, declaring, " Before you, my father, Great Sun Chief, I now adopt this young man as my son." The neophyte was then admitted to take part in several sacred songs, and to share the family meal, but his full initiation was deferred to a meeting of the tribe. Then he was again painted with the sacred paint, an Indian name was ceremonially given to him, and the arcana of the tribe were disclosed to him. These, the Medicine Bundle of the Beavers, consisted of a roll of skins, each of which had its own sacred chant and its dance, in which the adopted Blackfoot had to take his allotted part (M'Clintock, chaps. ii., v.).

In the great majority of savage and barbarous nations, the transition from childhood to adult life is marked by rites of INITIATION. The time of initiation generally corresponds roughly to that of physical maturity, but the two events do not necessarily coincide, any more than in Europe physical maturity coincides with legal majority. The main features of initiatory rites for boys are complete removal from the society of women, and seclusion for a longer or shorter period in a remote spot or a circumscribed area, in circumstances of more or less physical discomfort. When the novices emerge from their confinement they may not return to the unrestrained life they have hitherto led among the women and children. They have " been made men," and thenceforth they associate with other men, and enjoy the privileges and submit to the restrictions of adult manhood.

The initiatory rites vary in elaboration and severity. Where highly developed they usually include (1) tests of endurance and self-control, such as fasts and dietetic taboos, compulsory silence, concealment of fear or pain, and general unresisting submission to whatever may befall ; (2) physical operations, such as circumcision, or extraction of teeth—

perhaps only daubing with clay or with coloured pigments ; (3) instructions as to conduct, and especially as to the national or tribal marriage regulations ; (4) esoteric dramatic dances, in which the traditions of the tribe are enshrined and perpetuated ; and with these, the exhibition of sacred objects, which the youths are strictly enjoined to keep secret from the women. Sometimes a make-believe death and resurrection forms part of the proceedings ; often the novice receives a new name, and is never again known by his former one. It is obvious that severe initiatory rites tend to strengthen the power of the elder men, and therefore to stereotype the institutions of the country.

The full privileges of manhood are not always conferred on the youth at once. Sometimes the food-prohibitions are only gradually removed, successive ordeals must be endured, and the youth must show his prowess as a warrior before he is permitted to take a wife. Among the Masai and other tribes of East Africa the whole social and political system is based on this principle of successive stages or " age-classes." Among the A-Kikuyu and A-Kamba these are as follows : the circumcised adolescent first joins the ranks of the bachelor warriors (*mwanaki*). Later, he is advanced to the grade of *nthele*, or young married man. When he has in his turn circumcised children he retires into civil life and becomes an elder of the Council, (the Masai ceremony on the occasion is called " passing the fence "), first in the *kisuka* and then in the judicial or *nzama* grade. Finally, in old age he becomes an " elder of the shrine," (*ithembo*), whose office it is to offer sacrifices at the sacred groves. Thus, says Mr. Hobley, these successive stages " really compose a system of graduated initiation." (*J.R.A.I.* xl. 428.)

Where secret societies flourish, initiation into them replaces initiation into adult tribal life. Shorn of their savage features, initiatory rites are still retained by Freemasonry, and similar societies ; and they may also be said to survive in the rude jocular ceremonies which sometimes attend the admission of a newcomer into a band of workmen or an

old-fashioned convivial club. Otherwise they have disappeared from social life in Europe, though not from ecclesiastical life.

Girls are usually secluded on arriving at womanhood, and
they sometimes have also to submit to initiation rites as a
prelude to marriage. These usually include instruction in
conjugal duties, but they do not appear to have any religious
import. Much less is known about them than of the corresponding rites for boys.

As to MARRIAGE. There are in the lower culture four ways in
which a man may obtain a wife. First, by capture. Some
years ago this was supposed to have been the normal and
universal primitive method, but the point is now doubted. At
any rate, wife-stealing raids are not unknown in barbarous
states of society, any more than head-hunting, slave-hunting,
or cattle-lifting expeditions. The stories of the Benjamites
and of the Sabines would be sufficient to prove this. Secondly,
a wife may be procured by service, as Jacob obtained his
wives ; next, by barter, when two men exchange sisters, or
two fathers give their daughters to each other's sons, usually
betrothing them in early childhood ; and, lastly, there is the
most common method of all, marriage by purchase, when
the man pays a " bride-price " to the girl's family, or whatever other social group has rights over her. Not that she
generally becomes his absolute property as a slave. What
he buys is the right to her society and ministrations, and her
importance and dignity are in proportion to the price paid.
A fifth method sometimes occurs, in which the couple—
members of the same social group—are predestined to each
other, either from birth, as in " cross-cousin " marriage
between the son and daughter of a brother and a sister, or
in consequence of an untimely death, as in the " levirate "
custom, by which a man is bound to take his brother's widow
to wife. In such cases, of course, there is no question either
of capture or of a " valuable consideration " of any kind.

The negotiation of a treaty of marriage from its inception
to the establishment of the pair in their permanent home is

generally a lengthy process, and includes various stages of betrothal, temporary residence, and restricted privileges, before a final settlement is reached. Among the Bhotias of Tibet, for example, the customary procedure is as follows. First, astrologers are employed to decide whether the proposed match will be fortunate. Then go-betweens, generally the uncles of both parties, are called to meet at the young man's home, whence they are sent to that of the girl, to arrange the marriage. Her parents consult their relatives. If they consent, and the presents offered (white silk scarves) are accepted—this presentation is called the *nangchang*—the amount of the dowry is fixed and the go-betweens are entertained at a ritual meal accompanied by prayers (the *khelen*). After this the young couple are allowed to meet freely   A year later, the bridegroom's family provide a festival meal (the *nyen*), at which all the kindred on both sides are present and at which the bride-price is paid ; but the bride still continues to live in her parents' house. A second year elapses, and on a day determined by the astrologer the bride's family give a great feast (the *changthoong*), to which lamas are invited. Two men make a forcible entry and attempt or pretend to carry off the bride. A mock combat ensues, settled by a money payment made by the pretended robbers. The guests make presents to the bride and her parents, and she to them, after which she is conducted with singing, dancing, and the firing of guns to the bridegroom's home. His parents meet the procession on the way, conduct the party to the house, and feast them there for two or three days. Still the bride does not stay, but returns home with her friends. Another year expires, and the *palokh* completes the business. The bride's parents pay over her dowry, and she goes once more to the bridegroom's home, where at last she remains permanently (*Rep. Census of India*, 1901, vol. vi. App. xxviii. xxix). Thus the whole proceedings of betrothal and marriage occupy at least three years.

The actual rites of marriage cover the whole scale of ceremonial, from the bald simplicity of the Bororó (a matrilineal people of Central Brazil)—where the bride remains in her parents' hut, no consent being asked, no presents given, and no feast or other general intimation made ;—to the wearisome complexity of ritual practised by some Hindu castes, who pile invocations, sacrifices, and ceremonies one upon another without end. Slav weddings in the south-east of Europe, too, are almost interminable. To find a clue to such laby-rinths we must in the first place discriminate between the private and the public rites observed. *Publicity* is every-where the element which distinguishes a recognized marriage from an illicit connection. There is all the difference in the world between a ring given in secret and one put on before witnesses, between vows exchanged privately and those pronounced in public. And when we know which rites must be performed in the presence of witnesses, we are on the way to learn what are regarded as the essential features of a valid marriage.

In classical Sanskrit literature, says Dr. Winternitz (*Trans. FL. Congr.* 287), Agni, the Fire, is often called the witness of marriages, and a marriage witnessed by the fire, according to Hindoo ideas, cannot be annulled. The *confarreatio* of the bridal pair, witnessed by the assembled guests, was the final and sole proof of a Roman patrician marriage. Among some of the tribes of German East Africa, a marriage is not valid until—some months after the first wedding-feast, which is attended only by the kinsfolk—a second feast has been given, to which friends as well as kinsfolk are invited, and at which the bridegroom gives the bride a heavy copper bracelet, the usual African marriage-token (v. Gennep, 194). The would-be bridegroom among the Veddas takes a present of food to his future father-in-law. The latter summons his daughter, who brings with her a cord of her own twisting and ties it round the waist of her suitor, never to be removed ; and from that moment they are man and wife (Seligmann, *Veddas*, 97). A Chinaman when he removes his bride's veil in the presence of the friends who have accompanied them to the bridal chamber, and sees her face for the first time, gives her three taps on the head with his fan to display his marital authority. This makes the marriage indissoluble. (*FL. J.* v. 234.)

In all these cases, as well as in all those of cere-monially tying knots, joining hands, drinking from one cup, being publicly seated side by side, and the like, the crucial point, the essential feature, of the rite is that something is done, given, or shared, before witnesses, which marks or represents the new relations of the two parties to each other. But in the lower culture marriage is regarded less as a union between two individuals than as, to use an old-fashioned phrase, "a change of condition," a *transition* from one state of life to another—from single life to matrimony, from one family or social group to another, and often too from one locality to another. Even in the private and personal pre-parations for the event this idea of making "a new depar-ture" may be discerned. An English "peasant-bride about to dress for her wedding first strips herself of every article of clothing, and begins absolutely *de novo* to attire herself in new and unwashed garments, rejecting even pins that have been used before." (*Shr. FL.* 289.) On the same prin-ciple the Scottish fisherman, the night before his wedding, ceremonially washes his feet with the assistance of his com-panions (Gregor, p. 89). And among the public rites, those which emphasize or symbolize the transition should be dis-tinguished from the multitude of precautions and omens observed—the disguises, the taboos, the amulets, the bits of sympathetic magic, and all the endless things done to procure good luck or to avert bad—which are heaped upon and mingled with them.

In the lower culture such things accompany the commence-ment of every new era or undertaking—an expedition or a journey, the erection of a building, the cultivation of the ground, the entrance into a new year. Much more then, do they gather around that most momentous event in the life of man or woman, marriage. Then, if ever, enemies, human or superhuman, have an opportunity of wreaking their malice or obtaining their revenge; particularly on the bride, whose womanhood renders her specially liable to their attacks. Many of the Arab tribes of Morocco carry precaution to the point of conveying the bride to her new home shut up in a box and invisible to all. But this is not entirely for her own sake, for it seems to be thought that at this supreme crisis of her life the natural " sanctity " of womankind (cf. *ante*, p. 61), reaches such a height as to make her glance dangerous to the beholders (Westermarck, *Morocco*, ch. vi.). But much has already been said of such things in other connections. Here we will dwell chiefly on the rites which actually constitute the marriage and mark the change of status it involves.

Chief among these is the dramatic contest between the parties of the bride and the bridegroom, settled by gifts or money payments. This has been thought to be a relic of bride-capture. One example of it has already been cited in the account of the Tibetan marriage above, and others might be adduced by the hundred, for it is a very widespread custom, found in all stages of culture. In Mabuiag, for instance, the pair first exchange tokens in secret, but when their mutual relations come to the knowledge of their families, the girl's brothers attack and fight the young man till they have drawn blood from him. They then take their sister by the hand and give her to him. He next collects valuables, which she distributes to her brothers, and a feast concludes the affair (*Torres Straits*, v. 223). Sometimes, as among the Khonds, the contest is rather between the sexes than the families. Sometimes again the opposition is offered by the bride's fellow-villagers, who bar the road by which the young couple must depart and require payment for passage. In this form the custom is well represented in Great Britain, where it is commonly known as " chaining the path." In other cases the bride is hidden or disguised when the bridegroom's party come to fetch her away. This was a common practice at old-fashioned weddings in Wales, among other places. The bride is generally expected to make a great show of resistance to her departure, and to lament loudly. This is a marked feature of the marriage rites of Eastern Europe. Among the Mordvins of Simbirsk (Russia), she weeps and laments for two days beforehand. The bridegroom and his party, headed by the best man, have to pay a fee before they can even enter her parents' house ; and the bride has to be carried out by force, pinching and scratching her bearers and grasping at everything she can reach to delay the passage. She throws herself at the horses' feet, beseeching them not to carry her away, she declines to receive the ritual kiss from the bridegroom, or to sit beside him in the carriage. The girls at the bridegroom's house take her part and abuse him, till their silence is purchased with glasses of spirits and they are turned out of the room (*FL.* i. 430 *sqq.*).

The rites observed on arrival at the bridegroom's house as clearly symbolize—or effect—the bride's reception into a new society as do those at her parents' home her separation from an old one. Generally she is ceremonially lifted over the threshold—by her husband, by his maternal uncle (Khonds, *ut sup.*), by a married woman (China, *FL.* i. 278). As she enters, fruits or cereals are scattered over her. In ancient Greece figs and nuts were showered upon her. In Ireland, the bridegroom's mother scatters oatmeal and sprinkles holy water upon her (*FL.* xviii. 81) ; in the north of England cake is crumbled over her head and the plate on which it rested is broken (Henderson, p. 36). In north-east Scotland, the bridegroom's mother, or if she were dead, one of his nearest relatives, welcomed the bride at the door. A sieve containing bread and cheese was held over her head in the doorway, or oatcake was broken over it. The bridegroom snatched her from beneath the shower, and the company scrambled for the pieces. She was led straight to the hearth and the tongs were given to her, with which she made up the fire, or the besom (broom), with which she swept the hearth. The " crook " (pot-hanger) was then swung three times round her head with a solemn invocation, and finally her hand was pressed into the meal-chest and thrust deep into the meal (Gregor, p. 93). The Mordvin bride in some

cases enters the house under a shower of hops from one of
the bridegroom's female relations, a child is placed on her
lap, and she is carried to the stove, to which she bows, beseeching it to love and obey her, and not to dirty her ! Next
day she goes ceremonially with her mother-in-law to draw
water (*FL.* i. 442, 443). Or the mother-in-law leads her
to the stove, strikes her on the head with a loaf of bread,
and gives her a new name of auspicious meaning. Then
she feeds her, and desires her to stay (*ibid.* 449). The Manchu
bride worships Heaven and Earth with her husband on her
first arrival, and on the next day joins him in worshipping
his ancestors and hearth-gods, thus testifying to her adoption
into his family (*FL.* i. 488, 489).

The bridegroom's house is often the scene of the rites of
union already referred to ; and after the ceremonial reception
of the bride there is almost always a wedding feast, with
special viands and appropriate songs and dances.

The Christian marriage-ritual presents us with many of
the ancient features translated into a new atmosphere. It
is performed at the doorway of the church or chancel, and
it includes, in the Western Church, the presence of witnesses,
the formal surrender of the bride by her friends, and the
payment made by the bridegroom, together with the troth
plight, the mutual vows, the gift or exchange of marriage
tokens (rings) and even the concluding ritual feast ; to which
the Eastern Church adds the crowning of the bride and bridegroom and the pre-Christian religious rite of the procession
round the altar. When the ecclesiastical ceremony is performed actually *in transitu* from the bride's old home to
her new one—as among the Mordvins, in Cappadocia, and
formerly in north-east Scotland—the original significance of
the ancient household *rites de passage* and the fact that
the visit to the church is an addition due to an " intrusive
culture," are both very apparent. Not that the inclusion
of a religious element in the rites is peculiar to Christendom.
The Mordvins, for example, who were pagans down to the
eighteenth century, still intersperse their marriage rites with

prayers to the old gods. And where there is a regular priest-hood, the priest usually takes a leading part in the cere-monial. At the marriage of a Fijian chief, the priest, seated between the young couple, invoked the divine protection on them and joined their hands, exhorting them to be loving and faithful and to live and die together. In the Kingsmill Islands he pressed their foreheads together, poured coco-nut oil upon them, and sprinkled their faces with a branch dipped in water, while he prayed for their prosperity. Dr. Wester-marck cites other cases (*Human Marriage*, 422).

Some time often elapses before the young bride is admitted to full social rights in her new environment. The frequent prohibition to call her husband by name has already been mentioned (p. 49). Eating with or speaking to his near kin is also often forbidden. A feature of interest in a Cappa-docian wedding, says Mr. W. R. Halliday (*FL.* xxiii. 87, 88), " is the severity of the taboos on the bride. For forty days she is obliged to wear the veil. For two or three years she may not speak to her mother-in-law or the male relatives of her husband above the age of childhood. Any conver-sation which is necessary with her mother-in-law must be carried on indirectly through her sisters-in-law or the children of the house, to whom the words intended to reach the ears of the mother-in-law must be actually addressed. . . . For several years, again, the bride may not eat out of the common dish, and, even when she is at length admitted to this privilege, she must sit on one side and eat with her head turned away. . . . My informant's brother had been married for three years, and his sister-in-law has not yet exchanged a word with him."

The husband also often has to observe similar " customs of avoidance," the most common of which is that which forbids him to speak to—sometimes even to see or to name —his wife's mother. The wife's father is sometimes sub-tijtuted for or added to the mother, and the taboo occasion-sl y extends even to the blood-relations, such as brothers and sisters. The " mother-in-law taboo " is particularly strict among the Navaho Indians of New Mexico, where both parties are liable to be struck blind for even looking at each other (*Anthropos*, iii. 862). In New Britain a man's most solemn oath is " May I shake hands with my mother-in-law if——! " and even accidentally speaking to one's mother-in-law leads to the suicide of both parties (Frazer, *Taboo*, 85). The taboo is generally permanent, but among some peoples it may be terminated by gifts, by a public ceremonial, or on the birth of the first son (*Amer. Nat. Hist. Mus*. xviii. 10 ; *Peab. Mus*. iii. 132 ; Hobley, 103 ; Werner, *Brit. Cent. Afr.* 132 ; *J.A.I.* xl. 307).

When the wife continues to inhabit her parents' dwelling, other inconveniences are involved. Sometimes her husband may only visit her there ; perhaps by stealth, and under cover of darkness, as in the story of Cupid and Psyche. This is the permanent form of married life among the Synteng, a sub-tribe of the Khasis, among whom mother-right is carried to an extreme point (*v*. p. 170) ; but generally it is only a preliminary stage, and eventually either an independent household is set up, or the husband takes up his abode with his wife's people. His position in the household is naturally a subordinate one, but in varying degrees. At one end of the scale are the Romang men, of whom we are told that the husband loses all right in his parental house because he belongs to his wife's family (Hartland, *P.P.*, ii. 32). At the other are the Pueblo Indians, among whom the husband occupies the lowest place at the board and dare not lift a finger to chastise his unruly offspring, but must entreat their maternal uncle to do so for him ! *En revanche*, however, he retains his status in his mother's house, and wields the authority over his sister's children that is denied to him in the case of his own (*Oral inf*. B.F.-M.).

The rites of " matrilocal " marriage are necessarily somewhat dissimilar from those previously described, yet not entirely so. A single example must suffice. Among the Musquakie Indians the young man's mother opens the negotiations with the girl's mother. The matter having been agreed

upon between them and an interval for courtship allowed
the young man visits the girl's parents. Her mother ceremonially feeds him and bargains with him for the presents
she is to receive, after which her father and other male relatives dress him in a new suit of clothes (to be returned on
the morrow), and introduce him to their friends. On the
morning of the wedding-day the bridegroom goes to the
wigwam of the bride's parents to take up his abode there.
The presents agreed upon are handed over to her mother.
The bride ceremonially feeds the bridegroom, and the pair
sit side by side all day on a seat of honour, receiving the
congratulations of their friends. This completes the rites
(Owen, p. 72). Note the absence of any ceremonial combat.

DIVORCE is a much simpler business than marriage. It
is usually effected by reversing the more important of the
previous ceremonies, or by symbolic division, as in Java,
where the priest cuts the marriage cord literally (Crawley,
323). The most quaintly practical method, perhaps, is that
once in vogue in Orkney, where irregular marriages used to
be contracted by clasping hands through a hole in a great
" standing-stone," known as the Woden Stone. When the
couple tired of each other, they had only to attend an ordinary
service in a Christian Church and to leave the building by
different doors. This loosed the bond which the Pagan
monument had made (*County FL.* iii. 212, 214).

DEATH. And now we come to the last passage of all,
Death, which, regarded as the separation of soul and body,
involves rites for the proper disposition of both. These vary
with the habits and environment of the people who practise
them and with their beliefs as to the nature of the soul and
its life after death. Of these beliefs, and of their culmination
in exorcism of the ghost on the one hand and worship of it
on the other, something has already been said in chap. vi.

As to the disposal of the body, mankind for the most part
are divided between cremation and interment. Sometimes
both are combined—the buried corpse is exhumed and afterwards burnt. Sometimes it is thrown into water; pious Hindoos

throw their dead into the Ganges, the sacred stream. Other peoples, *e.g.* the Parsees and Tibetans, expose the corpse to be devoured by birds or beasts, and in some cases, chiefly in Africa, it is eaten by the relatives ! All these methods aim at separation, concealment, or destruction, of the remains, but an appreciable minority of peoples attempt the preservation of them ; sometimes by mummification, but more often merely by treasuring up the bones. Nomadic tribes frequently carry the bones of their dead about with them for years, as we preserve locks of hair. But the leading form of preservation is the conservation of the skull (cf. p. 53). The ancient Issedones, a remote tribe of Scythians, ate the body, but removed the head and preserved the skull as a memorial (Herod. iv. 26). According to Livy (xxiii. 24), the Boii of ancient Gaul also preserved the skull. So did the natives of the Torres Straits within living memory, as we shall see. The practice is common in Oceania, and the skulls, ritually purified, are frequently used for divination, propitiated, invoked—customs which obviously lean in the direction of ancestor-worship.

Ritual is largely governed by belief in all matters connected with Death. Belief as to the state of the soul departed influences the method of disposal of the body. If the Land of Dead is pictured as underground, we shall not be surprised to find interment customary ; if it is imagined as beyond the sea, the corpse may be laid in a canoe and set adrift on the waters. In some of the Polynesian islands, far distant from each other, two beliefs concerning the home of the dead have been recorded. The future abode of the chiefs is above the sky, that of the common people is in the Underworld. Accordingly, throughout Polynesia there is evidence that preservation of the dead above ground is the practice of chiefs, and interment in the sitting posture that of the common people (Rivers, *Melanesian Society*, vol. ii. p. 281). Where two forms of belief and practice are thus found in the same region an intrusive culture may be suspected. Yet this hypothesis does not meet every case. There are groups in India which, in one and the same group practise cremation, sepulture, and exposure, according to the manner of the death. Where belief in reincarnation occurs, the bodies of those who are expected to return to earth after a more or less prolonged sojourn elsewhere, are differently treated from those whose manner of death argues them to be dead socially as well as physically, to be put out of existence and altogether extinct. Sex also affects the matter. The belief that women do not reincarnate causes their obsequies to differ from those of the men. Peculiar funeral dispositions, such as cave-" burial " and tree-" burial," and details such as the position of the corpse, the orientation of the grave, the interment of stones with the dead body, all have their significance. In fine, the proper investigation of funeral rites demands that they should be examined in relation to belief, to environment, and if possible, to history.

Much *deathbed* ritual seems to be dictated by the fear of pollution, whether from the ghost of the dead man or from contact with the mysterious phenomenon of death itself, is not clear, but the practically universal existence of the dread is certain, whatever may be its object. When Pausanias, the traitor-king of Sparta, fled for sanctuary to the temple of Athene, he was blockaded there and starved almost to death, for no one dared to touch him, till at the last moment he was dragged out just in time to die outside and avoid polluting the temple. Cylon, who in the sixth century B.C. attempted to raise a rebellion in Athens, was actually killed in the temple of Athene Polias, and the whole city was thereby tainted with blood-guiltiness. Even when it had been ceremonially purified, the family chiefly concerned in the murder were stigmatized as " accursed " down to the time of Pericles (Thucydides, i. 126, 134). According to the Levitical law, any *uncovered* vessel in a tent in which one had died was unclean seven days (Numb. xix. 15). In savage society, the sick man is often removed to a separate hut to avoid polluting the dwelling by his ghost. (Old-fashioned folk in Staffordshire never allowed young chickens, cage-birds, or other domestic pets, to die in the house, possibly for the same reason.) In Europe, a dying man may be taken from his bed, on the pretext of letting him die more easily. Any supposed impediment to the flight of the soul is removed. Doors and windows are opened, locks and bolts loosed. A sod or a tile may even be taken from the roof, to give it free egress. Persons as well as buildings, vessels, and implements, are held to be contaminated by the death pollution. Among the Maoris, who carried *tabu* to an extreme point, " anyone who had handled a corpse, helped to convey it to the grave, or touched a dead man's bones . . . could not enter into any house or come into contact with any person or thing, without utterly bedevilling them. He might not even touch food with his hands," but must be fed by another, who himself became subject to severe restrictions thereby. " In almost every populous village there lived a degraded wretch, the lowest of the low, who earned a sorry pittance by thus waiting on the defiled." (*G.B.* i. 323.) On the death of a Kafir head-man, all those in the same kraal become unclean. They must shave their heads, and they may not drink milk nor transact business with other kraals until the medicine-man has cleansed them. Indeed, some anthropologists think that the primary intention of mourning garb is to proclaim to the world the mourner's state of taboo. Typically, it consists of creating a marked contrast to the mourner's ordinary appearance. Those who habitually shave, let their hair grow, those who plait it and bind it up, let it fall in dishevelled locks, and *vice versa*. The Ainu at a funeral wear their coats upside down or wrong-side before (Batchelor, 106).

Sometimes the mourning relatives discard clothes altogether and bedaub themselves with paint, or cut off a finger-joint, or gash their bodies with knives and let the blood flow over the grave. Often they must fast, or at least refrain from cooking food, until the funeral. The house-fire is either put out, or only kept alight as a protection against anything evil. The ceremonial lamentations and dirges begin from the moment of death, and the corpse is as a rule watched incessantly till the funeral. Before it is taken away there is usually a preliminary feast, in which the dead man is often supposed to share. The Kols of India invite a Mahali man (one of a mongrel tribe with whom they do not eat) to a meal in the dead man's house. He represents the deceased, and goes away when the feast is finished, instead of joining the funeral party. Until this is done, no meal can be eaten in the house, but thenceforth it is pure, and no longer haunted. (Hahn, 84.) Cases have been noted in India in which the sins of deceased Rajahs have been removed from the evil doers and communicated to Brahmans by a similar rite. (*G.B.* iii. 18.) On the Welsh border, in the seventeenth century, when the corpse was brought out of the house, a stranger, a quasi-professional ("a long leane, ugly, lamentable poor raskal" says Aubrey of one such), was paid to consume food and drink handed to him over the coffin "in consideration of which he took upon him (*ipso facto*) all the Sinnes of the Defunct, and freed him or her from walking after they were dead." (Aubrey, p. 35.) Ceremonial eating and drinking in the presence of the dead, sharing a loving-cup placed on the coffin, or handing doles to the poor across it, are by no means uncommon European customs. In Upper Bavaria the dough for the "corpse-cakes" was set to rise *on the dead body itself*, but the reason given was that they then "contained the virtues and advantages of the departed, and that thus the living strength of the deceased passed over by means of the corpse-cakes into the kinsmen who consumed them, and so was retained within the kin." (*FL.* iii. 149.)

The actual removal of the dead body from the dwelling is accompanied by many precautions against the spirit's return. Sometimes the limbs are tied together ; occasionally the corpse is dismembered or mutilated ; invariably it is carried out feet foremost ; not seldom it is conveyed to its resting-place by a circuitous route. Very generally it is removed, not by the ordinary exit, but by an opening made on purpose and afterwards closed up. The "corpse-door" in an old house in Jutland is figured in *FL.* xviii. 364. It is a bricked-up archway, opened to admit of the passage of the corpse and built up again before the return of the funeral party. Special corpse-doors may also be seen in houses at Zaandam, in Holland (*oral inf.* D.H.R.M.). Sometimes the house-door is guarded by a sharp axe laid on the threshold; in other places the seats and tables are overturned and any vessels which might serve as a lurking-place for the disembodied soul are turned upside down. The police of Arran Island, in 1889, buried the boots of a murdered man below high-water mark, to keep him from walking. (*FL.* i. 135.)

Provision for the future needs of the dead is common, whether dictated by affectionate care for their comfort in their new state of existence, or by the desire to give them no excuse for returning to their former one. Among such provisions may be noted that of putting a coin, ("Charon's obol"), into the coffin to pay the passage to the further shore, and that which St. Augustine (15th Discourse) denounced as "the pernicious error of putting together food and wine on the tombs of the dead, as if their souls come forth out of the bodies and want food." Such customs culminate in the tombs of ancient Egypt, which were practically dwellings elaborately furnished and provisioned for the use of the dead. The destruction of property after a funeral, sometimes prompted by desire to get rid of the death pollution, is in other cases the outcome of this care for the welfare of the dead. According to Herodotus (iv. 71), the death of a king of Scythia was accompanied by the sacrifice on his grave of one of his concubines, his cup-bearer, cook, groom, lacquey, and messenger, some horses, some golden cups, and selections from all his other possessions. Hideous hecatombs of a similar character have been reported from Africa. A last relic of this custom may perhaps be traced in that pathetic feature of a military funeral, the riderless horse led behind the coffin, with the dead man's boots significantly reversed in the stirrups.

The funeral feast is generally regarded as the necessary completion of the rites. The Melanesians of Aurora Island think that if they do not kill many pigs on this occasion " the dead man has no proper existence, but hangs on tangled creepers, and to hang on creepers they think a miserable thing." (Codrington, 282.) If the body after burial is exhumed and re-interred or otherwise disposed of, a second feast will usually be held when all is concluded. In any case a later memorial feast, often with subsequent games and dramatic dances, is customary. The Prussians in the sixteenth century held banquets on the third, sixth, ninth, and fortieth days after the interment, to which they invited the soul of the deceased. They drank his health, and threw morsels under the table for him and his fellows. When the meal was finished, the " sacrificer " swept the house with brooms. " And he casts out the souls of the dead with the dust, as if they were fleas, and prays them to depart, saying ' Ye have eaten and drunk, beloved souls, go ye forth, go ye forth ! ' " (*FL.* xii. 301.)

The mourning period generally has a ceremonial termination, at all events in the case of a widow or other principal mourner ; and the completion of the funeral rites marks a change in the attitude of the living towards the spirits of the departed. They are no longer thought of as inimical, but as friendly, and are invited to share in feasts held periodically in their honour, usually at the close of the Old Year ; and where the cult of the dead is developed, offerings are made at their tombs.

Finally, an account of the funeral customs of Mabuiag (Torres Straits), may be added in some detail. It will be observed that they constitute essentially a *rite de passage*. The soul is driven out from the body with blows, and becomes a " ghost-person," (*markai*), admitted to the society of the other world by a blow on the head from each senior *markai*, as youths are admitted to the society of men by blows and rough usage. Fire and food are provided for the newly dead, apart from the abodes of men, but as the people believe that the dead are able to find sustenance for themselves, the ritual does not include any provision for their permanent comfort. But that the mourning is very real and the family affection very genuine, is shown by the preservation of the ghastly memorials of the deceased, as well as by the frequent commemoration of them. And the confidence of the people in the efficacy of the rites is evidently complete, for though the ghost is avoided as long as it is thought to linger in this world, there seems to be no fear whatever of its return to injure survivors afterwards.

When a death occurred, it was the duty of the brother or brothers of the deceased man's wife formally to announce the fact to the kindred, by giving the nearest kinsman a touch on the head with a stick and saying " —— is a *markai* (ghost)." The kindred wailed and fasted while the brothers-in-law, officially entitled the *mariget* (literally, *ghost-hand*), made preparations for the funeral. The body was sewn up in a mat, the thumbs tied together, the great toes also. It was carried out of the camp feet foremost, " otherwise the *mari* (ghost) would find its way back and trouble the survivors," and was placed on a platform under a shed erected for the purpose. Food and water—perhaps the remains of the dead man's last meal—were provided, else the ghost would come back to the house for them ; and a fire was lit, for " dead man he cold." Then the relatives, summoned by well-understood pantomimic signals given by the *mariget*, assembled in mourning array of paint and mutilations, touched the corpse and shot arrows at the shed and at the leaders of the ceremonies (or *mariget*), who, still in pantomime, hushed their lamentations and made them take food ; then repeated ritual formulas of comfort. The mourners then went to the gardens and made havoc of the crops, " it was like goodbye." Later, the *mariget* danced, and the mourners cried. A heap of food was piled up near the shed and was divided among those present.

The corpse remained under the shed for several days, watched by the *mariget* to protect it from animals, and to see if anything happened to throw light on the circumstances of the death, for these people recognized no cause of death but sorcery. They made a noise to drive away the *markai* (or ghosts of other defunct persons) who might be about, and the chief *mariget* waved his hand over the body to feel the *mari* (disembodied soul). When decomposition had sufficiently advanced, the relatives returned, and mourned. The roof of the shed was beaten with a stick " to drive rest of devil out," and the first and second *mariget* took the head and lower jaw and placed them in an anthill to be cleansed by the insects. The rest of the body remained in the shed till the flesh had entirely decayed away, when the relatives deposited the bones in a crevice in the rocks.

When thoroughly clean, the head (skull and lower jaw) was formally presented to the relatives. The chief *mariget* painted it red and placed it in a decorated basket. A large mat was spread in the usual place of assembly, the chief mourner sat upon it, the male relatives round him, the women at a little distance. The *mariget*, painted black, their heads covered with masks made of leaves, came in procession, and were greeted by the mourners with a ceremonial flight of arrows. The head *mariget* went on to the mat and presented the basket to the chief mourner ; the others crowded round and cried over it. The *mariget* hushed them, and repeated the formulas of comfort as before. Each party formally presented the other with food, and all went home and had a concluding feast. (*Rep. Torres Straits*, v. 248-252.)

The *mari* (shadow, reflection, or disembodied spirit), was supposed to linger near the body for some days after death. Thence it went to the mystic invisible western island where the *markai* (ghost persons) dwell, and where on the first night of the next new moon it was admitted into the society of the *markai* by a blow on the head from each previous arrival. Till thus initiated a *mari* is " a very intangible sort of thing." (*Ibid*. p. 355.) Then it learns the arts and crafts of the new abode, and especially how to make waterspouts, by which the *markai* spear and suck up turtle and dugong. For the *markai* carry on an existence similar to that of this world, and at times appear to living men who have the power of communicating with them (*ibid*. p. 358).

From time to time a general funeral ceremony was held in the sacred islet of Pulu off the western coast, where the sacred treasures of the community were kept and the boys were " made men." Immediately before the rites of initiation, the Death-dance was performed in memory of those who had departed this life since the last occasion of meeting. The men who had recently acted as *mariget* at any funerals usually took the lead in getting it up. The women and youths were forbidden to see the men making the leafy masks (*markaikuik*) which were to be worn, and a great screen of mats was erected round the rendezvous where the preparations were made. The masked and costumed dancers who, of course, were all of the male sex, personated the ghosts of deceased men (*markai*) and women (*ipika-markai*) and a buffoon (*danilkau*). Both male and female personages were painted black and the male characters carried bows and arrows, excepting two, who carried brooms. They issued from the screened *kwod* in threes, two men with a woman (man in woman's clothing) between them, and danced before the spectators, each imitating the movements and gestures of the dead friend whom he represented, so that the relatives sitting at a little distance could recognise him. The last pair of men were those with the brooms, and behind them came the buffoon, with a coco-nut suspended from his waist, skipping, tumbling, and playing antics, to relieve the strain. The women and children were supposed to believe that the performers were really the ghosts of their deceased friends come to visit them, and to be comforted by the assurance that the departed were still alive. (*Ibid.* 251-256.)

See Questionary, pp. 329-334.

CHAPTER XIII.

OCCUPATIONS AND INDUSTRIES.

IT is an error to suppose that WARFARE is the normal condition of savage mankind. There are, it is true, predatory tribes and piratical sea-robbers who subsist by plunder; and there are private quarrels and chronic feuds. But organized warfare implies an organized community, and the most warlike nations are to be found among those who, like the Maoris and the North American tribes, have developed a certain amount of independent culture. Some tribes, such as the Wyandots (*supra*, ch. xi.) even have a separate organization for times of war, distinct from the ordinary civil government. The personal preparations of the warriors, their mode of life while on a campaign, and the rites performed on their restoration to civil life, show that war is to them by no means a normal condition, but an important enterprise not to be lightly entered upon.

In the early years of the nineteenth century, a Mr. John Tanner, who was for some time a captive among the Osage, described their preparations for a campaign. When war had been decided upon, the warriors painted themselves and held a war-dance. They then got ready their arms and munitions of war, separated from their wives, and underwent a course of fasting, purging, and " sweat-bathing," praying all the while for victory. They consumed a particular narcotic plant, anointed themselves with bear's grease, specially medicated, and finally held another war-dance in which all the actions of war were imitated. Thus equipped, they set out on the war-path, but throughout their campaign they were subject to a variety of prohibitions, intended apparently to guard against loss of strength or " virtue " by contact. (*G.B.* i. 327 : cf. pp. 122, 123.) Before their return they threw away the bowls out of which they had eaten during the campaign. In other tribes and countries we are told of victorious warriors obliged to remain in quarantine and to submit to ritual purification before they are received back to civil life. Numerous examples of these customs will be found in *G.B.* i. 330, *sqq.*

The conduct of the women at home during their husbands' absence at war is also apt to be an important matter. They are often expected to perform sympathetic rites and to observe corresponding prohibitions. " An old historian of Madagascar (1685) informs us that ' while the men are out at the wars . . . the women and girls cease not day and night to dance, and neither lie down nor take food in their own houses.' " . . . " ' They believe that by dancing they impart strength, courage, and good fortune to their husbands.' " . . . And " ' they would not for the world have an intrigue with another man while their husband is away at the wars, believing firmly that if that happened their husband would be either killed or wounded.' " (*G.B.* i, 31.)

Charmed weapons lingered in Europe into the late Middle Ages. Rites to render the warrior invulnerable are found from the Siege of Troy down to the Thirty Years' War (Aubrey, *Remaines*, 75, 152, 237). Or talismans may be carried into battle to give strength to the arms of the combatants and cause confusion in the ranks of their enemies. The helmet of a fallen Dervish from Omdurman, hung with no less than twenty-four cases for amulets, was exhibited to the Folklore Society, 19th May, 1909. Even the Palladium of a nation is sometimes carried forth, in the hope of bringing victory. We are familiar with the story of the Ark of the Israelites and its capture by the Philistines, and with the Battle of the Standard in our own history. It is only of recent years that it has become customary to place the flags of a regiment in safe keeping at home rather than expose them and their bearers to the chances of a battlefield. A remarkable example of a war-talisman, and at the same time of the genesis of a war-god, is found in what Professor Haddon calls "the Saga of Kwoiam," the legendary hero of the Torres Straits Islands. He, so Dr. Haddon thinks, was probably an Australian immigrant from Queensland, who dwelt apart with his maternal family on the southern promontory of Mabuiag. One day he killed his mother in a fit of passion, and then in a fit of remorse vowed to revenge her death. Thenceforward his hand was practically against every man of the neighbouring islands and their hands were against him. He slew all his opponents single-handed with javelins hurled by his Australian spear-thrower, till at length there came a day when, in fight with an invading party from Moa Island, the spear-thrower broke in his hand, and Kwoiam knew that his hour was come. He retreated slowly backwards up the hill and fell, facing the foe, just as he reached the summit. The Moa men dared not behead his corpse as was their wont with fallen enemies, and the Mabuiag men, his neighbours, came and buried him under a cairn, and treasured his magic *augud* on Pulu the sacred isle. These were two crescent-shaped ornaments made of turtle-shell, the shape of the new moon as Kwoiam saw it when he was making them. One, the *kutiku*, was worn on the upper lip ; the other, *giribu*, on the chest. They directed the wearer in the straight course and enabled him to be victorious in fight. Any woman who saw them became insane. They could move and turn at their own will. When men approached them to equip themselves therewith for war, they were restless in their receptacle, and when they had smelt fish they were ready for battle. The Mabuiag clans formed themselves into two phratries of *kutiku* and *giribu*, and on every outbreak of war the *augud* were brought out of their hiding-place with solemn ceremony and were carried into battle, each worn by the leader of its own phratry. "Spose we no got *augud*, how we fight ? " said the islanders, relating the story. And though one grieves to read of the desecration of Kwoiam's shrine and relics, yet the missionaries who destroyed them probably acted in the interests of peace. But the natives still point out the scenes of their hero's life and death, and say that the party who demolished the shrine on Pulu were nearly wrecked on their return voyage, and that the Samoan who actually committed the sacrilegious act was seized with mysterious illness that very night. (*Torres Straits*, v. 3, 67, 367.)

Preparations for HUNTING much resemble those for war. Many North American tribes hold solemn magico-religious dances before a hunt. They masquerade as the quarry they are in search of, and imitate its actions, hoping thus to bring the real animals within their reach. Before a bear-hunt the hunter sometimes addresses the bear, begging it not to be angry and fight, but to have pity and give itself up ; and after it has been killed, rites are performed to appease its spirit, as if it had been human or superhuman. (*Mem. Am. Mus. Nat. Hist.* i. Anthro., 347.) The Malay *pawang* takes a much higher line with the tiger; *e.g.* he says, "Ho, Sir Cruncher! Ho, Sir Muncher ! Let the twig break under the weight of the wild goose ! Fast shut and locked be your jaws by virtue of 'Ali Mustapha, OM. Thus I break the tusks of all beasts that are tusked, by virtue of this prayer from the land of Siam." After this the tiger cannot open his mouth to devour his victim (*M.M.* 167). Among the Bushongo, to secure the success of a hunt, you must *steal* a hen or a goat from another village (one honestly come by would be useless), and kill it by blows in the presence of the hunting-fetish. The fetish must be sprinkled with blood, and the flesh eaten by the hunters. The rites on returning from hunting last several days (Torday and Joyce, 121). The dogs used for hunt-ing come in for their share of treatment. In Uganda before hunting a dog was fed on the entrails of the kind of animal to be hunted, its eyes and nose were rubbed with " medicines " to quicken its sight and smell, and a " fetish " was tied round its neck to preserve it from snake-bites, and to enable it to catch its prey. Women were forbidden to step over the dog's fetishes, as that would break their charm (Roscoe, 424).

FISHING is accompanied by practices of a similar character. In the Torres Straits Islands, magico-religious dances are held from time to time to promote the success of the fisheries. Women are forbidden to enter the turtle-fishing canoes and are excluded from the company of the fishermen. The canoes are purified by the smoke of burning herbs, and the men are anointed with a mixture of turtle-fat and charcoal. Bull-roarers are swung at the departure of the expedition ; magical images are put on board and their spirits are invited to join the crew. (*Torres Straits*, v. 330.)

War and hunting have passed out of the dominion of the folk in Europe, but fishing has become a craft followed from father to son till the fisher-folk often form a quasi-caste apart from the landsmen. The Scottish fishermen used to distribute bread and cheese on launching a new boat, and sometimes to scatter barley over the boat itself. Talismans— a horseshoe, a silver coin, a lucky stone, etc., were, nay, still are, carried in it. When the herring-season was very backward, the fishermen of Buckie (Banffshire) dressed a cooper in flannel shirt with burs stuck over it and carried him in procession through the town in a hand-barrow, to bring better luck to the fishing. (*Ch. N.* 271, Gregor, 145.) The words *minister*, *salmon*, *pig*, and many others must not be spoken at sea. Meeting a woman on the way to the boats is a most unlucky omen. (Gregor, 199 : cf. *FL.* xiv. 300 ; xv. 95.) In this last detail the fishermen agree with the miners.

Little has been recorded of the folk-lore of English fishermen, but the two following items show that it is likely to repay investigation. A belief exists among East Anglian fishermen that the souls of their deceased comrades undergo trans-migration into gulls (*FL.* xiv. 64). On the first night of the mackerel-fishing season at Brighton, bread and cheese are distributed to the children on the beach, and on each night some form of the following charm or prayer is recited by the boat's crew while putting the nets into the sea :—

Captain. Now, men, hats off ! God Almighty send us a blessing, through, etc. Amen.

1st *Man.* Watch, barrel, watch ! mackerel for to catch !

2nd *Man.* White may they be, like a blossom on a tree.

3rd *Man.* Some by the head, (4th) Some by the tail,

5th *Man.* God send good mackerel may never fail !

6th *Man.* Some by the nose, (7th) Some by the fin,

8th *Man.* God send as many as we can lift in !

This rite is called *Bending-in,* perhaps for *Benediction.* (F. E. Sawyer, in *Journ. Brit. Arch. Asso.* 1886, p. 317.)

The customs of HERDSMEN have as yet been little studied. The Hindoo reverence for the cow is well-known ; and the Todas have elaborated the care of the milch-kine into an absolute cult. Not that they actually worship the sacred herd of buffaloes ; but the dairy is a sacred place, the dairyman a consecrated priest, and the daily routine of the dairy opera-tions a religious ritual. They use the milk of the buffaloes, but not the flesh, except when, at stated periods, a calf is killed in sacrifice. Even less has been recorded of shepherds' than of cowherds' lore, yet the pastoral life should yield a rich harvest to the enquirer. The wide-spread use of the blade-bone in divination is a significant item. In Africa, the Baganda women are forbidden to eat mutton, and a Baganda man killing a sheep stands behind it and stuns it by a blow on the head, because if it saw its slayer its ghost would haunt him. An axe once thus used is kept inside the door and called " the plague of the sheep." (Roscoe, p. 288.) The Wiltshire folk believe that a furious ghost may be safely encountered by anyone wrapped in a lambskin, or a sheepskin turned inside out. (*F.L.* xii. 74.)

Floral offerings to the waters at sheep-shearing feasts survived on the banks of the Severn in the middle of the eighteenth century. (Dyer.) Within the last half-century, if not now, a set of numerals was used in many English counties to count, or as it is called, to " score " sheep, which is based on an early Celtic system of numeration. It consists chiefly of old Welsh words corrupted into a sort of memorial rhythm, and bears witness to the unbroken existence of the shepherds' calling in these islands from perhaps pre-Roman times. (See A. J. Ellis, in *Trans. Phil. Soc.* 1877-79, pp. 316-372.)

The customs of HUSBANDMEN on the other hand have been the subject of much study. Mannhardt in Germany, and Dr. J. G. Frazer in England, have treated of them at length. The object of agricultural rites is, naturally, to promote the fertility of the soil, to secure good crops and safe in-gathering. One of the most famous of these rites is the human sacrifice offered to the Earth-Goddess by the Khonds. A *Meriah*, or human victim, was kept in confinement, often for years, before being sacrificed, and was treated with reverence and affection as a consecrated being. At the time of laying down the crops he was put to death with horrible tortures, his flesh was hacked from his body by the crowd and the shreds were buried in the fields. The head, bones, and intestines were burnt with a whole sheep as a funeral pile, and the ashes scattered over the fields, laid as paste over the houses or granaries, or mixed with the new corn to preserve it from insects. Here is a European parallel, one of many. At Spackendorf, in Austrian Silesia, on the morning of St. Rupert's Day (March 27th), a human effigy made of straw, sticks, and rags, dressed in a great fur-coat and cap and hung with iron chains, is fastened to a pole and carried with uproarious singing to an open space outside the village, where, with divers ceremonies, it is laid in a large grave. A fire is then kindled, and the figure is stripped, and thrown into it. Then begins a struggle for the burning rags, which are snatched from the flames with naked hands. Everyone who gets a piece ties it to a branch of the biggest tree in his garden, or buries it in the fields, in order that the crops may thrive the better. (*G.B.* iii. 244.) Thus civilization preserves while it mitigates barbaric custom.

Numerous examples of rites for the well-being of the growing crops are cited in *G.B.* vols. i. and iii. Most of them are sympathetic or symbolic. Women sow the grain with hair unbound, to make it grow luxuriantly: men throw the seed-bag into the air that the crop may grow tall. But there are other rites of an indeterminate character. Captain J. G. Bourke describes how, immediately before the snake-dance of the Moqui Indians—this is a rain-rite which consists in catching little snakes and sending them with messages to Big Snake to ask him to send rain—" one of the old men held up a gourd rattle, shook it, lifted his hands in an attitude of prayer towards the sun, bent down his head, moved his lips, threw his hands with fingers opened towards the earth, grunted to represent thunder, hissed for lightning, at the same time making a sinuous line in the air with the right index finger, and then, seeing that my attention was fixed on him, made a sign as if something was coming up out of the ground, and said, 'mucho maize, *lotamai*!'" (good!—the Hopi salutation. Bourke, 123). It is difficult to say whether such observances as these should be regarded as dramatic magic or as pantomimic prayer. Here " that blessed word " *Magico-religious* will come to the aid of the recorder, and will save him from following the example of a writer who, seeing Magic in one part of a rite and Religion in another, deliberately cut the account of it in half and placed the two portions in two separate chapters accordingly.

Rain-making rites, though not confined to agricultural peoples, may conveniently be dealt with here. The following series of examples will show how gradually, in the Lower Culture, Magic melts into Religion and Religion into Magic.

The Tully River natives of North Queensland, we are told (W. E. Roth, 167, 168) conceive of Rain as a person. Certain men and women who are named after him can make him come. The means usually adopted for this purpose are to hang an implement called a *whirler* (bull-roarer) in the water of certain pools. Even if the rain do not come for several weeks afterwards, when it does it is due to this cause. If thunder and lightning are desired, chips of a certain kind of wood are also thrown into the pool. On the Georgina River a more dramatic rite is employed. An artificial water-hole is made and the women are encamped a few yards away. The men dance and sing around the hole, and imitate the sounds and movements of ducks, frogs, and other aquatic creatures. They then form a line and encircle the women, over whom they throw crushed quartz-crystals, while the women hold shields, pieces of bark, and wooden troughs, over their heads, pretending to protect themselves from a shower of rain. Rain must indeed be dull if he mistake what is wanted ! (*ibid*).

In Africa, the dramatic appeal is not to Rain himself, but to the ruler or owner of the rain. On his first visit to the Shire Highlands, Dr. Livingstone noted that the Anyanja " believe in a supreme being called Mpambe." Some years later the Rev. H. Rowley thus described the rite of appealing to Mpambe for rain. " The principal part was taken by a woman, the chief's sister," (*i.e.* a princess of the blood-royal, the potential mother of kings). " She began by dropping *ufa* (grain) on the ground, slowly and carefully, till it formed a cone, and in doing this called out in a high-pitched voice, ' *Imva Mpambe ! Adza mvula !* ' (Hear thou, O God ! and send rain !). Beer was then poured out as a libation, and the people, following the example of the woman, threw themselves on their backs and clapped their hands (a form of salutation to superiors) and finally danced round the chief where he sat on the ground." When the dance ceased " a large jar of water was brought and placed before the chief ; first Mbudzi (his sister) washed her hands, arms, and face ; then the water was poured over her by another woman ; then all the women rushed forward with calabashes in their hands, and dipping them into the jar, threw the water into the air with loud cries and wild gesticulations." (Callaway, 125, quoting Rowley, *Universities' Mission.*)

Further south, as Mr. Garbutt relates (*J.R.A.I.* xxxix. 530-558), young girls are sent out to call the rain when the growing crops are threatened with drought. " They were almost naked and were striped with ash like zebras. They ran about from kraal to kraal, beating drums and singing

songs all along the edge of the cornfields, and on reaching
the leading kraal of the neighbourhood, or on returning to
their own kraal, the head man gave them corn, which they
would make into beer." One of their songs is to this effect :
" Oh, it's beginning to rain, let it rain very much without
stopping for a long time, let it rain, we rejoice ! "

In Mashonaland, if rain does not come when it should,
all the women of a kraal take small baskets full of grain to
the hut of the oldest woman in the kraal, who must be of the
same *M'tupo* (totem) as the tribe (? clan) of the *Mondoro*,
or god, who is to be appealed to. (Each " tribe " has its
own *Mondoro*, and each Mondoro has a " medium " through
whom he speaks (cf. ch. vii. p. 120). The old woman
pours the grain into a hollow in a flat rock, and walks round
it with a dipping calabash in her hand, calling on the Mondoro
to send rain, because his children are starving. If rain does
not follow within a few days, the whole kraal proceed to the
kraal of the " medium," make offerings of snuff to her, and
ask her to enquire what the people have done wrong. She
retires into her hut and the people remain outside all night
waiting for the spirit to enter into her. In the early morning
(usually), she rushes out foaming at the mouth and shouting,
and in answer to the people's questions tells them how they
have offended the Mondoro, and what offerings they must
make to him to get rain. (*Ibid.* p. 547.)

At Rudraganj in Bengal, in time of drought, all the outlets
of the temple of the god Rudradeva are closed up, and Brahmans pour water over the idol in the temple until it is immersed
to the chin. This process never fails ! (*FL.* ix. 278.)

Sometimes it is human blood that is " poured out like water "
in such rites. We may recall the story of the prophets of
Baal, who in a time of drought, leaped upon the altar, and
cut themselves with knives and lancets *after their manner*
till the blood flowed, in the vain endeavour to attract the
attention of their god. (I. Kings, xviii. 26-28.) The
suggestion that what we are in the habit of calling imitative
magic is really a kind of gesture-language, a sort of heavenly

signalling-system, evidently deserves investigation. In such
cases it should be noted : (1) whether the natives recognize
the existence of any personal heavenly Powers, and (2)
whether they communicate with their neighbours or with
strangers by means of a gesture-language.

The government of the weather is often the special province of the king or chief. (Cf. p. 179). In other places
a professional expert, or rainmaker, is employed, who in arid
climates is often an important personage, though his position,
depending as it does on his success, must necessarily be a
precarious one. But the prominent part taken by women
in rainmaking rites will strike everyone. We meet with it
even in India, where women do not till the soil. There, in
time of drought, women stripped naked draw a plough through
the fields at night. Even the high-caste Brahman ladies
condescend to perform this rite. (*G.B.* i. 98.)

The rain-charms practised in Europe are of a similar character. Water is thrown on a man or a girl covered with leaves,
or on a stone, perhaps one beside a holy well ; or sometimes
on a corpse exhumed from the grave. Welsh children are
chidden for spilling water or throwing stones into a well or
stream, lest rain should follow. (Trevelyan, p. 6.)

The firing of big guns in a battle or sham fight, and even
the playing of a brass band (this in London among other
places), are popularly supposed to cause rain. On the dry
and thirsty Rand, it seems, recourse is had to such methods
when rain is wanted. On August 5th, 1895, a petition from
Krugersdorp was presented to the Raad, praying that a law
might be passed to prohibit the sending up of bombs into
the clouds to bring down rain, as it was a defiance of God,
and would most likely bring down a visitation from the
Almighty. And from the discussion which followed it would
appear that attempts had really been made to influence the
weather in this way. (Fitzpatrick, 392-3.)

Space does not admit of more than a bare allusion to rites
of rain-stopping and procuring sunshine.

We come now to *Harvest.* The most noted, and perhaps

the most general, of Harvest rites is that of making a bunch
of the ears of grain into a rude likeness of a human being,
naming it the Doll, the Baby, the Maiden, the Old Woman,
the Harvest Mother, or some such name, and preserving it
till next year " for luck," as it is expressed in Great Britain.
The Malay rice-harvest shows us the significance of this
proceeding. When the rice is ready for harvesting, before
anything is cut, the *mother-sheaf* (a group of ears growing
in a particular form) is searched for and chosen. Then
the Pawang (who when Mr. Skeat witnessed the proceeding was a woman) comes attended by other women, and with
elaborate ceremony, repetition of charms, fumigation with
incense, aspersion with liquid "neutralizing rice-paste to
destroy mischief," she first plants a sugar-cane in the midst
of the "mother-sheaf" and explains to it that she gives
it a prop to lean against, as she has come to take away its
soul. "Cluck, cluck, soul!" she concludes. She then ties
a string round the growing sheaf, and cuts seven ears (the
Malays believe in the existence of seven souls) from the midst
of it. Still to the accompaniment of charms, incense, and
aspersions, she ties these together, wraps them in a white
cloth, sometimes making them into the shape of a little child in
swaddling clothes, (*M.M.* p. 226) and places them in a cradle.
With a final cry of "Cluck, cluck, soul!" they are carried
under the shelter of an umbrella to the house, where the wife
of the owner receives and welcomes them, saying "That,
methinks, is a child of mine!" and they are kept in the cradle
with all the forms observed in the case of a real baby. The
firstfruits of the crop are then reaped, cooked, and eaten at
a special feast (p. 226), but the mother-sheaf is left standing
and is eventually reaped by the wife of the owner. The
grain from it is mixed with the grain from the Rice-soul to be
used for seed-grain, and the empty ears made into a wreath
and kept in the rice-bin till next year (*ibid.* 235-247). It
is needless to cite any of the numerous European, and indeed
British, parallels to these rites. Where there is an interval
between reaping and ingathering, the observer should be

careful to note on which occasion each portion of the ritual is performed, as there is a confusion in some of the accounts.

In the lower culture, the firstfruits of a crop are a matter of supreme importance. They must be severed by a special person—chief, king, priest, or medicine-man—and until this has been done no one may touch the main crop. Sometimes they are reserved to the use of the sacred personage who cuts them, or are offered to a divine being. In other cases they are eaten ritually, generally by the whole of the household or other social group concerned. Sometimes, as in Pondoland and in Nigeria, this feast develops into a general harvest festival with many of the characteristics of a New Year celebration. Nor are such festivals confined to the cereal crops. Yams, where they form the staple food, are the subject of firstfruit ritual. The tobacco-harvest among the Black-feet may not be entered upon until the first plant has been ritually gathered (Grinnell, 270) ; and even the Ojibway and Dakota and others, who do not till the soil, hold a thanksgiving feast before they gather the wild rice which supplies their farinaceous food, and set apart the firstfruits (*Rep. Bur. Ethn.* xix. 1091).

In Great Britain, the firstfruits were formerly offered on the altar of the parish church on Lammas or Loaf-mass Day (August 1st), and the harvest-home rejoicing was a household festival, when the last load was brought home in triumph with shouts and songs and the subsequent meal was a joyous scene of equality and mirth. The ecclesiastical festival has long been disused ; the social one lingered within living memory.

ARTS AND CRAFTS. Other early industries would assuredly repay investigation. The governing council of the Bushongo includes representatives of sixteen different trades who, according to tradition, were added to it by Shamba Bo-logongo, said to have been an enlightened and reforming monarch of the Bushongo in the seventeenth century. They are as follows : the wood-carvers, who rank much before the others, the cap-makers, weavers, blacksmiths, leather-workers, singers, musicians, dancers, salters, fishers, hunters, boat-builders, oil-pressers, mat-makers, net-makers, and tailors. Monsieur Sébillot, whose *Légendes et Curiosités des Métiers* naturally deals mainly with France, treats of the following trades : millers, bakers, pastrycooks ; spinners and weavers ; tailors, sempstresses, hatters, milliners, lace-makers, laundresses ; shoemakers, glovers ; woodcutters, charcoal-burners, crate-makers, clog-makers, besom-makers ; carpenters, wheelwrights, cabinetmakers, coopers, and turners ; masons, stone-cutters, slaters ; blacksmiths, locksmiths, nailers, and tinkers. To this list we may add miners, potters, tanners and leather-workers, dyers, brewers, butchers, and chimney-sweeps.

It is obvious that no folklore of arts and crafts can date from the very earliest ages of human life : none, for instance, can be so old as beliefs about fire and water may be. At first, of course, all known arts would be practised by one person, or rather one household. They can only gradually have been differentiated into trades or crafts. Perhaps the arts of millers, bakers, spinners, weavers, woodcutters, potters, and blacksmiths, may be considered as among the oldest ; and as they developed into trades, they would carry the lore attached to the art with them. Ceremonies in felling trees, taboos on spinning, omens from baking, may thus be older than the existence of the separate crafts or callings of the woodcutter, the spinner, the baker. The millers' lore, on the other hand, seems only to date from the beginning of the craft. Everywhere, at some time or other, there must have been a period when the windmill or water-mill began to supersede the hand-quern, and this period of course marks the rise of the millers' trade. To this period also we must evidently refer the bulk of the millers' lore, which chiefly deals with the supposed existence of a supernatural being in the mill, and which brings one face to face with the time when wind and water were so newly-employed as motive powers, that what was effected by them must needs be set down to superhuman agency. In like manner Sir Richard

Temple avers that in the mind of the Asiatic peasant the railway train is propelled by a devil that sits in the engine, or the engine is a spirit controlled by the driver, " anything rather than the reality." (*FL.J.* iv. 196.)

It is an interesting point that the more modern trades (the printers, for example, for the origin of which a definite historical date can be assigned), have their own folklore as well as the ancient ones. They do not, it is true, appear in folk-tales and proverbs, like the blacksmith, the woodcutter, or the spinning-girl. But all crafts which are carried on in concert (such as printers, carpenters, and masons), have trade customs, practised in common, such as are not found among the solitary workers, like the old-fashioned weavers or tailors. Some crafts demand the aid of at least one assistant—the mason's server, the printer's devil, the miller's man, the blacksmith's boy ; and these lower grades often have separate characteristics and usages of their own. All this, of course, is the lore of the craftsman, as distinct from the lore of the art : and so is the position held by the craft in popular estimation. The blacksmith often has a reputation for occult powers, and practises as a healer or charmer. In the blacksmiths' own opinion, theirs is " the first of trades," because the others are dependent on it for their tools. (See *FL.J.* ii. 321.) Stone-cutters and masons (save for their eating and drinking powers) seem to be generally respected ; they have, perhaps, always, from the time of the mediæval freemasons, belonged to the superior class of artizans. But for tailors, weavers, and millers—for all, in short, who manufactured the raw material supplied by their customers—there is but one voice. " Put them all three in a bag and shake them, and the first that comes out will be a thief," is the gist of the proverbs of all nations on the subject. In the case of some trades the popular detestation is carried into action, and intermarriage is discouraged or forbidden between the families of the crafts-men and the agricultural peasantry. This is so in the case of the woodcutters, the charcoal-burners, and all the smaller trades which find a home within the bounds of a French forest. The rope-makers form almost an outcast trade. In Brittany, even in the nineteenth century, they were still obliged to bury their dead apart.

All crafts and organised industries seem indeed to have been in the first instance hereditary. In India they seem to have largely influenced the development of caste. Where anything approaching to the caste system is found, it should be dealt wth carefully, craft by craft ; and beliefs, rites, customs, stories, songs, and proverbs should be sought for as in the case of a tribe or a geographical area. In Europe, the history and lore of the mediæval trade-guilds should add immensely to the breadth and value of such a study.

See Questionary, pp. 334-339.

CHAPTER XIV.

CALENDAR FASTS AND FESTIVALS.

ONE cannot conceive a people so low as not to distinguish between day and night, or not to perceive that the alternations of day and night, light and darkness, are regulated by the seeming movements of the Sun. But beyond this point the Sun is not always the dominant factor in reckoning time. Solstices and equinoxes belong to temperate zones and high latitudes, and the solar year is necessarily unknown in tropical countries, with their changeless monotony of day and night. In such regions the " wet " and " dry " seasons are almost the only possible landmarks of the year. We are familiar with the Indian reckoning of " the hot weather," " the cold weather," and " the rains." In Uganda, where both a " wet " and a " dry " season are comprised in a period of six months, the natives think of six " moons " as constituting a complete year (Roscoe, p. 37). Among the Bushongo in the Congo basin, the dry season, in which no growth takes place, is not reckoned as part of the year, but is treated as having no existence for the purpose of calculating time (Torday and Joyce, 284). In New Guinea the year is calculated from yam-harvest to yam-harvest, and by some of the Massim tribes there the new year is known by the blossoming of a kind of flowering rush (C. G. S.).

The Basuto exhibit a higher degree of culture in the matter, and base their annual reckoning on the stars, beginning the year in August, *i.e.* in early spring. The Sandwich

Islanders, Society Islanders, and Maoris, as befitted maritime peoples, also based their reckoning on the stars. The half-yearly appearance and disappearance of the Pleiades on the horizon regulated their annual calendar.

But the Moon everywhere affords the most obvious natural measurement of time, and there are few peoples so low in culture as not to observe the changes of the Moon. The influence they are supposed to exercise on growth and increase causes agricultural operations to be largely affected by them. Most peoples also distinguish the Moons by name. The Sioux and Cheyenne Indians speak of the moon in which the leaves fall off, that in which the wolves run in packs, in which the ducks come, the grass grows green, the corn is planted, the buffaloes are fat, the plums red, etc. But the lunar month is by no means always definitely divided into weeks, and weeks, when they occur, vary in length. We reckon four weeks of seven days to a lunar month ; many West African tribes make seven weeks of four days. Other peoples calculate thirty days to the month and divide it into six weeks of five days ; or more rarely, five weeks of six days. These minor divisions of time, as bearing on the subject of the evolution or diffusion of culture, demand much more investigation than they have yet received.

Great difficulty has always been experienced in adjusting the lunar months to the solar year. Thirteen moons have been reckoned to the year ; " intercalary days " or months have been inserted, generally at the solstices. Perhaps the most ingenious device is that of the Bella Coola Indians of British Columbia, who calculate five moons in the spring and five in the fall, while the solstitial periods of Summer and Winter are allowed to last as long as may be necessary to make up a complete solar year. Julius Cæsar's bold stroke of abolishing the lunar months altogether, in favour of arbitrary " calendar " months, is rather a settlement than a solution of the problem.

In high latitudes the solar year is usually divided into two or four *Seasons*, viz. : winter and summer, with or without spring and autumn, or "fall," to use the old English word which still flourishes across the Atlantic. The Esquimaux, and also some of the tribes of British Columbia, regularly changed their whole social organization with the half-yearly change of seasons. The ancient Celtic calendar is especially interesting. When the Celts discovered or adopted the solstices must probably remain unknown, but the Irish certainly kept Midsummer as a festival as early as the eighth century. Their year was divided into *Geimhreadh* and *Samhradh*, the winter half and summer half, beginning respectively with the festival of *Samhain* on the eve of the first of November and with that of Bealtiane similarly on the 1st May. These were again divided on the 1st February, when the Spring quarter began, and on the 1st August, when the festival of *Lughnasadh*, corresponding to our Lammas Day, ushered in the harvest season. The modern Welsh name for July, *Gorphenaf*, literally means "end of Summer." Several of the months have native names in Irish, but in literary Scottish Gaelic the month-names are all borrowed from the Latin, and the native colloquial names for the internal divisions of the seasons represent, not months, but short spells of time of various lengths. "Computation of time by months and days of the month," says the Rev. J. G. Campbell (*Witchcraft and Second Sight*, p. 228), "was entirely unknown to the Highlander of former days, and even yet the native population do not say, ' on such a day of such a month,' but ' so many days before or after the beginning of Summer,' or other season, or before or after certain well-known term-days or festivals."

What were the internal divisions of the year among the Teutons and Scandinavians is not certain, but they appear to have begun it with the winter ploughing and sowing and ended it with the autumnal harvesting and threshing. Midwinter was the season of their chief annual festival.

Our British Calendar is in fact a palimpsest. Officially, of course, it is the Julian solar calendar, as modified by Pope Gregory XIII. in 1582. The Papal reform was not introduced into Great Britain till 1753, and the "New style" met with much opposition from the people. Numbers of fairs and village feasts are still dated by " Old style," and the annual accounts of the Imperial Exchequer itself are still made up to Old Lady Day, now the 5th April. Even the decennial census is taken on that morning. The reckoning of the year from the 25th March is due to the ecclesiastical " clerks " of the Middle Ages, who calculated " Anno Domini " from the Annunciation, as a regnal year is calculated from the day of the king's accession.

The " Moveable Feasts " are derived from the Jewish calendar, through the Christian Church. They cover a period of three and a half moons from the Shrovetide new moon to the full moon following Whitsuntide, and thus form a portion of a lunar calendar thrust into the midst of the Julian or Gregorian solar year, and impossible to amalgamate with it.

Beside all these reckonings by sun or by moon, we come upon traces of the old agricultural reckoning by seasons. In the Isle of Man it is a debateable question whether the 1st January or the 1st November is the true New Year's Day, for the latter is the date for entering on farm-holdings or farm-service. (Rhŷs, vol. i. p. 316.) The Mayors of English municipal boroughs hold office from November 9th. In their case the ancient New Year has now superseded previous local varieties of custom. The potters of North Staffordshire, whose craft is thought to have existed there from Celtic times, used to make their annual bargains at Martinmas (November 11th). In Scotland, Martinmas and Whitsuntide are even now the legal half-yearly terms for entering on tenancies or employments ; and May and Martinmas are the customary dates for hiring servants, especially farm-servants, throughout Wales and the north of England. The pasturage of cattle and the keeping-up of fires are still ruled by the same dates among old-fashioned people.

To appreciate the importance of particular days and seasons one must realize the position of a village community held in the iron grip of a system of common agriculture, under which everyone is obliged to do the same thing at the same time. (Even the geese, if they do their duty, are expected to lay at a certain date !) The plough-lands of the village lie in one or more common fields, and every man contributes his *quota* of draught-oxen to the common plough. Thus all must begin ploughing on the same day, and the whole plough-land must be fenced-in from the cattle at the same time. The reaping and harvesting are done by all together, and at a certain date the fences are thrown down and the cattle in charge of the common herdsman admitted to wander over the stubble. So also with the pastures. All but a few crofts and closes near the houses are common to the villagers at certain seasons of the year. At the beginning of summer the hay meadows are fenced-in, and the cattle are turned out upon the open commons, not to be re-admitted to the meadows till after hay-harvest, when the fences must be simultaneously removed as in the case of the stubble fields. Such was the yearly round of the agricultural community of northern Europe, among whom calendar observances may be said to have reached their height.

The transit from one season, month, or year to the next is commonly marked by public festival rites. The well-known Holi festival of northern India occurs in early spring at the full moon of the lunar month Phālgun. It belongs especially to the cowherding population, and has probably been adopted by the Hindus from the Dravidian tribes. Among the hill tribes of Mirzapur, the *Baiga* (" Devil-priest ") of the village then burns a stake, a rite which is called *Sambat jalana*, the burning of the Old Year, and from this date the New Year begins. In Nepal, a decorated wooden post is burnt in front of the palace at this date, which represents the burning of the body of the Old Year.

The Holi celebration is kept up for three days. " The central square of the little town," says an eye-witness of the scenes at Barsana, " is crowded with people, dancers with castanets, and clowns playing tricks and antics." On the first evening a mock fight takes place between the women of the village armed with bamboos, their faces wrapped in their mantles, and the men of a neighbouring village, carrying stags' horns and round leather shields. On the second evening the bonfire—the Holi fire—is lighted. It is made of wood which the village boys are permitted to loot unhindered in the neighbourhood, and is built between the temple of Prahlāda and an adjoining pond. The first-fruits of the sugar-cane, that have been offered to Vishnu at the preceding cane-harvest, are burnt in it, and omens of the prospects of the coming season are drawn from the way the smoke and flames ascend. It is supposed to prevent blight, and its ashes to cure disease. In Bengal, as we learn from another account, " a sort of Guy-Fawkes-like effigy, termed Holika, made of bamboo laths and straw, is formally carried to it and committed to the flames." (Wilson, *Religion of Hindus*, ii. 225.) As soon as it is lit the *Kherapat Panda*, or priest of Prahlāda, who is not a Brahman, but a low-caste man, dips himself in the pond and then runs through the fire. The boys run about it jumping and brandishing sticks : ribald songs are sung and much horseplay goes on. A favourite dance for the occasion is a circular one called the *Rāsa-mandala*, which represents the amours of the god Krishna with the Gopis, or dairymaids, of legend. On the third day the people threw red powder upon one another and up to the balconies of the houses. There was another mock combat between men and women, and when all was over many of the spectators ran into the arena and smeared themselves with the dust which had been hallowed by the feet of the dancers and the combatants. About Marwar, when the festivities are ended, the people bathe and change their garments, and the retainers of great men offer gifts to their masters.

Various myths are current as to the origin of the festival. According to one version, it was founded in honour of a female *Rakshasi*, or ogress, whose name meant " she who would otherwise destroy us." Another says that Holi was a witch who tried to destroy the infant god Krishna by suckling him with her poisoned milk, but that he slew her instead.

A more elaborate story relates that an ascetic claimed exclusive worship from all the world. His son Prahlāda apostatized to Vishnu, and the father, aided by his sister Holi, put him to the torture, but Vishnu saved him and slew the father. Holi then tried to burn herself and Prahlāda together in a fire, but he was saved and she alone was consumed. (Crooke. *Pop. Rel.* ii. 313-322, and *FL.* xxv. 55-83.) Fire festivals of a more or less similar character extend through Persia and Armenia, across Europe, even to *Ultima Thule.* (Cf. *G.B.* iii. 237 *sqq.*)

The *Walaga*, a spring full-moon solemnity customary at Bartle Bay, New Guinea, must rank as a calendar festival though not held regularly. Its significance is obscure, but probably has to do both with the food supply and the presence of the dead. Some six weeks beforehand, a self-sown mango-tree that has never flowered is chosen by a selected master of the ceremonies (the *taniwaga*), and his companions, and a circle is cleared round it, after which the men live apart in a state of strict taboo, and a party of women of the *taniwaga's* clan submit to similar but less strict taboos. The men erect a platform (*walaga*) in the village, on posts which have been carefully treated by the medicine-men to expel any souls of dead men which might be lurking in them. The tree is felled with a stone adze,—no iron may be used—and the chips are caught in nets and mats placed for the purpose. The greatest care is taken that neither they nor the tree itself shall touch the ground. It is then carried in procession to the village, together with the mats full of chips. The women dance backwards before it. Eventually it is set up in the midst of the platform in the village. (Cf. the bringing in of " that stynckyng ydolle," the Maypole.) The houses are decorated, the masters of the revels painted, the invited guests arrive bringing pigs, the dancing on the platform begins, and is kept up till sundown. At moonrise two chiefs mount the roof of a house and charge all evil spirits to keep away and the crowd to do nothing to disturb the general harmony. The dancing is kept up all night to the accompaniment of

singing by a party stationed in the midst of the platform.
At daylight next morning the pigs are killed, care being
taken that they should squeal long and loudly so that the
mango-tree may hear them. A chief climbs the mango-tree
and chants what sounds like a prayer, to which the people
on the platform respond. The pork is then distributed and
the guests disperse. In the afternoon the songs and dances
are renewed. On the third day, the mango-pole, wrapped
in new mats, is carried to the house of the " fasting-men,"
and slung from the roof. The fasting-men now return to
their several homes. At the end of some months they build
a new house to which the tree is removed in procession as
before. It is set down in the midst of the village, still without
touching the ground. The medicine-man cuts up a number
of green mangoes and puts them into the mouths of the
fasting-men, who chew them and sput them out towards
the setting sun, so that " the sun should carry them over
the whole country and every one should know." The
taniwaga breaks off part of the tree, which is burnt without
ceremony after sundown, together with the old mats, the
chips, the vessels used and refuse left by the fasting-men
while under taboo. The remains of the tree are wrapped
in new mats and hung over the fireplace in the *taniwaga's*
house (cf. our Kern-baby, mistletoe, and other talismanic
treasures). The ceremony is repeated at intervals as long
as the tree lasts. (Seligmann, 589-599.)

Annual Feasts of the Dead are found in Europe, Asia,
and Africa, and coincide with the end of harvest, or with
the end of the year (*Prim. Cult.* ii. 36). The Dīwāli, or
Feast of Lamps, of Northern India, is held on the last day
of the dark fortnight of the (lunar) month *Kārtik* (October-
November); *i.e.* on the night before the new moon. It is
rather a townsmens' than a villagers' festival. All the houses
are cleaned, set in order, and lighted up, to receive the
souls of the departed, who are expected (as in the corresponding European festival) to revisit their homes. The women
make " new-moon lamp-black " which is used throughout

the following year as a charm against the Evil Eye. Next morning the oldest woman in the house takes a winnowing-sieve and a broom, and beats them in every corner of the house, saying "God abide and poverty depart!" The sieve is thrown away outside the village, and carries poverty away with it. Sisters then mark their brothers' foreheads (with the lamp-black?) and make them swallow three grains of *gram* to ensure long life. They offer them sweetmeats and the brother in return gives his sister a present.

The story told of the origin of the feast is that a Raja was once warned by an astrologer that his Fate would come to him that night in the form of a snake, and must be received with illuminations of the town and palace, which was done accordingly. The snake was so much pleased that he bade the Rani ask a boon of him. She desired long life for her husband, and the snake contrived to bring back the Raja's soul from Yama, the lord of the Dead, for several more years. The feast is also said to be held in honour of Lakshmi the goddess of wealth, who is propitiated by gambling (as a form of divination?). (Crooke, *op. cit.* ii. 295-296.)

Ship processions, from their ascertained antiquity, are festival rites of especial interest. Representations of sacred boats drawn on wheels are found in Egypt dating from at least the seventeenth dynasty. Three such processions are still carried out at Luxor every year, the chief of which is nominally in honour of Abu'l Heggag, a local saint. Such rites extend at least as far eastward as Ceylon, where Dr. and Mrs. Seligmann witnessed one at Kandy on the 16th May, 1908. This also was professedly held in honour of a local saint. The festival of Dionysus in ancient Athens was celebrated in the same way, and many similar examples are found in modern Europe (cf. *FL.* xvi. 259, etc.). Presumably, the custom has been carried eastwards by Arab traders. Whether the western celebrations also spread from ancient Egypt is a question on which one cannot but speculate, but which Dr. Seligmann does not attempt to decide. (C. G. Seligmann in *Ridgeway Essays*, pp. 452-455.)

The Ibo of the Oka district of Southern Nigeria make offerings annually at the close of the year to a power whom they call *Aru*, the year. The women take their old clothes, old pots, and so on, and throw them upon the ground, in a certain spot, which is sometimes in the middle of the village, sometimes on the outskirts. In either case they are never touched or disturbed afterwards. At the same time they call upon *Aru* to give them children and relieve them of all pain and sickness. (N.W.T. *MS. note.* Cf. *G.B.* vol. iii. sections 14, 15.)

One season treads on the heels of another ; at the death of the Old Year the New Year is born. The routine of divinations, sacrifices, talismans, dances, fire and water ceremonies, recurs so frequently that it is not always easy to perceive whether a given festival is held to celebrate the end of one season or the beginning of the next. It may be tentatively suggested that mock combats, athletic contests, procuring visions, and all rites of destroying, burning, burying, or *carrying away* objects, or driving away men or animals, mark the end of the old year or season, while rites of *bringing in* boughs, trees, ships, ploughs, or what not, with processions and dances, " first-footing," offering gifts, feasting, and the like, celebrate the beginning of the new. Days of license, when the rights of property are disregarded, and when, in savage countries, the ties of matrimony are relaxed, perhaps denote an interval between the seasons, and correspond to M. van Gennep's period of *la marge* (cf. p. 194).

Seasons of fasting and abstinence must be noticed. The Nagas divide the year into the agricultural and the hunting seasons, in each of which all labour proper to the other is forbidden ; and their *gennas*, or seasons of abstinence, as already noted (ch. iv.), are periodical and general, as well as occasional and particular. These *taboo* seasons are reflected in European custom. Marriage was forbidden by ecclesiastical law in Lent and is avoided by popular prejudice in May. In England, spinning might not be done during Christmastide, nor laundry-work on Good Friday, but the latter day is held particularly favourable for sowing or planting vegetables.

Friday throughout the year is an unlucky day for the beginning of any enterprise.

The taboo-day and the rest-day imperceptibly develop into the unlucky day and the festival. (Cf. Hutton Webster, *Rest-days*.) The Congo women utilize the weekly rest-day, when they may not work in their gardens, as a market-day. In the early days of Christianity in England, Sunday was not infrequently thus utilized. The weekly market of Much Wenlock in Shropshire was held on Sunday till Henry III.'s time, when it was changed to Monday, on which day it still continues. In the same way, ecclesiastical holidays were selected as convenient days for the transaction of any public business, such as "wappenshaws" and perambulations of boundaries.

Local festivals seem generally to have had a religious origin. They often began as annual pilgrimages to sacred spots, which gradually developed into centres of commerce. In the hill-country above Chittagong there is a temple of Buddha, the Maha-Mouni Pagoda, in the neutral ground where the hillfolk and the plainfolk can meet. There a fair is held annually, beginning on the ninth day of the moonlight half of the month Asin. The people come village by village, carrying provisions for a three days' picnic. First they visit the great image of Gautama in the temple, and then stroll away to see the peepshows and exhibitions and the booths of the Bengali traders, "who drive a roaring traffic, for there are no shops among the hills." At dusk lighted tapers are carried round the temple, crackers are let off, and the fun goes on all night. The festival is closed by another visit to the temple, the offering of alms, and the reception of a ceremonial benediction from the priest (Lewin, 220). The Maha Mouni Fair seems to fall into line with the Breton Pardons, the Irish Patterns, and the Well-wakes so persistently denounced by the Anglo-Saxon Church. The famous mediæval fair at Stourbridge near Cambridge originated in the visits of young people to the springs at Barnwell, taken under the protection of the neighbouring house of

Augustinian Canons. In the Middle Ages nearly every municipal town in Great Britain had its own public holiday, celebrated with pageantry and processions, and every village its own yearly Feast or Wake in honour of the saint to whom the parish church was dedicated. Sometimes these became important local " events," sometimes they dwindled and died out. Probably the position of each feast in the calendar, if studied, would throw light on its *raison d'être* and its career.

Hitherto the favourite method of anthropological study has been that of tracking a single feature of a rite around the globe, over land and sea. This fascinating process has had valuable results in the discovery of certain principles of savage philosophy, such as that of " sympathetic magic," and the establishment of their position as the common property of the human race. But to comprehend the real object, the true significance, of a given rite, whether public or particular, occasional or periodical, it is obviously necessary to study the ritual of the occasion *as a whole,* and to take it in connection with the occasion on which it is performed, in short, to note the *when* as well as the *what.* Hence the paramount importance of ascertaining the *date* of every calendar observance and of noting its position in relation to the agricultural or other operations in connection with the food-supply, which after all cannot help being the chief preoccupation of mankind.

The Folklore Society is now taking steps to record the Calendar Customs of the British Isles, collating the existing printed evidence and supplementing it by oral information. The work is intended to cover not only Great Britain and Ireland, but the Isle of Man, the Shetlands, the Hebrides, the Scilly Isles, and the Channel Isles. The British Archipelago includes such a variety of racial elements that the work ought to prove a valuable ethnographical study of comparative folklore.

See Questionary, p. 339.

CHAPTER XV.

GAMES, SPORTS, AND PASTIMES.

GAMES are a more important section of folklore than might be supposed at first sight ; but their value to the folklorist is as unequal as their origins are varied. Enquiry will show that the majority are survivals of primitive conditions rather than subsequent inventions, and that they not infrequently had their beginning in magico-religious rites. Thus, what in one part of the world may be a prominent feature of serious or magico-religious ceremonial, as for instance the bull-roarer, (cf. ch. v.), in another land will have degenerated to a nursery game or a toy ; and it is possible that the nursery can supply a page from the past that History has not recorded. The counting-out rhyme may be a clue to primitive methods of reckoning ; early games of ball and other sports may find origin in martial exercises ; while in blindman's buff it has been suggested that the rudiments of sacrificial procedure may be traced.

The reason is not far to seek. Children are both mimetic and conservative. They imitate adult life in their games all the world over, and often retain features which have actually long ceased to exist. They play at courtship— " Poor Mary sits a-weeping " ; marriage—" Nuts in May " ; and burial—" Jenny Jones." The Scotch child's " Tappie, tappie tousie " perpetuates, in the line " Will ye be my mon ? " a formula of feudal days ; the " Three Knights out of Spain " represents marriage as a business transaction

between the bridegroom and the bride's parents—she has
no voice in the matter, but is purchased ; whilst " Draw
a Pail of Water " irresistibly suggests a primitive rite of
well-worship (cf. Lady Gomme, *s.v.*, and Haddon, 364).

The singing game itself is a survival among the children
of a custom otherwise extinct or nearly so, in Europe—that
of dancing to the accompaniment of the human voice only
(cf. ch. xvii.). Moreover, the singing-games are not only
narrative but dramatic. Each child enacts a different character, and the singing-game thus shows dance and drama not
yet separated from one another. Both indeed are methods
of emotional expression, and as such may be either secular or
religious. There is the Miracle Play as well as the tragedy,
comedy, and farce.

Dancing in connection with sacred ceremonial is to be
found in all climes and in every century. It is not extinct
in Europe. If Yorkshire apprentices no longer dance in the
Minster nave on Shrove Tuesday, Luxemburg has its dancing
procession of Jumping Saints (*springende Heiligen*) at
Echternach on Whit Monday ; and the choristers of Seville
dance in the nave before the High Altar of the Cathedral
at the Carnival, the Corpus Christi festival, and at one of the
feasts of Our Lady, in the presence of the Archbishop and
the Cathedral clergy. At Nola and other towns in Southern
Italy there are annual dances that find their counterpart in
Asia, for sacred images and shrines are carried through the
streets as a main feature of the performance, even as the
gods themselves are brought in palanquins to take part in
Raghunāth's festival dance during the great fair in Kulu.
(*FL.J.* v. 278, 300 ; *FL.* xvi. 243-259.) Thus we find the
ceremonial dance performed by all classes, as well as by the
priests alone, or by a particular sect, as in the cases of the
Lamas of Tibet, the Dancing Dervishes, or the Aissaoua
of Algeria. There is also the hired professional dancer.
In the Sahara, funeral dances are enacted by hired mourners.
These are women, but women are not permitted any share
in funeral dances held by some of the Assamese hill-tribes.

Débutante maidens, however, among those tribes in the Khasia Hills, select their life-partners at an annual dance. The Pueblo Indians dance to bring the early spring rains (B. F.M. in *Sociol. Rev.* 1911), as the natives of the Torres Straits perform their Saw-fish Dance to secure good harvest from the sea. (*Torres Straits*, v. 342.) Similarly, the devil-dance, the war-dance, and the hunting-dance have magical values wherever they exist, as have the anthropophagous dances of certain cannibal tribes. The dance is an inseparable feature of the ritual of the *shaman* of the Siberian wilds and of the medicine-man of North and South America (cf. ch. vii.) Nowhere is it a more important function than among the tribes of the great Amazon basin. Each tribe has its own dance. Some, like so many of the Bushman dances, are imitations of animal movements, as the Ackawoi dance, wherein every performer represents a different animal and carries its figure on a stick, which may be the origin of the Amazonian dancing-stick. (Im Thurn, 324.) Another mimetic dance is the Yacamí-cuñá dance of the Upper Amazon, imitative of the actions of yacamí, a tailless bird, according to the Indian tradition embodied in the dance. (Spruce, ii. 468.) A good example of the mimetic dance in Europe is the Fan-dance of Spain.

The dance indeed offers matter for exhaustive study. It may represent the latest development of a people, as among the Australian aborigines, who embody new ideas in new dances, or it may conserve traditions and even language the meaning of which is enitrely forgotten. Some of the Amazon tribes sing words that to them have no meaning, but are handed down orally as the correct accompaniments of certain tribal dances (*FL.* xxiv. 50). Or the dance may have an ethical value, as in the singing-combat, the drum-dance, whereby the West Greenlanders settle their quarrels. (D. Crantz, 164.) The Vedda and the Fuegian will dance to express gratitude; the Upper Kutenai in British Columbia dance when they gamble. (Appleton, pp. 8, 14, 23; Culin, xxiv. *Rep. Bur. Ethn.* p. 286.)

Among peoples of the higher cultures, the dance tends to become less ceremonial and more a matter of play. Not that there is no dancing for mere amusement among those of the lower cultures. Dancing may be a serious pursuit to a Vedda, but the solemnity of the Negro cake-walk is that of pure enjoyment, as much so as the delight of the Mohave-Apache " when some man or woman feels sad and wants the people to dance to make them happy." (B. F.-M. *op. cit.*)

The folk-dances of England among adults show three varieties. There is first the almost extinct old-fashioned country-dance of men and maidens dancing together for their own enjoyment, to the sound of instrumental music. Next come the morris-dances of southern England and the sword-dances of the north. These are performances by a fixed number of skilled dancers, men only, who dance for the amusement of the spectators and their own financial profit. They are accompanied by two or three disguised performers whom Mr. E. K. Chambers (*The Mediæval Stage*), terms " Grotesques " ; namely a Fool or Clown, a man in woman's clothing, and, more rarely, a Hobby-horse, *i.e.* a man disguised with a horse's head ; but these characters are not essential ingredients in the dance and are often found apart from it. The sword-dancers, instead of merely flourishing wooden swords or staves, as do the morris-dancers of the south, interweave real swords in elaborate designs to correspond with the various figures of the dance. They also introduce a rudimentary dramatic element. Each dancer is supposed to represent some character, named and described by the leader in an introductory song ; but there is no dramatic speaking or action with the exception of a few cases in County Durham, where the central incident of the Mummers' Play is introduced as an interlude in the dance (Sharp, p. 23). The Mumming Play itself is the third variety of these sports. The actors in it are often called morris-dancers by the folk, but the dramatic element of the performance has routed the dance, and they are more properly known as guisers (disguised men) or mummers. " Pace-eggers " and " plough-jags " are other names for them, derived from the different seasons of their performance. Under the cloak of the legend of Saint George, the Champion Saint of England, they enact the world-old story of the death of a hero in single combat and his resuscitation at the hands of a wonderworker. This is one of the most interesting features in the whole range of British folklore, and deserves more careful and minute study than it has yet received. The songs at the conclusion of the performance and the part taken by the " Grotesques " bring it into line with the morris-dance and the sword-dance.

As to the origin of games, that is a matter for the student, the expert with wider knowledge and facilities of research, rather than for the collector, properly concerned in the main with local details. Existing similarities do not necessarily argue a common descent. For instance, the German singing-game, " Would you know how the peasant sows his peas ? " may be instructive—there are games of instruction, *per ex.*, thieves play at pocket-picking to secure neat-handedness, and the Kullin (or Kallan) of Southern India become expert thieves by playing certain games—or it may be merely childish pantomime ; while one seemingly similar, the English " Oats and Beans and Barley " had possibly a magical signi-ficance in the first place, as still is the case with the Threading-the-Needle game danced by the peasants of Central France " to make the hemp grow." (Haddon, 341-345.) The need for accurate description of details is enhanced by the fact that the origin of a game, and hence much of its value to the comparative folklorist, may sometimes be determined by the identification not only of movements—always difficult to describe—but of the articles, instruments, implements, made use of in playing it. The netted hoop of the Iroquois' and other North American Indians' hoop-and-pole games is similar to the netted shield of the twin War-gods of Zuni mythology. Women are not allowed to play, nor—among the Apache, where the game retains a religious character—to be present within a hundred yards. Among the Hopi, however, a game with the same essentials is played by women

during the celebration of the *Oáqol* ceremony. According
to Fewkes, two women shoot a small package of corn-husks.
Their acts are said to typify lightning striking the cornfield,
which is considered the acme of fertilization (*J.A.F.L.* 1899,
p. 91).

The evolution of playing-cards, dice, and dominoes has been
traced back to the arrow. Cards were introduced into Europe
from China by Arabs or Gypsies, and the name of the Chinese
playing-card to-day is *tau tsin*, fighting tablets (an arrow
is *tsin*). The flattened ceremonial arrow became the bamboo-
slip, whence the domino and dice—or the cardboard strip,
whence the playing-card. The symbolic value of the arrow
is well shown by Mr. Cushing in a paper published in 1896,
where he states that " ceremonially they often stood for the
man himself even more intimately than our signatures stand
for us " (Cushing, *op. cit.* 881 ; cf. Culin, *Korean Games*,
xxi.). In form the cards are evidently copies of the slips
of bamboo used to this day as divining-lots by the Chinese,
and the design on their backs perpetuates the arrow-feathers.
The Korean playing-cards are in suits of ten ; the Korean
ceremonial quiver has ten bamboo arrows, each numbered
and marked with the owner's name and tipped with black-
topped feathers. In like manner the stave-dice of the Uinth
Utes are a connecting link between the long staves of the
Pai Utes and dice ; the American Indian, like the Korean
and the Chinese, deriving these and other variations from the
original arrow.

Similarity of origin for games may throw an occasional
side-light upon ethnological problems, but it does not
necessarily presuppose a common origin for the players.
It argues no connection between us and the Guaymis of
Chiriqui that the "Aunt Sally" of our village greens finds a
parallel in their game of *Batza*, varied in that the stick or
club is in Panama thrown at the legs of the adversaries,
not at a dummy figure. Equality of origin need not even be a
proof of equality of culture, any more than the possession of a
complicated toy is evidence of a high culture :—the Eskimo

are skilful constructors of mechanical toys. It must not
be overlooked in the consideration of games and their distribution, that though the essential unity of Folklore has for
its base the essential solidarity of human kind, the explanation
that men of equal culture will act and argue alike, must be
complicated by borrowed influences. Games can be learnt.
One race may introduce, or even impose, its own pastimes.
We owe the kite as well as the playing-card to the East.
Though the kite is found widely spread in Polynesia—the
Hervey Islands even possessing three different kinds—it did
not reach Europe before the seventeenth century. The idea,
however, finds parallel in the Greek play with captured
beetles, μηλολόνδη, and the Chinese to this day have their
chained butterflies and crickets. The ancient Mangaian
tradition has it that kites originated in the land of spirits
(Haddon, 250) ; and there certainly seems to be good reason
for the assumption that the kite was a religious symbol of
the primitive Indonesian race. Its use in Korea supports
this belief. On the fourteenth day of the New Year the
kite there plays the part of " scape-goat " to carry away
the year's ill-luck. (*Ibid.* 240.) Though in China and Japan
kite-flying is now done mainly for amusement only, abundant
traces yet linger of its ancient ceremonial use.

Cat's Cradle, far more highly elaborated among primitive
peoples than with us, is an almost universal game. Two
principal types have been distinguished, the Asiatic and the
Oceanic (A. C. Haddon in Jayne, p. xii ; cf. K. Haddon,
Cat's Cradles), and it is possible that this apparently trivial
game, when taken in conjunction with other evidence, may
supply some needed ethnological clue. Another very widely
distributed game is Hopscotch, which is played in Japan as
well as in the Indo-European area. It is probable that in
some remote spots a magical significance may be attached to
either or both of these games. Magical values may be attributed to almost any action, or connected with it by some
similarity or sympathy of idea. Take for instance our Cup-
and-Ball : a similar game is played among the Klamath

of the Gulf States with the suggestive name for one action of *Punch out the Moon,* that is, to hasten the advent of spring. (G. A. Dorsey, *Amer. Anthr.* 1901, p. 21.) It must also be remembered that everything which includes success or failure, not only winning or losing, can be used for divinatory purposes. Knucklebones are used to-day by the London street-child merely to play a game of skill and chance, but in Africa they are largely used for divination (cf. ch. viii.). A prehistoric knucklebone has been found at Cuzco in Peru ; they were used in ancient Egypt and are constantly referred to by classical authors ; they are known to the Arabs, Persians, and other peoples of Western Asia. Among all these they appear to take the place that dice occupy among the Mongolian peoples, for the dice found in Babylonia and Egypt seem to have been associated with foreign influences. That in ancient Greece knucklebones were played with by girls is evidenced by the well-known little statue of a girl throwing them as an English child would to-day.[1] In Cornwall a knucklebone is carried to prevent cramp, so that we get an English example of their dual use. (*FL.* v. p. 201.)

The Tug-of-War with us to-day is merely an "item" in the programme of athletic sports, but it was the occasion of an annual contest between two divisions of the town of Ludlow in Shropshire up to 1851, and at Presteign in Radnorshire up to 1884. The rope was pulled either down to the river by one party, or up to the higher ground within the town by the other (*Shr. FL.* 319, 320). This Shrovetide contest may be compared with the Tug-of-War played by the Eskimo of Baffin Land on the yearly festival of their superhuman being Sedna, which is held in the autumn. Those born in summer pull against those born in winter. If Summer wins there will be plenty of food during the coming year, but if Winter, the prospect of the food-supply is bad. The Tug-

---

[1] A copy may be seen in the Victoria and Albert Museum. The girl is seated on the ground exactly as I saw in 1911 two girls sitting on the pavement in Gray's Inn Road, playing knucklebones with the cheap earthenware discs sold on street stalls for the purpose.—(C. S. B.)

of-War appears here as a definite method of divination. In Japan and Korea it is a magic ceremony that secures a good harvest (Haddon, 275). In Burma it is an actual magical rite intended to produce rain. A rain-party and a drought-party tug against each other, the rain-party being allowed the victory. (*FL.J.* i. 214.) Our football matches, when played up and down the streets of a town between two sections of the inhabitants on a fixed day in early spring, fall into the same category. Even in their modernized form they represent the old-time faction fight, but the organization to-day exists first for the purposes of the game itself, and only in a secondary degree for the locality or division from which the players are drawn. (Gomme, *V.C.* 240, 246.) Another "Sports" item, Wrestling, is performed ceremonially by the Japanese in the Pavilions of the Four Directions (Culin, *Korean Games*, xxxv.).

The question may well be asked, how should the collector classify ball-playing, rope-pulling, and other divinatory games? for apparently the majority of games might be entered either under Divinations or Games. Here as elsewhere the rule holds good, *always to classify as found* : *i.e.*, where football is a game only, as now with us, it would be entered under Games ; but not where it is a religious performance, as in the Hopi Snake ceremony, for there the magico-religious element predominates. Take away that element and it is a game—an amusement, that is to say, which entails winning and losing. Without the factor of success or failure, plays are not games, but pastimes. The number of players concerned does not affect this : games may be won and lost by the solitary player, pastimes indulged in by hundreds ; but any simple pastime at once becomes a game by the addition of an element of contest. Clog-dancing, *per ex.*, is a game when a prize is competed for, a pastime when merely done because of the pleasure derived from the exercise. Sports, for the most part, consist of pastimes played with an element of rivalry, and thus rank as games. All plays that entail a penalty on the loser, and all plays with a reward to the winner or winners, are games proper. Hence we find that for purposes of collection, Games, Sports, and Pastimes group themselves roughly into the following classes :

Pastimes :

(*a*) Children's games. Nursery play, such as *Little Pigs went to Market*, which is common to Europe and Africa at least.

(*b*) Feats of skill, bodily or mental, performed individually or by combined action ; *e.g.* Cat's Cradle.

(*c*) Methods of locomotion employed as recreation, alone or in company, such as swimming, running, rowing, see-saw, swinging, stilt-walking, skating, etc.

(*d*) Rhythmic movements, such as children's singing-games ; and dancing, with the connection between dance and song, or instrumental music (cf. ch. xvii.).

(*e*) Mimicry. Children imitate adults, and both children and adults imitate animals. Imitation combined with rhythmic movement gives dramatic dancing, and eventually Drama is evolved.

In almost every case the introduction of an element of competition will convert the Pastime into a Game proper.

Games :

(*a*) Games with a *penalty on the loser*, or losers.

(1) Games of chasing, catching, seeking, finding ; *per ex.*, Blindman's Buff. These may have, as already suggested, a possible connection with sacrifice, or with the choice of a king.

(2) Forfeit games. In this section we get games which result in mockery of the loser, and so introduce a comic element, which is curiously lacking in the majority of games.

(*b*) Games which entail honour or *reward for the winner* or winners. These group themselves as follows :

(1) Mental contests ; puzzles, riddles.

(2) Physical combats ; such as wrestling, boxing, fencing, tilting. Feats of skill in which individual competitors vie with each other. Combats between animals : cock-fighting, bear-baiting, bull-baiting, bull-fighting, etc.

(3) Games of skill ; that is, feats organised into games with regular sides, opponents, and rules ; as base-ball, hockey, cricket, and other ball-games.

(4) Games of chance, and games of skill and chance combined. These are chiefly played with pieces on a board, as chess, draughts, backgammon, etc. ; or, more rudely, on areas marked on the ground, as Nine Men's Morris.

D. H. Moutray Read.

See Questionary, p. 341.

PART III.
STORIES, SONGS, AND SAYINGS.

"This is our track and story, this is the home of the true Rinds, a name exalted among tribes. If you do not believe it, no one has seen it with his eyes, there are no ancient documents or witnesses to attest it, but there are tales upon tales ; every one says that so it was!"

Peroration of Balochī Epic Song, *FL*. xiii. 274.

CHAPTER XVI.

STORIES.

THE intellectual efforts of peoples who have not acquired the art of writing, or who have at least made comparatively little use of it, have chiefly taken the shape of Stories, Songs, Proverbs, and Riddles. These things must not be despised as trivial. They represent the earliest efforts of mankind in the exercise of reason, memory, and imagination, and no student of psychology or ethnology can afford to disregard them.

Traditional stories may be roughly classified as Myths, Legends (including Hero-tales and Sagas), and *Märchen* or Folk-tales, with which last may be reckoned the minor varieties of Beast-tales, Drolls, Cumulative tales, and Apologues.

Myths are ætiological stories ; that is to say, stories which, marvellous and improbable though they may be, are nevertheless related in all good faith, because intended, or believed by the teller, to account for the existence of the Universe, of Life and Death, of men and beasts, of distinctions of race and species, of the different occupations of men and women, of sacred rites and ancestral customs, and the like mysterious phenomena. Some examples of cosmological myths have been already given ; *v.* the stories of Cagn (p. 111), of Unkulunkulu (p. 93) and of Puluga and the origin of fire (p. 110). They have been so plentifully recorded that they are evidently not difficult to collect. They are not always connected with sacred personages, nor is the whole work of creation always ascribed to one author. An animal makes the habitable world, and mankind issues from the joint of a reed, or is vomited up by a cow, and so on ; or a superhuman being creates mankind and the first man does the rest ; or a beneficent being passes from place to place on the already-existing earth, endowing each region with its special products, and then is no more seen. A god creates the earth and a demon makes the sea to drown it ; superhuman beings inhabit the dry land and bring the waters into existence for their own use ; or the waters are created first and the dry land is fished up from them by gods or heroes ;—such are a few of the many savage theories on the subject. The origin of remarkable natural objects, of local prehistoric monuments, of the form and colour of certain plants and animals, and the meaning of personal and local names, are fertile subjects of ætiological (*i.e.*, explanatory) Myths, even in Great Britain.

Legends are narratives told, not to explain anything, but simply as an account of things which are believed to have happened, such as a deluge, a migration, a conquest, the building of a bridge, or of a city. They are often told about events or persons who are in fact historical, though the legend itself may be inaccurate or even baseless, and may be told of other persons or places in countries far away. Legends which relate the exploits of a traditional hero, taking his existence for granted and not introducing him to account for the existence of something else, may be distinguished as Hero-tales ; and when a series of legends follows in detail the lives and adventures of characters who are probably historical, it forms a *Saga*. Professor Haddon groups together the stories of Kwoiam, the war-hero of the Torres Straits (*v.* p. 222) under the title of " The Saga of Kwoiam," but Hero-tales and Sagas are often not clearly distinguished.

" *Märchen*," (nursery-tales, fairy-tales, folk-tales), are stories told mainly for amusement. The Märchen is distinguished from the Hero-tale and the Saga, not only because it is not told seriously as they are, but because, first, the characters in the Märchen are mainly anonymous ; secondly, there is no note of time or place ; and lastly, the story has a definite theme and a plot worked up to its natural conclusion : while the Hero-tale merely narrates an adventure or a series of adventures and leaves off when the narrator has no more to tell. Unfortunately the word *Folk-tale* is often loosely used to include *Hero-tale* and *Saga*, thus leaving us without any exact English equivalent for the German *Märchen*, to which it would be convenient to restrict it.

Traditional stories thus seem to group themselves naturally into two classes—those *told as true* (myths, legends, hero-tales, sagas)—and those *told for amusement*—(folk-tales or Märchen in all their varieties). But convenient as this classification is to the white man, it probably does not represent anything to the mind of the native. To him, if the idea of classification occurred to him at all, the division would probably be between things sacred and things profane. For myths and legends frequently rank among the most sacred possessions of the tribe or other group which preserves them. This is a marked feature of North American culture. There, the Palladium that may not be touched, perhaps not even looked upon, the song that must not be uttered, save by him whose solemn charge it is, and the legend that may not be told, save to him to whose memory it is to be entrusted, combine to form a sacred deposit, handed down, sometimes from father to son, sometimes from initiated priest to initiated priest, from generation to generation. Miss Fletcher and her collaborateur draw an affecting picture of the last hereditary Keeper of the Sacred Pole of the Omaha, realizing that there could be no independent future for his people and resolving to entrust the " Venerable Man " which had been their rallying-point and guiding-star, into the hands of the white man. Even then, the faithful trustee could not bring himself to divulge the Sacred Legend until the solemn promise of his superior chief to hold him harmless emboldened him. Then, in the house of the chief, during three whole days he related to a small and sympathetic audience the history that had been kept secret so long. And within a fortnight the chief who had undertaken to bear any consequences of the disclosure, lay dead in the very room where the tale was told.   (Fletcher, *Omaha*, 224.)

The story itself was not, as might be thought, concerned with the doings of gods and heroes, but was a simple narrative of the history and wanderings of the tribe, and its gradual ascent from a condition of savagery to one of comparative comfort.   In like manner, when Mr. Torday had, at considerable expense, overcome the scruples of the Bangongo elders to divulge their sacred traditions, the secret that was revealed to him at an appointed spot in the bush, to which all the approaches were guarded from the curiosity of the common herd by the sticks of the elders laid across the pathway, was a narrative, distinctively mythological in character, of the history of the tribe when they dwelt on the other side of the river Sankuru.   About the supposed course of events since they migrated to their present abode there was no mystery, but the mythic or " Alcheringa " time, if we may so call it, was regarded with religious awe.   (Torday and Joyce, p. 37.)

It need hardly be said that stories which are likely to have any sacred character should not be asked for unless the enquirer is on thoroughly confidential terms with his informant ;   and any that may be obtained should be carefully distinguished from the ordinary popular tales.

The enquirer should not too hastily conclude that stories of wars, migrations, culture-heroes and the like are necessarily fictitious.   A story may embody true historical tradition, though parts of it are obviously impossible.   Some peoples possess bodies of men whose duty it is to preserve and transmit the traditions ;   as did the Druids of Gaul, the Brehons of Ireland, the colleges of the Maori priesthood (see Professor York Powell in *FL*. xv. 12-23).   Even in England, where no such school of tradition exists, and where the art of writing is supposed to have enfeebled the power of the memory, the memory of an event may be preserved by oral tradition for several generations.   Sir Laurence Gomme on the occasion of his marriage was presented by his father, as a family heirloom, with an old carved oak desk which had belonged to their ancestor Bernard Gomme, Secretary to the Protector Cromwell. Sir Laurence sent a tracing of the shield of arms carved on it to a friend at the Heralds' College for identification, and received in reply the question, " Where did you get that desk ? Those are Oliver Cromwell's arms ! " Thus was the family tradition corroborated.

In judging the age and comparative authenticity of stories, the channel through which they have reached us should be taken into account. It should be noted whether it could be to the interest of the custodians to garble or falsify the narrative. A defeat may be represented as a victory, or the numbers of the enemy may be exaggerated. Opposite parties will have different versions of the same event. In the case of peoples who preserve their genealogies with some care, it should be noted whether different informants tell the same story as having happened in the days of ancestors who were probably contemporary with each other. Now and then dates may approximately be fixed by references to recorded events, such as an eclipse, or a visit of white men.

Many of the local legends in which our own islands are so rich contain grains of historical fact embedded in a mass of unhistorical detail. Many are ætiological stories, folk-etymology, and the like ; others, such as the stories of Beddgelert, of Wayland Smith's Cave, or of the Pedlar of Swaffham, are folk-tales localised. The collector is advised not to attempt to classify them according to what he takes to be their component elements, but to set them down as what he finds them, simply as *Place Legends*. They will accumulate easily and rapidly on his hands in the course of visits paid in the character of the " intelligent foreigner " to remarkable natural objects, rude stone monuments, or places of historic interest.

Stories told for amusement are found in all stages of culture. They have an historical value notwithstanding their frankly fictitious character, for they are evidence of the manners of the time in which they took shape, and so they contribute to the social history of mankind. The acute intellect of the late Mr. Lang perceived that the prohibition laid by Urvasí, the prototype of Psyche, on her husband, to let her see him without his garments, " for that is the custom of women," was in reality a savage taboo, and that as a taboo its breach was supernaturally punished ; and that thus the central incident of the story as we have it, comes down from a savage state of society. (*Custom and Myth*, p. 71) ; and on the other hand he pointed out that the story of Cinderella " could not have arisen among a naked and shoeless people." (Cox, *Cinderella*, p. x.) Again, the situation on which the story of Catskin turns—the proposed marriage between a father and daughter—to us so repulsive, would not contravene the marriage laws of an exogamous people recognising only matrilineal descent. In fine, some of the strongest evidence for the theory, or rather the fact, of Survival in Culture is to be found in folk-tales.

How do the tales come to us ? Often, no doubt, by inherited tradition ; but folk-tales are very transmissible. The event of a canoe-load of visitors from another island— a common incident, as Dr. Rivers tells us, of Melanesian life—a stay of a single night, a sociable evening spent together, and a story may be left behind to be told and retold from generation to generation, and perhaps to afford evidence of former communication between peoples since separated by warfare, by migration, by wholesale shipwreck, or some other catastrophe. In recent ages the African slave-trade has been a powerful factor in the dissemination of folk-tales. The well-known Tar-Baby story, for example, current among Baronga, Basumbwa, Manganja, and Yao, on the eastern side of Africa, and among Hausas, Fantees, and many of the tribes of Angola and the Congo on the western side of the continent, has been inherited from them by the coloured population of the United States, and thanks to " Uncle Remus " is now familiar in English nurseries.

People who do not assimilate each other's customs may

assimilate each other's tales   A curious example of the effect of transplantation is the story of the *Three Sisters*, one of several Jamaican negro versions of the *Maid freed from the Monster* (as it might be entitled), which Miss Werner (in Jekyll, p. xxxvi) refers to an indigenous African prototype.   But in this variant the youngest sister escapes by outwitting the suitor (who turns out to be the Devil) in a riddling contest.   She quotes one of the riddles in the ballad of the *Elfin Knight*, singing it to an old " modal " air, with a burden evidently borrowed from an English original (*op. cit.* p. 286).   Here a European story which commended itself to African minds because its underlying idea was the same as one of their own, has been grafted on to an African root-stock.   Wherever the soil is suitable, there the seed germinates, though the blossom frequently takes its colour from its environment.   The Frog Prince of the German forests is a lobster in the Greek Islands, a snake in Zululand, a lizard in Burma.   The Swan-maiden of Germany is the Seal-woman of the Faroes and Shetland Islands.   In Europe the False Bride is a maid who attends the heroine on the journey to her wedding with her prince-bridegroom, as yet unseen.   On the way, the maid contrives, as she thinks, to drown her mistress, takes her clothes and possessions, and passes herself off as the bride ; but the heroine is rescued and eventually manages to prove her identity.   Among the Bantu Fiote, the heroine is the daughter of the goddess Nzambi, sent in charge of a slave to a distant town for the customary seclusion of young girls before marriage.   On the way the slave gradually gets possession of all her mistress's ornaments ; and when they arrive she is treated with honour while the princess is set to till the fields, until she finds means to send a message to her mother, who comes and rescues her. (Dennett, *FL.F.* 128.)   Among the wild and primitive Bushmen, the heroine is the wife of the " Dawn's Heart Star," (Jupiter).   The Hyena is jealous of her, and bespells her by mixing her own sweat with the other's food, so that her ornaments and skin garments fall off, and she is transformed into a lynx.   She lurks concealed among the reeds, while the Hyena, dressed in her bracelets and kaross, sits beside the fire with her back turned towards her husband. But the wife's younger sister takes her baby to her night and morning, and presently discloses the truth to the Dawn's Heart Star. The Hyena hurriedly decamps, leaving the kaross and ornaments behind her ; and they bring back the true wife, restored to human form all but the tufts of hair at the tips of the lynx's ears. (Bleek and Lloyd, 85.) The " Problem of Diffusion," in this and many another case, seems at present altogether baffling.

The study of the variations and areas of distribution of folk-tale themes is one of the most fascinating branches of the many-sided science of Social Anthropology, and is by no means the least useful. There are indications that the choice of themes depends not only on environment, but on racial character. One group of nations will be chiefly given to ætiological stories, another to didactic and moral stories, another to wonder-tales ; and they will assimilate stories from other cultures in accordance with their own idiosyncrasies as well as by adapting them to their own environment. Seventy types of Indo-European stories were enumerated by Mr. Joseph Jacobs in the first edition of this Handbook, and the list is reproduced in Appendix C. Time has, however, proved it to be far from complete, and similar classifications of African, American, and other stories are sadly to seek. The compilation of one or more such ethnographical classifications would be a praiseworthy work on the part of any young British folklorist. The international *Folkloristischer Forscherbund* of Northern Europe possesses an elaborate one, compiled by Herr Antti Aarne. But for the collector, as M. Sébillot remarks (*Le Folklore*, p. 30) it will usually be enough to arrange his " harvest " in the general groups we have indicated here, without further subdivision.

Beast-tales, namely, folk-tales in which the actors are animals, who speak and act like human beings, belong more especially to the savage stage of development. The savage mind seems unable fully to grasp the difference of kind, and the

personages of his folk-tales are represented as acting in ways
that their physical forms alone would render impossible.
" The hare and the elephant hire themselves out to hoe a
man's garden ; the swallow invites the cock to dinner, and
his wife prepares the food in the usual native hut with
the fireplace in the middle and the *nsanja* staging over it ;
the hare's wife goes to the river to draw water, and is caught
by the crocodile ; the tortoise carries his complaint to the
elders in the village smithy assembled, and so on." (Werner,
op. cit. p. xiii.)   Yet on the other hand their several mental
characteristics are often cleverly and convincingly drawn,
and with entire consistency.   One is strong, another cunning,
and another slothful.   The chief characteristic of Annancy,
the Spider, the central figure of Negro beast-tales on both
sides of the Atlantic, is trickery.   " A strong and good
workman, he is invariably lazy, and is only to be tempted
to honest labour by the offer of a large reward.   He prefers
to fill the bag which he always carries, by fraud or theft.
His appetite is voracious, and nothing comes amiss to him,
cooked or raw. . . . Sometimes he will thrust himself
upon an unwilling neighbour, and eat up all his breakfast.
At another time he carries out his bag and brings it home
full of flesh or fish obtained by thieving.   He is perfectly
selfish, and knows no remorse. . . . His only redeeming
point is a sort of hail-fellow-well-met-ness, which appeals
so much to his associates that they are ready almost, if not
quite, to condone his offences." (Jekyll, pp. 1-2.)

Drolls are comic stories, or intended to be comic.   They
are still current in England, where other folk-tales are now
rare.   The blunders of fools form their principal theme.   The
narration of a good droll will often penetrate the reserve even
of a north-country man, and cause him to divulge stores of
other folklore.

Cumulative tales are distinguished by form, not by subject.
At every step in the narrative all the previous steps are
repeated till the climax is reached, and the whole story re-
capitulated.   The *Old Woman and the Crooked Sixpence* is

a familiar instance. *The House that Jack Built* is another.
A Lushai example occurs in *FL*. xx. 389. Ritual formulæ
are sometimes built up on this plan.

Apologues are stories with a conscious purpose and a moral,
and are thus nearly allied to Proverbs (ch. xviii. *q.v.*). In
West Africa short stories are quoted in legal "palavers"
as *exempla* for the guidance of the Court. (*FL.F.* p. xi.) In
like manner did Jotham tell the men of Israel the famous
apologue of the Trees choosing the Bramble for their King.

In the matter of collecting stories, those that refer to any
person, place, rite, or object, regarded with reverence, must
not be lightly approached or treated, and it must be made
plain that any confidence is appreciated as it was meant to be.
Any other course is likely to be rewarded by inventions or by
feigned ignorance, if native ideas of courtesy forbid a blunt
refusal. But Myths about things indifferent may be obtained
by asking the reason or origin of this or that—the changes
of the moon, the cleft lip of the hare, the marks on the leaves
of the lungwort or the "holy thistle," the standing-stones,
the earthwork, and the like. Other tales should be listened
for when people are talking at leisure. The traveller should
be able to relate a few tales himself, to join in the conversation,
and to draw out his companions.

All tales should be written down with as little delay as may
be, preferably in the presence of the narrator, if possible
in the native language, and in any case with the native
idioms exactly rendered ; and should be read over to the
narrator for correction, if possible. The name, age, residence,
and occupation of the latter should be recorded, and it should
be stated whether he or she is bilingual, and if possible, where
and from whom either heard the story. Variants and fragments of stories should also be recorded ; but should be kept
separate, not pieced together or used to "correct" other
versions. Rhythms, long runs, and repetitions are tedious to
transcribe in full, but they should always be indicated as they
occur ; otherwise the literary structure of the tale is destroyed.

See Questionary, p. 342.

CHAPTER XVII.

SONGS AND BALLADS.

SONG is so many-sided and so all-pervading a form of human expression that it is hard to say from what point of view it may best be approached. Perhaps its beginnings first arose out of the perception by early mankind of the power of the human voice over animals, and then extended to belief in its power over other beings or phenomena. But this is, of course, conjecture. What concerns the folklorist is to ascertain the place of Song in the life of the people, and to note into what spheres of life it enters and what are the varying forms which it takes. With verse we include melody, for in the lower culture the two are inseparable ; and in view of the close association of musical and other artificially produced sounds with magico-religious rites, music deserves more attention than it has yet received from folklorists.

Song is used to communicate with other worlds—to address the Above-folk, as the Congo natives call the dwellers in the skies. The North American peoples always intone their prayers, says Miss Alice Fletcher (*Indian Story and Song*), and the same habit is found far into European higher culture. The incantations of the wizard, of whatever colour he may be, are almost always couched in rhythmical verse. War-songs, love-songs, cradle-songs, dirges, and epithalamiums, all no doubt had primarily a magico-religious value, and partook of the nature of charms. Oxen, in whatever quarter of the globe they are used, are coaxed and encouraged to labour by song, and milch kine are induced to yield their milk in the same way.

> " Cush-a-cow bonny, come let down your milk,
> And I will give you a gown of silk,
> A gown of silk and a silver tee (tie, chain),
> If you will let down your milk for me." (*FL.J.* iv. 261.)

> " Give thy milk, brown cow,
> Give thy milk, so abundant and rich,
> Give thy milk brown cow,
> And the gentles coming to the townland.
> 　　Ho, my heifer ! ho, my heifer fair !
> 　　Ho, my heifer ! (etc.).

> Give thy milk, brown cow,
> And that there is nothing for them but bread !
> Give thy milk, brown cow,
> Macneill ! Macleod ! Clanranald !
> 　　Ho, my heifer ! ho, my heifer fair !
> 　　Ho, my heifer ! ho, my heifer fair !
> 　　Ho, my heifer ! ho, my heifer fair !
> 　　　Thou heartling, heart, I love thee ! "

> > (Carmichael, *Report Crofter Commission*, quoted
> > in *Handbook*, 1st ed. p. 149).

Labour, and especially labour performed in concert, is very generally accompanied by song, probably in the first place for magico-religious reasons, but certainly also from the practical usefulness of music in inspiriting the workers and enabling them to keep time together. And on the other hand, the regular beat of the oars, the fall of the hammer, the tramp of the warriors' feet, naturally tend to promote the development of rhythm and metre in the songs. Rowing especially is ruled by song ; all over the world " our voices keep tune and our oars keep time." The " chanty " of sailors at the windlass is now perhaps the only relic of the use of labour-songs in England. The lifeboat crew at Criccieth were heard hauling up their boat after a practice, to the accompaniment of a chanty, in the summer of 1908. The leader gave the time with a solo (in Welsh), and the hauling party joined in the chorus.

It is the same with dancing; the accompanying song both inspirits the dancers and enables them to keep step. The dance-songs of savages are generally short strophes repeated again and again, like our choruses. The "ballads" of Northern and Western Europe, it need hardly be said, were originally dance-songs. They are still thus used in the Faroe Islands; and elsewhere the older and finer of them preserve the refrain, or burden, taken up in chorus by the dancers and marking the steps of the dance.

> " Now he has asked her father dear,
>   *With a heigh-ho! and a lily gay,*
> And the mother too, that did her bear,
>   *As the primrose spreads so sweetly.*
>
> And he has asked her sister Anne,
>   *With a heigh-ho! and a lily gay,*
> But he left out her brother John,
>   *As the primrose spreads so sweetly.*"

The refrains are sometimes onomatopeic, as in the case of the chorus of the Sussex blacksmiths' song, which imitates the sound of the bellows :

> " Twankidillo, twankidillo, dillo, dillo, dillo, dillo, dillo !
>   With a roaring pair of bagpipes made of the green willow ! "
>
>   (*FL.J.* ii. 324.)

Or they may contain unintelligible words, such as the famous " Lero, lero, lillibulero ! "—perhaps obsolete, perhaps derived from a foreign language imperfectly understood, perhaps never more than " mere vocables to carry the air," to quote Miss Fletcher again.

The " stem " or solo part, of chorus songs tends to become narrative. It may be improvised, especially in labour songs ; or it may relate a legend or a folk-tale. The story proceeds step by step ; not in a continuous narrative, but dramatically, in a series of little scenes, and with frequent iteration ; features which characterise the true ballad-form of song even when the burden is wanting. For instance, in the song-game of *The Maid Freed from the Gallows*, the heroine addresses her father, mother, brother, and sister, in turn, thus :

> " Oh, have you found my golden ball ?
> 　And are you come to set me free ?
> Or are you come to see me hanged
> 　All on the gallows-tree ? "

And each in turn replies :

> " Oh, I've not found your golden ball,
> 　And I'm not come to set you free,
> But I am come to see you hanged,
> 　All on the gallows-tree."

till the fifth comer, the lover, proclaims himself the successful finder.　Take another, and a beautiful example :

> " Oft have I ridden through Stirling town
> 　In wind and snow and sleet,
> But now I ride through Stirling town
> 　With fetters on my feet.
>
> Oft have I ridden through Stirling town
> 　In the sunshine and the rain,
> But now I ride through Stirling town
> 　Ne'er to return again.
>
> They brought unto the heading-hill
> 　His hounds within a leash,
> They brought unto the heading-hill
> 　His goshawk in a jess ;
>
> They led unto the heading-hill
> 　His horse and golden saddle,
> The nurse came to the heading-hill
> 　With his young son from the cradle.
>
> His wife came to the heading-hill ;
> 　' Adieu, dear love to thee ; '
> And for the words the queen had spoke
> 　Did brave Young Waters dee."

Of such ballads as this the late Andrew Lang wrote, " the heart of humanity is their maker."

Whether the European ballad arose from a religious beginning cannot be known, but the fact that the choral dances which seem to have been its source were held at night in churchyards, and were denounced by the clergy as impious (Prof. W. P. Ker, in *Proc. Brit. Acad.* vol. iv.) suggests a connection with pagan ritual. If the ballads developed out of a kind of pagan *Danse Macabre*, it might account for the tragic character of the ballad-stories compared to that of the prose folk-tales, which so puzzled Mr. Lang. None of them can be older than the twelfth century, the date at which rhymed metre supplanted alliterative rhythm, but the comparative antiquity of individual ballads may to some extent be arrived at from internal evidence. The ballad of the *Cruel Brother*, cited above, is cast in the typical form, with repetitions, progression by single steps, and independent burden. In it, the bride's brother, to revenge the slight put upon him by the bridegroom in omitting to ask his consent to the marriage, stabs the bride to the heart on the wedding-day, and the act, though blamed, is accepted as natural. But in *Katharine Janfarie*, a ballad with no burden or chorus, but with that unmistakeable mark of a "minstrel" ballad, the address to the audience at the close, a more modern phase of public opinion appears. The suitor who "asked her father and mother and a' the lave o' her kin" is ridiculed, and the fortunate lover is he who

> " Asked not her father or mother
> Nor the chief o' a' her kin,
> But he whispered the bonnie lassie hersel'
> And did her favour win."

Far later than either of these are the doggrel ballads of the pedlar or the street-singer, in which the "proud porter" of the castle appears as an important personage.

But of the very early character of the ballad form of narrative song there can be no doubt. We find the same characteristic features of the narration, step by step, of a legend or folk-tale sung to the accompaniment of dancing—or of acting and dancing, as in the children's song-game cited above—in the songs of the New Guinea people studied by Dr. Landtmann (*FL.* xxiv. 284-313). In the men's house (*darimo*) legends are narrated in song and dance. A " precentor " if we may so call him, sings each verse, and the dancers repeat it after him, slowly moving round the room two and two, after the manner of a Russian polonaise. Here are some stanzas, in the " pidgin English " into which the natives themselves rendered it, of a ballad of over sixty verses, relating the building and destruction of a *darimo* on the mainland opposite the island of Kiwai (where the song was sung), by the " people " of their Culture Heroine, Abere, and the subsequent adventures of the party :

> " People belong Abere cut him bush what place they want him make darimo.
> People belong Abere burn him bush now for darimo.
> People belong Abere clear him ground now for darimo.
> People belong Abere go cut him post now for darimo.
> People belong Abere cut him post now belong darimo.
> People belong Abere cut him other end belong post.
> People belong Abere carry him post now.
> People belong Abere dig him hole now for post.
> People belong Abere put him up *abo* (the short posts to support the floor).
> People belong Abere put him *mao* (the horizontal beams) on top *abo*.
> People belong Abere dig him hole and put him up *saro* (the tall posts supporting roof).
> People belong Abere put him *mao* (the horizontal beams) on top of *saro*.
> People belong Abere put him up post belong wall.
> People belong Abere make fast all wood belong on top."

and so on through every step of the processes of flooring and thatching. Then the house proves unsatisfactory, and is pulled down step by step in reverse order.

> " People belong Abere take him out altogether wood belong on top (the rafters).
> People belong Abere take him out altogether *mao*.
> People belong Abere take him out altogether *te* (the floor).
> People belong Abere pull him out *saro*.
> People belong Abere pull him out *abo*.
> People belong Abere put him all the post together."

The story next turns to the building of a raft, loading it with yams, bananas, and so on. The raft is wrecked, but

Abere changes herself from a fish to various birds in turn, rescues her people and they reach Kiwai, where she directs them to plant such of the plants as have been saved from the wreck.

Snatches of verse interspersed in prose folk-tales have a wide popularity, ranging from the *cante-fable* of *Aucassin et Nicolette* to the lament of the forsaken mother in the Australian (Dieri) story, who sinks underground in search of her lost children, singing :

> " Earth I, clay seeking, under go,
>   Backwards down go,
>   Hard earth splitting yes, I down go,
>   After me drawing, yes, I go,
>   Blood in streaks, yes, I down go,
>   Earth depth I back again go."   (*FL.* xiii. 416.)

It is a long way from such artless compositions as this to the intermediate stage of barbaric culture at which we find poetry erected into an independent art practised simply for the pleasure and amusement of the singer and his hearers. Narrative poetry in the form of rude epics is then deliberately composed and recited to keep alive the memory of the heroes of the nation and their deeds and sufferings. At this stage a professional class of Bards arises, sometimes in the direct pay of the sovereign, sometimes dependent only on popular support. Such are the Doms of Balochistan, a tribe of wandering professional minstrels who sing, or rather chant in a sort of recitative, to the accompaniment of rude stringed instruments, songs which are the work of native Baloches and are always given with scrupulous acknowledgement of their authorship. The poems and songs are recorded solely by oral tradition, and though they are formed on strictly defined metrical models they owe nothing to Indian or Persian literary culture. Here are some specimens, literally translated by Mr. Longworth Dames.

" Gwaharam sings of the day on which Mir-Han was slain :

" Let us meet on the bare desert foot-hills, and have our interview on the barren plain, the grazing ground of wild asses. Let the Rinds and Dombkis come together, let the Bhanjars and Jatois repeat their gibes! The Rinds came with booted feet, with their slaves they alighted. From every hamlet they took their blood, and the far-famed Malik Mir-Han was slain! Chakur fled thence by night; he took a stick in his hand to drive the cows and to graze the slate-coloured buffaloes! Whither went Rehan and mighty Safar, Ahmad and lordly Kalo?

" What was the matter with you, thick-beards? [an epithet of the Rinds.] Was not your tribe established in Bheni; had you not in your hands wealthy Bingopur? Your place was with your love on the coloured bedstead!

" For the innocent blood of Malim the Khan Gwaharam tightened his saddle-girths, and let his mare go to the Mullah Pass! " (Longworth Dames, *Poetry of Baloches*, p. 20.)

The following are love-songs from the same source :

> " My ring is on thy finger, do not now go back,
> Thou art my old love, do not now go back.
> Thy pledge is on my finger, do not now go back,
> Thou wast never false yet, do not now go back." (p. 186.)

> " My riding is on swift mares,
> My love is by the green water-springs ;
> For a short moment I will sit there,
> I will look upon her wandering face,
> I will put an end to the black delay." (p. 190.)

> " When the horseman comes I shall be happy,
> With the piper for my love I shall be wealthy,
> Give me the dumb ring and speak to me,
> Give me the ring of betrothal." (p. 193.)

Modern Greek folk-song reaches a higher plane.

> " How peaceful all the mountains lie, how peaceful lie the meadows !
> It is not death that they await, old age does not afflict them.
> The springtime only they await, and May, and summer sunshine,
> To see the Vlachs upon the hills, to see the fair Vlach maidens.
> And listen to the music sweet that with their pipes they'll waken.
> While graze their sheep, around whose necks the heavy bells are
>   tinkling.
> Again they'll set their sheepfolds up, and set up their encampment.
> Again the young Klepht boys will come for frolic and for dancing.
> The Klepht bands, too, will scour again the fields of fair Phar-
>   salia.

Their Turkish foes to catch alive, and when they're slain to strip
  them.
And golden sequins carry off, and then divide and share them ;
And give perhaps some two or so to fair and kind Vlach maidens
When stealing from them kisses two, with sweetest fun and frolic."
(Garnett and Glennie, *Greek Folk Songs,* 246.)

Independent songs, like stories, are very transmissible, and
may be conveyed to remote nooks and corners by nomads,
sailors, or slaves. " Occasional " songs should not be recorded
with them, but always in connection with the rites, days,
festivals, or other occasions, to which they belong.

Of lullabies and nursery songs space fails us to say anything,
save that a rich harvest awaits the collector who turns his
attention to them. Nor can we do more than mention the
unsuspected wealth of English folk-songs revealed by the
researches of the Folk-Song Society and the independent
enterprise of Mr. Cecil Sharp.

See Questionary, p. 343.

CHAPTER XVIII.

PROVERBS AND RIDDLES.

" THERE is a matter," says Father de Clercq, "which is worthy of the most minute examination and which almost enters into the region of religion,—I mean the morality of the natives. What do they think good, what evil? What do they advise and what condemn? Who is in their eyes a respectable man, and whose conduct do they disapprove? These are questions which every missionary should be able to answer. He will find the answer in their proverbs and popular sayings, as also in their moral tales." And he proceeds to summarise the Baluba code of morals, as evidenced in their proverbial sayings. (*Anthropos*, vol. viii. p. 22.)

Among the intellectual efforts of the backward races, proverbs have in fact been too little regarded. But they deserve careful study, because they represent, not forgotten ideas surviving in practice, but the actual views of those who use them, their practical philosophy of life, and their principles of action.

Racial and national character are revealed in proverbs. Oriental fatalism speaks in the Punjâbi saying, " Life and death, fame and dishonour, are in the hands of Fate." And again in " There is no remedy for Fate." But the European under various figures affirms that, " Heaven helps them who help themselves." Japanese courtesy says, " Sword-wounds may be healed, word-wounds are beyond healing." The grim humour of the Spaniard rebukes avarice with " Shrouds have no pockets." Scottish caution peeps out in the saying, " Friends are like fiddle-strings, they maunna be screwed ower tight ; " and Irish happy carelessness in " Time enough to bid the Devil good-morrow when ye meet him."

Social systems give birth to many proverbs. " To love the king is not bad, but to be loved by the king is better," is the outcome of the West African experience. The elaborate civilization of China meets us in the Chinese aphorism, " Without the wisdom of the learned, the clown could not be governed ; without the labour of the clown the learned could not be fed." Their " Master easy, servant lazy," is as obviously a maxim of the upper classes, as the Egyptian, " He strikes me, and says, ' Why does he cry out ? ' " is the wail of the down-trodden Fellahin. " Never take a wife from a hall or a pig from a mill," (because neither will be satisfied in their new quarters), speaks the experience of the English cottager (Staffordshire). Other proverbs are the coinage of sex. " When ye tak' a man, ye tak' a maister," (Fife) ; " A noggen (wooden) mother is better than a golden father," (Salop) ; and, " Children be first an arm-ache and then a heart-ache," (Wilts), betray female authorship as plainly as the plentiful jests at women do masculine.

Very many proverbs are due to occupation and environment. " Every one cannot have his house on the piazza," says the Italian city-dweller ; " By going and coming the bird builds its nest," says the Negro trader, journeying to and fro in the West African forest. " Make not friends by the way lest you lose your knife," and " No one gives his pig to the hyena to keep," are other dicta from the same source. Again, ideas identical in themselves are translated into terms of locality or occupation. The Frenchman says " You cannot make an omelette without breaking the eggs ; " the Norwegian, " You cannot climb a mountain by a level road." " Don't count your chickens before they are hatched," becomes in Holland, " Do not cry your herrings before they are in the net ; " and in Scotland, " Dinna gut your fish till ye get them ; " while the Italian says, " Do not sell the

bird on the bough," and " Do not part with the bear-skin
before you have caught the bear ; "—hunters' proverbs both.
One might continue this theme *ad infinitum.*

Various schemes have been proposed for the classification
of proverbs, but all of them are better suited to an exhaustive
study of the subject than to the simple record which is all
the collector desires to make. This he will find it best to
arrange according to the *form*, rather than the matter of his
material. Proverbs naturally fall into two groups, viz. I.
Proverbs proper, that is to say, proverbs which form complete
sentences for citation, and II. Proverbial Phrases, or expressions consisting of parts of sentences only, which may be woven
into the speaker's own remarks, as did Samson, when he said
to the men of Timnath, " If ye had not *ploughed with my
heifer*, ye had not found out my riddle."

I. *Proverbs proper* may be further divided into simple
Maxims or Aphorisms, *i.e.* direct statements of the matter
in hand ; and Metaphorical statements, which involve
reasoning by analogy. For examples of the first class, take
the following :—

> " Choose a horse made and a man to make."
> " Good and quickly seldom meet."
> " Honesty is the best policy."
> " Love and a cough cannot be hid."
> " Praise the day at night, and life at its close." [1]
> " Punishment is lame, but it comes."
> " Threatened men live long."
> " Waste not, want not."

while the following are examples of metaphorical proverbs
(by far the largest and most interesting class) :—

> " A cat in pattens catches no mice."
> " A curst cow hath short horns."

---

[1] In the *Elder Edda* this runs :
> " Praise day at even, a wife when dead,
> A weapon when tried, a maid when wed,
> Ice when 'tis crossed, and ale when 'tis drunk."

" A feather in the hand is better than a bird in the air."

> (George Herbert, *Jacula Prudentum*.)

" It's a long lane that has no turning."

" Let sleeping dogs lie."

" Little dogs start the hare, great dogs get her."

" Once bitten, twice shy."

" One dog, one bone," (*i.e.* fair play).

" You a lady, I a lady, who shall drive the pigs afield ? "

> (Spanish.)

" The Jackal dipped himself in indigo and then thought he was a peacock." (Persian.)

II. *Proverbial phrases* may be divided into Metaphors and Similes. The following are examples :—

Metaphors.

" To draw the long bow."

" To put the cart before the horse."

" To plough the headlands before the butts."

" To praise one's pasture."

" To look for a needle in a bottle of hay."

" To run with the hare and hunt with the hounds."

" To save at the spigot and waste at the bunghole."

Another class of Metaphors, nearly related both to Riddles and to Nicknames, is represented by the following :—

" The blacksmith's daughter," (a padlock).

" The Franciscan's hackney," (his feet).

" Shanks's pony," (ditto).

" A wooden suit," (a coffin).

Similes.

" As right as a trivet."

" As drunk as a lord."

" As hungry as a hunter."

" As mad as a March hare."

" As quiet as a lamb."

" As poor as a church mouse."

"As dead as a door nail."

"As big as the parson's barn," (*i.e.* the tithe-barn).

"Like a chip in milk, neither good nor harm."

"In and out, like a dog at a fair."

"In and out, like a crooked road," (or, a dog's hind leg).

"As queer as Dick's hatband, that went nine times round and then wouldn't tie."

This last introduces us to a group of sayings which connect the Proverb with the Apologue or Fable ; those, namely, which are attached to an anecdote of which they form the climax. "A moral proverb," says Father de Clercq, "is generally a synthetic formula in which the natives sum up— or as they say, abridge—a moral story ; so that to appreciate the exact bearing of the proverb you must begin by obtaining the story or parable which give rise to it and of which it constitutes the summary. These stories cannot be better collected than at the palavers, for it is then that an elder will cite them, more or less paternally, to his clients." (*Anthropos*, vol. viii. 21.)

Egyptian proverbs frequently take this form. An English example is the well-known "The case is altered, quoth Plowden." We know the story, variously told, that Judge Plowden, being informed that his tenant's beast had gored his own, decreed that the tenant must pay damages, but when it appeared that it was his own beast that has injured the other's, " 'Oh, then the case is altered,' quoth Plowden." Local historians of Plowden's native county (Shropshire) have expended much pains in trying to decide which is the "authentic" version of this story. Meanwhile Professor Sayce has discovered an equally "authentic" version at Cairo. (*FL.* xvii. 191.)

RIDDLES in the lower culture are not mere *jeux d'esprit*, but problems for solution. While the proverb states a fact or expresses a thought in vivid metaphor, the riddle describes a person or a thing in more obscure metaphor, calculated to exercise the intellectual skill of any who attempt to solve it. Thus making and guessing riddles becomes a trial of wits, a dialectic combat ; and riddles are in fact used by various peoples not only as a form of amusement, but as a means of education, a kind of " mental gymnastics," and even as a serious test of intellectual ability. In folk-tales, we find the youth who can guess the riddle is rewarded with the hand of the princess, and the reputed sage who fails is sentenced to death as a charlatan. In real life, riddles " are set like exercises to whole companies of puzzled [Basuto] children." (*Prim Cult.* i. 91.) The value placed on them by our own fore-fathers is shown by the number that are included in the collec-tion of Anglo-Saxon poems known as the *Exeter Book.*[1]

The problems themselves strictly follow the type of the famous riddle of Œdipus, " What goes on four legs in the morn-ing, on two legs at noonday, and on three legs at night ? " *e.g.*, " There is a thing that travels fast without legs or wings, and no cliff nor river nor wall can stop it," (the voice ; Basuto). " There is a long slender trading-woman who never gets to market," (a canoe,—it stops at the landing place ; Yoruba). "What is it we get into by three parts and out of by one ? " (a shirt ; ancient Mexico). " Guess ye some men who are many and form a row, they dance the wedding-dance, adorned in white hip-dresses," (the teeth ; Zulu). And in England we find " A troop of white horses around a red hill, now they go, now they go, now they stand still," (the teeth). " It goes round the house and round the house, and leaves a white glove in the window," (snow). " It goes upstairs red and comes down black," (a warming-pan).

> " I heard a rickety-racket,
> Pulled off my shoes and run a'ter it, and couldn't o'ertak' it."
>   (A railway train.)

The modern date of the last example shows that the mytho-poeic faculty is not yet dead in England.

Having once heard a riddle proposed, it is easy to ask for

---

[1] A transcript of these with an Introduction and Notes and a full Bibliography, by Mr. Frederick Tupper, was published by Ginn & Co., London, 1910.

more, to note those contributed in response, and to propose them on similar occasions, asking again for contributions. But proverbs are more difficult to collect. They can only be listened for, and noted whenever they are incidentally cited. Then, as opportunity occurs, those already noted may be made the topic of conversation ; and eventually perhaps some intelligent native may be induced to collect and supply others. But in such a case it would probably be wise to verify his statements by comparison with those of other informants. " When a poor man makes a proverb, it does not spread," complains the Oji of West Africa, and not every wise and witty saying can claim to be ranked as a proverb.

Residents have a great advantage over visitors in collecting proverbs. Their fuller knowledge of the local dialect makes it easier for them to observe and catch the proverbial expression incidentally let fall, and intimate acquaintance with the speaker will enable them to distinguish between the accepted proverb and the pithy and picturesque impromptu of the local sage himself. " The tide never goes out so far but it comes back again," said a Cornish fisherman when Mr. Albany Major condoled with him on the badness of the fishing season ; but Mr. Major, a temporary visitor only, could not tell whether this bit of cheerful philosophy was an apt quotation or an original remark.

CHAPTER XIX.

PROVERBIAL RHYMES AND LOCAL SAYINGS.

JINGLES and other sayings in rhyme or rhythm, even when unmeaning to those who repeat them, sometimes have considerable significance for the scientific enquirer. The incantation or invocation in rude verse is an essential part of ancient ritual, and from its form often has a quality of endurance which causes it to outlast the ceremonial or custom of which it originally formed a part. It then comes down to us on the lips of the people, sometimes associated with observances less ancient than itself, sometimes as the formula of a game, as a nursery rhyme, or simply as a trifling catch-word. These formulæ though probably not very important in savage folklore, bulk largely in that of European countries. The older of them bear witness to former social conditions, the more modern reveal the mental preoccupations and idiosyncrasies of the folk. In either case, therefore, they must not be overlooked.

Examples of formulæ used for magical purposes, both to hurt and to heal, and especially to call up visions, have been given in previous chapters. And rhythmical formulæ were equally in use in legal matters. The phrase " to have and to hold," which occurs not only in the conveyance of property but also in the marriage service, retains the old alliterative rhythm ; and still more did that earlier form in which the bride vowed to be " bonnair and buxom at bed and board." Sir Henry Maine comments on the fact that the

Laws of Manu are in verse, and Sir Francis Palgrave observes that the marked alliteration of the Anglo-Saxon laws is to be referred to the desire for an aid to memory, and notes that in the Frisic laws several passages are evidently written in verse.

The verderer in the mediæval forest knew that he was justified in the summary execution of an offender, if he found him in any of the following circumstances :—

> " Dog draw, stable stand,
>   Back berend, and bloody hand."

The rhyme inscribed beneath the effigy of King Athelstan in Beverley Minster commemorating his traditional grant to the inhabitants,

> " Als fre mak I the
>   As heart may think or eigh may see,"

perhaps, says Sir Laurence Gomme, records the ancient form of manumission or enfranchisement.

Banffshire schoolboys ratified a bargain, says Dr. Gregor, by linking their little fingers, moving their hands up and down, and repeating :

> " Ring, ring the pottle bell !
>   Gehn ye brak the bargain
>   Ye'll gang t' hell."

It was regarded as the height of wickedness to break a bargain thus sealed. Another form was :—

> " Ring a bottle, ring a bell !
>   The first brae it ye cum till
>   Ye'll fa' doon an brack yer neck,
>   And that'll the bargain brak."

A third form ran :—

> " ' Will ye brak the bargain ? '
>   ' No.'
>   ' Swear then.'
>   ' As sure as death
>   Cut ma breath
>   Ten mile aneath the earth,
>   Fite man, black man, burn me t' death.' "

If the bargain was broken, the doom of the breaker was looked on as sure, and with awe. (*Handbook*, 1st ed., pp. 153-157.)

There seems little difficulty in believing that these boyish formulæ were once the property of grown men.

Memorial rhymes are the natural expedient of unlettered folk for preserving the knowledge of anything deemed worthy of record or remembrance. Most of our popular rhymes are concerned with the weather and the crops, with good and bad luck, and with observations of natural history. They form a vade-mecum for the conduct of affairs.

> " On St. Valentine's Day
> Cast beans in the clay.
> But on St Chad
> Sow, good or bad."

> " Cuckoo oats and woodcock hay
> Make the farmer run away."

> " If the cuckoo comes to an empty thorn
> Sell your horse and buy your corn."

> " A wet March and a windy May,
> Plenty of good grass and little good hay."

> " A swarm of bees in May is worth a load of hay,[1]
> A swarm in June is worth a silver spoon,
> A swarm in July is not worth a fly."

> " If the cock crows on going to bed.
> He's sure to rise with a watery head."

> " A man had better ne'er been born
> Than on the Sabbath pare his horn."

Sometimes popular rhymes commemorate historical circumstances. The following lines,

> " Ring-a-ding ding, I heard a bird sing,
> ' The Parliament soldiers are gone for the king ! ' "

(with which, late in the nineteenth century, an old woman in

---

[1] " Worth a noble the same day." (Clee Hills, Shropshire.) The last king of England under whom nobles were coined was Henry VIII.

the Staffordshire Potteries was heard hushing a baby), must undoubtedly refer to the action of General Monk in 1660.

Usually, however, such rhymes record matters of merely local interest.

> " *Saltash* was a borough town
> When Plymouth was a furzy down."
> (Said also of *Plympton*.)

> " While muir grows moss, and nowt grows hair,
> A Roddam of Roddam for ever mair."
> (Northumberland. *Nowt*, neat cattle.)

> " While ivy is smooth and holly is rough,
> There'll always be a Blest of The Hough."
> (Staffordshire.)

A rhyme may enumerate the boundaries of a franchise or the number of farms in a valley, or record the characteristics of neighbouring places and their inhabitants.

> " We go from Beckbury and Badger to Stoke upon Clee,
> Monk Hopton, Round Acton, and so return we."

> " An otter in the Wear you may find but once a year,
> But an otter in the Tees you may find at your ease."

> " Sutton for mutton, Tamworth for beef,
> Walsall for bandy-legs, and Brummagem for a thief."

> " A new church, an old steeple,
> A drunken parson, a wicked people." (Said of many places.)

Local gibes in verse or prose are to be found everywhere, and especially where a number of small communities are situated within a short distance of each other. Then each will probably have its nickname, and one will be the butt of all the rest. Every neighbourhood too has its natural barometer, its " weather-hole," or its cloudy peak.

> " Wenn Pilatus trägt sein Hut
> Dann wird das Wetter gut.
> Aber wenn er nimmt sein Degen
> Kommt es Regen."

War-cries, " slogans," family nicknames and sobriquets,

proverbial epithets,—"the gay Gordons," "the gallant Graemes," and the like—none should escape the collector's watchful care. Even "bell-jingles," or the words which the different peals of church-bells are supposed to "say," may be admitted for the sake of "Oranges and lemons, say the bells of St. Clement's."

Not a little social history lies hidden beneath these trifling "relics of an unrecorded past." They reflect the rural life of past generations, with its anxieties, its trivialities, its intimate familiarity with Nature, and its strong local preoccupations. And, to quote once more words read too long since to trace their source now, "if it be true that nothing human is without interest to a man, then that which tells us of the thoughts and ways of our forefathers should be of the deepest and nearest interest to us, for it has had something to do with making us what we are."

* The task of rewriting the brave little pioneer work of 1890 is now concluded, but the writer cannot lay down the pen without expressing a final hope that the compressed form in which it has been necessary to present the various examples cited, will not mislead any reader into supposing that such summaries are all that it is needful to give of any scenes of the kind which he or she may be so fortunate as to witness, and that minute particulars would only be tedious. On the contrary, the fuller the details supplied, the more welcome will the record be to the scientific world.

THE END.

APPENDICES.

APPENDIX A.

TERMINOLOGY.

It will help to make descriptions both of social groups and magico-religious functions intelligible if the commoner technical terms are used in accordance with the definitions and explanations given below. These have been drawn up by a conference representing the Editors of *Notes and Queries on Anthropology* and also of this volume, for the common use of both works. Provisional definitions framed by this conference were submitted also on its behalf to experienced students of social anthropology, and amended to give effect as far as possible to their recommendations. It is hoped, therefore, that the result may be generally accepted as a standard vocabulary.

Tribe. A group of a simple kind, nomadic or settled in a more or less definite locality, speaking a common dialect, with a rude form of government, and capable of uniting for common action, as in warfare.

Clan. An exogamous division of a tribe, all the *clansmen* or members of which are held to be related to one another and bound together by a common tie of *clanship*. This tie may be a belief in common descent from some ancestor, real or mythical ; it may be the common possession of a totem ; or it may be of some other kind. In some cases the most obvious tie is the common habitation of a village or district, but in such a case there is little doubt that the real tie has been of some other kind.

Sept, Gens, and *Totem-kin* have been used synonymously, but *Clan* is recommended. Some American authors use *Gens* only where there is patrilineal descent, *Clan* where there is matrilineal descent.

In some cases Clans are grouped in *Phratries*.

Phratry. An exogamous division of a tribe, which division is sub-divided into *clans* or *classes*; though it may sometimes happen that, owing to the disappearance of clans, a phratry may have only one clan. When there are only two divisions, admitting of no further sub-division, in a tribe, they may be called *Moieties*.

Non-Exogamous Divisions such as are often found to exist in a tribe, will usually be found to be based on the principle of locality, and in that case may be called **Local Divisions.**

Caste should be limited to the institution as it exists in India, and to similar forms which may be found elsewhere.[1]

Class should be limited to the matrimonial classes of the Australians, or to similar groups which may be found elsewhere.

Family. This term should be limited to the group consisting of parents and children; including all children (adopted or other) who are treated by law and custom as *conventional* descendants of the person, whether father or mother, through whom descent is traced.

Kindred may be used for a group of persons descended, or regarded as descended, from the same grandfather or grandmother, or more distant progenitor, where the descent can be demonstrated genealogically and is not mythical, as is often the case with the *clan*. Occasionally the clan and the kindred may coincide with each other.

Kin and kinship should be limited to relationship, real and conventional (see *Family* above), which can be demonstrated genealogically.

Clansmen and **Clanship** should be used for the relationship set up by membership of the Clan (*v.* above).

The kindred, when living under one roof, may be called the **Undivided Household.**

[1] [Mr. Gait defines a Caste as " an endogamous group, or collection of such groups, bearing a common name and having the same traditional occupation, who are so linked together by these and other ties, such as the tradition of a common origin and the possession of the same tutelary deity, and the same social status, ceremonial observances, and family priests, that they regard themselves, and are regarded by others, as forming a single homogeneous community." *Indian Census Report,* 1911, vol. i. p. 367.—E. S. H.]

Polygamy is a generic term including **polygyny** and **polyandry.** *Polygyny* is a union of one man with two or more women. *Polyandry* is a union of one woman with two or more men. When the husbands are brothers the polyandry is called *adelphic* [or *fraternal*]; when one or more of the husbands has a position superior to the others it is *disparate*. Polygyny is disparate when one or more of the wives has a position superior to the others.

Supplementary Unions may be described as follows: when a man has one or more supplementary partners, they are his *concubines*, and their status is *concubinage*. Supplementary unions by which a woman has one or more supplementary partners or *cicisbei* are described as *cicisbeism*.

Group-Marriage has been used to denote a form of marriage in which all the men of a definite social group are the husbands of all the women of another social group. No such form of marriage is known to exist at present.

Cross-Cousin Marriage. Marriage between children of a brother and sister, *i.e.* one in which a man marries the daughter either of his mother's brother, or of his father's sister.

Marriage is **Matrilocal** when the husband lives, temporarily or permanently, with the group of his wife: **Patrilocal** if the wife lives, temporarily or permanently, with the husband's group.

Patrilineal or Matrilineal Descent should be used to express that membership of the family or other social group is reckoned through the father or the mother.

Authority in the family or kindred should be described as **Patripotestal** or **Matripotestal:** in the latter case it should be noted whether the authority is in the hands (1) of the actual mother; (2) of the maternal uncle; (3) of the mother's relatives in general, and so on.

Mother-Right may be used to describe a state of society characterised by the presence of two or all of the three conditions, *Matrilineal Descent*, *Matrilocal Marriage*, and *Matripotestal Family*. The old terms *patriarchal* and *matriarchal* should be avoided altogether, as they have become ambiguous through inexact use in the sense of either *-local*, or *-lineal*, or *-potestal*.

Totemism (pp. 41-43). Three chief features of the relation between human beings and their *totem* seem to be essential to totemism in its normal form:

(1) The *totem* (generally a class of animals, plants, or inanimate

objects; occasionally an individual animal or thing) is connected with a definite social group, and in the typical form of the institution this social division is exogamous. Often the group takes its name from the *totem*, or uses it as a badge, but these points are less constant and essential.

(2) The members of the social group believe themselves to be related to the *totem* or " of one flesh " with it, and not infrequently they believe that they are descended from the *totem*.

(3) There is a magico-religious bond between them; the members of the social group look for protection from their *totem* and show respect to it, and the most usual method of showing this respect is the prohibition to eat, kill, or injure the *totem*.

When a clan or corresponding social group owns more than one totem, these totems should be spoken of as *Associated Totems*. When one of these is more important than the rest, the latter should be called the *sub-totems*. When different parts of an animal are associated with different divisions of the social group, they should be called *Split Totems*.

Soul, Ghost, and Spirit. It is convenient to limit *soul* to the separable personality of the living man or other being; *ghost* to the same thing after death; *spirit* to a soul-like being which has never been associated with a human or animal body. *Soul, ghost,* and *spirit* are all essentially of the same type, representing a personality independent of a body though usually possessing an apparitional form of its own (*e.g.* like a dream-image or a shadow).

Familiar is preferable to *demon* as the name for the spirit attached to a person or a rite.

Animism is " the belief in spiritual beings " (E. B. Tylor). This includes soul, ghost, and spirit, as above defined.

Animatism is the attribution of life and personality to things, but not of a separate or apparitional soul.

Fetishism has been used in so many different and contradictory senses that it is very likely to be misunderstood. Its use should therefore be avoided. Even the word *Fetish* should only be used in its historic sense, to describe a limited class of magical objects in West Africa.

Anthropomorphic should be limited to outward shape, not used to describe the attribution of human behaviour or thought. Similarly, the terms *Zoomorphic, Phytomorphic, Hylomorphic,* mean that something is conceived or represented as having the outward shape of an animal, a plant, or an inanimate object.

Rite : a customary practice of a magico-religious character. (The word *ceremony* has lost this special sense.) A rite may consist of a number of *ritual acts*. There may be a *negative ritual*, consisting in refraining from doing things for magico-religious reasons, as well as a positive ritual.

Prayer should be used in the English sense, and not used to cover every sort of oral rite.

Sacred may be used of all persons or things set apart from the *profane* by reason of the possession of supernatural power inherent or derived.

Sacrifice includes any kind of magico-religious rite of which the essential feature is that something is consumed. It may embody various purposes, being intended, for instance, as a communion feast, or as an offering to propitiate a supernatural being, or as an expiation.

Tabu should be limited to describe a prohibition resting on a magico-religious sanction. Various other prohibitions are observed in uncivilized society ; *e.g. Legal Prohibitions*, put forth by authority ; and *Customary Prohibitions*, which appear to rest simply on social disapproval ; but the term *tabu* should be restricted as above.

[The following additional suggestions may be useful :]

Votive Offering, an object dedicated in consequence of a vow. This frequently takes the form of an image or *simulacrum*.

Wizard, a professor of occult science.

Conjurer, cunning man, wise man, dialectal equivalents for wizard.

Sorcerer, a wizard who is chiefly concerned with evil.

Shaman, a wizard or wizard-priest who is liable to be possessed by a god or spirit (Siberia, North America).

Medicine-man, a wizard who endues material objects with magical power.

Witch, a practitioner of evil magic, an enemy of society. Formerly used of both men and women ; still so used in South Africa, and dialectally in England.

Spell, (1) a form of words having magical power to impose a curse, or its equivalent; (2) the work of a witch, an enchantment.

Charm, a form of words having magical power to convey a blessing, or its equivalent. *N.B.*—The practice of carrying such formulas about in writing has led to a confusion between the charm and the amulet. The word *charm* should never be used in the latter sense.

Charmer, white witch, a practitioner of healing or counter-acting magic, often including divination.

Myth, a story told to account for something.

Legend, a story told as true, but consisting either of fact or fiction, or both indifferently.

Folk-tale, a popular story; often used as equivalent to the German *Märchen*.

APPENDIX B.

QUESTIONARY.

Let it be clearly understood once for all that these questions are not intended to be addressed to the persons from whom information is sought. Formal questioning, and especially direct questioning, is the sure road to failure and disappointment. The Questionary is intended as a summary of the points to be noted by the observer, and his notes made on the spot may be usefully compared with it afterwards, with a view to discover and supply any omissions. An endeavour has been made to render it fairly complete, but in the present state of our knowledge it is unlikely that the attempt has been altogether successful. In any case, the observer should not allow it to limit the scope of his investigations, but should try to follow up all clues and take advantage of all opportunities, whether they come within the prescribed curriculum of enquiry or not.

The following practical hints are summarized from a paper by Father Augustin de Clercq (*Anthropos*, vol. viii. pp. 12-22), which embodies the result of many years' experience as a missionary in the Belgian Congo.

In putting questions, remember three things:

1. The native has not the methodizing power which intellectual culture has bestowed on you; he cannot synthetize or combine ideas.

2. It is pretty certain that he will never have heard the question you put to him, and that he would never have put it to himself.

3. No native knows everything.

Therefore; (1) Avoid general questions (such as: " On what occasions do the people offer sacrifice ? "), and never ask for definitions. (2) Do not limit your enquiries to one individual, village, or district ; the replies from different persons or places will illustrate and explain each other and may suggest new lines to follow.

The best way is to lead your informant up to the subject gradually and unconsciously to himself and let him speak spontaneously. You can then believe what he says.

The worst way is, in hopes of getting the most information in the shortest time, to send for a native, interrogate him according to your pre-arranged Questionary, and take down his answers. He will say anything that comes into his head, in order to get quit of you, and you will only obtain blunders and inventions.

A third way, which looks promising at first sight, is to get a number of natives together and question them all, with the idea that what one does not know another will. The effect of this will be that they will squabble among themselves and you will learn nothing at all.

I. THE EARTH AND THE SKY, pp. 23-30.

(*1st Edition : " Great Natural Objects."*)

The Sun, Moon, and Stars. Note what actions or kinds of work should be done before or after noon, sunset, or sunrise, in the waxing or waning of the moon, at the new moon, the full moon, " the dark of the moon " ; movements to be made with the sun's course or contrary to it, the point of the compass faced in funeral or other rites ; prohibitions connected with the sun, moon, or stars (seeing, pointing, counting, etc.) ; influence of the stars on human life, of the moon on health or weather ; uncanny powers of midnight or noon ; omens from the appearance of sun, moon, or stars ; lucky actions or acts of reverence towards them ; prayers ; salutations ; dances ; things done during an eclipse of the sun or moon ; seasons and festivals dated by or held in honour of sun, moon, or stars (cf. ch. xiv.).

Give the names applied to sun, moon, stars, and sky. Are they masculine or feminine ? Are they regarded as gods, or as governed by special gods ?

What is supposed to be the origin of the heavenly bodies ? What are supposed to be the origins of day and night ? of the changes of the moon ? the seasons ? eclipses ? comets ? shooting stars ? the Milky Way ? (what is this called ?). Is the sky regarded as a person or a place ? Is there supposed to be a land above the sky ? who lives there ? has anybody ever been there ? what were his adventures ? Is the Land of the Dead above the sky ? Give any myths or legends concerning the sky or the several heavenly bodies.

Atmospheric Phenomena. Note any signs of fear, reverence, anger, etc., shown to winds, storms, rain, thunder, lightning, the rainbow, waterspouts, sandstorms, mirages, the Aurora Borealis, or the Ignis Fatuus ; any names or nicknames applied to them ; powers ascribed to them. What should be done on seeing a rainbow, mirage, etc. ?

Note omens drawn from them, or from the weather on particular days or occasions ; and any other weather-omens.

Note what things should be done or avoided during tempest. How can storms be raised or allayed ? are they thought to come of their own will or to be sent by anyone, and for what reason ? What persons, human or otherwise, have influence over them ? (cf. ch. ix. xiii.). Is there a Storm-god ? a Thunder-god ?

Are there any myths or sayings connected with any of the above ? or with clouds, snow, hail, or ice, or other atmospheric phenomena ? (cf. ch. xix.).

Fire. How is fire procured ? Are ritual fires kindled by different means from domestic fires ? Is there any perpetual sacred fire ? where ? by whom tended ? Is there any annual rite of kindling new fire ? Are special fires lighted on special occasions ? If so, are existing fires extinguished and is the new fire kindled in any special or archaic manner ? and by whom ? Is moral, physical, or sexual purity required when kindling ceremonial fires ? Are any rites practised in connection with such fires ? leaping over them, dancing round them, driving cattle through them, or through the smoke ? walking on hot stones or embers ? Are noxious animals, or effigies of offending persons, etc., consumed in such fires ?

Note all uses of fire or smoke, including tobacco-smoke, incense, etc., in sacrifice, purification, exorcism, festivals (public or domestic), leechcraft, etc. (See Hearth-fire, p. 313.) Is Fire personified ? Is there a Fire-god ? Is there any myth or story of the origin of fire ?

The Earth. Note any sites or spots inherently sacred or permanently *taboo*. Are trees and plants growing on them also sacred ? Are there any areas in which animals may not be hunted or killed, or where rulers have no authority ? How are obstinately-barren patches of ground accounted for ?

Note any occasions on which contact with the earth is either enjoined or forbidden (such as sleep, marriage, planting, warfare, worship, etc.). May sacred objects or vessels containing holy water or drugs be set on the ground ? What is the effect of spilling blood on the ground ? Is there anything else which must not touch the ground ?

Note any ceremonies connected with disturbing the earth (by ploughing, digging, sinking a new shaft or a well, opening a quarry, choosing a site or laying the foundation of a building).

Give names, habits, powers, and attributes, of any subterranean beings. Do they inhabit mines or caves ? How is their presence or existence known ? Are they feared, reverenced, or worshipped in any way ? What is supposed to be the cause of earthquakes ? Are volcanoes the abode of superhuman beings ? Note any traditions or practices connected with them (cf. Mountains, *infra*).

Give names applied to the earth. Is there an Earth-god or Earth-goddess ? how worshipped ?

Note any legends of the Creation of the Earth, and give any traditions about ancient earthworks.

Mountains, Hills, and Forests. Note any signs of fear or reverence towards mountains or forests. Are the people afraid to approach or ascend the mountains or traverse the forests ? Always ? or at special times ? Is it customary to leave offerings at special places in the mountains or forests (sticks, stones, flowers, leaves, shreds of dress, or other offerings) ?

Note any shrines in the mountains or forests : to whom dedicated, by whom resorted to ? when and what for ? Any annual assemblies held on the mountains and hills ; when, where, and what for ? Are any figures cut on the hillsides ?

Are the mountains personified ? spoken of as if living beings ? Give the names of any mountains, etc.

Are there special gods of the mountains, hills, or forests ? Are they the abode or the trysting-place of any superhuman beings or of ghosts or witches ? Are there any beliefs or practices connected with echoes ? Are they ever resorted to as oracles ? or for healing purposes ?

Give any myths or legends connected with the mountains or forests, or their origin or creation, fabulous height, etc. ; any connection with the birth of mankind ; legends of giants or heroes entombed within the mountains, of an invisible axe heard in forests, etc.

Rocks, Stones, Minerals, etc. Note any marks of reverence paid to rocks, boulders, great standing-stones, or stone circles. Record their names and any legends about them ; or about peculiar marks on them. Are such stones supposed to move ? What would be the consequence of injuring them ? Note any rites practised in connection with any of the above, or with clefts in rocks (healing, marriage, divination, ordeals, chastity tests, rites to obtain children). Are offerings made to them? with what intent?

Note whether caves are regarded as sacred, used for burial, thought to be inhabited by superhuman beings, supposed to extend for unknown distances, or to give access to the Underworld. Has anyone tried to explore them? What happened to him?

Note whether the principal actor in any rite, or the subject of the rite, stands or sits on a stone. Any stone or a particular one? Does standing on a particular stone convey a challenge?

Note any practices with regard to Cairns. What do they commemorate? Is it customary to add a stone when passing a cairn? Is it an honour or an insult?

Ascertain if stones are believed to grow or multiply. Is magic or curative virtue attributed to special stones? Are aerolites, belemnites, ammonites, or naturally " holed " stones reverenced or treasured? Are stone amulets carried? stone implements used in ritual? What precious or semi-precious stones are worn as jewels? Do they influence health or fortune? special stones in special ways? Do they act as oracles or talismans? What virtues are attributed to minerals (gold, silver, iron, salt), or to coral, amber, jet? Are they potent against witchcraft, illness, bad luck? How are they used?

Islands. Note any sacred islands, islands used as burial-places, rites performed on uninhabited islands, islands believed to be inhabited by superhuman beings.

Give any stories about phantom islands, sunken islands, islands inhabited only by women. Is the Land of the Dead believed to be an island?

Seas, Rivers, Lakes, Springs, etc. Note all ritual uses of water (drinking, bathing, purification, lustration of persons or things). Is it thought wrong to take payment for water? Has running water any special properties? Running in a particular direction? Must it be dipped up with or against the stream? Can ghosts, demons, witches, or criminals cross running water?

Note any practice of throwing particular objects overboard when crossing the water. Is the first fish caught returned to the water? Is it unlucky or forbidden to rescue a drowning person? Are ghosts " laid " under water? witches or scolds dipped in it? dead bodies or their ashes thrown into it? Stagnant or running water?

Note healing wells or springs, wishing wells, holy wells, wells which give children. Is the " life " of a well or spring thought to be an animal, or spirit in animal form, living in it? Note rites performed (for what purpose?), small objects or more valuable offerings left there, apparitions seen there ? shrines erected ? annual assemblies held ? Is rain-water collected in the hollow of a rock thought to have special properties ?

Give the native words for the sea, rivers, lakes, springs, etc., and proper names, if any, of any local rivers, etc. Are seas, lakes, rivers, cataracts, etc., regarded as personages or as places ? are any of them regarded as specially sacred ? Note any signs of fear or marks of reverence paid to them. Are they supposed to be inhabited by any superhuman beings ? Give particulars of their names, forms, and attributes, the occasions of their appearances, any reverence or worship paid to them ? stories connected with them ? Is there a sea-god ? a river-god ?

Give any stories of the origin of the sea, lakes, rivers, etc. the cause of the tides and waves, whirlpools, cataracts, rapids. Why is the sea salt ? Is the sea supposed to have existed before the earth ? What are its relations with the earth ? Give any legends of sunken cities, etc.

II. THE VEGETABLE WORLD, pp. 31-39.

Note native or dialectal names of Trees, Plants, Herbs, and Fruits, and identify them by their Latin names when possible.

Note Trees, Plants, Herbs, and Fruits, used for food or forbidden to be so used, with particulars of the prohibitions : poisonous and narcotic plants and their use ; medicinal plants and their use. Is there any sound knowledge of medicinal herbs ?

Note trees and plants used to make ordeal drinks, thought potent against lightning, credited with marvellous properties (as of drawing out iron nails, discovering springs, hidden treasure and lodes of ore, causing forgetfulness, insanity, invisibility, pregnancy) ; used in divination or other magical or religious rites, in initiation, marriage, or funeral ceremonies ; marriage of girls to trees ; practices of placing afterbirth or corpses in trees ; transference of evil to trees or plants.

Note kinds of wood used for rods, brooms, sticks, whips, amulets, talismans, sacred poles or posts, images, altars, or ritual implements of any kind, or forbidden to be so used ; practices of rubbing or touching wood, ritually switching girls or cattle, aspersing persons or things with sprinklers made of sprigs or boughs. What plants are used in each case ?

Note species of trees or plants forbidden to be cut down or injured, planted or transplanted, taken inside buildings ; ceremonies on felling trees ; kinds of wood used for fuel or forbidden to be so used, with the reasons given by the people themselves for the restriction ; individual sacred trees, sacred groves and sanctuary trees (how guarded ? what would be the result of

injuring them ?) ; ceremonies observed in groves, offerings made
to trees, rags, etc., hung on them, ceremonies or festivals celebrated under or beside them ; trees thought to be embodied
spirits or the abodes of spirits, reputed to be the " life-index "
of any person or community ; plants fabled to be connected with
childbirth, or thought to influence the produce of domestic
animals.

Note myths or legends about trees or plants, their origin,
forms, marking, or other peculiarities ; stories of haunted trees,
the birth of mankind from trees or plants, the transformation of
human beings into trees, the connection of special families, clans,
or individuals with special trees (name, reverence, reputed descent,
etc.). See *Totemism*, p. 308.

Obtain photographs or portions of unknown species for identification.

III. THE ANIMAL WORLD, pp. 40-46.

(*Beasts, Birds, Reptiles, Fishes, Insects.*)

Give the native or dialectal names or nicknames of different
species.

Note omens drawn from the sight, movements, or cries of
animals. On what occasions ?

Note domestic or semi-domesticated animals ; whether informed of family events ; ears and tails cropped, etc. (cf. ch. xiii.).

Note use of animals in medicine ; use of animal amulets (teeth,
fur, claws, horns, feathers, figures of animals) ; if for protection
or to bring luck ? horns or skulls set up on or inside houses ;
dances or other occasions when men dress as animals (wear
horns, fur, or feathers). By whom worn ? Try to get specimens.

Note any marvellous powers attributed to certain species of
animals, human or superhuman knowledge (*e.g.* perceiving spirits,
weather wisdom, medical knowledge, understanding of human
speech, etc.). Why do certain species migrate ?

Note any beliefs as to the social systems of particular species ;
as that they have a king, laws, etc. ; that they are human beings
" in their own country."

Note any persons having power over animals, understanding
their speech, curing their bites, etc. How acquired ? Over certain species or all ?

Note belief in possible transformation into animals, descent of
mankind, clans, classes, or families from animals, reincarnation
of departed souls as animals. If the animal dies, what happens
to the soul ?

Note animals used as food ; forbidden as food ; to everyone
or to certain persons or in particular circumstances ? usually

avoided but feasted on once a year. Animals forbidden to be
injured ; killed whenever seen ; the first seen of the species
killed ; killed once a year ; hunted once a year (wherever found,
or in a particular spot ?) ; ceremonially expelled once a year.
Give dates and other particulars of such ceremonies.

Note names of animals tabooed ; offerings made to animals.
On what occasions ?

Note signs of awe of animals, as distinct from physical fear.
Is laughing at them forbidden ?

Note animal sacrifices (give full details). When ; what kind
of animals, how and by whom slaughtered ; for what purpose ?
omens drawn from behaviour of victim ; previous treatment of
victim ; general treatment of species at other times ; what is
done with each part of the carcase ; who shares in the sacrifice ;
is it, or is it not, connected with any personal deity ? (cf. ch. vii.).

Note animal gods ; animals associated with particular gods ;
animals revered by special social groups, classes, or individuals ;
men ? women ? etc. (See *Totemism* below.) Animals kept in
temples, used in magical rites, associated with witchcraft.

Note any stories ascribing the creation of the earth or of mankind to animals ; myths of animals bringing fire, babies, souls,
etc., animal characters in folk-tales, fabulous animals ; myths
as to migration of species ; myths accounting for peculiarities
of certain species.

Totemism (pp. 41-43).

Give the names of the clans with the English equivalents as
far as can be ascertained. If the clans are associated with any
species of natural objects, plant, or animal (*Totem*), give the
generic name equivalent to totem. Give the names of the several
totems. Are these the same as the names of the clans ? Is
the totem, or part of it, used as a badge ? cut or tattooed on the
body ? carved or painted on posts or on personal property ?
Has the clan more than one totem ? If so, what is the cause,
actual or reputed, and what are the relative positions of the
several *associated* totems ? (See Appendix A, *Terminology*.)

(*a*) **Exogamy.** Is marriage or sexual intercourse allowed between men and women of the same totem and clan ? If the
latter, under what limitations or restrictions ? Do the same
rules hold good in the case of persons of different tribes but
having the same totem ? What would be the consequence of
offending against the marriage regulations ?

(*b*) **Consanguinity.** Do the clan think themselves related to
the totem ? descended from it ? Do they ever speak of it as

their grandfather, grandmother, etc. ? Do they claim or endeavour to resemble it, physically or mentally ? Have they
any legends about it ? Can they or could their ancestors transform themselves into its shape ? Do their souls migrate into
it after death ? How is the totem of an individual determined ?
By parentage (father's or mother's side ?) ; or circumstances of
birth ? Are children subject to the totemic tabus ?

(c) **Mutual relations.** What are the mutual relations between
the totem and the clan ? May the clansmen kill or injure their
totem ? or eat it ? What happens when the totem is a valuable
food-animal ? If a member of a fish totem catches his totem,
what does he do ? If a man of another clan should kill the
totem, how would the clansmen take it ? Do they lament over
a dead totem ? give it honourable burial ? Is the totem animal
ever kept in captivity, fed and petted, addressed by titles of
respect ? Has the head man of the clan any special office with
regard to the totem ? Does the totem befriend the clan, help
them in war or hunting ? Do the clansmen perform rites to
increase the supply of the totem ? Do they disguise themselves in the form of the totem in dances ?

How do husbands regard their wives' totems ? children their
parents' (not being their own), and *vice versa* ?

Are *sex-patrons* revered, or have any individuals *animal guardians* ? How acquired ? What are their relations to the totem ?

Enquire into all similar taboos and observances ; give a full
account of all rites, and give concrete examples whenever possible.

IV. HUMAN BEINGS, pp. 47-63.

(1st Edition : " Superstitions Generally.")

Human Life and Death. What is the accepted theory of the
origin of mankind ? Give any stories of the creation of mankind
as distinct from the rest of the universe. Note whether cannibalism is practised ; on whom ? friends, enemies, children, adults ?
When ? what parts are eaten ? what persons abstain ? Note
any trace of human sacrifice. How is the victim disposed of ?
How is murder regarded ? must it be expiated ? is vengeance
taken for it ? by whom ? Is there a distinction between murder
within and without the social group, or between murder and
manslaughter ? Head-hunting : is it practised ? with what
object ? if in revenge does it placate the *manes* of the dead ?
what is done with the heads ? Is bloodshed or contact with dead
bodies defiling ? what purification is necessary ? Infanticide :
is it practised ? with what motives and limitations ?

Names and Effigies. Note the system of personal nomenclature; when the name is given, by whom? how chosen? Is it ever changed? on what occasions? Are nicknames usual? Do people conceal their names? Have they one secret name and another for use? May the names of the dead be uttered? Are words in ordinary use changed to avoid mentioning names of certain persons; living or dead? Are women forbidden to pronounce men's names? or those of certain relatives? or relatives by marriage? *Vice versa?*

Is there any objection to having one's portrait taken? to seeing oneself in a mirror? Give particulars.

Note any ideas or observances connected with the shadow.

Special Innate Powers. Note whether any groups or individuals are credited with inborn occult powers: over the elements, witches, disease, the lower animals; prophetic or visionary powers; the power of the Evil Eye. (Has the colour of the eye anything to do with this?) Are such powers hereditary or personal? Are any such powers ascribed to kings or priests? Note all signs of veneration paid to particular persons or offices.

Abnormal persons. Note how lunatics are regarded; epileptics, idiots; twins, first-born children, others in order of birth? Detail any ceremonies or beliefs connected with twins. How are abnormal births regarded? (*e.g.* with teeth, with a caul, feet foremost, posthumous, etc.). How are personal peculiarities regarded? dwarfs, albinoes, red-haired, black-haired, beardless, squinting, blue-eyed, black-eyed, blear-eyed, one-eyed, blind, deaf, dumb, lame, flat-footed, left-handed, ambidextrous, humpbacked, pockmarked, persons? Are they lucky or unlucky? to themselves or others?

Outsiders. Observe how foreigners and strangers are regarded? Are they feared? despised? supposed to be wizards? credited with malformations? or reverenced as possibly superhuman? How is communication with strangers carried on? Is there a recognized code of gestures or signals? Is the " Silent Trade " known? How are neighbouring social groups regarded? Are they mocked at? nicknamed? credited with malformations? Are there any local Gotham stories?

Women. What is the division of labour between men and women? Do women bring good or bad luck? on what occasions? old, young, married, and unmarried alike? Are special prophetic or magical powers ascribed to women? Have the women a language peculiar to themselves? Note any rites (of

initiation or otherwise) at which women, or men, are forbidden
to be present. Do men ever avoid women ? all women ? their
wives ? certain relations ? relations by marriage ? On what
occasions ? Give particulars of the extent of the avoidance in
the several cases (cf. chs. xii. xiii.).

Food. Note whether the men and the women eat together ;
whether persons who eat together acknowledge a common bond ;
whether the " stranger at the board " is thereby secure from
injury ; for how long ? Whether any etiquette or order of precedence is observed in eating or drinking ; a loving-cup passed
round ? any ceremony performed before eating or drinking ?
whether omens are drawn from accidents at table ? Are any
persons or classes of persons forbidden to eat or drink together ?
Do any persons eat or drink alone ; object to be seen eating or
drinking ? What is done with the remains of the meals ? Are
certain kinds of food or drink, otherwise wholesome, abstained from
at certain times, or by certain persons ? What, when, by whom,
and for what reason ? (See *Totemism*, above.) Note whether
certain kinds of food or drink, not usually consumed, are partaken
of at certain times, or by certain persons. Give particulars. Are
any prohibitions or other observances confined to, or intensified
in the case of, certain persons (as chiefs, priests, medicine-men,
mourners) ? When is fasting resorted to ? and what effect is
it thought to have ? Should certain things be done or not done,
before breaking one's fast ? What is thought to be the consequence of accepting food from fairies, demons, the ghosts of the
dead, etc. ?

The Human Body. Note reverence paid to the head ; *e.g.*
forbidding to touch it, to pass over it, swearing by it (one's own
head or another's) ; use of skulls, bones, or other human remains,
in magic or medicine ; reverence shown to any other parts of
the body ; any trace of phallic worship. Is passing over another's
body or legs prohibited ? is it ever ritually performed ? on what
occasions ? What part of the body is regarded as the seat of
life ? Are there any beliefs or taboos as to the hands or fingers ?
Note magical or ritual use of hair-ropes ; observances as to cutting
the hair or nails ; what is done with the clippings ? with cast
teeth, amputated limbs, bones accidentally discovered, human
excreta ? Are locks of hair, teeth, or impressions of teeth, used
to authenticate messages ? Must one avoid spilling blood upon
the ground ? Why ? Is there something more impalpable
than blood—a sort of vapour or essence arising from it which has
a power of its own and clings to the spot where anyone has been
killed ? How is the blood of sacrificial victims disposed of ? Is

blood-letting practised, ritually or medically ? with what ceremonies, on what occasions ? What is the consequence of accidental bloodshed ? Note whether " blood-brotherhood" is
practised (by transfusion, swallowing, or swearing ?), and what
privileges or disabilities it confers ; how it affects the relations of
the parties with each others' kindred or enemies ; whether blood-
feuds are customary, and how ended ; give particulars of any
existing feud. Note all uses of saliva ; in magic, medicine, exorcism, blessing, bargaining, etc. (must it be " fasting spittle ? ") ;
any beliefs or sayings about sneezing, yawning, whistling, or
kissing ; omens drawn from moles, birth-marks, spots on nails,
itching of the nose, right or left ear, hand, foot, etc.

Marks and Mutilations. Note any mutilations practised (circumcision, filing or knocking out teeth, cutting off a finger-joint,
boring the ears, nostrils or lips). When are these done ? by
whom performed ? with what ceremonies ? for what alleged
reason ? what is done with the severed parts (see chap. xii.) ?
Note any marks made on the body (tattooing, scarifying), on
what parts ? of which sex ? when made, by whom, and why ?
Are the patterns tribal or individual ? Give photographs or
drawings if possible. Note whether the body is ever painted,
daubed with moist earth, whitened, or blackened ; what parts,
what colours, when, and why ? Note any austerities practised—
fasting ? self-torture ? (as of the Indian fakirs). By whom
and when ? Are they supposed to increase magical power or
sanctity ?

Clothing. Note what clothing is usually worn ; what changes
of costume or hairdressing are made on reaching manhood or
womanhood, on marriage, parentage, mourning, etc. ; whether
any article of clothing or personal ornament is never taken off ;
whether amulets are worn and for what purpose (cf. chs. ix.
x.) ; whether rings, bracelets, or necklaces are worn for ceremonial, magical or medicinal purposes ; whether crowns, wreaths,
girdles, or caps of office are ceremonially worn, when and by
whom ? Note any observances, ceremonies, or omens connected
with headgear or footgear, with girdles, garters, veils ; things
to be said or done on putting on any article of clothing for the
first time ; omens drawn from accidents in dressing ; practices
of reversing articles of clothing. Are men ever dressed as women
or women as men, little boys as girls or girls as boys ? when
and why ? Are there any games or festivals at which men
and women exchange clothing ? Can men's garments protect
women from harm, or women's men ? (In New Guinea a woman
can save a wounded warrior by throwing her petticoat over him.)

Are men's garments used to facilitate childbirth ? Are there any rites in which nudity is required, or dancing barefoot ?

V. THINGS MADE BY MAN, pp. 64-74.

(1*st Edition* : " *Superstitions Generally.*")

The Dwelling and its Contents. Note how the site of the building is chosen, ceremonies performed ; who erects it (the owner and his household, friends and neighbours, professional workmen ?) ; things done on laying the foundation (things buried under it or under the threshold), on raising the ridgepole, covering in the roof, completing the chimney (if any), kindling the first fire on the hearth ; ceremonies on entering into possession ; "first foot," fumigations, blessings, talismans, feasts. Does building a house entail a death ? whose death ? Is a house ever pulled down when a death has taken place in it ? If this is customary, how are exceptions made possible ? When pulling down a house, must a portion be left standing ? what for ?

Note whether any part of the dwelling is considered specially sacred, whether there is anything on which the *luck* of the dwelling specially depends. How can the luck be taken away ? In which direction should the house be swept and what should the broom be made of ? Is the threshold or the doorway the scene of any cult or ceremony ? is it adorned with boughs or flowers or guarded by amulets ? What parts of the house are assigned to men, women, parents, children, or guests respectively ?

The Hearth. Observe whether the hearth is the object of any cult or ceremony. Who tends the hearth-fire ? Is it kept always burning ? What happens if it goes out accidentally ? Is it ever purposely extinguished and re-kindled ? when and how ? Is it unlucky to give fire or light ? Always or when ? Are ashes used for divination ; omens drawn from the way the fire burns ? Is there a household familiar ? is the hearth his abode ? what are his habits ? is food left for him ?

The Furniture. What part of the household goods is provided by the husband, and what by the wife ? Is a special place or position assigned to any part of the furniture, *e.g.* the bed ? Note beliefs, observances, or prohibitions, connected with ladders, staircases, windows, mirrors, lamps, candles, clocks, books, brooms, sieves, shears, cooking vessels, knives, pins, other tools or implements. (The crook or chain on which the pot hangs over the fire is in many countries intimately connected with the most important events of family and domestic life.) Are omens drawn from accidents, breakages, misplacing of tools or utensils or the like ?

Cookery and other Household Work. Note all observances connected with grinding, baking, and cooking ; [1] by whom the work is done ; whether indoors or out-of-doors ; charms repeated or other precautions taken against witchcraft : omens drawn from the progress or appearance of the work. Note use of alcoholic drinks ; from what they are made ; by whom and how prepared ; with what precautions, etc. ; observances in drinking.

Note days when particular kinds of household work (*e.g.* washing) are forbidden, (cf. p. 340). See *Churning*, p. 337 ; *Handicrafts*, p. 339.

Manufacture of Magico-religious Objects. Observe what talismans or sacred objects are displayed or magical or other figures drawn, in the dwelling or elsewhere. Are the objects natural or artificial ? How are they obtained ? Who makes them ? How ? Are old or new materials preferred for them ? Is purity of substances used important ? What gives them their mystic power ? What special influence is attributed to them ?

N.B.—It is impossible to give hints as to inquiry into secret treasures : household, village, or tribal. The observer must keep his eyes and ears open, and only venture a remark or a question on what he sees when he feels sure it will not be resented as a liberty. It may even be years before he succeeds in being taken into confidence. Some such objects, however, are displayed openly ; *e.g.* the favourite British horseshoe. (How must this be procured ? Is it hung heels upwards or downwards ?)

VI. THE SOUL AND ANOTHER LIFE, pp. 74-89.

Ascertain the words for *breath, shadow, reflection* (in a mirror or in water) : for *soul, life, spirit.* Is the word for image or reflection the same as that for soul ? If not, carefully distinguish between them.

What is thought to leave a man's body at death ? What becomes of it ? What is it like ? Has a man more than one ? What are they respectively called ? What becomes of them after death ? Can (——) leave his body during life, and return ? What could hinder its return ? Have animals, plants, other

---

[1] Inchi Sawal, a noted Guru of Kuching, made a preserve of half-ripe oranges for the Ranee of Sarawak : " A good deal of religion was mixed up with the cooking of those small bobbing green balls as they simmered in the boiling syrup. A number of invocations to Allah secured a good result to his labours . . . a grave religious aspect seemed *de rigueur* as he leant over the pot." *My Life in Sarawak,* p. 161.

things, also got —— (supply the native word) ? Note any show of scruple to awaken a sleeping man and enquire into it. Enquire as to dreams : what are they ? whence do they come ? who sends them and for what purpose ? What are shadows or reflections supposed to be ? What would happen to a man if his shadow were to leave him ?

When the (——) leaves a man's body at death, where does it go ? Does it stay there, or go somewhere else after a time ? Is it ever seen again ? In what form ?

If possible, be present at a funeral, and from observing, and ascertaining the reasons of, the mode of disposing of the body, try to ascertain what is thought to become of the (——) ; whether it is reborn in this world, as animal or human being ; if it goes to another. Where is that other, and how does the (——) get there ? Does the completion of the funeral rites affect the character or condition of the dead ? Has anyone ever visited the Land of the Dead ? what were his adventures ? Do the souls ever return from the Land of the Dead ? Are they feared or welcomed ? honoured, feasted ? Periodically ? Is prayer made to them ? sacrifices or offerings given to them ? To the souls generally or to individuals ? Do they take part in domestic or communal events ? share in festivals ? Is the cult of the dead a communal worship, or special to a Society, or confined to the descendants of the deceased ? Are the remote ancestors or the recently dead chiefly venerated ? Do they become the guardian genii of the family ? warn them of coming evil, etc. ?

Relate any stories of ghosts, wraiths, double-gangers, apparitions, spectres or spectral appearances (*e.g.* phantom funerals). Note the reasons why ghosts return, the form in which they appear, the places they haunt, the method of exorcising or " laying " them ; by whom performed ? Are they dangerous to survivors generally, or only to particular persons or in special circumstances ? Are women specially dangerous ? women dying in childbirth, unmarried women ? To whom ? How may ghosts be guarded against ? Is it thought safe to speak to a ghost ? is there anything peculiar in a ghost's mode of speech ? What should be done on seeing one ? Have any individual persons or animals special powers of seeing them ? Is there any mode of summoning them to appear ? What will cause them to vanish ?

Do belief in re-incarnation and belief in a Land of the Dead occur together ? Observe birth-rites in connection with reincarnation.

N.B.—European ghost-stories often resemble the stories of old pagan deities, and so may have been derived in the first place from that source and not have been originally stories of ghosts.

But it is best to set them down as what they are *now* accounted to be, and not to attempt to assign each to its origin. Whenever there is a *living belief* that a certain spectre or apparition of the dead may be seen any day (or night), it should be recorded as one of belief in " another life."

VII. SUPERHUMAN BEINGS, pp. 90-123.

(1st *Edition* : " *Goblindom.*")

Names. Give the generic term for god or deity, state what deities are recognised and what are their personal names, with the meanings if possible. May their names be spoken ? Have they secret names in addition to the ordinary ones ?

Form. Note what is their supposed form, human or animal, beautiful or monstrous, male or female ? Are they inanimate objects ? Are there any pairs of gods or goddesses, husband and wife, brother and sister, or twin brethren ?

Abodes. Where do they live ? How do they occupy themselves ? Do they ever appear to man ?

Means of Communication. How can they be communicated with ? by signals, actions, sounds, speech, or song ? What persons know how to communicate with them ? Note by what titles they are addressed, and compare these with modes of address used to human beings. How do they make known their wishes, their satisfaction or dissatisfaction ?

Powers. What are their powers ? Did they or any of them create the earth or mankind ? Do they still exist ? how is their existence known to man ? are they ever seen ? can they be present in several places at once ? Are they kindly or malicious ?

Functions. What are their several functions and spheres of action ? Are they connected with the elements, the heavenly bodies, or the forces of nature ? Are they limited to certain places or persons, groups of persons, particular spheres of nature or of life ? Can they be offended ? if so, by what acts ? Have they any restraining influence on conduct ?

Worship. How are they worshipped ? Are oaths taken by them ? are they consulted ? enquired of ? How ? Are any gods known but not worshipped ? Are the gods of other nations recognised as real and powerful ?

Prayer. Is prayer offered to the gods ? for what benefits, material or moral ? Is it common or individual prayer ? Are forms of prayer used, extempore prayer, ejaculations, responses, unintelligible formulas or syllables ? Are the prayers sung or said ? are there any rites of praise and thanksgiving ?

Sacrifice. Is sacrifice offered ? human, animal, firstfruits, portions of food ? How are vegetable or other food-offerings disposed of ? What is the object of the sacrifice ? To whom was it offered ? is it a gift with a view to benefits in return, payment of dues, propitiation of unfriendly beings, communion with the god, fulfilment of vows ? Describe in detail any sacrificial rite witnessed ; note the scene of the rite, who attended it, what implements were used. Was any preliminary purification necessary ? fasting, bathing, fumigation, brushing, sweeping, aspersion, or washing ? What was the victim offered ? how was it selected, how previously treated, what points were necessary qualifications ? is the species commonly used for food ? How was it slaughtered ? by whom, with what ceremonies ? was there any altar ? by whom was it made ? of what ? How was the carcase divided and disposed of ? the head, blood, entrails, flesh, and bones ? what was the god's portion, and how was it supposed to be conveyed to him ? What was the priest's portion, and what the worshippers' ? Was prayer offered ? by whom, to what effect ? Give the words if possible. Were libations made ? was incense used or any fragrant smoke ? were omens observed or rites of divination performed ? How ? (see next chapter). What was the demeanour of the worshippers ? Note any other details you observed. Are the creatures used for sacrifice held sacred at other times ? What would be the ordinary consequence of killing and eating one ? Who would enforce the penalty, if any ? Are they sacred to any particular god ? Have they themselves any divine character ? Does any direct benefit accrue to the worshippers from the actual partaking of the sacrifice ? Was the rite in question a definite offering to a personal god (so far as you can ascertain), or was it rather a solemn ritual feast without reference to any special deity ?

Priests. Is there a priesthood ? is it hereditary ? if not, how is it recruited ? what are the necessary qualifications for the office ? how is the priest trained, instructed, initiated, consecrated ? What privileges has he ? to what prohibitions is he subjected ? what purificatory or other rites must he observe ? what are his priestly garments or insignia, his dues or emoluments, his duties (divination, exorcism, blessing, cursing) ? What part does he take in sacrificial rites ? What sacred objects or ritual secrets are committed to his charge ? Does he administer ordeals ? oaths ? receive and release from vows ? is he subject to " possession " by his god ?

Temples. What places are held specially sacred ? Are there temples ? What decides the site of a temple or shrine ? by whom are they erected or repaired ? What rites are performed in building a temple ? do they differ from those used for an ordinary house ? What is kept in the temple or shrine, or near it ? images, emblems, relics, votive offerings, sacred birds, beasts, or reptiles ?

Idols. Are idols known ? what are they made of ? who makes them ? Is their shape human ? partly or wholly ? What makes an image into an idol ? any ceremony ? Is the idol (i) the embodiment, or (ii) the abode of the god ? occasional or permanent ? or does the idol *become* the god ? Are images credited with powers of consuming food, giving oracles, speaking, nodding, or moving in any way ? are any stories told of such things ? of wonder-working images ? or accounting for the attitudes or characteristics of images ? stories of images being found, falling from heaven, arriving by sea or the like ? What reverence is paid to images or idols ? are they ever beaten or maltreated ? Are they, or other sacred objects, exhibited, carried in processions ? when, how often, and for what purpose ? Are pilgrimages made to tombs, wells, or shrines ? Give particulars.

Festivals. What festivals are observed ? with what rites ? fire ceremonies, water ceremonies, tree and plant ceremonies ? Give full details. Are public fasts, or penitential or rest-days observed ? periodically or on special occasions ? (See chap. xiv. p. 339.)

Dances. Is dancing a religious exercise ? is it connected with " possession " ? Who takes part in it ? Is it performed by special companies or secret societies ? on what occasions ? Are the dancers masked or disguised ? Is the performance dramatic ? What does it represent ? What is the object of it ? Describe it in detail. (Cf. ch. xv. p. 341.)

Mysteries. Are any austerities practised ? fasting, celibacy, solitude or self-tortures of any kind ? Are there any " mysteries " or secret rites of worship ? where are they held ? who may be initiated into them ? State anything that can be ascertained about them.

Special and Individual Cults. Do the several social groups— the caste, the clan, the family—practise special cults apart from the general community ? What, where, and how ? Is there a fire-god, a household familiar, or a hearth-cult ? Detail the rites. Has each individual his guardian genius or patron saint ? how are these chosen, and how honoured ? To whom or what is appeal made in moments of distress or emergency ?

Deified Men. Are any deceased human beings worshipped or venerated ? (1) Ancestors, (a) the founder of the tribe or family ; (b) the recently deceased. (2) Saints or heroes. (3) Restless and malicious ghosts. Give particulars of the rites and legends.

Demons. What kinds of malignant or hostile demons (not being ghosts) are recognised ? In what forms do they appear ? is their form constant or can they vary it at pleasure ? how do they act ? how are they guarded against or propitiated ? Is there any belief in *incubi* or *succubi* ? what persons are specially subject to their attacks ? Any belief in demons who cause nightmares—how can they be caught ? demons who devour dead bodies—what can be done to banish them ? demons who haunt solitary or uncanny places—in what form or forms do they appear, and how must they be treated if encountered ? Can any demons be compelled to the service of men (wizards) ? (Cf. ch. ix.) Do men or women enter the service of demons ? On what terms ?

Female Demons. Are there any races of female demons ? what is their origin ? are they beautiful or hideous ? do they wander about, or haunt special places ? are they dangerous ? how should they be treated if encountered ?

The Elfin World. Is there any belief in the Elfin World, or in a race or community of anthropomorphic, but not human, yet not divine, beings, generally invisible but sometimes seen ? terrestrial or subterranean beings ? Where do they dwell ? is the way to their abode known ? has anyone visited it ? what were his or her adventures ? What are the appearance and stature of the elves or goblins ? what is their character and disposition ? are they fond of music and dancing ? Do they love, marry, keep house, bear children, as do human beings ? Do they ever love and intermarry with human beings ? what is the consequence of such marriages ? Do they steal human beings ; infants, women in childbirth ? Are they generally on good terms with mankind ? Do they borrow human implements, or lend them ? have human beings ever rendered them assistance or service ? are they grateful ? Is it safe to accept food or other gifts from them ? Are they rich ? What are their habits and occupations ? Do they avoid special objects, materials or words ?

have they special names for any objects ? Do they use special implements ? Do they frequent pre-historic grave-mounds or other ancient remains ? Do they hate the dominant religion of the country ? Have they souls ? are they mortal ? How is their origin accounted for ?

Spectres. Is there any belief in an ancestral spectre who appears to give warning of death ? any legend of a vanished hero who is still living and will one day return ? of a spectral huntsman and hounds seen riding through the air ? or of a beautiful female spectre, with or without a train of attendants, wandering about the country ? Are there any stories of spectral fights, spectral ships, spectral funerals, spectral lights, or any other apparitions not already mentioned ?

VIII. OMENS AND DIVINATION, pp. 124-133.

(1st Edition : " *Magic and Divination.*")

Note all omens from the sight, appearance or movements of beasts, birds, reptiles, insects, persons, the heavenly bodies, etc., *and record them under those several headings.*

State on what occasions Omens are particularly observed, and for what purposes—public or private, legal, medical, religious or other—Divination is resorted to ; what particular times or seasons are thought especially suitable for divination ; what colours or numbers are reckoned lucky or unlucky ? Is the *first* occurrence of any act or event specially ominous ?

By whom are rites of Divination performed ? by the persons interested, by priests or others connected with the religious system of the community, by specially-gifted seers, or by professional experts ? Are they performed publicly or secretly ? reckoned holy or unholy ?

What methods are used and what implements ? Describe them if possible minutely. Are there rules of augury, or are the methods automatic ? Is any form of words used ? If so, try to obtain it. Does the same diviner use several methods, or does each man confine himself to one only ? (See list of methods, p. 133.)

Are any Oracles consulted ? if so, with what rites and in connection with what Powers or what worship ?

IX. THE MAGIC ART, pp. 134-151.

(*Sorcery, Witchcraft, and Charming.*)

Give the generic names for wizard, witch, charmer, etc. Mention any famous individuals you can hear of. Is the wizard a public

functionary or an independent practitioner individually resorted
to ? on what occasions and for what purposes ? Is he rewarded
or ill-treated according to his success or failure ? Does he work
for good or for evil or for both ? if for evil, is the *désorcheleur*
(Channel Islands) or charmer resorted to, to counteract his doings ?
Are the *sorcheleur* and *désorcheleur* distinct personages or not ?
are they male or female or of both sexes ? How does a man or
woman become a wizard (sorcerer, witch, or charmer) ? by
inheritance, austerities, initiation, instruction, transmission ?
Is there any connection between magical and political power ?

What are the powers of the wizards ? Are they general, or
limited to particular spheres, as the weather, or disease ? Do
the wizards prophesy, divine, exorcise, work evil, or counteract
evil ? Can they transform themselves ? into what shapes ?
Can they become invisible, transport themselves through the
air, travel long distances in a moment of time, control the weather,
raise storms, cause earthquakes ? Have they compelling power
over spirits and demons, over diseases ? Have they familiars,
in animal form or otherwise ? what animals are associated with
them ? Do they abduct men's souls, cause insanity, transform
men into beasts ? Do they avenge injuries or affronts offered
them, cause illness (especially in children), check the bodily
powers and functions, injure domestic animals, steal the milk
of cattle ? Is their power constant or intermittent ? do they
act individually or in concert ? do they form a " craft " or
fraternity, hold secret assemblies, meetings with demons ? Do
they belong to the community or tribe ? If not, are they members
of some more or less inferior and outcast body (like the Gypsies).
Are the wizards of any particular district or people supposed to
be specially powerful ? Does the sorcerer believe in his own
sorcery ? How are witches recognized ? By what ordeals are
they tested ? How are they treated when discovered ?

Magical Rites. Note *what, when, where, how,* and *what for* in
each case. Was the rite described public or secret ? what was
its object or purpose ? Note the *dress and apparatus* of the
wizard, or principal performer, and his assistants ; feathers,
claws, amulets, etc., rod, staff, drum, bell, rattle; broom,
sieve, shears, cauldron, etc. ; the *preparations* for the rite ; whether
ceremonial purity is insisted on and in what it consists ; purify-
ing ceremonies, taking omens, fumigations, drawing the magic
circle, etc., precautions taken for the safety of the wizard ; the
actions of the wizard (as symbolic tying of knots, etc.) ; the use
of *gestures* (*e.g.* dancing) ; protective gestures, as the " horns,"
the cross, etc. ; the use of *sounds,* singing, muttering, ventriloquism, mechanical and musical sounds ; the use of *names, words,*

and *formulas* (obtain all these if possible) ; the *materials* used, as iron, salt, blood, parts of human bodies, animal or vegetable matter, fire ; the *colours, numbers,* and *odours* used. What would be the result to the wizard of any mistake in the ritual ? Were spirits supposed to be raised or not ? was their assistance procured ? were they banished ? was any person or thing exorcised ?

Record any instances of the leading forms of magic arts ; such as tying and loosening knots, making and injuring figures and representations of persons to be injured ; sticking pins or thorns into any object ; boiling iron nails with animals' hearts, etc. ; causing or removing sickness or plagues of vermin by incantations ; "medicining," or charming, natural objects to convey hurt or help to those who touch them ; magically treating human hair, nail-clippings, remains of food, to affect the owner sympathetically. Make every effort to obtain the words of magical formulas, whether spells or charms. What is supposed to be the effect of *counting* ?

Record magical practices for killing or injuring enemies, blighting crops, injuring domestic animals, injuring other peoples' property ; practices used by thieves, *e.g.* to make themselves invisible, to cause others to sleep, to distract their attention ; examples of talismans carried, or magical ceremonies or actions used in ordinary life, to bring luck ; *e.g.* to bring prosperity generally, to bring luck in games or sports, success in journeys or business enterprises, to gain customers, to obtain the favour of the great, to win the affections of the other sex, to preserve beauty, chastity, conjugal fidelity. Is expert aid required in such cases ?

Record examples of ceremonies, actions, gestures, formulas, or amulets used to avert evil ; *e.g.* to protect houses, animals, crops, other property, from witchcraft, fire, the elements, or any accident ; to protect travellers, women in pregnancy or childbirth, infants and young children, from accidents, enemies, or superhuman beings ; movable property from theft ; roads, boats, bridges, etc., from accident or injury. Is expert aid required ?

Amulets. Note what natural objects are worn as amulets or talismans ? Are they animal, vegetable or mineral ? Are they whole objects or parts of larger ones (shells, teeth, claws, seeds, etc.). Do they owe their virtue to their rarity, shape, colour, or what ? Are holed stones worn ? bezoar stones ? stones or substances found in the bodies of animals ? precious or semi-precious stones or gems ; beads, etc., made of coral, amber, jet, crystal, mother-of-pearl ? What artificial objects are worn, what are they made of ? what do they represent ?

From whom are the amulets obtained ? must they be given by persons of the opposite sex ? may they be purchased ?

Is the virtue of the amulets innate? or how is it imparted?
How may it be lost? and how renewed? Is there a special
virtue in things stolen? or found accidentally? is there any
virtue in special ornamental patterns? With what object are
the talismans or amulets worn; for protection, cure, or luck?
How are they worn, openly or concealed? Do they change their
appearance to give warning of evil? Are written charms worn?
on what are they written? are they kept in cases? are they
worn openly or secretly? are the words kept secret? are they
taken from books? are regular charm-books in use, either published ones, or manuscript compilations, such as, perhaps, have
been handed down from one wizard to another?

Are protective figures (*e.g.* the cross, swastika, pentacle, magic
square, open hand, etc.) drawn on walls, doors, lintels, etc., or
otherwise used?

X. DISEASE AND LEECHCRAFT, pp. 152-158.

Nature and Cause of Disease. Is disease personified, thought
to afflict victims by its own volition? If not, how is it caused?
by breach of taboo, by an offended deity, displeasure of the
dead, by demon or evil spirit inside or outside the body, absence
of the sufferer's soul, sorcery (cf. pp. 77, 145) or other causes? Is
any disease regarded as a mark of divine favour? How are
insanity and idiotcy regarded? is any attempt made to cure
them? Is death ever supposed to occur from natural causes?
If the cause of the disease be doubtful, what steps are taken to
ascertain it? is a professional diviner called in? if so, does he
also treat the disease?

The Leech. What persons have power over disease? how
are their powers acquired? by inheritance; by circumstances
of birth (*e.g.* a seventh son, a " left " or surviving twin, England);
by voluntary action (*e.g.* riding a piebald horse, marrying one
of the same name, England; eating eagle's flesh, North Wales;
having a certain kind of caterpillar die in your hand, Hebrides);
by transference or bequest, by possession of talismans, by professional skill, either in exorcism or medicine? What are the limitations of their powers? over certain diseases only, at certain times
only, over patients of one sex only? May they take payment?

Methods of the Leech. Describe the proceedings of the diviner
or medicine-man in detail (cf. pp. 153, 154). Has he an assistant?
does he require a fee, does he use ordinary household tools or
implements kept specially for the purpose? Are the whole
household or family treated as well as the patient?

Cures. Describe any cures by (*a*) exorcism, or by musical or other sounds, (*b*) by transference of the disease to some other body, animate or inanimate, (*c*) mock-birth (creeping through holes, clefts in rocks, etc.), mock-burial and resurrection, change of name, etc. ; any cures by sympathy ; " salving the weapon and not the wound," or bringing the affected part into contact with some decaying, dying, or dead substance ; cures by sacrifice to, or invocation of, gods or saints, application of sacred relics to the part affected, visits to sacred shrines or holy wells ; cures by charms, spoken or written (is secrecy enjoined ?) ; or by amulets or rings (see p. 149 ; how are they made and procured ?) ; cures by administration of drugs, is any formula repeated over them ? do they involve the principle that " like cures like," or otherwise ?

Materia Medica. What plants are used in folk-medicine ? what is their appearance, and have they any real medicinal qualities ? What animal or mineral substances are used ? How are the *materia medica* procured ? with what ceremonies, and at what times and seasons ? Should they be stolen ? How are the drugs administered, when, how often ? Is fasting prescribed ?

Other Conditions. Note the use of *colours* and *numbers* in folk-medicine ; the influence attributed to the sun, moon, stars, rainbow, tide, season of year, on disease ; the influence attributed to the sex, status, or person, of patient or doctor ; *e.g.* are different drugs administered to men and women ? may medical knowledge be communicated by men to men, or women to women ? Are salves, unguents, plasters, poultices, baths, blood-letting, cauteries, in use ? is painting or tattooing the body, piercing the ears, etc., considered prophylactic ? What remedies may be administered without professional aid ? Note any signs of observation, experiment, reasoning from evidence, in medical practice. Are any restrictions placed on diet during illness or after recovery ? other restrictions ? Are any rites of purification observed on recovery from illness ? Are the sick waited on, visited, or avoided ; placed in special houses, or allowed to remain at home ? How are the aged or incurable treated ? if abandoned, are any special ceremonies performed ? (cf. ch. xii.).

XI. SOCIAL AND POLITICAL INSTITUTIONS, pp. 161-192.

(1st *Edition* : " *Local Customs.*")

Begin by making a rough plan of the village or settlement, showing every dwelling, and ascertain to what clan (etc.) each householder belongs (and what totems he owns). Later, you can identify the individual householders and proceed by the genealogical method (see p. 168).

Social groups. Ascertain into what social groups the people are divided. Give the generic and proper names of each group with the meanings if possible. Ascertain what is the mutual tie that holds each group together ; a common name ? (supposed) common descent ? reverence for a (supposed) common ancestor or other object of worship ? residence in a common locality ? or ties of blood genealogically proven ? Note whether the groups are totemic, that is to say, are they associated with some species of animal, plant, or other natural object ? (See *Totemism*, pp. 41-43.) Note whether the several groups have special functions to perform for the welfare of the community ; whether they practise special arts and crafts ; if so, do they keep their methods secret ? Are the groups recruited by adoption ? if so, who may be adopted, when, and by whom ? Is a lengthened term of residence necessary, and a formal ceremony ? or does intermarriage suffice to give the stranger rights in the group ?

Slavery. Note whether slavery is practised, domestic or communal. How are the ranks of the slaves recruited (as by capture in war, by inability to pay debts, by purchase) ? What is the status of the children of a freeman, or freewoman, and a slave ? Have the slaves any special duties to perform in public functions, especially in magico-religious rites ? Are slaves owned by any superhuman powers or by temples ?

Marriage System. Is group-marriage known ? (See *Terminology*, p. 297) ; or, on the contrary, is marriage permitted only to one member of each group (*rare*) ? Is the marriage system one of endogamy or exogamy, with regard to (*a*) the caste, (*b*) the clan, (*c*) the family, (*d*) the village or district. If exogamy rules, are certain groups allotted to each other, or is choice free ? Is polygamy customary, if so, in what form ? polygyny (many wives), or polyandry (many husbands) ? In this case, must a woman's husbands or a man's wives belong to one particular group or family, or are they selected promiscuously ? If polygyny rules, do the wives live separately or together ? Does the husband take up his abode with each in turn ? Are they regarded as of equal status ? If not, how is the principal wife chosen or distinguished ? What is the position of the supplementary wives and of their children ? Are concubines recognized ? and may the women correspondingly have *cicisbei* ? or do they in fact, though not openly ? Note any prohibited degrees of marriage, any relations-in-law (or blood-relations) with whom intercourse is forbidden, or towards whom any sort of reserve is practised.

Give particulars. Are any marriages compulsory or recommended ? such as with a brother's widow (called the Levirate), or between " cross-cousins." Is a woman obliged to marry into a rank above her own (hypergamy) ? If certain matches are reckoned the " best," does the bride-price or the dowry differ from that paid in other cases ?

State whether (1) the husband leaves his own social group, temporarily or permanently, to reside with that of his wife, or *vice versa* ?

Note whether (2) descent is reckoned in the male or female line, or in both ; whether children belong to their mother's social or local group or their father's.

Note whether (3) the authority over the family or kindred is exercised by the father, or eldest male member ; by the mother, her brother or maternal uncle, or her relations generally.

What special duties or privileges belong to collateral relatives ? (*e.g.* the mother's brother, father's sister, sister's son, or brother's daughter).

What is the position of widows ? Do they belong to the deceased husband's group, or return to their own ? may they re-marry ? if they may, is it by different ceremony, and how does the ceremony differ from that of a first marriage ? what becomes of their dowry ? of their children by either husband ?

Property and Inheritance. Note what kinds of property belong to the men, and what to the women ; who inherits a woman's property, and who a man's ; whether individuals can leave their goods as they please ; if the children inherit, whether they take equal shares, or whether the firstborn or lastborn has special claims ; whether sons and daughters share alike ; whether the family property is divided on the death of the head, or held in common. Give details of the rules of inheritance as far as possible.

Land. To whom does the land belong ? to the tribe, to the community, to the family, or to individuals ? How is the right to occupation determined ? and what is the consequence of ceasing to occupy or cultivate ? Does ownership of the land also carry with it ownership of the crops (*e.g.* fruit-trees), and *vice versa* ? Can a man or a community part with land ? Where a supreme chief exists, note what are the respective rights of the chief and of the people in the land, cultivated and uncultivated (cf. *A. N. & Q.* p. 168).

> *N.B.*—(A right understanding of the native laws of property is of the first importance in countries where white men govern or have settled among coloured races.)

Contracts. Note how contracts are made and enforced, between master and servant, owner and tenant, buyer and seller; what pledges are given, and what penalties exacted for a breach of agreement, etc. (cf. ch. xii. p. 193).

Authority. Ascertain who is responsible for the maintenance of law and order; who takes cognizance of breaches of law and custom; who decides questions of (*e.g.*) war and peace, of holding assemblies or other public functions. Note whether there is any assembly of elders or of the whole community, how summoned and constituted; when does it meet, and where, with what ceremonies? Must its decisions be unanimous? how are they enforced? is there a separate organization for war and peace?

Law and Justice. Ascertain what offences are major, and what minor crimes? Which are offences against the individual and which against the community? What punishments are inflicted in each case? Is murder a matter for private revenge, or a question for public justice? If so, is the *lex talionis*, blood for blood, enforced, or is a fine (*blód wite*) imposed? Who sees to the enforcement of the penalty? What is the judicial procedure? the ceremonial of a court of justice? are oaths taken (by what?), ordeals submitted to, oracles consulted? Give details. How is the verdict arrived at and how is the judgment enforced?

Sanctuary. What places or persons have the right of sanctuary? churches, temples, shrines, desert spots, stables, women or women's apartments, guests? All such, or individuals only? Does the refuge protect against the law or only against private foes?

Kings and Chiefs. Ascertain what are the powers and duties of the chief or king, and how his political powers are limited; whether he is expected to control the weather, held responsible for any failure in the crops, or other public misfortune, supposed to possess special powers of healing or of divination. Does he officiate in the public magico-religious rites? Is the chief's office hereditary? if not, how is he chosen? Observe with what ceremonies he is installed in his office; what are the insignia of his office; have the insignia any special powers?

What physical disabilities disqualify a man from being king? Is the king or chief subject to any special prohibitions? State them. Who would be injured by any breach of them? the king, the offender (who saw him eat, partook of his food, etc.), or the commonwealth? Does the king reign for life or only for a fixed term ?   Is he got rid of at the end of the term, or when his physical powers fail ? if so, how ?

Societies (p. 183).   Is there a bachelors' house ? does it serve as a guest-house ? is it the scene of any special rites ? is it the resort of all the men of the community or of certain societies only ? Have the societies (if any) any other rendezvous ?   Who may belong to these societies ? what is their object or purpose ? do they include different grades or ranks ?   Is membership voluntary ?   Are they secret as regards the members (*i.e.* is it known who belongs to them ?) or only as regards the proceedings at the meetings ? are the performances public ?   Are they connected with the ghosts of the dead ?

Social Life, Regulation of. What is the code of manners practised ? and what rules are observed in greeting equals, saluting, or receiving superiors or inferiors, giving and receiving presents, method of conducting interviews, duration of interviews.

What are the local rules of hospitality ? does it include lending of wife (or other woman) ?   Is the person of a guest sacred ? for how long ? how long is hospitality incumbent on the host ? What rules are observed in the sending of messages from one tribe to another ? in the reception of embassies ?

What ceremonies are observed on setting out on a journey ? on arriving in a strange country or district ? on leaving it ? on returning home ?

What ceremonies are observed in buying and selling ? making known the goods offered ? the price asked or offered, the conclusion of the bargain, the receipt of the payment, taking possession of the property, etc.   (See *ante, Contracts*, p. 327, and ch. xiii. pp. 335-337, for ceremonial of travel.)

The Village Community in England (p. 188).

Ascertain the position of the ancient Common Fields (arable) ; the common pastures (" Dolemoors," " Lammas lands," and the like), and their situation with regard to the village.   Note the course of old roads, lanes, and paths ; the relative positions of the church and the manor-house ; the sites of the mill and the smithy ; of houses known as the Lodge, the Park, the Grange, or the Dairy House ; names of fields indicating obsolete crops or customs—*e.g.* the Hempbutt, the Herdsman's Croft ; and any other points discoverable from old maps or Enclosure Acts. Enquire for Manor Court Rolls and Churchwardens' Accounts, and note anything that may help to reconstitute the obsolete local social system ; services and payments due; when due ?

heriots, privileges of the lord of the manor, ecclesiastical rights and dues, and the like. Note any peculiar tenures, rose-rents, etc.; peculiar customs of inheritance, borough English, dower; rights of annual entry into enclosed ground (when, and for what purpose); common-rights, hearth-rights, "keyhold tenure," privileges confined to one part of the village or township, local rivalries, traditions of old local contests. Village officers, how chosen, how paid; their duties. The pound, the stocks, the village green, tree, or well; the courthouse or other meeting place of the court, indoor or outdoor; the name and position of the village inn. Local weights and measures (these varied surprisingly). Fairs or markets, past or present; when held, how opened, any special laws or privileges during the fair. Kind of business transacted, hiring servants, ceremonies and terms of contract. The dedication of the church (is it the original dedication?). Annual feast or wake; any special ceremonies (choice of a Mock Mayor, etc.), games, performances, or festival viands. (See *How to Write the History of a Parish*, by Dr. J. C. Cox. London: Geo. Allen & Sons, 1909.)

XII. RITES OF INDIVIDUAL LIFE, pp. 193-219.

(1st Edition: "Ceremonial Customs.")

Birth. Note how sterility is regarded; what practices are resorted to to obtain children. Describe what a woman should do when she finds that she is pregnant, what precautions or prohibitions she must observe during pregnancy, what her husband must observe, what methods are practised for divining the sex of the unborn child, and what is done to procure an easy delivery. Note where the birth takes place; in a dwelling specially provided, at the woman's own dwelling, at her mother's, or where? Who acts as midwife, is this the duty of any particular relative? What is done with the after-birth, with the umbilical cord? has any special person the charge of the latter? Note any belief about birth with a caul, what is done with the caul? What is done in the case of birth of twins, deformed infants, infants born feet foremost, or other abnormal births? Give the reasons assigned.

Note restrictions, prohibitions, length of separation or seclusion of the mother. Does the father submit to a period of seclusion or restriction? Give particulars. Describe supernatural dangers to which mother and infant are exposed; things done to protect them from witchcraft or other evils, rites or ceremonies performed or submitted to before resuming ordinary life, things done to promote or check the flow of milk; ceremonies at weaning.

Are omens drawn from the time or circumstances of birth ? What is the first food given to the child, by whom is it given ? How is the child received or treated when first taken abroad ? is any public exhibition made of it to the community, or to the sun and moon ?

Note any beliefs connected with the cradle, and enquire for cradle-songs and lullabies (cf. chs. xv., xvii.).

Describe the ceremony of naming the child. When does it take place, how is the name selected, by whom given ? Do the parents change their names on the birth of the first child (cf. p. 310) ? Is the name-giving accompanied by any other rite ? purification ? circumcision ? Is there any rite, unconnected with naming, performed for a young child, boy or girl ? any ceremonies connected with the first tooth, first hair-cutting, etc. ? What amulets or talismans are worn by children ? To what prohibitions or restrictions are they subjected ? How long do they last ? till weaning, end of first year, change of teeth, or when ? What is done with the cast milk-teeth ? Is there any difference in the rites observed for boys and girls, for the first-born infant and succeeding children ?

Are children preferred or required as priests or priestesses ? or to perform any special rites, and if so, on what occasions ? or to do any act which would be injurious if done by an adult who may have violated some prohibition ?

What becomes of women who die in childbirth, or children who die in infancy ? How are their corpses disposed of ?

Adoption. Is this customary ? when ? with what ceremonies ? what change of status do they convey ? what rights do they confer ? Who may adopt and who may be adopted ?

Initiation. What is the customary age of initiation ? is it compulsory ? does it admit the candidate to clan, tribe, or society ? Describe the rites, especially noting (1) endurance ordeals, (2) instructions in conduct, belief, and morality, (3) dramatic representations, (4) communication of secrets, (5) physical operations, (6) subsequent restrictions or privileges. Describe any special dances, and compare with death-dances. Note any ceremonies representing death and resurrection : are they connected with the initiation rites ? are women and the uninitiated made to believe that the candidates are put to death and raised to life again ? does the candidate receive a new name ? does he afterwards affect forgetfulness of his former life ? Is initiation repeated on admission to successive social grades or " age-classes " (cf. ch. xi., *Societies*).

Are girls secluded on arriving at womanhood ? Where, for

how long, and under whose charge? What ceremonies do they
go through? To what prohibitions and restrictions are they
subjected? are these repeated periodically? Do they undergo
any further rites, physical or other, previous to marriage? Are
they collected in a " school " under superintendence, and instructed in womanly duties?

Marriage. Note any love-charms or love-divinations in use.
Ascertain the customary age for marriage, what liberty of choice
is permitted to the parties, whether infant betrothal is customary,
(if so, at what age the marriage is consummated), what relatives
have the right of disposing of the hand of a girl, of a boy; who
makes the first overtures, how, and to whom? Is there any
ceremony of betrothal? of what does it consist? what rights
does it confer? Is pre-nuptial chastity desired? is proof of
it required? does the validity of the marriage depend on it?

What special duties in connection with the marriage devolve
upon the father and mother or the several paternal and maternal
relatives of the bride and bridegroom respectively?

Is there more than one form of marriage? if so, what is the
status of the wife (or husband) in each? Is a bride-price paid,
or a bridegroom-price? (how much? what does it consist of?
who finds it and who receives it?) Does the bride receive a
dowry? (*ibid.*).

Is there a special season for marriages? What are auspicious
days for it? what omens are observed in connection with it?
Note the preparations for marriage. What ceremonies, purificatory or other, do the bride and bridegroom undergo? what
precautions are taken to ensure good luck or avert evil, what
prohibitions are either subjected to; before, during, and after
the marriage ceremonies? what presents do they exchange?
what special garments does either wear? Is the bride veiled?
Is the bride or the bridegroom required to satisfy any test or to
perform any feat?

Does the bride go to the bridegroom's home or he to hers?
Do they remove at once or after an interval? Is the first removal
temporary only? Is any opposition offered to the entrance of
the bridegroom or the departure of the bride? Is she hidden
or disguised? How does she behave? What companions
accompany them? What does she take with her? How are
the pair conveyed? Describe all the ceremonies connected with
the change of domicile both at the departure and subsequent
reception Is the marriage consummated at once, or after what
delay?

Where is the bridal feast held? Is there more than one?
What guests are present? what special viands are provided?

what special songs, dances, or games are performed? Does the chief, the priest, or medicine-man take a leading part in the rites?

Give all the ceremonies in order of time, and state which is the essential part of the rite, which makes the marriage binding. In the case of *matrilocal* marriage record all the details with special care, and state whether there is any mock-fight or ceremonial change of domicile. Note what is the subsequent status of the husband (see p. 209).

What changes of costume or of hair-dressing do men or women make on marriage, or on widowhood? What marriage-tokens are worn?

What are the bride's relations with her husband's mother, father, brothers, sisters, or other relations? what are the bride-groom's with hers? If prohibitions occur, give particulars, and say how long they last and how they may be removed.

Is it customary to repeat the marriage ceremony after the birth of a child? Are conditional, temporary, or irregular marriages entered upon? on what terms and with what rites?

Remarriage of widows, see p. 326.

Divorce. What causes are held to justify divorce or separation? Is divorce at the will of one party only? or of either? Is the consent of any other persons needed? With what ceremonies is it effected? What are the consequences of divorce, (*a*) to the parties themselves (how soon can they re-marry?), (*b*) to the children, (*c*) to the bride-price?

Death (cf. chs. vi., x.). What events give warning of death (cf. ch. viii.)? When death is imminent how is the sick man treated? is he abandoned, buried alive, or put to death? is he removed from the house or bed? is anything done to ease or expedite the departure of the soul?

Ascertain what is the first thing to be done after a death. Are deaths formally announced? how, by whom, and to whom? To what is death attributed? Are any steps taken to find out the cause? or (if attributed to witchcraft) the author? Is there any idea of death from natural causes?

How is the corpse prepared for the funeral? washed? (what is done with the water?), clothed, adorned, bound, mutilated, embalmed? in what position? Is food offered to it? is it watched? Does it sit or lie in state? how long, and with what ceremonies? How is the corpse disposed of?

How is the body disposed of? by *interment* (temporary or permanent? in extended or contracted position? describe position in detail); *cremation* (where? detail the ceremonial; who lights the fire, by what method, with what fuel, how are the

ashes disposed of ?) *exposure* (on what and for how long ?) ;
immersion (where ?) ; *preservation* (by desiccation, or other
means ? detail them. What parts are preserved, how adorned
or painted, where kept, for what purpose and for how long ?)
If more than one mode of disposal is in use what determines the
choice in each case ? sex, status, mode of death ?

State the exact relationship to the dead man of gravediggers
and others who perform specific functions in connection with
the death. Note all observances or prohibitions with regard to
fire, water, salt, food, and cookery.

Lamentations and dirges : are these formal ? by hired
mourners ? extempore or in a set formula ? Give the words.
When do they begin and how often are they repeated ?

How long a time elapses between the death and funeral ?
What is the usual hour for funerals ? Is there a preliminary feast ?
who is invited, or comes ? Is the deceased supposed to partake
of it ? Is a portion given to the domestic or semi-domestic
animals, or doles to the poor ? Must the guests touch the dead ?

Are coffins used ? How is the corpse taken out ? feet foremost ? by what exit ? Note any precautions taken on the
threshold. May the house door be shut ? What route is taken
to the grave ? any beliefs about it ? Does the corpse show any
reluctance to go ?

The grave : what are its locality, shape, position, orientation ?
its furniture—food, drink, wives, dependants ; effigies of above ;
property : tools, weapons, ornaments, children's toys ? whole or
broken ? Are the objects used in the funeral rites destroyed at
the grave-side ? any other property destroyed ? What is the
tenor of the farewells at the grave ? How soon is the soul supposed to be at rest ? Is the burial permanent ? or is the corpse
afterwards exhumed and re-interred ? In this case, are any
bones retained by the relatives ? Which bones ? and what for ?

If *cremation* is practised, how are the ashes disposed of ? where,
and with what ceremonies ?

What is done in the case of suicides, women dying in childbirth,
uninitiated persons, slaves, criminals, persons dying by lightning
or other " visitation of God," or " evil death."

Note any ceremonies performed or undergone by the attendants
at a funeral on their return.

What special duties are incumbent on particular relatives in
connection with a death ? what signs of mourning are used or
worn ? do they differ according to degree of relationship ? How
long are they continued ? what prohibitions does a state of
mourning involve ? State exactly whose duty it is to remove
the signs of mourning. Is this done publicly ? with any special
ceremony or feast ?

Is there a second or third funeral feast ? after what intervals ? Who provides and who partakes of them ? Are any games, dances, dramatic performances, held ? Describe them. Do they make any difference to the state of the soul of the deceased ? Where is the soul supposed to be between death and the completion of the funeral rites ? Is there any attempt to drive away the soul, or to retain it ? is any receptacle provided for it (image, tablet, etc.) ? In the case of death away from home, is anything done to recall the soul ? is a cenotaph erected for it ? Is any memorial (stone, cairn, etc.) set up to the deceased ? if so, describe it. Are tombs cared for or neglected ? Compare the beliefs as to another life with the funeral rites (pp. 75-89).

XIII. OCCUPATIONS AND INDUSTRIES, pp. 220-235.

War. Ascertain whether there is any definite military organisation ; how war is declared ; are enemies surprised, or is notice of attack given ? Note what preparations, positive or negative, are made for war ; sacrifices offered, war-dance performed, omens taken, separation of the sexes enforced, weapons blessed or " medicined " ? Are magical formulas engraved on sword-blades, etc. ? Do the warriors take any means to make themselves invulnerable, invisible ? do they carry amulets, talismans ? Is any sacred object carried by the army to the battlefield ? Note whether the warriors are subject to any prohibitions previously or while on the war-path. Are they accompanied by priests or medicine-men ; with what object ? Are their wives subject to any prohibitions during their absence, or are any particular actions enjoined on them ?

Note how the bodies of slaughtered enemies are treated, and what trophies the victors bring back ; is head-hunting practised, with what object ? Must the warriors observe any particular rites or prohibitions on their return ? How is peace settled ? is there any ceremony of declaring a peace or truce ?

Hunting. Ascertain whether there is a class of professional hunters ; what days or times are thought auspicious for hunting ; what are the preliminaries of a hunting expedition ; what previous preparation do the hunters undergo, and with what object ? (to give skill, ensure safety, procure success ?) what amulets, if any, are carried ? To what prohibitions are they subjected, as to diet, actions, relations with women, etc. Are the traps, or weapons, charmed, " medicined," or treated in any way ; is any sort of personality attributed to them ? How are the dogs treated, are they also charmed, etc. ? are they rewarded with a portion of the game ? Note whether anything is done before the party starts to attract the game ; dances or masquerades, sacrifices offered or charms recited ? Are pantomimic representations of the catching and killing of the game enacted ? Give full particulars of the rites. Note any acts or conduct prescribed or forbidden to women and others left at home ; whether any words or names are prohibited while out hunting ; whether any ceremony is observed after killing the game. How is it divided ? who has a right to share in it, and to receive what portions ? Are any parts (horns, teeth, claws, whiskers, etc., etc.) preserved as amulets or talismans, or simply as trophies ? Is there any ceremony in eating game, particularly the first of the season ? How are the bones treated ? What is done to a new hand the first time of going out hunting ?

Fishing, Fishermen, and Sailors. Note whether there is a professional class of fishermen, whether their occupation is hereditary, whether they intermarry with other classes or trades, whether they live in a separate district or area, whether they have any special festival or religious patron apart from the rest of the population. What part do the men take in the industry, and what the women ? Note rites performed to attract the fish ; lucky or unlucky omens observed on going fishing ; anything done to bring luck and anything forbidden ; acts prescribed or forbidden to the women in their husbands' absence ; ceremonies practised in launching boats, especially new boats ; articles taken in the boat to bring luck, and articles prohibited ; words or names which must not be spoken at sea. Must silence be observed while letting down or hauling in the nets ? Note charms repeated or anything said or done to obtain a good haul ; what is done with the first fish taken ; any fish returned to the water (particular kinds ?) ; kinds of fish or other objects which it is unlucky to find in the haul ; kinds of fish which may not be eaten ; what is done with the bones, blood, entrails and eyes of the fish eaten ; anything said or done on salting, smoking, selling, or buying fish. Is there any annual ceremony of blessing the sea ? any ceremony in eating the first fish of the season caught ? How are the bones treated or disposed of ?

Describe rites of building or launching boats. Is their ultimate fate foretold from accidents during building or launching ? Have they personal names ? how bestowed ? Are eyes painted on them ? Why ? Are they personified, supposed to have special characters, to be individually lucky or unlucky ? What amulets are carried on board ? Note any peculiarity about the shape or material of the vessel or fishing-rod, the make of the net or fish-hook, etc., which brings luck or the reverse ; any days specially lucky or unlucky for putting to sea.

Is labour, such as rowing, weighing anchor, hauling on ropes, accompanied by songs ? traditional or improvised ? sung in chorus or as a solo with a chorus burden ?

Note what is done to a new hand on joining the vessel, on first seeing open sea, first going up the rigging, first crossing the Line, etc. ? Are sailors tattooed ? are the patterns original or copied from each other ? have they any significance ? does each man choose his own pattern or is some special pattern allotted to him by right ?

Are any talismans carried to prevent wreck or drowning ? Are any spots haunted by mermen or mermaids ? do they drag unwary victims under the water ? can these be rescued ? how ? Is it unlucky or unlawful to save a drowning man ? how is wreckage regarded, and wrecks ?

Note things done to influence the weather ? Does whistling affect it ? Do witches control it ? do they raise storms ? do sailors buy favourable winds of them ? Note what persons or animals are unlucky passengers (natives of certain countries, clergy, women ; a corpse ; etc.). Are any noted landmarks saluted in passing ? how ? Describe rites relating to the birth of an infant at sea, a death and burial at sea ; can the captain of a vessel celebrate marriages at sea ? Note what rites are observed on landing, or returning from a voyage. Describe them. Note any legends told by sailors of ghostly ships, the Flying Dutchman, the sea-serpent, or other marvels. Have they any special songs ? How are they regarded in folk-tales, songs and proverbs ?

Flocks and Herds. Note what domestic animals are kept and who attends to them, men or women ? or both ? whether cattle are housed during part of the year and pastured during the other part ; whether they are pastured in the uplands and lowlands at different seasons ; rites and ceremonies observed on changing pasture. Are the cattle ever driven through fire or smoke ? What is done in case of murrain ? Enquire into veterinary practice (cf. *Leechcraft*, ch. x.). What is done to preserve the cattle from witchcraft ? to secure fecundity ? Are strange births ominous ? What is done to prevent abortion ? if it occurs, how is the immature fœtus disposed of ? How is the after-birth disposed of ? What is done to console a cow for losing her calf or a ewe her lamb ? Who milks the cattle or sheep ? men, women, or young children of both sexes ? Are charms or songs used to induce the cows, etc., to give their milk ? Is milk used for human food ? note any taboos in connection with it. May other food be taken before it is believed to have passed out of the system ? may it be boiled ? is butter or cheese made from it ? Do witches and demons steal milk, prevent butter

" coming " ? what precautions are taken against this, or remedies used ? Note method of churning and all observances connected therewith ; is the presence of strangers objected to ? are charms, amulets, or benedictory gestures used ? Is the flesh of cattle, etc., eaten ? is the flesh of any animal forbidden to women ? Nòte whether there is a special slaughtering season ; what is done with the old bulls and rams, are they subjects of sport or public amusement ? whether any domestic animals are sacrificed, annually or occasionally ? with what object ? killed in any special way ? with any special implement ? what is done with the different parts of the carcase ? Note whether the herdsmen have any special festivals, guardian deities, or patron saints ; any annual ceremony of blessing flocks or herds ; any festival on the occasion of sheep-shearing. Note what wood is used to make drovers' sticks or shepherds' crooks, whether they are carved, with what patterns ? Are there any stories or songs celebrating pastoral life ? do the herdsmen tell stories of the superhuman knowledge or sagacity of their charges ? Do herdsmen and husbandmen intermarry ? Is there any rivalry between them ?

Agriculture. Ascertain what is the system of land-tenure, as regards the actual cultivators ; communal or individual ; what crops are grown (grain, vegetables, fruit ?) ; what implements are used (hoes, ploughs ?) ; what beasts draw the plough, if used ; whether men or women till the ground, or is the work shared ? if so, how ? Note any rite performed to increase the fertility of the soil ; observances connected with the dunghill ; the proper date for beginning ploughing ; is the plough wetted before putting it into the ground ? is liquor from a festive meal ever poured over it ? is food eaten beside it ? is anything said ? is it ever carried about in procession ? When and with what ceremonies ? Is any part of the field purposely left untilled ? What for ?

Note lucky or unlucky days for sowing, planting, and grafting ; the proper period of the moon, the good or evil omens observed. Is anything special mixed with the seed grain ? is it carried to the field by any special person, or in any special receptacle ? Is anything said or done on beginning sowing ? on completing the sowing ? Who sows the seed ? if a patch is missed, does it portend death ? to the sower or to someone else ? Must the sexes be separated at sowing-time ? or on the contrary, is license enjoined or recommended ? Must young plants be planted by women ? Are any rites performed, or talismans used, to protect crops or fruit from animals, birds, insects, or other dangers, or to make the newly-sown crops grow, the vines and fruit-trees bear ?

are they ever abused and threatened ? Note all observances connected with orchards. Is bloodshed enjoined or forbidden at seed time or harvest ? What is said when the wind waves the growing grain ?

With what implements are the grain-crops cut ? Is the grain bound up in sheaves at once or allowed to lie on the ground ? All crops alike ? Do the same persons both cut and bind the corn, or is the work divided between men and women, paid labourers and volunteers, men specially hired and regular labourers, or the like ? Observe how a new workman is " hanselled," made to " pay his footing," or otherwise made free of the harvest-field ; any pretext of " shoeing the colt," " horning the ox," or any such ceremony ; any drinking ceremony ? When the master enters the field how is he received ? is a gift of money demanded of him ? How are passing strangers treated ? are they roughly handled ? What compensation is demanded of anyone who treads down the growing crop ? Is one of the reapers chosen to be " lord," and one of the women his " lady " ? What do they do ? have they any special privileges ? are they disguised in any way ?

Firstfruits.—Does any special person cut the *first* ears (or firstfruits of the crop) ? Is anything special done with the *first* sheaf (or first fruit gathered) ? is it preserved ? consumed ? by whom ? If eaten, must anything be said or done ?

What is the *last* sheaf called ? Who cuts it ? how ? Do the reapers all throw their hooks at it ? What is the man nicknamed who cuts it ? Is any dialogue or rhyme repeated, or song sung ? What is done with the last sheaf ? is it made into an effigy of any sort ? what is it then called ? What does the successful reaper do with it ? to whom does he give it ? must it or he be drenched with water ? what eventually becomes of it ? Note whether such an effigy is made from each crop or only from the staple crop of the district. Is a corner of the field left unreaped ? what for ? what is it called ?

Harvest-home. When the field is finally cleared, what re-joicings take place ? Is there any ceremony of shouting or triumphing over others more backward ? Is the last load carried home with shouting, dancing, and singing ? (Give the words of the songs.) Is it known by any special name, as " hock-cart " or " hawkey " ? Must the master treat his men to a feast ? with any special delicacy ? If a load is upset, do the men forfeit it ? if the master neglects to give the feast can they exact any penalty ? Are there any games or masquerades proper to the occasion ? any sort of Saturnalia or temporary abolition of rank or order ? In cultivating common fields, who takes the part otherwise taken by the owner or master ? Are bonfires lighted

in the arable fields or the orchards ? any effigy or other object
burnt in them ? At what time of the year is this done ?

Rain-making, etc. Note and describe all rites performed to
produce or stop rain, or to cause sunshine. Who performs them ?
a clan, or other section of the community ? members of one or
the other sex ? persons having innate powers that way ? the
king or chief ? or one or more professional experts (cf. ch. ix.) ?

Handicrafts. Note whether the craftsmen are nomadic,
itinerant, or stationary ; whether they inhabit a special quarter
of the town or district ; whether the craft is practised by men
or by women or both ; whether it is hereditary ; whether the
craftsmen intermarry with the rest of the population ; have
any social customs differing from the rest of the population.
Describe any ceremonies practised on initiation or apprentice-
ship. Note whether the craftsmen have any special cult or
worship ? do they revere any special deity, guardian genius,
or patron saint ; have they any festivals peculiar to themselves
(see ch. xiv.) ? Note any legend about their craft ; days or
seasons on which it is forbidden to exercise it ; omens they
specially believe in ; practices on beginning or leaving off work ;
superstitions or animistic beliefs about their tools or machines ;
forfeits or penalties for handling tools without admission to the
craft, or wrongly after admission. Do they show any marks of
reverence to their tools ? do they worship them ? When ?
Have they any legend of the origin of particular tools ? Give
the words of any songs accompanying their labour ; songs about
the craft, in praise of it or otherwise ? How is the craft regarded
by the rest of the population ? held sacred, tabooed, feared,
respected, despised, thought to be under a curse ? Are the craftsmen credited with powers over disease, or over certain diseases ?
Is the craft mentioned in folk-tales or proverbs ? to what effect ?

XIV. CALENDAR FASTS AND FESTIVALS, pp. 236-248.

(1*st Edition :* " *Festival Customs.*")

Is time reckoned by the sun, moon, or stars, or by seasons
and harvests ? Have the " moons " names ? and are they
divided into weeks ? if so, how many, and of what length ?
Are the solstices observed ? How are the lunar months accom-
modated to the solar year ?

Note what kinds of occupations, labour, or sport, are pursued
in the several seasons, what engagements are entered into or
terminated with them, what fasts or festivals mark the several
seasons.

Ascertain what event or circumstance dates the beginning of the year; how many festivals there are in the year, and what they are called. Give an account of each festival; state how long it lasts, where it is held, who attends it, what part the priests or other officials take in it, what the lower classes of the community. Does it specially belong to any one class, sex, trade or occupation? Is it generally observed in the district or confined to one place or community only? What is the occasion or object of the festival and what the central feature of the celebration? Narrate the several incidents or ceremonies in their order as they occur.

Note things brought in, things burnt, things carried out; use of flowers, boughs, garlands; distribution of flowers, fruit, feathers or other objects (are they kept for good luck? how long? and how finally disposed of?): processions, perambulations, official or religious, to guard boundaries or bless crops: begging expeditions (*quêtes*), (what is begged for? materials for the approaching feast? liquor? money?): things carried about and exhibited: is a reward asked for, is the demand enforced by threats, bugbears, or any terrorism? Whipping customs? Masquerades, men and women exchanging clothes, buffoonery; dramatic performances, songs, dances, special games (between what parties and where played, are auguries drawn from the result? see ch. xv.). Auguries generally as to love, marriage, death, harvest, general prosperity in the coming year or season (what methods of divination are used, and when?). Luck-bringing rites, "first-footing," exchange of gifts: courtship customs, kissing practices, choosing partners for the year, by lot or otherwise. Feasting; what viands are provided, and by whom? are any special ceremonies observed in preparing them? are they eaten in common, or household by household? is a portion allotted to the poor, the domestic animals, the dead, non-human beings? Drinking customs: is any special drink provided, are healths drunk? is intoxication allowed, enjoined, or approved? Fire-customs: ritual in lighting of new fires, things burnt in bonfires, omens from fire, jumping over fires, or through smoke, fumigation. Water customs: bathing, drinking, aspersion; visiting wells, springs or rivers. Kinds of work enjoined or forbidden; freedoms permitted, tricks played, ordinary laws suspended. Is there a leader of the revels? what is he called, how chosen, what are his powers? how long does his authority last? "Mock mayors"; enquire into the history of any such customs. Seasons of abstention from work, food, or society; dates when payments are due, contracts entered upon, servants hired, etc.: particulars of such customs (cf. ch. xi.).

XV. GAMES, SPORTS, AND PASTIMES, pp. 248-258.

Games. Record all games played in the district by (*a*) children, (*b*) adults (men, women, or both together ?). Describe them, and note local variants and their probable causes (season, climate, sex of players). Record *Pastimes* : infants' plays with fingers and toes, etc. ; feats of skill, as cats' cradle (see *A. N. and Q.*, p. 229), cup-and-ball ; sportive exercises and methods of locomotion, as see-saw, swinging, swimming, stilt-walking, and skating ; children's singing-games and dances. Record *games with a penalty on the loser* ; hide-and-seek, blindman's buff, forfeits. *Games with a reward for the winner* ; mental contests, puzzles, riddles ; physical contests, wrestling, boxing, fencing ; games of skill, with organized sides, rules, and opponents (polo, cricket) ; games of chance, or of skill and chance combined (nine men's morris, backgammon, cards).

Note all " *ditties* " or songs used in games, with tunes if possible. Give " counting-out " formulas. Describe any *implements* or apparatus used (balls, bats, tops, kites, hoops, nets, whistles, horns, skipping-ropes, swings, etc., etc.) ; and say of what made and how procured.

Are there any *public games* ? who regulate and manage them ? Is there any customary public playground ? At what time of year and on what occasions is each game played ? Note games played annually between two communities or two divisions of a community ; on what date ? how are the sides chosen ? what is the goal or trophy played for, and what the result or effect of victory ?

Note all *sports with animals*, baiting or torturing them, or setting them to fight each other : races. Are these sports held annually ? at what date ?

Gambling. Does this enter into any games, or is it independently pursued ? By players or by spectators ? Is it an old or a new habit ? Is it regarded as a religious act ?

Luck. Does luck in other things follow or affect luck in games, or the contrary ? What affects luck in games, and how can ill-luck be altered ?

Dancing. Note whether dancing is performed for spectators or simply as a pastime for the dancers : whether performed (*a*) as a magico-religious exercise or solemnity (see ch. vii.), or (*b*) for amusement. Do the steps or figures differ accordingly ? Describe them. Who are the dancers ; children, or adults (men, women, or both ?), initiated persons ? What is the accompaniment ? vocal or instrumental ? Give words of songs (see ch. xvii.). What dress or decoration is worn ?

Note articles made use of in the dance ; worn, carried, waved, etc. (are bells worn, or anything else to produce sound ?). How are they made or procured ? by or from whom ? are they kept from performance to performance ? Is the dance dramatic, or imitative of anything ? are the dancers disguised ? do they wear masks or animal relics ? Is it restricted to time, place or season ? connected with a particular festival ? Do they vary the performance from year to year ? give new steps ?

See *A. N. and Q.*, p. 224, for technical directions on recording dances.

Drama. Where and on what occasion is it performed ? For pleasure, or for what other object ? Who are the actors, men, women, or both ? Who take the female parts ? Describe the plots ; how are they procured ? Is there any use of songs, music, or dancing ? Are the performers amateur or professional ? How dressed or disguised ? Are there any puppet-shows ?

XVI. STORIES, pp. 261-270.

On what occasions are stories told ? Is there a story-telling season ? Do particular stories belong to particular occasions ? For what purpose are they told ? for instruction or warning, or simply for amusement ?

Ascertain whether there is a class of *professional story-tellers* ; if so, how recruited and rewarded ? whether each has a *répertoire* of his own ; whether there is any sort of property in stories ; whether special or different stories are told by men, women, and children respectively. Are any stories not told before elders, or concealed from women, children, strangers, or outsiders ?

What kinds of phenomena form the subject of myths ? things ordinary and constant, or things fitful and irregular ? novelties or accustomed objects ? natural phenomena or social institutions ? Are there opening and concluding formulas (" once upon a time "— " they lived happy ever after ") ? Are snatches of verse or song interspersed in the stories ? Is there any attempt at dramatic narration ? imitation of the cries and gestures of animals or the like ? Take note of all such features.

Relate the stories as nearly as possible in the speaker's own words, do not try to harmonise versions, and do not reject fragmentary stories because they are not complete. Give the name (not necessarily for publication), age, and status of the story-teller, and state whether he or she is bi-lingual, and, if possible, the source from which he learnt the story.

XVII. SONGS AND BALLADS, pp. 271-279.

What kinds of labour, of recreation, of religious and other solemnities, are accompanied by songs ? Are songs sung as an independent form of recreation, and not only as adjunct to something else ? At what times or on what occasions ?

Is there a class of *professional singers* ? If so, how are they remunerated ? Do they compose their own songs, or sing those of others ? Are they retained in the service of the kings or chiefs ? Do they wander from place to place ? Are the subjects of their songs topical or historical ? Are there any competitive prizes for singing, or singing festivals ? Are the songs traditional, modern, or improvised ? Are there burdens, refrains, or choruses ? Do they contain any nonsense words, obsolete words, or words and phrases not understood by the singer ? Are there any set forms or rules of rhythm and metre ? Do men, women, and children sing different songs ? Does each singer claim property in his songs ? Are songs put into the mouths of the characters in prose-tales ? Is song supposed to have an influence over animals or over the elements ?

All songs should if possible be taken down exactly, noting the occasions of hearing them.

It is best if two persons can combine in this work, one to give attention to the words, the other to the melody. Let the singer go straight through the song without stopping him or asking for repetitions. Then ask for the first verse (or strophe) to be repeated, as often as may be necessary to get the air on paper. Give your attention to the intervals at one repetition, and the rhythm at another. When you have set down the air as correctly as you can, ask to have the whole song repeated, to verify your transcript.

If only one worker is available he should take down the words and the music at separate repetitions. If no one competent to transcribe the air is available, do not therefore omit to secure the words.

Do not ask the singer to repeat the words without the air, as it is likely to confuse him, but take them down as he sings them, before or after you have recorded the tune. If you fail to catch any words ask to have the *whole verse* repeated, not part of it. Get any information you can as to the history of the song, where the singer learnt it, and from whom ; and give the name, age, status, etc., of the singer, as in all other cases.

N.B.—The address of the Folk Song Society, from one of whose leaflets the above hints are summarized, is 19 Berners Street, London, W.

APPENDIX C.

SOME TYPES OF INDO-EUROPEAN FOLKTALES.

(Revised by Mr. Joseph Jacobs for the original edition of the *Handbook*, from the classification by the Rev. S. Baring-Gould in the 1st Edition of Henderson's *Folklore of the Northern Counties*.)

1. *Cupid and Psyche type.*
   1. A beautiful girl is beloved by a man of supernatural race.
   2. He appears as a man by night, and warns her not to look at him.
   3. She breaks his command and loses him.
   4. She goes in quest of him, and has to surmount difficulties and accomplish tasks.
   5. She finally recovers him.

2. *Melusina type.*
   1. A man falls in love with a woman of supernatural race.
   2. She consents to live with him if he will not look on her upon a certain day in the week.
   3. He breaks her command and loses her.
   4. He seeks her, but never recovers her.

3. *Swan-maiden type.*
   1. A man sees a woman bathing, with her charm-dress on the shore.
   2. He steals the dress and she falls into his power.
   3. After some years she succeeds in recovering the dress and she escapes.
   4. He is unable to recover her.

4. *Penelope type.*
    1. The man goes on his travels, and the wife is left at home.
    2. She awaits his return in fidelity.
    3. He returns to her.

5. *Genoveva type.*
    1. The man goes to war, and the wife remains at home.
    2. A false charge is brought against the wife, and he orders her death.
    3. She is driven away, but not killed.
    4. The husband on his return discovers his mistake.
    5. He finds her again, and they are reunited.

6. *Punchkin or Life-Index type.*
    1. A giant with his soul hidden in some external object (" Life Index ") marries a woman who has a lover.
    2. The lover seeks and finds her, and urges her to kill her husband.
    3. She tries to discover where the Life-Index is, and the giant puts her off several times, but at last tells the secret.
    4. She destroys the Life-Index, and thus kills her husband, and
    5. Elopes with her lover.

7. *Samson type* (cf. 6).
    1. The husband has giant strength residing in some external object.
    2. The wife, unfaithful to him, asks him his secret ; he refuses long to reveal it, and at last does so.
    3. She betrays the secret to his enemies, and he is ruined.

8. *Hercules type.*
    1. The husband has giant strength.
    2. A former lover of his wife, who is true to him, determines to cause his death, and persuades the wife to make him a present.
    3. She does so without intending harm, and he is killed by it.

9. *Serpent Child type.*
    1. A mother has no child. She says she would like to have one, were it a serpent or a beast.
    2. She is brought to bed of a child as she had desired.

3. The child she marries to a man or woman, and by night it assumes human shape.

4. She seizes the skin and burns it. Thenceforth her child leaves the serpent or bestial form.

10. *Robert the Devil type.*

1. A mother or father vows a child, if they have one, to an evil being.

2. The child is born, and the being claims it.

3. The child escapes, fights with, or tricks, the evil spirit, and

4. Finally overmasters it and frees himself.

11. *Goldchild type.*

1. A mother desires a certain food ; it makes her pregnant.

2. She casts some of the food away ; part is eaten by a mare or bitch, and part grows ; the mare or bitch is also pregnant.

3. The child and the foal, or the whelp and the plant, are twins with strong sympathies.

4. The mother seeks the death of her child, but his twin brother, the foal or the whelp, saves him.

5. They have further adventures.

12. *Lear type.*

1. A father has three daughters. He puts their love to the proof, and as the youngest does not profess much love, he drives her away.

2. The father falls into trouble, and the two elder daughters refuse him assistance, but he obtains help from the youngest.

13. *Hop o' my Thumb type.*

1. The parents, very poor, desert their children.

2. The youngest child leads the rest home several times, but at last fails to do so.

3. They fall into the power of a supernatural being, but the youngest robs him and they all escape.

14. *Rhea Sylvia type.*

1. The mother is either killed, or leaves the children for a few minutes.

2. They are suckled by a wild beast.

3. They pass through various adventures, and

4. Are finally recognised and raised to the throne.

15. *Juniper Tree type.*

   1. A stepmother hates her stepchild, and accomplishes its death.

   2. Marvellous circumstances follow, through the transmigration of the soul of the child into 1st, a tree; and 2nd, a bird.

   3. Punishment of the stepmother.

16. *Holle type.*

   1. A stepmother makes her stepdaughter the slave of the house.

   2. Great good-luck falls to the lot of the girl by her amiability.

   3. Misfortune befalls the other daughter through her evil temper.

17. *Catskin type.*

   1. A father, having lost his wife, vows to marry one who resembles her.

   2. Decides on marrying his daughter.

   3. She flees with three smart dresses.

   4. She marries a prince in a foreign land.

18. *Goldenlocks type.*

   1. Three princes set off to obtain a bride. The two first fail.

   2. Third succeeds in winning the bride.

   3. The two elder waylay him, half kill him, and steal the bride.

   4. He recovers and puts his brothers to flight.

19. *White Cat type.*

   1. A king sets his sons a task, and promises to the successful son that he shall succeed him.

   2. The two eldest are enchanted; the youngest breaks the enchantment, liberates them, and accomplishes the task.

20. *Cinderella type.*

   1. The youngest of three sisters is employed as kitchen-maid.

   2. The eldest sisters go to a ball. By supernatural means the youngest obtains a gorgeous dress, and goes as well.

   3. This happens three times. The last time she leaves her slipper.

   4. The Prince, by means of the slipper, discovers her and marries her.

21. *Beauty and Beast type* (cf. 1).

   1. The youngest of three sisters despised.

2. The father goes a journey and promises them each a present. The youngest asks for a flower only.

3. In obtaining the flower, the father falls into danger, and saves his life by the promise of the surrender of his daughter.

4. The daughter is in great prosperity thereby, and obtains a handsome lover.

5. The sisters injure the lover, and nearly cause his death.

6. The youngest saves his life.

22. *Beast Brothers-in-law type.*

1. A brother has several sisters who are married to beasts.

2. The young man has a task to perform.

3. He accomplishes it by the aid of his beast brothers-in-law.

23. *Seven Swans type.*

1. A sister has seven brothers who are turned into birds.

2. She seeks their release at the cost of silence.

3. She falls into great peril and is nearly lost, but succeeds in releasing them.

4. She marries a king.

24. *Twin Brothers type.*

1. Two brothers love one another dearly. They part on their journeys.

2. Before parting they give each other a token by which either may know the health and prosperity of the other.

3. One brother falls into danger. The other ascertains this

4. And saves him.

25. *Flight from Witchcraft type.*

1. A brother and sister (or two lovers) are in the power of a witch or stepmother, or giant.

2. The brother learns witchcraft, or the sister obtains these powers.

3. By means of spittle, or apple pips, they deceive their keeper and escape.

4. They are pursued, and transform themselves repeatedly (or interpose obstacles) to elude pursuit.

5. Finally they kill the pursuer.

26. *Bertha type.*

1. A prince sends for a princess whom he will marry. She sets off accompanied by her maidservant.

2. The servant throws the princess out of a ship, and passes herself off as the bride.

3. The princess seeks the king, and the fraud is discovered.

27. *Jason type* (cf. 25).

  1. A hero comes into a strange land and falls in love with a princess.

  2. The king sets him tasks, and these he performs by the aid of the lady.

  3. He elopes with her and is pursued.

  4. He deserts the bride (*a*) either through no fault of his own, being rendered oblivious of the past by a kiss from his mother, (*b*) or wilfully.

  5. The bride either breaks the enchantment or revenges herself.

28. *Gudrun type*.

  1. A bride is carried off by a monster or a hero.

  2. And is recovered, or is the cause of misfortune and ruin on the ravisher.

29. *Taming of the Shrew type*.

  1. She is proud and shrewish.

  2. The husband tames her by violence.

30. *Thrush-beard type*.

  1. A king, angry with his daughter, for her pride, marries her to a beggar.

  2. The beggar makes her into a slave and breaks her spirit.

  3. He then discovers himself to be a king, whose suit she had formerly despised.

31. *Sleeping Beauty type*.

  1. A princess warned not to touch a certain article.

  2. She does what she is forbidden and falls asleep.

  3. A prince discovers her sleeping after the lapse of many years, kisses her and wakes her.

32. *Bride Wager type*. Bride (more rarely husband) obtained by—

  1. Answering a series of riddles.

  2. Performing several tasks.

  3. Fighting with a monster.

  4. Making her laugh.

  5. Discovering a secret.

33. *Jack and Beanstalk type*.
  1. A man climbs a tree, or a rope, or a glass mountain, and reaches a land of wonder.
  2. He steals from it a harp, money, a golden egg, or a princess.
  3. He returns to earth.

34. *Journey to Hell type*.
  1. A man descends by an underground passage to a mysterious land.
  2. He has several narrow escapes.
  3. He rescues from beneath a princess.

35. *Jack the Giant-Killer type* (cf. 43).
  1. A man is matched with giants or devils.
  2. He deceives them by his superior cunning.
  3. He makes them kill themselves.

36. *Polyphemus type*.
  1. A man is kept in durance by a giant.
  2. He blinds the giant.
  3. He escapes by secreting himself under a ram.
  4. The giant endeavours to deceive him in turn, but is outwitted.

37. *Magical Conflict type*.
  1. Two persons with supernatural powers test them against one another.
  2. They pass through various transformations.
  3. The good person overcomes the wicked one.

38. *Devil Outwitted type*.
  1. A compact entered into between a man and the devil.
  2. The man outwits the devil.

39. *Fearless John type*.
  1. A lad knows not fear. He is brought into contact with (1) men, (2) dead bodies, (3) spirits.
  2. He has three adventures with spirits in a haunted house, and wrests from them gold.
  3. He learns how to shiver, by a pail of goldfish being upset over him in bed.

40. *Prophecy Fulfilled type.*
   1. A prophecy is made by a supernatural being, that a certain child will either kill a king or will marry his daughter.
   2. The king seeks the death of the child.
   3. The means he used to accomplish this purpose turn to bring about the fulfilment of the prophecy.

41. *Magical Book type.*
   1. A man obtains power over evil spirits by certain means.
   2. He is unable to control the means, and they ruin him.

42. *Master Thief type.*
   1. A youth goes forth to learn thieving.
   2. He steals from a farmer to establish his credit as a thief.
   3. Accepted as robber chief, he outwits the band.
   4. He returns home and asks the squire's daughter for wife.
   5. He is set tasks, which he accomplishes.

43. *Valiant Tailor type* (cf. 35).
   1. A tailor kills seven flies at a blow, and believes himself to be a hero.
   2. He outwits (1) giants, (2) men.
   3. He marries the princess.

44. *William Tell type.*
   1. A tyrant sets an archer the task of shooting an apple or nut from the head of his own son. He accomplishes the task.
   2. He is asked the use of the additional arrows in the archer's belt, and is threatened.
   3. The archer kills the tyrant after the lapse of years.

45. *Faithful John type.*
   1. A prince has a faithful servant, who saves him from danger.
   2. The prince mistakes the act and punishes the servant, who is turned into stone.
   3. The servant released from enchantment by the tears of the prince and his bride.

46. *Gelert type.*
   1. A man has a faithful hound, which saves his child from danger.
   2. The man mistakes the act and kills the dog.
   3. When too late he discovers his error.

47. *Grateful Beasts' type.*
    1. A man saves some beasts and a man from a pit.
    2. The beasts make their preserver wealthy, but the man tries to work his ruin.

48. *Beast, Bird, Fish type.*
    1. A man does a kindness to a beast of the earth, a winged creature of the air, and a denizen of the water.
    2. He falls into danger, or has tasks to perform.
    3. He escapes, or succeeds, by aid of the thankful creatures.

49. *Man obtains power over Beasts.*
    1. By his cunning.
    2. By his musical powers.

50. *Aladdin type.*
    1. A man has a treasure of supernatural properties, or a family has a gift given by spirits which will bring luck.
    2. By folly this is lost.
    3. It is recovered.

51. *Golden Goose type.*
    1. A man has a similar treasure.
    2. By folly it is lost.
    3. It is never recovered.

52. *Forbidden Chamber type.*
    1. A girl (or man) marries one of superior station.
    2. She (or he) is allowed free access to every room in the new house but one.
    3. The forbidden chamber is visited and found full of horrors.
    4. The spouse discovers this, and in trying to punish is killed.

53. *Robber-Bridegroom type.*
    1. A girl is engaged to a disguised robber.
    2. She visits his castle and discovers his occupation.
    3. She convicts him before her relatives by some token, and he is killed.

54. *Singing Bone type.*
    1. A brother (sister) slays another through envy or jealousy.
    2. After many days a bone of the victim, when blown through, declares the murder.

55. *Snow White type.*
  1. Step-mother hates her step-daughter, and plots her death.
  2. Step-daughter at last succumbs.
  3. But is restored to life by hero, and the step-mother is punished.

56. *Tom Thumb type.*
  1. A mother wishes for a son, even if no bigger than her thumb.
  2. Such a son is born, who performs many exploits through his cunning and small size.

57. *Andromeda type.*
  1. A dragon ravages a country, and requires a maiden to be exposed for him.
  2. The king's daughter has to be thus exposed.
  3. The dragon is slain by hero, and he marries king's daughter.

58. *Frog-Prince type* (cf. 21).
  1. A prince is transformed into a loathsome beast.
  2. He does some kindness to a girl, on condition she does his bidding for one night.
  3. She does so ; he is unspelled and they marry.

59. *Rumpelstiltskin type.*
  1. A girl is set tasks to do.
  2. She is helped by a dwarf on condition she discovers his name.
  3. She does so by his accidentally revealing his name to others, and escapes falling into his power.

60. *Language of Animals type.*
  1. A son apprenticed to a wizard learns language of animals.
  2. Is cast forth by his father for saying he will be superior to him.
  3. Achieves tasks by knowledge of animal language.
  4. Becomes superior to his father (Pope, King), and is reconciled to him.

61. *Puss in Boots type.*
  1. A youngest son has only a cat left him.
  2. The cat induces the king to believe its master has large possessions.
  3. The cat's master marries the king's daughter.

62. *Dick Whittington type.*

   1. A poor lad becomes possessed of a cat.
   2. He sends the cat abroad as a venture.
   3. The cat is sold for a large price in a country infested with mice, and the lad becomes rich.

63. *True and Untrue type.*

   1. Two companions set out on a journey, one good tempered, the other surly.
   2. The surly one at first gets advantage, but the other obtains fortune by overhearing demons, etc.
   3. The surly one tries to do the same, but is destroyed by the demons.

64. *Thankful Dead type.*[1]

   1. Hero pays debts of an unburied man, who is by this means buried.
   2. The ghost helps him to achieve tasks.

65. *Pied Piper type.*

   1. A magical musician frees a town from vermin.
   2. He is refused his promised reward, and in revenge decoys all the children away.

66. *Ass, Table, and Cudgel type.*

   1. A lad, in reward for his services, receives an ass that drops gold, and then a table which is covered with food at word of command.
   2. Both are stolen from him by a rascally innkeeper.
   3. As a third gift he receives a cudgel that lays on at word of command, and with this makes the innkeeper restore the other two gifts.

67. *Three Noodles type* (Droll).

   1. A gentleman is betrothed to a girl who does some silly thing.
   2. He vows not to marry till he has found as great sillies as she.
   3. He finds three noodles, returns and marries her.

[1] Studied by Professor G. H. Gerould, *The Grateful Dead.* Folklore Society's Publications No. LX. 1908.

68. *Titty Mouse type* (Accumulation Droll).
  1. Animals set in partnership ; one dies, the other mourns.
  2. Other objects mourn in sympathy till there is universal calamity.

69. *Old Woman and Pig type* (Accumulation Droll).
  1. Old woman cannot get pig over stile ; she asks dog, stick, fire, water, ox, butcher, rope, rat, cat to help her.
  2. Cat does so on condition, and sets rest in motion till pig jumps over stile.

70. *Henny-Penny type* (Accumulation Droll).
  1. Hen thinks sky is falling, goes to tell king, and meets cock, duck, goose, turkey.
  2. At last they meet fox, who leads them to his own den and eats them up.

APPENDIX D.

AUTHORITIES CITED.

ABBOTT, G. F. *Macedonian Folklore.* Cambridge : 1903.

ALLDRIDGE, T. J. *The Sherbro and its Hinterland.* London : 1901.

(*Amer. Anthr.*) *The American Anthropologist.* Organ of the Anthropological and Ethnological Societies of America. New York : 1899—proceeding.

Anglo-Saxon Leechdoms. *v.* Cockayne.

(*Ann. Soc.*) *L'Année Sociologique.* Publiée sous la direction de Emile Durkheim. Paris : 1898—proceeding.

A.N. and Q. *v.* Notes and Queries.

Anthropos. Ephemeris Internationalis Ethnologica et Linguistic. Saltzburg, Oesterreich : 1906—proceeding.

APPLETON, L. ESTELLE. *A Comparative Study of the Play Activities of Adult Savages and Civilised Children.* University of Chicago Press : 1910.

ARBOUSSET, T. *Narrative of an Exploratory Tour to the North East of the Colony of the Cape of Good Hope.* Translated from the French by J. C. Brown. Capetown : 1846.

AUBREY, JOHN. *Remaines of Gentilisme and Judaisme.* Edited by J. Britten. Folklore Society, No. IV., 1881.

BATCHELOR, THE REV. J. *The Ainu and their Folklore.* London : 1901.

B.B.M.M. *v.* Dennett.

BLEEK, DR. W. H. I., and LLOYD, L. C. *Specimens of Bushman Folklore.* London : 1911.

BOURKE, CAPTAIN J. G. *The Snake-Dance of the Moquis of Arizona.* London : 1884.

BOURNE, THE REV. H. *Antiquitates Vulgares.* Newcastle-on-Tyne : 1725.

BURNE, C. S. *Shropshire Folklore.* Edited by C. S. Burne from the Collections of G. F. Jackson. London : 1883–1886.

Bur. Amer. Ethn. v. Reports.

CALLAWAY, THE REV. CANON H. *The Religious System of the Amazulu.* Folklore Society, No. XV., 1884.

CAMPBELL, THE REV. J. G. *Witchcraft and Second Sight in the Highlands and Islands of Scotland.* Glasgow : 1902.

CAREY, E. F. *Guernsey Folklore.* Edited by E. F. Carey from MSS. of Sir Edgar MacCulloch. London and Guernsey : 1903.

CARR, THE REV. W. *The Dialect of Craven in the West Riding of York.* Two vols. London : 1828.

CASALIS, EUGENE. *Les Bassutos : 23 années au Sud de l'Afrique.* Paris : 1859. (English version. London : 1861.)

Caste in India. v. p. 164 *n.*

Celtic FL. v. Rhŷs.

CHAMBERS, E. K. *The Mediæval Stage.* Oxford : 1903.

(*Ch. N.*) *Choice Notes from Notes and Queries.* London : 1859.

CLODD, EDWARD. *Tom Tit Tot.* London : 1898.

COCKAYNE, THE REV. O. *Leechdoms, Wortcunning and Starcraft of Early England.* Three vols. London : 1864–66.

CODRINGTON, THE REV. DR. R. H. *The Melanesians : Studies in their Anthropology and Folklore.* Oxford : 1891.

County Folklore. Vol. I. (*Suffolk*). By Lady Camilla Gurdon. Folklore Society, No. XXXVII., 1893.

—— Vol. II. (*North Riding of Yorkshire, York and the Ainsty*). By Mrs. Gutch. Folklore Society, No. XLV., 1899.

—— Vol. III. (*Orkney and Shetland Islands*). By G. F. Black. Edited by Northcote W. Thomas. Folklore Society, No. XLIX., 1901.

—— Vol. V. (*Lincolnshire*). By Mrs. Gutch and Mabel Peacock. Folklore Society, No. LXIII., 1908. (Cited as *County FL.*)

COURTNEY, M. A. *Cornish Feasts and Folklore.* Penzance : 1890.

COX, THE REV. DR. JOHN CHARLES. *How to write the History of a Parish.* Fifth edition. London : 1909.

COX, M. ROALFE. *Cinderella.* Folklore Society, No. XXXI., 1892.

CRAWLEY, A. E. *The Mystic Rose : a Study of Primitive Marriage.* London : 1902.

CROOKE, W. *The Popular Religion and Folklore of Northern India.* Two vols. London : 1896.

CRANTZ, DAVID. *The History of Greenland.* London : 1820.

CULIN, S. *Korean Games.* Philadelphia : 1895.

CULIN, S.   In the Twenty-Fourth Annual Report of the Bureau of American Ethnology, 1907.

CUSHING, F. H.   *Zuni Folk Tales.*   New York and London : 1901.

DAMES, M. LONGWORTH.   *Popular Poetry of the Baloches.*   Folk-lore Society, No. LIX., 1905.

DARWIN, CHARLES.   *The Voyage of a Naturalist.*   London : (1890 Edition).

DEENEY, DANIEL.   *Peasant Lore from Gaelic Ireland.*   1900.

DE LAVELEYE, E.   *Primitive Property.*   London and Cambridge : 1878.

DENHAM TRACTS.   *A Collection of Folklore by Michael Aislabie Denham reprinted from the original tracts.*   Edited by Dr. James Hardy.   Folklore Society, No. XXIX., 1891.

DENNETT, R. E.   *Notes on the Folklore of the Fjort.*   (*French Congo.*)   Folklore Society, No. XLI., 1879.   (Cited as *FL.F.*)

—— *At the Back of the Black Man's Mind.*   London : 1906. (Cited as *B.B.M.M.*)

DORSEY, G. A.   *Traditions of the Skidi-Pawnee.*   Memoirs of the American Folklore Society, Vol. VIII., Boston : 1904.

—— in *Amer. Anthr.*   1901.

DOUTTÉ, EDMOND.   *La Société Musulmane du Maghrib : magie et religion dans l'Afrique du Nord.*   Alger. : 1908.

DURHAM, M. E.   *High Albania.*   London : 1909.

DYER, THE REV. JOHN.   *The Fleece : a Poem.*   1757.

ELLIS, A. J.   " The Anglo-Celtic Score " in *Transactions of the Philological Society,* 1877–79.

ELLIS, A. B.   *The Yoruba-speaking Peoples of the Slave Coast of West Africa.*   London : 1894.

ELLIS, THE REV. W.   *Polynesian Researches.*   Four vols.   London : 1831.

ELWORTHY, FREDERICK THOMAS.   *The Evil Eye.*   London : 1895.

Encycl. Rel.   *v.* Hastings.

ENDLE, THE REV. SIDNEY.   *The Kacháris.*   1911.

FISON, LORIMER, and HOWITT, A. W.   *Kamilaroi and Kurnai.*   Melbourne : 1880.

FITZPATRICK, SIR J. P.   *The Transvaal from Within.*   London : 1899.

FL.   *Folk Lore : the Transactions of the Folklore Society,* 1890 —proceeding.

FL.J.   *The Folklore Journal.*   Organ of the Folklore Society.   Seven vols.   1883–1889.

FL.F. *v.* Dennett.

FLETCHER, A. C., and LA FLESCHE, F. *The Omaha Tribe.* Bureau of American Ethnology, XXVII. Washington: 1911.

FLETCHER, A. C. *Indian Story and Song from North America.* Boston, Mass.: 1900.

FRAZER, DR. J. G. *The Golden Bough : a Study in Magic and Religion.* (Cited as *G.B.*) Second Edition. Three vols. London: 1900.

—— *Totemism and Exogamy.* Four vols. London: 1910.

—— *Taboo and the Perils of the Soul.* (*Golden Bough.* Part II. Third Edition, 1911.)

Fritillary, The. Organ of the Union of Women Students, Oxford: privately printed.

GARDINER, CAPT. ALLEN F. *Journey to the Zulu Country.* London: 1836.

GARNETT, L. M. J., and GLENNIE, J. S. S. *Greek Folk Songs from the Turkish Provinces of Greece.* London: 1885.

G.B. *v.* Frazer.

VAN GENNEP, A. *Les Rites de Passage.* Paris: 1909.

GOMME, A. B. (LADY). *The Traditional Games of England, Scotland and Ireland.* Two vols. London: 1894.

GOMME, SIR G. L. *The Village Community.* (Cited as *V.C.*) 1890.

GOODRICH-FREER, A. G. *Outer Isles.* London: 1902.

GREGOR, THE REV. DR. W. *Notes on the Folklore of the North-East of Scotland.* Folklore Society, No. VII., 1881.

—— *Kilns, Mills, Millers, Meal and Bread.* London: 1894.

GRINNELL, G. B. *Blackfoot Lodge Tales.* London: 1893.

GROOT, J. J. M. DE. *The Religious System of China.* Five vols. published. Leiden: 1892–1907.

Guernsey FL. *v.* Carey.

GURDON, MAJOR P. R. T. *The Khasis.* London: 1907.

HADDON, DR. A. C. *The Study of Man.* London: 1898.

HADDON, KATHLEEN. *Cats' Cradles from many Lands.* London: 1911.

HAHN, F. *Einführung in das Gebiet der Kolsmission.* Gütersloh: 1907.

HARTLAND, E. S. *The Legend of Perseus.* Three vols. London: 1894–6. (Cited as *L.P.*)

—— *Primitive Paternity.* London: 1910. Two vols. (Cited as *P.P.*)

HASTINGS, J. *Encyclopædia of Religion and Ethics.* Edinburgh: 1906.

HARRISON, JANE E. *Ancient Art and Ritual :* in *Home University Library.* London : N.D.

HENDERSON, W. *Notes on the Folklore of the Northern Counties of England and the Borders.* Second Edition. Folklore Society, No. II., 1879.

HERBERT, GEORGE. *Jacula Prudentum.* Second Edition, 1651.

HILDBURGH, W. L. " Japanese Household Magic " in *Transactions of the Japan Society,* Vol. VIII., 1908.

HOBLEY, C. W. *Ethnology of A-Kamba and other East African Tribes.* Cambridge : 1910.

HODSON, T. C. *The Naga Tribes of Manipur.* London : 1911.

HOLLIS, A. C. " Nandi Prayers," in *Trans. 3rd Internat. Congr. Rel.*

HOWITT, A. W. *The Native Tribes of South-East Australia.* London : 1904.

—— *v.* Fison.

HYDE, DR. DOUGLAS. *Beside the Fire.* London : 1890.

HUNT, R. *Popular Romances of the West of England.* London : 1881.

H. W. *v.* Webster.

IM THURN, SIR EVERARD. *Among the Indians of Guiana.* London : 1883.

J.A.I. *Journal of the Anthropological* (now *Royal Anthropological*) *Institute of Great Britain and Ireland.* London : 1872—proceeding.

JAUSSEN, LE P. ANTONIN. *Coûtumes des Arabes au Pays de Moab.* Paris : 1908.

JAYNE, C. F. *String Figures.* New York : 1906.

JEKYLL, W. *Jamaican Song and Story.* Folklore Society, No. LV., 1904.

JONES, PETER. *History of the Ojebway Indians.* London : 1861.

J.A.FL. *Journal of American Folklore.* Organ of the American Folklore Society. Boston : 1888—proceeding.

J.R.A.I. *v. J.A.I.*

JUNOD, HENRI A. *Les Baronga.* *Étude Ethnographique.* Neuchatel : 1898.

—— *The Life of a South African Tribe.* Two vols. Neuchatel : 1912–13.

KER, PROFESSOR W. P. *On the History of the Ballads.* 1100–1500. London : 1910. Reprinted from the *Proc. of the British Academy.* Vol. IV.

KINGSLEY, THE REV. CHARLES. *The Hermits.* London : 1868.

KINGSLEY, M. H. *Travels in West Africa.* London : 1897.

KUHN, F. F. A. *Die Herabkunft des Feuers.* Gütersloh : 1886.

LADY GOMME. *v.* Gomme, A. B.

LANG, ANDREW. *Custom and Myth.* London : 1884–5.

LEATHER, E. M. *The Folklore of Herefordshire.* London : 1912.

LEGGE, JAMES. *Chinese Classics.* London : 1867–76.

—— In *Sacred Books of the East* (Vols. III. and XXVII.). Fifty vols. Oxford : 1879–1910.

LEWIN, COL. T. H. *A Fly on the Wheel, or, How I helped to govern India.* London : 1885.

LLOYD, L. C. *A Short Account of Further Bushman Material.* London : 1889.

MACCLINTOCK, W. *The Old North Trail.* London : 1910.

Man ; a Monthly Record of Anthropological Science. Royal Anthropological Institute. London : 1901—proceeding.

MAINE, SIR H. *Ancient Law.* With an Introduction by Sir F. Pollock. London : 1906.

MARRECO, B. FREIRE-. " Two American Indian Dances," in *The Sociological Review*, October 1911.

MARETT, DR. R. R. *The Threshold of Religion.* Second Edition, London : 1909.

MATHEW, THE REV. J. *Eaglehawk and Crow.* London : 1899.

(*Mem. Am. Mus. Nat. Hist. I. Anthro.*) *Memoirs of the American Museum of Natural History ; Anthropology, Vol. I.*

M.M. v. Skeat.

MOFFAT, THE REV. DR. R. *Missionary Labours and Scenes in Southern Africa.* London : 1842.

Nagas. v. Hodson.

Notes and Queries on Anthropology. (Royal Anthropological Institute.) Fourth Edition, 1912. (Cited as *A.N. and Q.*)

ORPEN, J. M. In *The Cape Monthly Magazine*, July 1874. Cape-town.

Outer Isles. v. Goodrich-Freer.

OWEN, M. A. *Folklore of the Musquakie Indians.* Folklore Society, No. LI., 1902.

PARTRIDGE, CHARLES. *Cross River Natives.* London : 1895.

PLOWDEN, W. C. *Travels in Abyssinia and the Galla Country.* Longmans, 1868.

POLACK, J. S. *Manners and Customs of the New Zealanders.* Two vols. London : 1840.

Pop. Rel. v. Crooke.

POST, DR. A. H. *Afrikanische Jurisprudenz.* Two vols. Olden-burg and Leipsig : 1887.

Prim. Cult. *v.* Tylor.
P.P. *v.* Hartland.
P.R. *v.* Skeat.

RANEE OF SARAWAK, THE. *My Life in Sarawak.* London : 1913.
(*Rep. Bur. Amer. Ethn.*) *Reports of the Bureau of American Ethnology.* Washington : 1879—proceeding.
Report of the Census of India, 1901 : *ditto,* 1911.
Report of the Cambridge Anthropological Expedition to the Torres Straits. Vol. V. Cambridge : 1904.
(*Rep. Nat. Mus.*) *Report of the United States Museum.* Washington, Vol. III.
(*Rep. Amer. Nat. Hist. Mus.*) *Report of the American Natural History Museum.* Vol. XVIII.
(*Rep. Peab. Mus.*) *Papers of the Peabody Museum of American Archaeology and Ethnology.* Harvard University. Cambridge, Mass. : 1888—proceeding.
Revue des Traditions Populaires. Organ of the Société des Traditions Populaires. Paris : 1886.—proceeding.
RHŶS, SIR JOHN. *Celtic Folklore, Welsh and Manx.* Two vols. Oxford : 1901.
RIVERS, DR. W. H. R. *The Todas of the Nilgiri Hills.* London : 1906.
—— *Kinship and Tribal Organisation.* London : 1914.
—— *The History of Melanesian Society.* (In the Press.)
—— " The Genealogical Method of Anthropological Enquiry," in *Soc. Rev.,* January, 1910.
ROSCOE, THE REV. JOHN. *The Baganda : their Customs and Beliefs.* London : 1911.
ROTH, H. LING. *The Natives of Sarawak and British North Borneo.* Two vols. London : 1896.
ROTH, WALTER E. " Tully River Natives." In *Ethnological Studies among North-West Central Queensland Aborigines.* Brisbane : 1897.
ROUTLEDGE, W. SCORESBY and KATHLEEN. *With a Prehistoric People : the Akikúyu of British East Africa.* London : 1910.

ST. JOHN, CHARLES. *Short Sketches of the Wild Sports and Natural History of the Highlands.* London : 1849.
SAWYER, F. E. " Sussex Songs and Music." In *Journal of the British Archaeological Association,* Vol. XLII., 1886.
SCHEFFER. *Lappland. Das ist : Neue und wahrhaftige Beschreibung von Lappland und dessen Einwohnern.* Franckfurt am Mayn und Leipzig : 1675.

SÉBILLOT, PAUL. *Légendes et Curiosités des Métiers.* Paris : N.D.
—— *Le Folklore.* Paris : 1913.
SELIGMANN, DR. C. G. *The Melanesians of British North Guinea.* Cambridge : 1910.
—— In *Essays and Studies presented to William Ridgeway.* Cambridge : 1913.
—— and B. Z. *The Veddas.* Cambridge : 1911.
SHARP, CECIL. *The Sword Dances of Northern England.* London : N.D.
SHARP, DAVID. *The Cambridge Natural History.* London : 1899.
SKEAT, W. W. *Malay Magic.* (Cited as *M.M.*) London : 1900.
—— and BLAGDON, C. O. *Pagan Races of the Malay Peninsula.* (Cited as *P.R.*) Two vols. London : 1906.
Shr. FL. v. Burne.
SMITH, W. ROBERTSON. *Lectures on the Religion of the Semites.* Edinburgh : 1889.
(S. and G.) SPENCER, BALDWIN, and GILLEN, F. J. *The Native Tribes of Central Australia.* London : 1899.
(*Soc. Rev.*) *The Sociological Review.* Organ of the Sociological Society. London and Manchester : 1908—proceeding.
SPRUCE, R. *Notes of a Botanist on the Amazon and Andes.* Two vols. Macmillan, 1908.
STOW, G. *Native Races of South Africa.* London : 1905.

TANNER, JOHN. *Captivity and Adventures among the North American Indians.* New York : 1840.
THORPE, BENJAMIN. *Northern Mythology.* Three vols. London : 1851–1852.
Todas. v. Rivers.
TORDAY, E., and JOYCE, T. A. *Les Bushongo.* (Documents Ethnographiques concernant les populations du Congo Belge. Tome 2. Fasc. 1.) Brussels : 1910.
Torres Straits. v. Reports.
(*Trans. FL. Congr.*) *Papers and Transactions of the International Folklore Congress.* 1891. Edited by Joseph Jacobs and Alfred Nutt. London : 1892.
(*Trans. 3rd Internat. Congr. Rel.*) *Transactions of the 3rd International Congress of Religions.* Oxford : 1908.
TREVELYAN, MARIE. *Folklore and Folk Stories of Wales.* London : 1909.
TRUMBULL, THE REV. DR. HENRY CLAY. *The Blood Covenant and its Bearing on Scripture.* Third Edition. Philadelphia : 1898.
TURNER, THE REV. G. *Samoa a Hundred Years Ago and long before.* London : 1884.

TYLOR, SIR E. B. *Primitive Culture.* Fourth Edition. Two vols. London : 1903.

—— *Researches into the Early History of Mankind.* London : 1878.

WADDELL, COL. L. A. *Lhasa and Its Mysteries.* London : 1905.

WARDE FOWLER, W. *The Roman Festivals of the Period of the Republic.* London : 1899.

WEBSTER, HUTTON. *Primitive Secret Societies.* New York : 1908.

—— *Rest Days : a Sociological Study.* Nebraska University Studies, Vol. XI., 1911.

WEEKS, THE REV. JOHN H. *Among Congo Cannibals.* London : 1913.

—— *Among the Primitive Bakongo.* London : 1914.

WERNER, ALICE. *The Natives of British Central Africa.* London : 1906.

WESTERMARCK, DR. E. A. *History of Human Marriage.* London : 1901.

—— *The Origin and Development of the Moral Ideas.* Two vols. London : 1906–8.

—— *Marriage Ceremonies in Morocco.* London : 1914.

WHEELER, GERALD C. *The Tribe and Intertribal Relations in Australia.* London : 1910.

WHITE, THE REV. GILBERT. *The Natural History of Selborne.*

WIEDEMANN, A. *Religion of the Ancient Egyptians.* London : 1897.

WILSON, H. H. *Essays and Lectures, chiefly on the Religion of the Hindus.* Twelve vols. London : 1862.